PENGUIN CLASSICS

THE PENGUIN BOOK OF PIRATES

KATHERINE HOWE is a bestselling and award-winning historian and novelist who is a direct descendant of a nineteenth-century sailor who battled pirates on the high seas as well as three women who were tried for witchcraft in Salem. She is the editor of *The Penguin Book of Witches*; the author of the novels *A True Account: Hannah Masury's Sojourn Amongst the Pyrates, Written by Herself* and *The Daughters of Deliverance Hobbs*, the *New York Times* bestselling novels *The Physick Book of Deliverance Dane* and *The House of Velvet and Glass*, and the young adult novels *Conversion* and *The Appearance of Annie van Sinderen*; and the coauthor with Anderson Cooper of the *New York Times* bestsellers *Vanderbilt: The Rise and Fall of an American Dynasty* and *Astor: The Rise and Fall of an American Fortune*. A native Houstonian, she lives and sails with her family in New England.

T0049091

The Penguin Book of Pirates

Edited by
KATHERINE HOWE

PENGUIN BOOKS

PENGUIN BOOKS
An imprint of Penguin Random House LLC
penguinrandomhouse.com

Introduction, notes, and selection copyright © 2024 by Katherine Howe
Penguin Random House supports copyright. Copyright fuels creativity, encourages diverse voices,
promotes free speech, and creates a vibrant culture. Thank you for buying an authorized edition of
this book and for complying with copyright laws by not reproducing, scanning, or distributing any
part of it in any form without permission. You are supporting writers and allowing
Penguin Random House to continue to publish books for every reader.

LIBRARY OF CONGRESS CATALOGING-IN-PUBLICATION DATA

Names: Howe, Katherine, 1977– editor of compilation.
Title: The Penguin book of pirates / edited by Katherine Howe.
Other titles: Book of pirates
Description: 1st edition. | New York : Penguin Books, [2024] |
Includes bibliographical references and index.
Identifiers: LCCN 2023042182 (print) | LCCN 2023042183 (ebook) |
ISBN 9780143137511 (paperback) | ISBN 9780593511596 (ebook)
Subjects: LCSH: Pirates—History. | Pirates—Biography.
Classification: LCC G535 .P425 2024 (print) |
LCC G535 (ebook) | DDC 910.4/5—dc23/eng/20231016
LC record available at https://lccn.loc.gov/2023042182
LC ebook record available at https://lccn.loc.gov/2023042183

Printed in the United States of America
1st Printing

Set in Sabon LT Pro

*For ZGL
and CGHH*

Many of the published reports, exaggerated beyond reason, were subsequently found to have been based upon terrified imagination; but on the other hand, there is no doubt that much valuable information was covered up, some of the pirates, also, were lost at sea, with all their booty and all knowledge of the vessels they had plundered and destroyed.

—Francis B. C. Bradlee,
Piracy in the West Indies and Its Suppression

The night before he died, Blackbeard was up drinking, knowing sloops were on the way to engage them. One of his crew asked Blackbeard if his wife knew where he had buried his money. Nobody but himself and the Devil knew where it was, and the longest Liver should take all. There was even an account among his surviving crew that a spectral man unknown to all of them was seen lurking about the ship, and more than one man among them swore it was the Devil himself.

—Anonymous (Captain Charles Johnson),
*A General History of the Pyrates, from Their First Rise and
Settlement in the Island of Providence, to the Present Time*

Contents

THE PENGUIN BOOK OF PIRATES

The Seventeenth Century and Before

The Golden Age

The Nineteenth Century

Introduction

Every Halloween, toddlers in peg legs and eye patches take to the streets among the dinosaurs and ghosts and Harry Potters and Marvel superheroes, and we all recognize them, and we all say "yaaaaar" to them, even though American ports are no longer peopled with men whose bodies have been mutilated by work on a tall ship and whose accents bear the strange extra-national marker of membership in the fellowship of the sea.

Most of us don't know much about pirates beyond the Halloween or Hollywood stereotype. We don't know that a man's body was hanged in chains as a warning against piracy on a rock at the mouth of Boston harbor in 1726, or that pirates along the Texas-Louisiana border did a brisk business selling enslaved people who had been kidnapped from Spanish ships in 1821. We don't know about the notorious pirate town full of Europeans and Americans and Africans on a tiny tropical paradise off the coast of Madagascar, or the women who disguised themselves as men and raided up and down the coast of Jamaica, or the Englishman who converted to Islam and terrorized the Barbary coast. We are romantic about pirates in part because we don't know anything about them. But we are romantic about them too because of what they represent: "A merry life, and a short one, shall be my motto," as Captain Bartholomew Roberts famously put it. Pirates in the Age of Sail lived under a set of shared principles—resistance to hard labor and desire for self-governance, money, and drink chief among them—and shared risks—of dismemberment or death at sea and of execution by the maritime powers whose authority they directly challenged on land.

Most interestingly for our moment, pirates occupied a constantly shifting littoral space that existed outside national boundaries and identities. Pirate crews were often multiethnic, multilingual, multinational, and, on rare occasions, even multi-gendered. Records of men tried as pirates often list their ports of origin rather than their countries of birth; a pirate could be "late of Barbadoes" and have been Scottish or English or Moorish. The organization of a pirate ship was egalitarian in comparison to a naval or merchant ship, and so has more than once been pointed to as a kind of utopian experiment, a proto-democracy. That conception might be a stretch, but certainly a sailor going out "on the account" would expect to reap the rewards of his labor and his risk more directly than if he were serving at the pleasure of a corporation or a government.

The tension at the heart of the pirate story stands at the intersection of extreme conditions of freedom and unfreedom. Men who turned to piracy often did so out of mutiny from "hard usage," or were men who had been press-ganged or forced into naval service against their will. Samuel Johnson famously noted that "no man will be a sailor who has contrivance enough to get himself into a jail; for being in a ship is being in a jail, with the chance of being drowned. . . . A man in a jail has more room, better food, and commonly better company." For men in jail with the added risk of being drowned, turning pirate consisted of a movement from unfreedom to freedom. Even if that freedom was fleeting.

But piracy during the Golden Age was also dependent on unfreedom, being bound inextricably with the transatlantic slave trade. Pirates often raided "Guineamen," in one horrifying instance renaming the seized slave ship *Batchelor's Delight* (from the *Delight*) because of the opportunities for rape of enslaved women they found on board. The fate of enslaved people on pirate prize ships is an opaque one. The coding in the contemporary database Slave Voyages, which attempts to catalogue the outcome of every slave-trading journey made in the Atlantic from the 1500s through the 1800s, tags 153 instances of pirate-related activity out of 36,108 total voyages, which seems impossibly low, given the value of enslaved people and the necessity of merchant ships traveling heavily armed.[1] Of course, a ship being taken by pirates would leave a record of its seizure only if someone survived to talk about it; dead men tell no tales, after all. Another possibility is that the insurance underwriters who insured slave voyages might have had a different risk profile for piracy than they had for loss at sea or to weather or acts of God. We know that insurance underwriters in some instances gave rich rewards—money, fancy silver services, acclaim—to ship captains who successfully repelled piratical attack. Perhaps the disappearance of pirate prize slave ships is hidden in the paperwork, coded as something else.

In some instances, we do know the outcome when the radically free met the radically unfree. Sometimes the ships were reclaimed by the owners with the human cargo intact. In other instances the enslaved people may have joined the crew: William Kidd, when he was finally waylaid by the authorities after turning pirate, was found to be leading a crew that consisted of "ninety Moors." On some occasions, the seized human cargo were laundered and sold on the black market; Jean Lafitte infamously ran a pirate slave market over the Sabine River border from Louisiana, in Mexican Texas, after the importation of enslaved people had been banned in the United States. He reportedly sold his human prizes for a dollar a pound. More often than not, however, the fate of human cargo seized by pirates is a mystery.

The Penguin Book of Pirates illuminates the truth—often brutal, sometimes sympathetic, more often harrowing—behind the romance we attach to pirates. It contains a selection of primary sources excerpted from contemporaneous nonfiction, trial transcripts, journalism, and ship logs, with occasional recourse to secondary sources, organized in chronological order, beginning in the 1570s and ending in the middle of the nineteenth century. It is organized into three parts: the 1500s and 1600s, when some of the most widespread and notorious pirates achieved legendary status; the Golden Age (which was the eighteenth century, broadly speaking), when a whole new generation of pirates modeled themselves, to some extent, on the stories of the previous generation; and the nineteenth century, when piracy started to fade as a maritime threat but became firmly fixed in the popular imagination. Geographically, the text focuses primarily on the Atlantic world, the Caribbean, the Mediterranean / Barbary Coast, and Madagascar, with quick detours to the South China Sea and Sumatra, for those regions were all linked by a constantly moving population of sailors who were more citizens of the oceangoing world than any nation where they may have been born.

The selections have been chosen mainly to be a good read, with some dialogue and action where possible. The volume also contains a short appendix that excerpts two of the most entrenched fictional sources of the pirate imaginary: Long John Silver from Robert Louis Stevenson's *Treasure Island* and Captain Hook from J. M. Barrie's *Peter and Wendy*, better known as *Peter Pan*. Both these fictional pirates are familiar to us, one even lending his name to a chain of fish fast-food restaurants, the other leering in a flowing Restoration-era wig, splashed across every Disney property known to man. And yet they are both strangers to us. They simultaneously gesture to the true horrors of piracy in the Golden Age of Sail— the threats they pose to children, their avarice and desire for revenge, the mutilation of their bodies over the course of their lives on the sea mirroring, or perhaps signifying, the mutilation of their souls. But they are also denatured, safely consigned to history, bested by clever young boys, made alternately harmless (John) or ridiculous (Hook). They are worth revisiting in the context of their historical antecedents, to understand how cultural myths are made.

I confess that part of my pirate obsession stems from thinking about the remarkable life of my fifth-great-grandfather, a mariner from Beverly, Massachusetts, named Zachariah Gage Lamson, who in the course of his checkered career at sea from 1797 to his death from fever in Grenada in 1846 did battle against pirates twice. When I was a child, my grandmother used to say he had been "strung up by his thumbs" by the pirates, though it turns out he was actually hanged by his neck from the yardarm, choking, before being cut down, apparently in an attempt to get him to confess where any valuables were hidden on board. After that experience, he resolved never to be so mistreated by pirates again, and so when his ship the *Belvidere* was attacked on a voyage from Port-au-Prince to New Orleans, he was ready for them (see the entry for the *Belvidere* in Part III: The Nineteenth Century, on page 286). That defense was met with such success that he was awarded a coin silver service by the insurance company that underwrote his voyage, two pieces of which I now possess. He sailed out of the same waters in Massachusetts where I sail today, and the one time I kissed my keel off a rock outside of Beverly Harbor, I'm pretty sure I heard him laughing at me.

Beyond my own personal and professional pirate obsession, I think we are living in a moment that is ripe for piracy. Supply chain disruption has brought about a new awareness of the strange ocean world outside our own homes and borders. Pirates now active in the Indian Ocean pilot lightning-fast motorboats and brave water cannons to seize the container ships that carry global wealth from port to port, or they collect money from desperate migrants to ferry them in dangerously overloaded boats across the Mediterranean in a different, but still dangerous, model of human smuggling. Popular culture too seems not to be finished with pirates, as *The Hollywood Reporter* writes that the Pirates of the Caribbean film franchise has raked in over $4.5 billion, making it one of the most successful film franchises in history.[2] We, as a culture, cannot shake pirates. From where I sit even now, writing this introduction, I spy a hat sticking out of my son's dress-up box, a black bicorne with gold piping and red sash trim, marked with the skull and crossbones that is the flag of death.

So let us take a closer look at them and see the truth, as the mysterious Charles Johnson put it, about how "these Wretches passed their Lives, with very little Pleasure or Satisfaction, in the Possession of what they violently take away from others, and sure to pay for it at last, by an ignominious Death."

KATHERINE HOWE

NOTES

1. Data drawn from "Trans-Atlantic Slave Trade–Database," Slave Voyages, accessed November 28, 2022, https://www.slavevoyages .org/voyage/database.

2. Vlessing, Etan, "Margot Robbie Says Disney Has Moved on From Her 'Pirates of the Caribbean' Spinoff," *The Hollywood Reporter*, accessed December 6, 2022, https://www.hollywood reporter.com/movies/movie-news/margot-robbie-says-disney -has-moved-on-from-her-pirates-of-the-caribbean-spinoff-12 35261421/.

Suggestions for Further Reading

Antony, Robert J. *Pirates in the Age of Sail*. New York: W. W. Norton & Co., 2007.

Bassi, Ernesto. *An Aqueous Territory: Sailor Geographies and New Granada's Transimperial Greater Caribbean World*. Durham, NC: Duke University Press, 2016.

Bentley, Jerry H., Renate Bridenthal, and Kären Wigen, eds. *Seascapes: Maritime Histories, Littoral Cultures, and Transoceanic Exchanges*. Honolulu, HI: University of Hawai'i Press, 2007.

Bolster, W. Jeffrey. *Black Jacks: African American Seamen in the Age of Sail*. Cambridge, MA: Harvard University Press, 1997.

Burgess, Douglas R. *The Pirates' Pact: The Secret Alliances Between History's Most Notorious Buccaneers and Colonial America*. New York: McGraw Hill, 2009.

Chambers, Anne. *Grace O'Malley: The Biography of Ireland's Pirate Queen 1530–1603*. Dublin: Gill Books, 2019.

Clifford, Barry. *The Lost Fleet: The Discovery of a Sunken Armada from the Golden Age of Piracy*. New York: William Morrow, 2002.

Clifford, Barry, and Paul Perry. *Expedition Whydah: The Story of the World's First Excavation of a Pirate Treasure Ship and the Man Who Found Her*. New York: Cliff Street Books, 1999.

Cordingly, David. *Seafaring Women: Adventures of Pirate Queens, Female Stowaways, and Sailors' Wives*. New York: Random House, 2001 and 2007.

Cordingly, David. *Under the Black Flag: The Romance and the Reality of Life among the Pirates*. New York: Random House, 1995.

Creighton, Margaret S., and Lisa Norling, eds. *Iron Men, Wooden Women: Gender and Seafaring in the Atlantic World, 1700–1920*. Baltimore, MD: Johns Hopkins University Press, 1996.

Davis, William C. *The Pirates Laffite: The Treacherous World of the Corsairs of the Gulf.* Orlando, FL: Harcourt, 2005.

Dolin, Eric Jay. *Black Flags, Blue Waters: The Epic History of America's Most Notorious Pirates.* New York: Liveright, 2018.

Dow, George Francis, and John Henry Edmonds. *The Pirates of the New England Coast, 1630–1730.* New York: Dover Publications, 1996.

Duncombe, Laura Sook. *Pirate Women: The Princesses, Prostitutes, and Privateers Who Ruled the Seven Seas.* Chicago: Chicago Review Press, 2019.

Ellms, Charles. *The Pirates Own Book: Authentic Narratives of the Most Celebrated Sea Robbers.* New York: Dover Publications, 1993, facsimile of Marine Research Society edition of 1924.

Exquemelin, Alexander O. *The Buccaneers of America.* Mineola, NY: Dover Publications, 2000.

Flemming, Gregory N. *At the Point of a Cutlass: The Pirate Capture, Bold Escape, and Lonely Exile of Philip Ashton.* Lebanon, NH: ForeEdge Press, 2014.

Geanacopoulos, Daphne Palmer. *The Pirate Next Door: The Untold Story of Eighteenth Century Pirates' Wives, Families and Communities.* Durham, NC: Carolina Academic Press, 2017.

Graeber, David. *Pirate Enlightenment, or the Real Libertalia.* New York: Farrar, Straus and Giroux, 2023.

Hanna, Mark G. *Pirate Nests and the Rise of the British Empire, 1570–1740.* Chapel Hill, NC: University of North Carolina Press, 2015.

Howe, Katherine. *A True Account: Hannah Masury's Sojourn Amongst the Pyrates, Written by Herself.* New York: Henry Holt & Company, 2023.

Johnson, Charles. Sometimes credited as Daniel Defoe. *A General History of the Pyrates, from Their First Rise and Settlement in the Island of Providence, to the Present Time.* Mineola, NY: Dover Publications, 1999.

Johnson, Steven. *Enemy of All Mankind: A True Story of Piracy, Power, and History's First Global Manhunt.* New York: Riverhead, 2020.

Kilmeade, Brian, and Don Yaeger. *Thomas Jefferson and the Tripoli Pirates: The Forgotten War That Changed American History.* New York: Sentinel, 2015.

Konstam, Angus. *Blackbeard: America's Most Notorious Pirate.* Hoboken, NJ: John Wiley & Sons, 2006.

Kritzler, Edward. *Jewish Pirates of the Caribbean: How a Generation of Swashbuckling Jews Carved Out an Empire in the New World in Their Quest for Treasure, Religious Freedom—and Revenge.* New York: Doubleday, 2008.

McDonald, Kevin P. *Pirates, Merchants, Settlers, and Slaves: Colonial America and the Indo-Atlantic World.* Oakland, CA: University of California Press, 2015.

Orihuela, Sharada Balachandran. *Fugitives, Smugglers, and Thieves: Piracy and Personhood in American Literature.* Chapel Hill, NC: University of North Carolina Press, 2018.

Pennell, C. R., ed. *Bandits at Sea: A Pirates Reader.* New York: New York University Press, 2001.

Rediker, Marcus. *Villains of All Nations: Atlantic Pirates in the Golden Age.* Boston: Beacon Press, 2004.

Skowronek, Russell K., and Charles R. Ewen, eds. *X Marks the Spot: The Archaeology of Piracy.* Gainesville, FL: University Press of Florida, 2006.

Snelders, Stephan. *The Devil's Anarchy: The Sea Robberies of the Most Famous Pirate Claes G. Compaen & the Very Remarkable Travels of Jan Erasmus Reyning, Buccaneer.* Brooklyn, NY: Autonomedia, 2014.

Wilson, Peter Lamborn. *Pirate Utopias: Moorish Corsairs & European Renegadoes.* Brooklyn, NY: Autonomedia, 1995 and 2003.

A Note on the Text

In compiling the following accounts from the various sources I consulted, I have used an ellipsis to indicate missing text, from either illegibility in the original source or selective redaction of long passages that don't materially add to the comprehension or enjoyment of the narrative. In some instances I've modernized the spelling and punctuation of primary sources for the ease of contemporary readers, making exceptions for examples in which period spelling doesn't interfere with comprehension. I have, however, added explanatory endnotes on locations, historical definitions, and especially nautical terminology, useful for anyone (like your editor) who has trouble keeping straight the difference between a brig and a brigantine. In some cases I have enclosed uncertain words in brackets when I have made an educated assumption about what the word probably is, and when in doubt, have included an endnote to elucidate my thinking. When long passages of text have been redacted, I have on occasion included a summary of what's missing within the brackets.

Each primary source selection is headed by either a pirate name, when the name is known, or by the name of a ship if the pirates in question are not known, followed by a broad theater of operations and a date or span of dates. Each entry is also introduced by brief contextualizing remarks. The chronology privileges dates of purported activity over dates of original publication.

Acknowledgments

My greatest thanks go first to my editor, John Siciliano, for being amenable to my working up a pirate volume for this wonderful series; to my agent, Suzanne Gluck, at WME, for patiently putting up with my ongoing pirate obsession; to my husband, Louis Hyman, for thoroughgoing research assistance and access to Cornell University libraries; and to my son, Charles, for having such great taste in hats. I am grateful to Anne Chambers and her publishing house, Gill Books, for their permission to reproduce Anne's thoughtful transcription of Grace O'Malley's interrogation, which saved me a very long plane ride and probably a change in my eyeglasses prescription. Thanks go also to Melanie Locay and the staff at the Center for Research in the Humanities at the New York Public Library, which provided workspace, research support, and access to documents without which this volume would not have been possible. Thanks also to the many friends on the water who have generously shared their sailing knowledge and passion with me over my years as a sailor. Space does not permit my listing all the scholars whose work on pirates and piracy has informed my thinking and whose work I greatly admire, but the suggestions for further reading highlight many of them. Thanks to Hannah Augusta Masury for reasons she would understand if she were here. And finally, thanks to all the readers I have encountered over the years, of both fiction and nonfiction, for making life in this scurvy world more merry. A bowl of punch for the lot of you rogues.

The Penguin Book
of Pirates

THE
SEVENTEENTH
CENTURY
AND BEFORE

FRANCIS DRAKE

"El Draque"

The Golden Hind

1570s

Sir Francis Drake was many things: an expert mariner, captain, privateer, slave trader, and possibly a pirate too, certainly from the standpoint of the Spanish, whose ships, cargoes, and settlements he attacked. His chief claim to fame was his circumnavigation of the globe, undertaken in a single expedition between 1577 and 1580, the first one completed by an Englishman, and only the third one undertaken in the history of seafaring.[1] Drake's explorations of the Pacific stirred further conflict with Spain, which had laid claim to the western coast of North America, which is one reason for his fearsome Spanish nickname: "El Draque," or "the Dragon." As Elizabeth I rewarded his exploits with a knighthood in 1581, so King Philip II levied a substantial price on his head for his capture or death.

Drake was born in Devon, England, sometime in the 1540s, before moving with his family to Kent. As a child, he was apprenticed to the master of a bark (sometimes spelled "barque," a general term for a small sailing vessel suitable for coastal cruising) engaged in trade across the English Channel with France. Eventually, Drake came into ownership or control of the bark himself. One of his early associates, John Hawkins, schemed to break the Portuguese monop-

oly on the West African slave trade, and Drake's involvement with this successful enterprise led him to become one of the very first English slave traders. From the outset, we cannot think about the history of piracy without considering its connection to the history of enslavement.

In the 1560s, Drake was part of an expedition that raided Portuguese slave ships off the coast of Africa and then transported the enslaved captives to sell in the Spanish colonies of the Americas. While captaining one of the ships in Hawkins's convoy, Drake and some others were forced by bad weather and captive resistance to put in at the port in Veracruz for repairs. While they were there, a fleet of Spanish warships attacked them, and the vessel on which Drake had shipped was burned to the waterline. He reportedly survived the attack by swimming away. After this, Drake turned his ambitions away from slaving and toward raiding shipping along the Spanish Main, an English term for the Isthmus of Panama, which served as the landing point for loading treasure galleons for transport across the Caribbean Sea.

The following account provides a Spanish perspective on Drake, which illuminates some elements of his character that might account for his fearsome, and piratical, reputation.

LETTER FROM DON FRANCISCO DE ZARATE TO DON MARTÍN ENRIQUEZ, VICEROY OF NEW SPAIN, GIVING AN ACCOUNT OF WHAT HAPPENED TO HIM WITH FRANCIS DRAKE IN THE SOUTH SEA[2]

Realejo, Nicaragua
16th of April, 1579

I sailed out of the port of Acapulco on the twenty-third of March and navigated until Saturday, the fourth of April, on which date, half an hour before dawn, we saw, by moonlight, a ship very close to ours. Our steersman shouted that she was to get out of the way and not come alongside of us. To this they made no answer, pretending to be asleep. The steersman then shouted louder, asking them where their ship hailed from. They answered, "from Peru," and that she was "of Miguel Angel," which is the name of a well-known captain of that route. The spokesman on the ship was a Spaniard, whose name I will tell Your Excellency further on.

The ship[3] of the adversary carried her bark[4] at her prow[5] as though she were being towed. Suddenly, in a moment, she crossed our poop,[6] ordering us "to strike sail" and shooting seven or eight arquebus[7] shots at us.

We thought this as much of a joke as it afterwards turned out to be serious.

On our part there was no resistance, nor had we more than six of our men awake on the whole boat, so they entered our ship with as little risk to themselves as though they were our friends. They did no personal harm to any one, beyond seizing the swords and keys of the passengers. Having informed themselves as to who were on board ship, they ordered me to go in their boat to where their general was—a fact that I was glad of, as it appeared to me that it gave me more time in which to recommend myself to God. But in a very short time we arrived where he was, on a very good galleon,[8] as well mounted with artillery as any I have seen in my life.

I found him promenading on deck and, on approaching him, I kissed his hands. He received me with a show of kindness, and took me to his cabin where he bade me be seated and said: "I am a friend of those who tell me the truth, but with those who do not I get out of humor. Therefore, you must tell me (for this is the best road to my favor), how much silver and gold does your ship carry?" I said to him, "None." He repeated his question. I answered, "None, only some small plates that I use and some cups—that is all that is in her." He kept silent for a while, then renewing the conversation asked me if I knew Your Excellency. I said, "Yes." "Is any relative of his or thing pertaining to him on this ship?" "No, sir." "Well, it would give me a greater joy to come across him than all the gold and silver of the Indies. You would see how the words of gentlemen should be kept." I made no reply to this. He then stood up, and bidding me go with him, led me to a cabin situated in the poop below deck, where there was a prison by them called "the ballast."[9] In it, at its end, was an old man. He said to me: "Sit down, for it is here that you will have to remain." I took this in good part, and was about to sit down, when he detained me and said: "I do not want you to try this just yet, but only want you to tell me who that man is in there." I answered that I did not know him. "Well," he said, "know that it is a pilot named Colchero, whom the Viceroy was sending to Panama to convey Don Concalo to China." He then had the pilot released from the prison and we all went up on deck. This was the man who had spoken to us from the galleon when we were taken. We talked for a good while before it was time to dine. He ordered me to sit next to him and began to give me food from his own plate, telling me not to grieve, that my life and property were safe. I kissed his hands for this.

He asked if I knew where there was water to be had about here, adding that he needed nothing else, and that as soon as he found some, he would give me leave to continue my journey. I did not dare to ask aught of him at that moment. Awaiting an opportunity, I begged him not to oblige us to pass the Gulf of Tehuantepec[10] again. He answered that he would see and that he would dispatch me shortly.

On the following day, which was Sunday, in the morning, he dressed and decked himself very finely and had his galleon decorated with all its flags and banners. He also ordered that all the men on our ship be passed to another one of his, which he had taken on this same coast, and which had served for this purpose since he reached the coast of Chile, where he had on his hands a ship laden with a large quantity of gold and many others laden with silver. He had entered the port of Callao de Lima[11] and cut the cables of all the ships that were in port. As the wind was from the land, they all went out to sea, where he had time to sack them at his will. Before he proceeded to do the same to ours he said to me: "Let one of your pages come with me to show me your apparel."[12] He went from his galleon at about nine in the morning and remained until towards dusk, examining everything contained in the bales and chests. Of that which belonged to me he took but little. Indeed he was quite courteous about it. Certain trifles of mine having taken his fancy,[13] he had them brought to his ship and gave me, in exchange for them, a falchion and a small brazier of silver, and I can assure Your Excellency that he lost nothing by the bargain.[14] On his return to his vessel he asked me to pardon him for taking the trifles, but that they were for his wife. He said that I could depart the next morning, when the breeze would rise, for which I gave him thanks.

The next morning, which was Monday, he gave back to some of the passengers who were there, their boxes, and thus occupied himself until the hour for dinner. He ordered that this be served as the wind was rising. After this had been done he said that he himself wanted to take me aboard. He ordered his sloop to be prepared and manned with two dozen archers. He had one of the artillery men called and ordered him to carry aboard half a dozen pieces of artillery. This done, he told me to embark with him, as all was in readiness. I did so, and on arriving at our vessel he boarded her first and having all our sailors called together, he gave each one a handful of reals. He also gave the same to some other men who appeared to him to be the most needy. He commanded that one of those sailors should embark with him so as to show him where water was to be obtained. All excused themselves, saying that they did not know where water was to be had, so he caused Juan Pascual to be put by force in his sloop saying that he would hang him if he replied a word. With this he took leave of me, and his last words were to beseech me, earnestly, to tell certain Englishmen who were in Lima that I had met him on April 6th and that he was well. From this it is to be inferred that he has spies in all this realm and in Peru. I can assure Your Excellency that two or three of those who came in his service have already navigated, where I have, on this route of New Spain.

He left Colchero with me, and after this set sail. I understand that he carries three thousand bars of silver, and twelve or fifteen chests of pieces of eight, and a great quantity of gold. He is going straight to this country, and I believe that no vessel that went after him could possibly overtake him. He has an intense desire to return to his own country.

This general of the Englishmen is a nephew of John Hawkins, and is the same who, about five years ago, took the port of Nombre de Dios.[15] He is called Francisco Drac, and is a man about 35 years of age, low of stature, with a fair beard, and is one of the greatest mariners that sails the seas, both as a navigator[16] and as a commander.

His vessel is a galleon of nearly four hundred tons, and is a perfect sailer. She is manned with a hundred men, all of service and of an age for warfare, and all are as practiced therein as old soldiers from Italy could be. Each one takes particular pains to keep his arquebus clean. He treats them with affection, and they treat him with respect. He carries with him nine or ten cavaliers, cadets of English noblemen. These form a part of his council which he calls together for even the most trivial matter, although he takes advice from no one. But he enjoys hearing what they say and afterwards issues his orders. He has no favorite.

The aforesaid gentlemen sit at his table, as well as a Portuguese pilot, whom he brought from England, who spoke not a word during all the time I was on board. He is served on silver dishes with gold borders and gilded garlands, in which are his arms. He carries all possible dainties and perfumed waters. He said that many of these had been given him by the Queen.

None of these gentlemen took a seat or covered his head before him, until he repeatedly urged them to do so. This galleon of his carries about thirty heavy pieces of artillery and a great quantity of firearms with the requisite ammunition and lead. He dines and sups to the music of viols. He carries trained carpenters and artisans, so as to be able to careen[17] the ship at any time. Beside being new, the ship has a double lining. I understood that all the men he carries with him receive wages, because, when our ship was sacked, no man dared take anything without his orders. He shows them great favor, but punishes the least fault. He also carries painters who paint for him pictures of the coast in its exact colors.[18] This I was most grieved to see, for each thing is so naturally depicted that no one who guides himself according to these paintings can possibly go astray. I understood from him that he had sailed from his country with five vessels, four sloops (of the long kind)[19] and that half of the armada belonged to the Queen. I believe this to be so for the reason that I am about to relate to Your Excellency.

This Corsair, like a pioneer, arrived two months before he intended to pass through [the strait] and during that time for many days there were great storms. So it was that one of the gentlemen, whom he had with him, said to him: "We have been a long while in this strait and you have placed all of us, who follow or serve you, in danger of death. It would therefore be prudent for you to give order that we return to the North Sea, where we have the certainty of capturing prizes, and that we give up seeking to make new discoveries. You see how fraught with difficulties these are."

This gentleman must have sustained this opinion with more vigor than appeared proper to the General. His answer was that he had the gentleman carried below deck and put in irons. On another day, at the same hour, he ordered him to be taken out, and to be beheaded in the presence of all.

GRACE O'MALLEY

"The Pirate Queen"

1580s

Grainne Ni Mhaille, commonly Anglicized to Grace O'Malley or Granuaile, was for many years consigned to a haze of rumor and myth, and like Francis Drake her status as "pirate" is to some extent dependent on one's point of view. Her biographer prefers to refer to her as a "dissident" or a "radical" or even as a feminist. What's not subject to debate is that she was a formidable leader of an oceangoing Irish clan, operating well beyond the shores of the region of her birth, in a relationship with the law that is a matter of perspective. To call her a "pirate queen," as folklore has taken it upon itself to do, is perhaps an overstatement, as so many things piratical so often are. But she is certainly legendary.

Born around 1530 in what is now County Mayo, she joined her clan's sea-trading enterprises—some legitimate, some less so—among Ireland, Scotland, and Spain before having an arranged marriage. A possibly apocryphal story holds that when she was a child, she wanted to go with her father on a trading voyage to Spain. When he denied her, claiming her hair would get caught in the lines on the ship, she cut her hair off, buying herself the nickname "Grainee Mhaol," from "maol," meaning "bald."[1] When her father died, she assumed control of her clan's interests on land and sea, including collection of taxes from fishermen who wished to trawl the seas over which the clan's castles looked. Her eventual disap-

pearance from more official histories of Ireland speaks to the dominance of English narratives over Irish histories. O'Malley lived and ruled in a period of a politically fragmented Ireland riven by infighting, bent under the eventual conquest of Elizabeth I. Her biographer notes that in 1593, a court accused her of piracy among many other "disloyal" activities, "a director of thieves and murderers at sea."[2] She sailed her own galleon to England to defend herself before Queen Elizabeth I.

The spellings of her name and those of her family and confederates are extremely variable, due to the age of the original documents and also the Anglicization of Irish spellings, which remains at issue because her life is largely documented in English records rather than Irish ones. I have largely retained the name spellings in this transcription of her 1593 court appearance before Queen Elizabeth I, reproduced with permission from O'Malley's preeminent biographer, Anne Chambers.

THE EIGHTEEN "ARTICLES OF INTERROGATORY," JULY 1593[3]

To be answered by Grace O'Malley

1. Who was her father and mother?
2. Who was her first husband?
3. What sons had she by him? What be their names and where do they live?
4. What countries they have to maintain them withal?
5. To whom they be married?
6. What kin was O'Flaherty, her first husband, to Sir Mourrough M'Ne Dough O'Flaherty that is here now at the court?
7. To answer the like question for her husband and for his sons and their livings.

8. If she were to be allowed her dower, or thirds of her husband's living, of what value the same might be of?

9. Where upon the Composition of Connaught there hath been any provisions for the wives?

10. Whether it be not against the Customs of Ireland for the wives to have more after the deaths of their husbands than they brought with them?

11. How she hath had maintenance and living since her last husband's death?

12. Of what kindred is Walter Bourgh FitzTibalds and Shane Bourke McMoyler to her son?

13. What captains and countries lie next to her husband's possessions?

14. Who doth possess the house of Moriske upon the seaside in Owle O'Malley?

15. What lands doth McGibbon possess in that country?

16. Who doth possess the country named Carramore and Mayn Connell?

17. Who doth possess the island of Achill and Kill castle?

18. What kin was her last husband to Walter and Ulick Bourke?

Answers of Grace O'Malley to the Articles

To the first

Her father was called Doodarro O'Malley,[4] sometime chieftain of the country called Upper Owle O'Malley, now called the barony of Murrisk. Her mother was called Margaret O'Malley,[5] daughter to Conogher O'Malley, of the same country and family. The whole country of Owle O Mailly aforesaid have these islands vis. Inish Bofyne Cleria Inish Twirke Inisharke Caher Inishdalluff Davellen and other small islands of little value which and the rest of the mainland are divided into the towns to the number of twenty and to every town four quarter or ploughs of land is assigned; out of every such quarter of land is yearly paid to her Majesty ten shillings called the composition rent. There is also in Connaught a country called Owle Eighter, otherwise the Lower or Nether Owle, containing fifty towns at four quarters the town, yearly paying the same rent, whereof the Bourkes of MacWilliam count other twenty towns and the Earl of Ormond ten towns.

To the second

Her first husband was called Donell Ichoggy Offlaherty[6] and during his life Chieftain of the Barony of Ballynehenssy, containing twenty-four towns at four quarters of land to every town paying yearly the composition rent aforesaid. After his death Teige Offlaherty the eldest son of Sir Morough now at court entered into Ballynehenssy aforesaid there did build a strong castle and the same with the domain lands thereof kept many years. Which Teige in the last rebellion of his father was slain.

To the third

She had two sons by her said first husband the eldest called Own Offlahertie[7] married Katherine Bourke daughter of Edmond Bourke of Castle Barry by her he had a son named Donell Offlahertie, now living which Owen all his lifetime remained a true subject to Her Majesty under the government of Sir Nicholas Malby while he lived and under Sir Richard Bingham until July 1586 at which time the Bourkes of the MacWilliams country and the sept of the Shoose [Joyce?] began to rebel. The said Owen, according to Sir Richard's special direction, did withdraw himself his followers and tenants, with all their goods and cattle into a strong island for their more and better assurance. Then having been sent against the said rebels five hundred soldiers under the leading of Captain John Bingham appointed by his brother Sir Richard Bingham as the lieutenant in those parts. When they missed both the rebels and their cattle they came to the mainland right against the said island calling for victuals; whereupon the said Owen came forth with a number of boats and ferried all the soldiers into the island where they were entertained with the best cheer they had. That night the said Owen was apprehended and tied with a rope with eighteen of his chief followers; in the morning the soldiers drew out of the island four thousand cows, five hundred stud mares and horses and a thousand sheep leaving the remainder of the poor men all naked within the island [they] came with the cattle and prisoners to Ballynehenssy aforesaid where John Bingham aforesaid stayed for their coming; that evening he caused the said eighteen persons without a trial or good cause to be hanged among whom was hanged a gentleman of land and living called Thebault O Twohill being of the age of four score and ten years. The next night following a false alarm was raised in the camp in the dead of the night the said Owen was cruelly murdered having twelve deadly wounds and in that miserable sort he ended his years and unfortunate days—Captain William Mostyn now at court and Captain Merriman and Captain Mordant were of that company. Her second son called Moroghe Offlahertie[8] now living is married to Honora Bourke daughter to Richard Bourke of Derivillaghny in the Magheri Reagh within the county of Galway.

To the fourth

Moroghe her second son aforesaid and Donell son to her first son the aforesaid Owen murdered do possess and enjoy the fourth part of Barony of Ballynehenssy aforesaid unto them descended from their ancestors which is all the maintenance they have.

To the fifth

This is answered more at large to the third article.

To the sixth

Her first husband by the mother's side of Sir Moroghe now at court was his cousin german and also cousins both being descended of one stock and root of nine degrees of consanguinity asunder.

To *the seventh*

Her second husband was called Sir Richard Bourke Knight[9] alias McWilliam chief of the Bourkes of Nether or Low Connaught by him she had a son called Theobald Bourke[10] now living he is married to Mewffe O'Connor sister to O'Connor Sligo now at court, his inheritance is about 40 quarters of land situated in the three baronies of Carry [Carra], Nether Owel and Galling [Gallen].

To *the eighth*

The countries of Connaught among the Irishry never yielded any thirds to any woman surviving the chieftain whose rent was uncertain for the most part extorted but now made certain by the composition and all Irish exactions merely abolished.

To *the ninth*

The Composition provided nothing to relieve the wife of any chieftain after his death wherein no mention is made of any such.

To *the tenth*

Among the Irishry the custom is that wives shall have but her first dowry without any increase of allowance for the same time out of mind it hath been so used and before any woman do deliver up her marriage portion to her husband she received sureties for the restitution of the same in manner and form as she hath delivered it in regard that husbands through their great expenses especially chieftains at the time of their deaths have no goods to leave behind them but are commonly indebted; at other times they are divorced upon proof of precontracts; and the husband now and then without any lawful or due proceeding do put his wife from him and so bringeth in another; so as the wife is to have sureties for her dowry for fear of the worse.

To the eleventh

After the death of her last husband she gathered together all her own followers and with 1,000 head of cows and mares departed and became a dwelling in Carrikhowlly in Borisowle parcel of the Earl of Ormond's lands in Connaught and in the year 1586 after the murdering of her son Owen, the rebellion being then in Connaught, Sir Richard Bingham granted her his letters of tuition against all men and willed her to come and dwell under him, in her journey as she traveled she was encountered by the five bands of soldiers under the leading of John Bingham and thereupon she was apprehended and tied in a rope, both she and her followers at that instant were spoiled of their said cattle and of all that ever they had besides the same and brought to Sir Richard who caused a new pair of gallows to be made for her last funeral where she thought to end her days, she was let at liberty upon the hostage and pledge of one Richard Bourke otherwise called the Devil's Hook when he did rebel fear compelled her to fly by sea into Ulster and there with O'Neill and O'Donnell stayed three months; her galleys by a tempest being broken. She returned to Connaught and in Dublin received her Majesty's pardon by Sir John Perrot six years past and so made free. Ever since she dwelleth in Connaught a farmers life very poor bearing cess[11] and paying Her Majesty's composition rent, utterly did she give over her former trade of maintenance by sea and land.

To the twelfth

Walter Bourke FitzThebalt and Shane Bourke FitzMeiller are cousins german removed of one side vis. Walter son to Thebault, son to Meiller son to the said Walter Faddy. Thebault Bourke mentioned in the seventh article and borne by Grany Ny Mailly [Grace O'Malley] is sone to Sir Richard Bourke her last husband, which Sir Richard was brother to the said Walter Faddy.

To the thirteenth

The country of her first husband is situated between Owle O'Mailley on the north west part, MacWilliam's country to the north east towards the country of Sligo, Sir Moroghe Offlaherties country on the east side towards Galway and the great bay of Galway on the south.

To the fourteenth

The castle town and lands of Morisky is possess by Owen M'Thomas O'Mailley now chieftain by the name of O'Mailley.

To the fifteenth

The Mac Gibbons have no lands by inheritance in any part of the country; farmers they are at will both to the Bourkes and to the O'Maillies.

To the sixteenth

She doth not know or understand Caremore or Moinconnell.

To the seventeenth

The island of Ackill is occupied by some of the Mailleys as tenants to the Earl of Ormond, as for Kill Castle, she knoweth no town of that name.

To the eighteenth

Her last husband had two brothers Walter and Ulligge [Ulick] Bourke both died before she married Sir Richard Bourke, her said husband, their father was called David Bourke.

A set of 18 questions by Lord Burghley, the Lord Treasurer of England, dated July 1593 with appropriate answers by Granuaile.

JACK "CHAKOUR" WARD

Tunisia

1605–1610

One fascinating element of many of the stories of piracy that we find in the seventeenth century and later is the way that pirates come to occupy a space or identity that is decoupled from land-based notions of territory. Jack Ward is one such example. Probably born in Kent, the same region where Francis Drake spent his boyhood, Ward would go on to embark on a career as a Barbary Coast pirate operating mainly in the region of Tunis, eventually "turning Turk," i.e., converting to Islam, and taking the name Yusuf Reis. He was born sometime in the 1550s, and as the ensuing account will demonstrate, he was a pretty hard character. The Spanish Armada tried and failed to invade England in 1588, after which time many men in coastal fishing communities like Ward's turned to privateering, claiming letters of marque (commissions, essentially) from the Crown to raid Spanish shipping under a veil of legitimacy. James I, however, ended hostilities with Spain upon his accession to the throne in 1603, and many of those mariners, like Ward, who had been squeezing their living out of privateering, continued their line of work, now outside the law as pirates.

The below account describes Ward's first determination to turn pirate. It paints a colorful picture of his habits of drinking and carousing and raises some interesting hypotheses about his sexual proclivities as well. By 1606 he and his crew had seized a dhow, or a thin-hulled, shallow draft sailing vessel commonly used in trade along the Barbary Coast and in the Red Sea, loaded with Catholic enslaved people. He arranged with Uthman Dey, the military commander of Tunis, to use Tunis as a safe haven for his raiding operations in the Mediterranean in exchange for the Dey's having right of first refusal over his spoils. The international character of maritime trade appears in the ships Ward and his company attacked: English merchantmen and rich Venetian traders, with enough value that England began to be concerned that Ward was a political liability. After his conversion he acquired the nickname "Chakour," supposedly because he resorted to an axe in his depredations on shipboard. He took an Italian wife while still supposedly sending money home to the English woman he had left behind, and was the subject of several plays and pamphlets during his lifetime. He retired, in a manner of speaking, around 1612, choosing instead to impart his wisdom to younger would-be corsairs, finally dying around 1622, possibly of the plague.

Some Turkish newspapers and other sources have suggested that Jack Ward was the inspiration for Captain Jack Sparrow[1] in the Pirates of the Caribbean films, though other sources claim that Johnny Depp based his performance on a combination of the Rolling Stones' Keith Richards and Pepé Le Pew.[2]

THE TRUE REPORT OF CAPTAIN WARDS PIRACIES, DONE BY ANDREW BARKER, MR. OF A SHIP, AND WHO WAS LATELY PRISONER IN TUNIS[3]

Sir, I have received your letter, and herein am glad to consent to your request, which was, (that since so many flying fables, and rumoring tales have been spread, of the fame, or rather indeed infamy, over the whole face of Christendom, of this notorious and arch pirate Ward) myself, who had even known him to be a knave, and of late (yet too soon) had proved him a thief, whose fortunes had been so much decayed by his prosperity, and who so long had been held his prisoner [. . .] who had there seen, abroad heard, and at Sea felt, the ability of his strength, the ordering of his actions, and the unjustness of his proceedings. I might best gratify my friends, and most truly satisfy the world, and their greedy and avidous expectation, what injury he hath done, daily doth, and still endeavoreth to do, to rich estates, and provident Sea-farers, to the venturing Merchant, and the careful Sailor, to poor wives and distressed children; how like a villain, and an apostate he lives, and how like a reprobate in persisting, he resolves to die.
[. . .]
This Ward, who now hath achieved to himself, the title of Captain, whose desperate actions hath caused terror to travelers by Sea, and whose name hath bred fear in the Merchants at home. In the last year of her late Majesty's reign,[4] was resident, and had his dwelling, (as by my own knowledge I can certify) in the West country at the haven Town of Plymouth, a fellow, poor, base, and of no esteem, one as tattered in [. . .], as he was ragged in conditions, the good past, that he could boast of himself, might be, that he was borne in a Town called Feversham[5] in Kent, and there lived as a poor fisherman, and the virtue present, that he durst talk of was, he had abiding in Plymouth, wherefore a while keeping house, although I have never heard that he paid his rent, all the day you should hardly fail but find him in an alehouse: but be sure

to have him drunk at home at night. Oaths were almost as ordinary with him as words, so that he seldom spake a sentence, but one was a syllable, he would sit melancholy, speak doggedly, curse the time, repine at other men's good fortunes, and complain of the hard crosses attended his own. All the virtue that any man could perceive might grow out of his whole course, or reckon out of his whole life was, that hitherto he loved not to be noted a quarreler: for rather then he would fight, he would be beaten by anyone. He was commonly called by the name of Jack Ward, one that was welcome into any tap-house, more for love of his coin, than love of his company, and all the reputation that his own crew held of him, was but this, that he was a mad rascal, would swear well, drink stiff, stick toot,[6] and like a good cock, he would never out of their damnable pit, if there were either money in his purse, or credible chalk in his hosts hand, being once in.

So that continuing thus for a reasonable season, in the same town drinking and swearing, the two twins, that such damnable wombs are ever in labor with, and not without wonder of a number, by what possible means he could get chinks,[7] so lewdly to consume his time withal. It at last so happened, that in the beginning of the King's reign,[8] he found means to be employed for service, in a small ship of his majesty's, commonly called by the name of the Lion's Whelp, in which employment, persisting as before, in his melancholy disposition, not contented, with that good and honest means was allowed him, and satisfied far better men, to defend themselves and the necessity of their charge: But having new reaches working in his brain, he one day selected out a choice crew, but of such, whose dispositions he perceived were as untoward as his own, when the poison of his heart disgorged itself thus.

"My mates," quoth he, "what's to be done? Here's a scurvy[9] world, and as scurvily we live in't, we feed here upon the water, on the King's salt beef,[10] without ere a penny to buy us bissell[11] when we come ashore, here's brine, but to revel, sup, and be merry, everyone at the proper charge of his own purse. So that this following night, when the Captain and Officers shall conjecture nothing, but that we are drawing dry the pot, we'll be diving arm deep in the Fugitives bags."

With which hopeful project, their resolutions being confirmed, and with the former purpose, getting ashore to their host's house, (which they chose to be without the walls[12] of Portsmouth) after some half a dozen of damnable oaths tane[13] down, they agreed amongst them, that with full cans, for the devising and foreseeing into this beneficial business, they freely, and of their own accord would elect Ward for their Captain, and which dignity accordingly (being down on their knees) with drink they performed, which installment done, and considering with themselves how they might best provide themselves of a boat, which the next full Sea should set them aboard the bark,[14] they resolved at a sortable hour to begin their ransack.

But see how it happened: A kinsman of this gentleman's, who had intended his departure, and furnished himself to this voyage for France, seeing the day before they attempted this Piracy, this Ward consorted with a crew of Scattergoods[15] and swaggering Rascals, and knowing fully of the charge that his friend had aboard, and withal nothing such a crew of desperates, mustering about Town, more then in one knot had been accustomed, and with such uncivil behavior, he began to be jealous they had some project in hand: whereupon he advised his friend to disbark[16] his money again, till the very instant that the wind served, and to lodge it in some place of more safety, to prevent the danger he stood in doubt of.

"For," quoth he, "yourself may witness what a knot of these knaves are linked together, who having not some intelligence, or but at least suspecting what substance you bear along with you, they will not stick to venture their bodies, I and it were to hazard their souls for money wherewithal to maintain their riot. So that I pray you Sir, be advised by my counsel: Redeem your money out of the Bark, and prevent their purpose, lest your repentance come too late."

Which counsel of his friends, setting some suspicion in the gentleman's head, and being the rather confirmed and grounded, through the disorders he beheld them continue in, and more than they were accustomed to exercise, he resolved himself to his friend's advice, and privately (either without knowledge or suspicion) landed his money and most estimable riches, and stored them in the Red Lion, (contenting themselves, then suspectless, to see what would be the issue of these fellows) and until the wind and tide should help fair for their departure.

Which defense of this gentleman's this new Captain Ward nothing at all suspecting, with his Command (as he before had determined) in the dead of night, and having so much experience to know when the tide and time was best for his advantage, he presently came and laid the Bark aboard, and entered his men in the hold of the Vessel, where he found none to resist him, but only two poor s[]ekes,[17] who belonged to the Bark, whom he straight shut under deck, and commanded them, not to squeak like Rats (in danger of their lives) whereby, upon their disturbance, the watch upon the first Blockhouse might have warning, and so with their Potguns[18] disquiet their peace. So presently weighing Anchor, and setting his sails, to Sea goes he. Only before his departure (yet not till he found himself out of their reach) he takes his farewell aloud, and very kindly bids me the watch good night. So that being now clear, and out of danger of their summons, and likewise come forth, without the Isle of Wight, like a Captain indeed, who now had command, he demands for the two men were lodged in his bark, and who, according to his call, were brought to his sight, when most Commander like, he began to question them, as they loved their safeties, to deliver truly unto him, in what place of the Bark was the Papists treasure hid, for that was the chief matter they came for, and that must be the means to make them merry withal, when these poor wretches shaking for fear before this terrible thief, they replied, that his expectation was herein frustrate, store of riches they must confess there was indeed, but upon what reason they knew not, it was the day before landed again.

At which unsatisfied news, and finding by search their words to be true, the whole crew having this cake of Ice for Sunshine

gold to chaw down, and comfort their stomachs withal. The
Rogues all, began now to be rank mad, there was then, such
Cursing, such Swearing, such Banning.

There was "a pox of thee, a pox of thee, and a plague of us
all, what shall now become of us? The Goldfinches we came
for, were flown out of their nest, little succor is to be found
here, and to go ashore we shall be sure to be hanged there, here
we are fallen desperately into the pitfall, and there we have
brought our necks just to the noose."

Yet at last, when their fury like an Hostler,[19] had walked
them awhile, and the heat of their bloods was grown a little
calmer, they agreed amongst themselves, that since their
pretense was to come for somewhat, they would at last see
what was there to be found. In which search, there was
presently laid open to their Ravening eyes, a couple of Venison-
Pasties, divers Turkey-pies, Capons, Hens, and such other
choice viands, as the forecited Gentlemen, had stored in the
bark for his own provision, to conduct him into France and of
every sort whereof, them was great store.

At the sight of which, Ward raps out oaths like pellets out of
a piece, that fly as swiftly as they can pass one after another,
and calls, "Come, let's be merry my hearts, although the birds
be flown, we came far, and we have found nothing but the
empty nest, come, let's be merry, & freely fat ourselves with
their fodder, here is good cheer, it was provided for us, and
we'll eat, an ounce of sorrow will not pay a penny debt. It is
bootless in these days, to lie in a ditch and cry for help, since
every man is bound to thrust out his hand to help himself, and
therefore my hearts let us be frolic with this, and live in hope
that our fortunes will be better."

At which (as if they had forgot already what they had done,
and not fearing what might follow) with this encouragement
they fell roundly aboard, when anon Ward called to them
again, "what, say you my bloods, who would be aboard of the
Lion's Whelp, with bare and hungry allowance of cold fish and
naked cheese, and may as we do thrust up their arms to the
elbow in a Venison pasty?"

And with that, breaking up a case of bottles, which were presented full of wine to his thieveship's hand, "here my mates," quoth he, "here is a health to our good fortunes, and a pox of the Hang-man, we know the worst, and let's therefore hope for the best, we'll be merry tonight with wine and Venison, and tomorrow take counsel what's best to be done."

SAMUEL PALACHE

The Pirate Rabbi

Morocco

1603–1614

Samuel Palache was born in the Jewish quarter of Fès, into a family with a longstanding rabbinical tradition. Jewish people had lived in the North African diaspora for hundreds of years, often in roles as moneylenders or dealers in gold and silver, which were jobs forbidden to their Muslim neighbors. This work also extended to backing sultan-supported corsair raids on Spanish shipping in the Mediterranean and along the Barbary Coast. Palache was one of a pair of brothers who traveled to Spain in January of 1603, offering news of a plan to halt the Ottoman advance on the North African coast in exchange for a right to settle there. After Spain denied him, he eventually settled in Holland, becoming one of the founders of Amsterdam's Jewish community, and helping to broker a treaty of friendship between Morocco and Holland. In 1614, while raiding with Dutch backing under the flag of Morocco (and with a kosher cook on board),[1] he was forced by bad weather to land in Plymouth, England, with three Spanish prizes he had taken, and was tried there for piracy at the urging of the Spanish Ambassador to England.

Palache is another example of a marine raider whose status as "pirate" is clouded by politics and perspective, largely because of his connections— both claimed and legitimate—to various conflicting imperial interests. He died in 1616 in Amsterdam, a respected rabbi, his black-draped coffin followed through the streets by Prince Maurice of Holland and more than a thousand mourners from the Jewish community he had founded.[2]

LETTER FROM LONDON, DATED NOVEMBER 4, 1614, FROM JOHN CHAMBERLAIN TO HIS FRIEND SIR DUDLEY CARLETON, THE BRITISH AMBASSADOR TO VENICE[3]

Here is a Jew Pirate arrested that brought three prizes of Spaniards into Plymouth . . . he shall likely pass out of here well enough for he has league and License under the King's hand for his free egress and regress which was not believed till he made proof of it.

ACTS OF THE PRIVY COUNCIL, DECEMBER 23, 1614

Privy Council to Sir William Craven, Alderman:

The Lordships give order for the restraint and safe keeping of Samuel Palache, a Jew, lately arrived at Plymouth [charged with] committing piracy and outrage upon the subjects of the King of Spain. . . . Palache hath alleged that he is a servant unto the King of Barbary, and by him employed as his agent unto the States United,[4] and that from the said King his master he had received commission for the arming and setting forth of ships of war, by virtue of which commission (together with license of the States United) he pretends the fact to be justifiable and no way with the compass of piracy.

WILLIAM JACKSON

Roatán

1630s–40s

Another example of piracy as a matter of perspective emerges with William Jackson, an English privateer based on Roatán, an island off the coast of Honduras. Jackson was an agent of the Providence Island Company, a Puritan colonial enterprise that sought to settle a Caribbean island along the same religious and financial principles as the Massachusetts Bay Colony with which most of us are more familiar. In effect, Providence Island became a pirate nest, albeit with such stringent moral laws that its failure was almost assured. While engaged with the Company, Jackson raided a Spanish slave ship out of Honduras and was rewarded with a cargo of indigo and two thousand Spanish reals (pieces of eight).

We don't have much information about Jackson, and there is a possibility that there were two different William Jacksons operating in the same waters around the same time. Broadly speaking, from the Spanish point of view Jackson was a pirate, lawlessly plundering along the Spanish Main. From the English perspective, he was essentially acting in the national interest. What follows is an account of his attack on Jamaica.[1]

Thus they continued in a seeming good Correspondence, and undisturbed, till about the Year 1635, when Colonel Jackson, with a small Fleet, set out from the Leeward Islands, with a Design upon Jamaica; he had not many Companions, but they were brave, resolute and daring, and such as he knew would not mind the Danger, if they were sure of a rich Purchase. With the Company he landed, which did not exceed 500 Men, and immediately attacked 2,000 Spaniards at Passage-Fort. They received him with Courage enough, and for a short time sustained the Fury of the Onset with abundance of Resolution; but that brave Few fought with such Spirit, that the Spaniards began to retire, and at last fled. Several Hundreds were killed in the Engagement and Pursuit. The English, having gained this Advantage, did not delay a Moment to prosecute the good Consequences of the Victory: they marched to St. Jago at about the Distance of six Miles, briskly stormed the Town, and notwithstanding the Opposition they met with, soon entered it Sword in Hand, and pillaged it of everything that was valuable: The Spoil was divided among the Soldiers, and the Spaniards were glad to agree for a certain Sum, to save the City from being burnt; which they soon paid, and the brave Colonel retreated to his ships without the least Disturbance, having, in all this Expedition, lost no more than Forty Men.

THOMAS VEAL

Lynn, Massachusetts

1658

In the spirit of fictional pirate stories being so often presented as fact, I now present a story that is almost certainly untrue. The following account, claiming that a pirate named Thomas Veal had been trapped with his treasure in a cave collapse at a formation that came to be called Dungeon Rock in Lynn, Massachusetts, in 1658, began to circulate in the 1820s.[1] Was there really an earthquake in New England, a nonseismic region, in 1658 that was strong enough to entomb someone in a cave? Doubtful. Did Thomas Veal exist? A Thomas Vealy had his will probated in Salem, Massachusetts—one town over from Lynn, in the same county—in 1714 and signed by his mark, rather than by his own hand, which indicates he wasn't literate.[2] But that's a generation later. The story specifically mentions the Saugus Iron Works, a seventeenth-century iron foundry that lives on today as a National Historic Landmark in Massachusetts. But that doesn't make it true.

A writer in 1865 set out to investigate this story, and found no record in the courts, nor at the Iron Works. But that did nothing to dispel widespread public interest in the story.

In the 1830s—a time, as we will see, in which real piracy still plagued the Caribbean—on the North Shore, where many real people who had personally encountered pirates on the high seas still lived, two

*separate attempts were made to discover the trea-
sure by blowing up the collapsed cave mouth with
powder kegs of explosive. Then, in 1852, Hiram
Marble, an avid spiritualist, purchased the property
on which the remnants of the cave stood and began
tunneling his way inside. He told onlookers that he
was digging there on the instructions of the ghosts of
the pirates, exchanged through notes on small folded
slips of paper.*

*The project dragged on for years, devouring Mar-
ble's savings, and he finally began marketing the tunnel as a tourist attraction called Pirates' Glen. Tours
cost a quarter, or would-be investors could buy a
bond for a dollar that promised them a share of the
treasure when it was recovered.*

*Marble never gave up his quest. He died in 1868,
having burrowed a tunnel 174 feet long and high
enough for an adult to stand in. His son Edwin never
lost his faith in his father's ghost-fueled vision of pirate riches either, and when he died himself in 1880,
he was buried at Dungeon Rock with a pink marker
for his tombstone. Dungeon Rock still exists today,
part of the Lynn Woods Reservation, and reportedly
the tunnel is open for visits during daylight hours. If
you go and find any treasure, please let your editor
know.*[3]

In the year 1658 there was a great earthquake in New England.[4] Sometime previous, on one pleasant evening, a little
after sunset, a small vessel was seen to anchor near the mouth
of Saugus River. A boat was presently lowered from her side,
into which four men descended, and moved up the river a considerable distance, when they landed, and proceeded directly

into the woods. They had been noticed by only a few individuals; but in those early times, when the people were surrounded by danger, and easily susceptible of alarm, such an incident was well calculated to awaken suspicion, and in the course of the evening the intelligence was conveyed to many houses. In the morning, the people naturally directed their eyes toward the shore, in search of the strange vessel—but she was gone, and no trace could be found either of her or her singular crew. It was afterward ascertained that, on the morning one of the men at the Iron Works, on going into the foundry, discovered a paper, on which was written, that if a quantity of shackles, handcuffs, hatchets, and other articles of iron manufacture were made and deposited, with secrecy, in a certain place in the woods, which was particularly designated, an amount of silver, to their full value, would be found in their place. The articles were made in a few days and placed in conformity with the directions. On the next morning they were gone, and the money was found according to the promise; but though a watch had been kept, no vessel was seen. Some months afterward, the four men returned and selected one of the most secluded and romantic spots in the woods of Saugus for their abode. The place of their retreat was a deep narrow valley, shut in on two sides by craggy, precipitous rocks, and shrouded on the others by thick pines, hemlocks and cedars, between which there was only one small spot, to which the rays of the sun at noon could penetrate. On climbing up the rude and almost perpendicular steps of the rock on either side, the eye could command a full view of the bay on the south, and a prospect of a considerable portion of the surrounding country. The place of their retreat has ever since been called the Pirates' Glen, and they could not have selected a spot on the coast for many miles, more favorable for the purposes both of concealment and observation. Even at this day, when the neighborhood has become thickly peopled, it is still a lonely and desolate place,[5] and probably not one in a hundred of the inhabitants has ever descended into its silent and gloomy recess. There the pirates built a small hut, made a garden, and dug a well, the appearance of which is still visible. It has been supposed that they buried money; but though people have dug there, and in many other places, none has ever been found. After residing there some time, their retreat became known, and one of the king's cruisers appeared on the coast. They were traced to their glen, and three of them were taken, and carried to England, where it is probable they were executed. The other, whose name was Thomas Veal, escaped to a rock in the woods, about two miles to the north, in which was a spacious cavern, where the pirates had previously deposited some of their plunder. There the fugitive fixed his residence, and practiced the trade of a shoemaker,[6] occasionally coming down to the village to obtain articles of sustenance. He continued his residence till the great earthquake in 1658, when the top of the rock was loosened, and crushed down into the mouth of the cavern, enclosing the unfortunate inmate in its unyielding prison. It has ever since been called the Pirates' Dungeon. A part of the cavern is still open, and is much visited by the curious.

This rock is situated on a lofty range of thickly wooded hills and commands an extensive view of the ocean, for fifty miles both north and south. A view from the top of it at once convinces the beholder that it would be impossible to select a place more convenient for the haunt of a gang of pirates; as all vessels bound in and out of the harbors of Boston, Salem, and the adjacent ports can be distinctly seen from its summit. Saugus River meanders among the hills a short distance to the south, and its numerous creeks, which extend among thick bushes, would afford good places to secrete boats, until such time as the pirates descried a sail, when they could instantly row down the river, attack and plunder them, and with their booty return to the cavern. This was evidently their mode of procedure. On an open space in front of the rock are still to be seen distinct traces of a small garden spot, and in the corner is a small well, full of stones and rubbish; the foundation of the wall round the garden remains, and shows that the spot was of a triangular shape, and was well selected for the cultivation of potatoes and common vegetables. The aperture in the rock is only about five feet in height and extends only fifteen feet into the rock. The needle is strongly attracted around this, either by the presence of magnetic iron ore or some metallic substance buried in the interior.

The Pirates' Glen, which is some distance from this, is one of Nature's wildest and most picturesque spots, and the cellar of the pirates' hut remains to the present time,[7] as does a clear space, which was evidently cultivated at some remote period.

HENRY MORGAN

Jamaica

Knighted in 1674

From an imaginary pirate to a legendary one, we now come to Henry Morgan, who was so much more than the brand of rum by which he is presently remembered. Morgan might be better understood as a seventeenth-century soldier of fortune, like an operative with Russia's Wagner Group today. Born in Wales, he would end his days in Jamaica, knighted for his service to the Crown, and having served as Jamaica's lieutenant governor. He made his base of operations the infamous pirate nest Port Royal and used his booty to obtain capacious sugar plantations, which he ran in his retirement. As always, piracy and enslavement cannot be disentangled.

Morgan's early years are somewhat hazy, though the following account claims authority on his origins. He was likely born in the 1630s in a region of Wales that is now part of Cardiff. It is not known with certainty what circumstances first took him to sea or to the Caribbean specifically. By 1667, as tensions were once again rising between England and Spain around shipping and sovereignty, Morgan acquired a letter of marque to permit his raiding along the Spanish Main. Under English authority he led successful attacks on areas in modern-day Cuba and Panama, another example of one country's pirate being another country's national hero. When once again the political weather between England and Spain shifted, leaving Morgan outside the boundary of legality, he was arrested in 1672 and placed on trial, though he was received in England with great admiration and fanfare, including by Charles II.

By 1674 he had been knighted and returned to a life of prosperity, politics, and plantation ownership in Jamaica until his death in 1688. Much of his piratical reputation rests on the publication in 1684 of a book by Alexander [Alexandre] Exquemelin, who had been one of his shipmates, first published in Dutch and called in various translations a version of The Buccaneers of America. *The account of Morgan in that book was unflattering to the point of brutality. Morgan successfully sued Exquemelin's publishers[1] for libel, but Exquemelin's remains the dominant account of Morgan's life as a pirate and is the source of one of the two excerpts below. The first is an unsparing account of Morgan's courage, and pitilessness, taken from a history of Jamaica first published in 1740. The second account covers some of the same period of Morgan's life as the first, only rendered from Exquemelin's perspective. The reader may judge for herself which account of Henry Morgan to trust.*

Libelous claims notwithstanding, don't mistake Morgan for a nice guy. In his role as plantation owner he led several campaigns to attack a community of Jamaican "Maroons," free Black descendants of self-liberating people who established communities in Jamaica's Blue Mountains. At the time of his death, 131 enslaved people of African heritage were working on his sugar plantations, of whom 33 were children.[2]

First, from a history of Jamaica:[3]

SIR, I am now to present you with an Abstract of a Life, that, in all its Parts, is extraordinary and surprising; a Man born of mean and obscure Parents, without Learning, or any thing else but his Courage to support him, advanced to the Dignity of a Lieutenant-Governor, over one of the finest Colonies in America, performing Actions almost incredible; with a desperate Few, storming Towns, and defeating Thousands, carrying the Terror of his Name to the remotest Corners of the New World, and making Viceroys tremble at the Head of Armies!

Such a one was Sir Henry Morgan, born in the Principality of Wales. His Father was a Farmer, of pretty good Repute, who designed his Son for the same way of Life; but his Inclinations were turned another way; and finding his Father positive in his Resolution, bid him adieu, and rambled to Bristol, where he bound himself a Servant for four Years, and was transported to Barbados; there he was sold,[4] and served his Master with a great deal of Fidelity. But his Term of Years was no sooner expired, than he shipped himself off for Jamaica, resolving to join the Pirates, and push for a Fortune along with them. He found Entertainment immediately on his Arrival, on Board a Sloop, which was to cruise upon the Spanish Coasts; and behaved with such Resolution and Courage, that he soon became famous. Having made several prosperous Voyages, he took care to secure his Share of the Booty in good Hands. He saw the Excess and Debauchery of his Fellows, and that they became soon reduced to the lowest Shifts, by their lavish Expenses on their Arrival: But he, having vast Designs in View, lived moderate, and got soon together as much Money as purchased a Vessel for himself; and, having got a fine Crew, put to Sea. His Success was at first but small, but afterwards he took several Prizes, which he carried to Jamaica, and disposed of. He made afterwards many successful Expeditions, and his Name grew so famous, that Mansvelt,[5] an old Pirate, having equipped a considerable Fleet, with a Design upon the Spaniards, pitched on Morgan to be his Vice-Admiral: They sailed from Jamaica with fifteen Ships and five hundred Men, and arrived at the Isle of St. Catharine's,[6] situated near the

Continent of Costa Rica. Here they landed, and made such a furious Attack, that they obliged the Castle and Garrison to surrender: They became entire Masters of the Island, and resolving to preserve it for their own proper Use, placed an Hundred of their Men in one of the Forts, entirely demolishing all the rest.

There is a small Island adjoining to St. Catharine's, which is so near, that a Bridge may reach betwixt them; this they likewise took, and having pillaged the Island of every thing of Value, retired to their Ships, leaving proper Orders with the Garrison they had placed in the Castle. They carried off a great many Spanish Prisoners; and judging it imprudent to allow them to continue in the Island, for fear of their creating a Disturbance, they steered for Puerto Velo, where the Spanish Prisoners were set ashore; and thence began to cruise on the Coasts of Costa Rica, designing to proceed a great deal further in Pursuit of new Conquests. But the Governor of Panama, having Intelligence of their Arrival and Designs, prepared to give them a very warm Reception; and having got together a great Body of Men, resolved to march, and drive them to their Ships. But they did not think it proper to wait his Coming; for knowing they were discovered, and that they had not sufficient Force to fight him, they retired to their Ships, and put to Sea.

They made directly for St. Catharine's, where they found their Garrison in Health, and everything in an extraordinary good Situation. Le Sieur Simon, a Frenchman, whom they had left to command, had performed his Part to their entire Satisfaction. Mansvelt would fain have kept the Island, it being so convenient for his Designs, and, for that Reason, applied to the Governor of Jamaica for Assistance; but his Excellency well knew, he durst not countenance them in such an open manner: Neither would it have been of Advantage to Jamaica; for the Pirates had infallibly made St. Catharine's their Place of Rendezvous; and by this means that Stream of Riches, which flowed so plentifully by their means into Jamaica, had been diverted into another Channel.

Mansvelt applied next to the Governor of Tortuga, but with like Success. Soon after he ended his wicked Life, and the Island of St. Catharine's was retaken by the Spaniards. Morgan did

all he could to prevent its falling into their Hands, but to no
Purpose; yet notwithstanding he retained his Courage and
Spirit, and began to equip another Fleet, in order to carry on his
Designs.

In less than two Months he saw himself at the Head of Twelve
stout Ships, and 700 fighting Men; and, now judging himself
sufficiently strong to attempt something himself of Consequence, he was at first for attacking the Havannah;[7] but, on
cooler Thoughts, seeing the Danger of such an Enterprise, he resolved to attempt some other Place.

After a great many Opinions were heard, they at last agreed
to storm Puerto del Principe, which is a fine island Town in the
Island of Cuba. Here the Pirates hoped for a rich Booty, and
having directed their Course of that Part of the Coast which lies
nearest it, resolved to land in El Puerto de Sancta Maria Bay.
But their Designs had like to have come to nothing, and the Expedition to have proved fatal to them all; for a Spaniard, whom
they detained as a Prisoner, having found means to escape, ran
directly to the Town, and gave the Alarm. The Governor immediately put the Place in a Posture of Defense, and did all that
Prudence or Courage could inspire. He raised and armed the
People of the City, both Freemen and Slaves; ordered vast Quan-
tities of Trees to be cut down, and laid cross the Roads, to ob-
struct their Passage; placed several Ambuscades[8] in convenient
Places; seiz'd an advantageous Pass, thro' which the Pirates were
expected to march; and, with the rest of his Forces, encamped
on a fine Plain, from whence they could see the Pirates advanc-
ing a great way off.

Morgan, with his Party, was surprised to find the Avenues
rendered impassable; they well knew they had been discovered,
but it was now too late to think of a Retreat: They animated
each other, and resolved to face all the Difficulties in their way;
and turning out of the common Road, they travelled thro' the
Woods, and so escaped the Ambuscades; and with a great deal
of Difficulty reached the Plain, where the Spaniards lay in-
camped.

The Governor immediately charged them, and a desperate
Fight began. The Spaniards behaved very well; but there was no

standing against the Fury of the Pirates, who fought like so many Madmen; and understanding exactly how to handle their Weapons, killed a vast number of Spaniards. The Engagement lasted four Hours. The Governor, and a great many Gentlemen of Note, were killed on the Field of Battle. At last the Rout began, the Spaniards fled, and were briskly pursued by the victorious Pirates. The People in the Town made a very good Defense, but were forced to surrender. The Town was taken, and soon became a Prey to the rapacious Conquerors: They drove the Men, Women and Children, promiscuously into the Churches, where they shut them in, and fell to Feasting and Riot, while they allowed their Prisoners nothing to support Nature. They continued amassing up all the Wealth they could get, and dispatched Parties into the Country, which returned with great Booty. At last, they began to think of removing; but first used the most inhuman Methods to persuade the poor half-starv'd Spaniards to discover their Money, tormenting them to that Degree, that many died, besides a vast Multitude, who perished of their Famine.

Provisions beginning to grow scarce, the Pirates resolved to retreat; but having demanded a Ransom for the Town, a few of the Prisoners were set at Liberty, to endeavor to procure the Sum. At this time a Negro was caught with Letters from the Governor of St. Jago,[9] to some of the principal Inhabitants of the Town; wherein he acquainted them with his Intention of coming very speedily to their Relief, and desiring them not to enter into any Agreement with the Pirates, but put off their Demands by repeated Excuses, till he should get to their Assistance. This unseasonable Piece of News put the Pirates in a kind of Terror; but concealing their Intelligence from the Townsmen, when their Deputies returned, and told them their Endeavors had been ineffectual; for they could not find Means to raise the Money; Morgan seemed good-natur'd all of a sudden, and told them, he would depart, if they would only provide Five hundred Beeves,[10] and salt them, for victualling his Ships. This they readily consented to, and accordingly performed in a few Days. He then set Sail; but an unhappy Division falling out among his Crew, on account of a Frenchman's being basely stabb'd by one

of the English Sailors, the French parted from Morgan, notwithstanding he used the utmost Art to keep them with him. The
Criminal he put in Chains, and carried to Jamaica; where he
caused him to be hanged. The Prize they took at Puerto del Principe, did not amount to more than Fifty thousand Pieces of
Eight,[11] which, when it came to be divided, was scarce sufficient
to defray their Debts in Jamaica; therefore they instantly resolved to go in quest of some new Adventure; and being encour-
aged by Captain Morgan, they resolved to be led by him,
without inquiring into his Designs, having an entire Reliance
upon his good Conduct, Courage, and Abilities.

Having his Crew so much at Command, he set Sail with Four
hundred and Fifty Men in Nine small Ships, and made towards
Costa Rica; there he imparted his Design of attacking Puerto
Velo to his whole Company. Several objected against the Attempt, because they had not sufficient Number to think of Success against so strong a City. But Morgan replied, "If our
Numbers are small, our Hearts are great; and the fewer we are,
the better Shares we shall have in the Spoil."

The Hope of Riches made them quit their Fears, and they
showed an Ambition of daring the Danger. Indeed, if we consider the Boldness of this Attempt, it will scarce find a Parallel in
History.

Puerto Velo is about Fourteen Leagues[12] from the Gulf of
Darien,[13] and Eight Westwards of the Nombre de Dios, and is
one of the strongest Places in the West-Indies: It is guarded by
Three Castles, which are almost impregnable, Two of them situated at the Entry to the Port, so that no Ship or Boat can pass
without Permission: These are not only well-garrisoned, but the
Town consists, besides, of near Five hundred Families. The Merchants have here their Chief Ware-houses, and 'tis a Place of extraordinary Trade.

Morgan was perfectly well acquainted with all the Avenues to
the City. 'Twas Night when he came to Puerto de Naos, about
Ten Leagues West of Puerto Velo: They sailed up the River from
thence to Puerto Pontin, where they came to an Anchor. They
took Boats, and about Midnight came to Estera longa le Mos,
where they all went ashore, and marched by Land to the first

Posts of the City. An Englishman, who had been a Prisoner in this Place, served them for a Guide.

This Fellow had Abundance of Courage, and was fit for the greatest Attempts: Besides, he was pushed on the Desires of Revenge; for the bad Usage he had met with from the Spaniards, had inflamed his Mind to such a Degree, that he listed a Pirate, with no other View than to be revenged; and this being the Place where he was formerly confined, he exerted himself, on that account, with the greatest Courage, as well as Art and Dexterity.

There were only Three more, daring like himself, who offered themselves to go and secure the Sentry. They went on with the greatest Caution; for, on their artful Management of this first Attempt, the whole Success of their Expedition depended: When they were got near enough, they at once laid hold of the Sentinel, and that so suddenly, that he had not Time, or Presence of Mind, to give the Alarm, by firing his Musket; and they provided against any other Noise, by gagging him.

Having thus successfully finished what they were commanded, they returned to Morgan with their Prisoner. The poor Wretch, being terrified with their Threats, freely discovered all he knew, told them in what Situation the Castle and Garrison were, and everything else which they demanded. On the welcome Intelligence he gave them, they instantly marched, carrying the captive Spaniard along; and, having got close to the Castle, entirely surrounded it; and by this means effectually prevented any from going in, or coming out.

The Spaniard, whom they had taken, was commanded to bid them surrender, and, if they refused, to threaten the utmost Severity; but he had no other Return, but from the Mouth of their Cannon. This gave the Alarm to the City; and the Pirates, afraid lest a superior Force from that Quarter should attack them, made a furious Assault, and carried the Place. They were not sooner in Possession, but they drove the miserable Spaniards into one Place, and instantly set Fire to the Magazine of Powder, which in an Instant destroyed them.

[. . . Morgan proceeds to sack the city, including houses and churches, and drives nuns and priests out of monas-

teries to force them to help affix ladders to the city walls
to help with their havoc. . . .]

The Place being now in their Power, they fell to their usual Debaucheries, committed the most horrid Rapes and Murders, tortured the Prisoners, and barbarously derided them in their Misery; till at last they began to think of retreating, which they offered to their Captives, if they would pay 100,000 Pieces of Eight for their Ransom. Two of that miserable Number were deputed from the rest to go to Panama, to raise the Sum; but the President, having raised a large Body of Men, was on his March to encounter the Pirates. The Deputies waited the Event, which proved fatal to the President's Party; for a Hundred Pirates beat and dispersed them, having killed an incredible Number in the time of Engagement. This disaster convinced these Gentlemen, who had been sent to procure the Ransom, that there was a Necessity of complying with Morgan's Demands; therefore, having raised the Sum, they returned, and gave it into his Hands.

Having victualled his Ships, he set Sail, but first dismounted the great Guns on the Castles, and leveled several Redoubts which had been raised by the Spaniards. He soon got to Jamaica, and found his Purchase amount to 250,000 Pieces of Eight, besides all other Merchandizes. Thus successfully ended one of the boldest Attempts that perhaps was ever made: Four hundred Men, to attack a strong and populous City, guarded by Three Castles well garrisoned, and abounding with all manner of military Stores, while the Pirates had nothing but Sword and Pistol to fight with! What will not such Resolution surmount?

And now, here is Exquemelin's take:[14]

CAPTAIN HENRY MORGAN was born in Great Britain, in the principality of Wales; his father was & rich yeoman, or farmer, of good quality, even as most who bear that name in Wales are known to be. Morgan, when young, had no inclination to the calling of his father, and therefore left his country, and came towards the seacoasts to seek some other employment more suitable to his aspiring humor; where he found several ships at anchor, bound for Barbados. With these he resolved to go in the service of one, who, according to the practice of those parts, sold him as soon as he came ashore. He served his time at Barbados, and obtaining his liberty, betook himself to Jamaica, there to seek new fortunes: here he found two vessels of pirates ready to go to sea; and being destitute of employment, he went with them, with intent to follow the exercises of that sort of people: he soon learned their manner of living, so exactly, that having performed three or four voyages with profit and success, he agreed with some of his comrades, who had got by the same voyages a little money, to join stocks, and buy a ship. The vessel being bought, they unanimously chose him captain and commander.

With this ship he set forth from Jamaica to cruise on the coasts of Campechy,[15] in which voyage he took several ships, with which he returned triumphant. Here he found an old pirate, named Mansvelt [. . .] busied in equipping a considerable fleet, with design to land on the continent, and pillage whatever he could. Mansvelt seeing Captain Morgan return with so many prizes, judged him to be a man of courage, and chose him for his vice-admiral in that expedition: thus having fitted out fifteen ships, great and small, they sailed from Jamaica with five hundred men, Walloons[16] and French. This fleet arrived, not long after, at the isle of St. Catherine, near the continent of Costa Rica, latitude 12 deg. 30 min. and distant thirty-five leagues from the river Chagre.[17] Here they made their first descent, landing most of their men, who soon forced the garrison that kept the island to surrender all the forts and castles thereof; which they instantly demolished, except one, wherein they placed a hundred men of their own party, and all the slaves they had taken from the Spaniards: with the rest of their men they marched to another small island, so near St. Catherine's, that with a bridge they made in a few days, they passed thither, taking with them all the ordnance they had taken on the great island. Having ruined with fire and sword both the islands, leaving necessary orders at the said castle, they put to sea again, with their Spanish prisoners; yet these they set ashore not long after, on the firm land, near Puerto Velo: then they cruised on Costa Rica, till they came to the river Colla, designing to pillage all the towns in those parts, thence to pass to the village of Nata, to do the same.

The governor of Panama, on advice of their arrival, and of the hostilities they committed, thought it his duty to meet them with a body of men. His coming caused the pirates to retire suddenly, seeing the whole country was alarmed, and that their designs were known, and consequently defeated at that time. Hereupon, they returned to St. Catherine's, to visit the hundred men they left in garrison there. The governor of these men was a Frenchman, named Le Sieur Simon,[18] who behaved himself very well in that charge, while Mansvelt was absent, having put the great island in a very good posture of defense, and the little one he had caused to be cultivated with many fertile plantations, sufficient to revictual the whole fleet, not only for the present, but also for a new voyage. Mansvelt was very much bent to keep the two islands in perpetual possession, being very commodiously situated for the pirates; being so near the Spanish dominions, and easily defended. Hereupon, Mansvelt determined to return to Jamaica, to send recruits to St. Catherine's, that in case of an invasion the pirates might be provided for a defense. As soon as he arrived, he propounded his intentions to the governor there, who rejected his propositions, fearing to displease his master, the king of England; besides, that giving him the men he desired, and necessaries, he must of necessity diminish the forces of that island, whereof he was governor

Hereupon, Mansvelt, knowing that of himself he could not compass his designs, he went to Tortuga; but there, before he could put in execution what was intended, death surprised him, and put a period to his wicked life, leaving all things in suspense till the occasion I shall hereafter relate.

Le Sieur Simon, governor of St. Catherine's, receiving no news from Mansvelt, his admiral, was impatiently desirous to know the cause thereof: meanwhile, Don John Perez de Guzman, being newly come to the government of Costa Rica, thought it not convenient for the interest of Spain for that island to be in the hands of the pirates: hereupon, he equipped a considerable fleet, which he sent to retake it; but before he used violence, he writ a letter to Le Sieur Simon, telling him, that if he would surrender the island to his Catholic Majesty,[19] he should be very well rewarded; but, in case of refusal, severely punished, when he had forced him to do it. Le Sieur Simon, seeing no probability of being able to defend it alone, nor any emolument that by so doing could accrue either to him, or his people, after some small resistance delivered it up to its true lord and master, under the same articles they had obtained it from the Spaniards; a few days after which surrender, there arrived from Jamaica an English ship, which the governor there had sent underhand, with a good supply of people, both men and women: the Spaniards from the castle having espied the ship, put forth English colors, and persuaded Le Sieur Simon to go aboard, and conduct the ship into a port they assigned him. This he performed and they were all made prisoners. A certain Spanish engineer has published in print an exact relation of the retaking of this isle by the Spaniards, which I have thought fit to insert here:

A true relation, and particular account of the victory obtained by the arms of his Catholic Majesty against the English pirates, by the direction and valor of Don John Perez de Guzman, knight of the order of St. James, governor and captain-general of Terra Firma, and the Province of Veraguas.

The kingdom of Terra Firma,[20] which of itself is sufficiently strong to repel and destroy great fleets, especially the pirates of Jamaica, had several ways notice imparted to the governor thereof, that fourteen English vessels cruised on the coasts belonging to his Catholic Majesty. July 14, 1665, news came to Panama, that they were arrived at Puerto de Naos, and had forced the Spanish garrison of the isle of St. Catherine, whose governor was Don Estevan del Campo, and possessed themselves of the said island, taking prisoners the inhabitants, and destroying all that they met. About the same time, Don John

Perez de Guzman received particular information of these robberies from some Spaniards who escaped out of the island (and whom he ordered to be conveyed to Puerto Velo), that the said pirates came into the island May 2, by night, without being perceived; and that the next day, after some skirmishes, they took the fortresses, and made prisoners all the inhabitants and soldiers that could not escape. Upon this, Don John called a council of war, wherein he declared the great progress the said pirates had made in the dominions of his Catholic Majesty; and propounded "that it was absolutely necessary to send some forces to the isle of St. Catherine, sufficient to retake it from the pirates, the honor and interest of his Majesty of Spain being very narrowly concerned herein; otherwise the pirates by such conquests might easily, in course of time, possess themselves of all the countries thereabouts."

To this some made answer, "that the pirates, not being able to subsist in the said island, would of necessity consume and waste themselves, and be forced to quit it, without any necessity of retaking it: that consequently it was not worth the while to engage in so many expenses and troubles as this would cost."

Notwithstanding which, Don John being an expert and valiant soldier, ordered that provisions should be conveyed to Puerto Velo for the use of the militia, and transported himself thither, with no small danger of his life. Here he arrived July 2, with most things necessary to the expedition in hand, where he found in the port a good ship, and well mounted, called the *St. Vincent,* that belonged to the company of the negroes, which he manned and victualled very well, and sent to the isle of St. Catherine, constituting Captain Joseph Sanchez Ximenez, major of Puerto Velo, commander thereof. He carried with him two hundred and seventy soldiers, and thirty-seven prisoners of the same island, besides thirty-four Spaniards of the garrison of Puerto Velo, twenty-nine mulattoes of Panama, twelve Indians, very dexterous at shooting with bows and arrows, seven expert and able gunners, two lieutenants, two pilots, one surgeon, and one religious, of the order of St. Francis, for their chaplain.

Don John soon after gave orders to all the officers how to behave themselves, telling them that the governor of Carthagena[21] would supply them with more men, boats, and all things else, necessary for that enterprise; to which effect he had already written to the said governor. July 24, Don John setting sail with a fair wind, he called before him all his people, and made them a speech, encouraging them to fight against the enemies of their country and religion, and especially against those inhuman pirates, who had committed so many horrid cruelties upon the subjects of his Catholic Majesty; withal, promising every one most liberal rewards, especially to such as should behave themselves well in the service of their kind and country. Thus Don John bid them farewell, and the ship set sail under a favorable gale. The 22nd they arrived at Carthagena, and presented a letter to the governor thereof, from the noble and valiant Don John, who received it with testimonies of great affection to the person of Don John, and his Majesty's service: and seeing their resolution to be conformable to his desires, he promised them his assistance, with one frigate,[22] one galleon,[23] one boat,[24] and one hundred and twenty-six men; one half out of his own garrison, and the other half mulattoes. Thus being well provided with necessaries, they left the port of Carthagena, August 2, and the 10th they arrived in sight of St. Catherine's towards the western point thereof; and though the wind was contrary, yet they reached the port, and anchored within it, having lost one of their boats by foul weather, at the rock called Quita Signos.

The pirates, seeing our ships come to an anchor, gave them presently three guns with bullets, which were soon answered in the same coin. Hereupon, Major Joseph Sanchez Ximenez sent ashore to the pirates one of his officers to require them, in the name of the Catholic King his master, to surrender the island, seeing they had taken it in the midst of peace between the two crowns of Spain and England; and that if they would be obstinate, he would certainly put them all to the sword. The pirates made answer, that the island had once before belonged unto the government and dominions of the king of England, and that instead of surrendering it, they preferred to lose their lives.

On Friday the 13th, three negroes, from the enemy, came swimming aboard our admiral; these brought intelligence, that all the pirates upon the island were only seventy-two in number, and that they were under a great consternation, seeing such considerable forces come against them. With this intelligence, the Spaniards resolved to land, and advance towards the fortresses, which ceased not to fire as many great guns against them as they possibly could; which were answered in the same manner on our side, till dark night. On Sunday, the 15th, the day of the Assumption of our Lady, the weather being very calm and clear, the Spaniards began to advance thus: The ship *St. Vincent,* riding admiral, discharged two whole broadsides on the battery called the *Conception*; the ship *St. Peter,* that was vice-admiral, discharged likewise her guns against the other battery named *St. James*: meanwhile, our people landed in small boats, directing their course towards the point of the battery last mentioned, and thence they marched towards the gate called Cortadura. Lieutenant Francis de Cazeres, being desirous to view the strength of the enemy, with only fifteen men, was compelled to retreat in haste, by reason of the great guns, which played so furiously on the place where he stood; they shooting, not only pieces of iron, and small bullets, but also the organs of the church, discharging in every shot threescore pipes at a time.[25]

Notwithstanding this heat of the enemy, Captain Don Joseph Ramirez de Leyva, with sixty men, made a strong attack, wherein they fought on both sides very desperately, till at last he overcame, and forced the pirates to surrender the fort.

On the other side, Captain John Galeno, with ninety men, passed over the hills, to advance that way towards the castle of St. Teresa. Meanwhile Major Don Joseph Sanchez Ximenez, as commander in chief, with the rest of his men, set forth from the battery of St. James, passing the port with four boats, and landing, in despite of the enemy. About this same time, Captain John Galeno began to advance with the men he led to the forementioned fortress; so that our men made three attacks on three several sides, at one and the same time, with great courage; till the pirates seeing many of their men already killed, and that they could in no manner subsist any longer, retreated towards Cortadura, where they surrendered, themselves and the whole island, into our hands. Our people possessed themselves of all, and set up the Spanish colors, as soon as they had rendered thanks to God Almighty for the victory obtained on such a signalized day. The number of dead were six men of the enemies, with many wounded, and seventy prisoners: on our side was only one man killed, and four wounded.

There were found on the island eight hundred pounds of powder, two hundred and fifty pounds of small bullets, with many other military provisions. Among the prisoners were taken also, two Spaniards, who had bore arms under the English against his Catholic Majesty: these were shot to death the next day, by order of the major. The 10th day of September arrived at the isle an English vessel, which being seen at a great distance by the major, he ordered Le Sieur Simon, who was a Frenchman, to go and visit the said ship, and tell them that were on board, that the island belonged still to the English. He performed the command, and found in the said ship only fourteen men, one woman and her daughter, who were all instantly made prisoners.

The English pirates were all transported to Puerto Velo, excepting three, who by order of the governor were carried to Panama, there to work in the castle of St. Jerome. This fortification is an excellent piece of workmanship, and very strong, being raised in the middle of the port of a quadrangular form, and of very hard stone: its height is eighty-eight geometrical feet, the wall being fourteen, and the curtains seventy-five feet diameter. It was built at the expense of several private persons, the governor of the city furnishing the greatest part of the money; so that it cost his Majesty nothing.

[. . .]

CAPTAIN MORGAN seeing his predecessor and admiral Mansvelt were dead, used all the means that were possible, to keep in possession the isle of St. Catherine, seated near Cuba. His chief intent was to make it a refuge and sanctuary to the pirates of those parts, putting it in a condition of being a convenient receptacle of their preys and robberies. To this effect he left no stone unmoved, writing to several merchants in Virginia and New England, persuading them to send him provisions and necessaries, towards putting the said island in such a posture of defense, as to fear no danger of invasion from any side. But all this proved ineffectual, by the Spaniards retaking the said island: yet Captain Morgan retained his courage, which put him on new designs. First, he equipped a ship, in order to gather a fleet as great, and as strong as he could. By degrees he effected it, and gave orders to every member of his fleet to meet at a certain port of Cuba, there determining to call a council, and deliberate what was best to be done, and what place first to fall upon.

HENRY
"THE DREAD PIRATE"
MAINWARING

HMS *Resistance*

Newfoundland

1610s

Like Henry Morgan, Henry Mainwaring occupies a shifting sphere of legality and illegality, depending on who is looking at him—a parallax of piracy. Born in the late 1580s, active in the 1610s and '20s, he even sat in the House of Commons, and after his career in piracy he also enjoyed a career in the Royal Navy. He turned his expertise into a tract on piracy and its suppression, which also included accounts of his own life on the high seas. This excerpt is unusual in that it offers a pirate's own account of himself, rather than the account of an observer. It is presented as a letter of advice to King James I, to help him better understand what would cause a man to turn pirate.

Mainwaring's shifting relationship with piracy began around 1610, when he received a commission to hunt pirates in the Bristol Channel, which separates Wales from southwest England. He went nominally hunting for a pirate thought to be based out of Newfoundland, but once underway decided that he and his crew would raid Spanish ships whenever they found them. In 1614 he raided the cod-fishing fleet

*in the Grand Banks off the coast of Canada, and
then crossed the Atlantic to raid off the coast of
Spain, using a port in what is now present-day Morocco as his base of operations (once again, the littoral space of the ocean crossing boundaries of nation
or culture). Mainwaring was a formidable enough
pirate that Spain and England competed to offer him
pardons in order to be spared from his depredations.
He was eventually knighted in 1618.*[1]

*His nickname, if we trust that he was in fact called
this, persists in popular culture as "the Dread Pirate
Roberts" in the book (1973) and film (1987) of* The
Princess Bride, *the pirate who never takes prisoners
but who has actually been long retired and living in
Patagonia.*

OF THE BEGINNINGS, PRACTICES, AND SUPPRESSION OF PIRATES[2]

To my most Gracious Sovereign, that represents the King of
Heaven, whose mercy is above all his works.

Give leave I humbly beseech your Grace to me your own
Creature (being newly recreated and restored by your gracious
Pardon to that life which was forfeited to the Law) humbly to
offer with a faithful, loyal, obedient and a thankful heart to
your Majesty's favor, this, as some oblation for my offences,
and a perfect sign of the true and hearty acknowledgment I
make of your Highness' grace unto me. I am so far from
justifying my own errors, that I can scarce afford them those
reasonable excuses, which might be perhaps allowable in any
other man.

As that I fell not purposely but by mischance into those
courses; being in them, ever strove to do all the service I could
to this State, and the merchants.

*[. . . Mainwaring then lists what he has done to make up
for his crimes . . .]*

These truths though they cannot expiate yet they might extenuate the offence in another man, and may be called *Pulchrum Scelus*,[3] but in me so little, that did not the laws of Christianity and Nature interdict me I could easily be evidence, jury, judge, and executioner to myself. I trust your Majesty will not undervalue, but rather esteem me the more for having refused the free and voluntary pardons with proffers of good entertainment from other Princes, as namely the Duke of Medina sent to me, that if I would deliver up Mamora[4] to the King of Spain, that I should have a great sum of money for me and my company, with a free pardon to enjoy all our ships and goods, and good entertainment if I would command in the King's ships.

The Duke of Savoy sent me my pardon. The Duke of Florence sent me my pardon, and gave leave to the ship to wait on me till I was willing to come in, which did so for a great while. The Dey of Tunis[5] eat bread and salt and swore by his head (which is the greatest asseveration they use) that if I would stay with him he would divide his estate equally with me, and never urge me to turn Turk,[6] but give me leave to depart whensoever it should please your Majesty to be so gracious as to pardon me. These I know of mine own knowledge and so do many more.

And since my coming home I have heard that the Condé of Porto Legro[7] after I had put off 5 sail of the King of Spain's men of war (being in fight with them all midsummer day last) myself having but 2 he offered that if any would go out and advertise me he would get me my pardon, and give me 20,000 ducats a year, to go General of that Squadron. Monsieur Manti[8] was met in the Straits with my protection from the Duke of Guise. I forbear to speak how willing the Spanish Ambassador seemed to my brother,[9] to have me serve his Master at that time when he moved him for his consent to my pardon. By these it may appear to your Majesty that I did not labor my Pardon as one being banished from all Christian Princes, but as a dutiful subject preferring the service of my country and my particular obedience to your Royal person

before my own ends. In this respect I doubt not but your
Majesty hath many malicious informations of me from other
States, who being themselves refused would by disgracing me
in your Majesty's favor, make me incapable of it. But let me
humbly beseech your Majesty, that since life and honor are
Individual Comities in every honestly resolved spirit, and that
your gracious favor hath restored the one, so likewise to do the
other, by your favorable acceptance of me, and that they may
either live or die together by your Majesty's command. Though
my course I confess were not honorable, yet since it was
ordained to be unfortunate I am glad 'twas in a way which
hath somewhat enabled me to do your Majesty service if
occasion were given. This small discourse, of a boisterous
argument, and as roughly handled (as also so unworthy your
Majesty's eye) of myself I durst not have presented but at the
commandment of one of your Majesty's most worthy servants.

Your Majesty's new Creature,

HENRY MAINWARING.

Of the Beginnings, Practices, and Suppression of Pirates.

The purpose of this discourse consists in showing:

Cap. I.

Their beginnings, and how they relieve themselves within
your Majesty's Dominions.

Cap. II.

The ground of opinion which encourages men in this course of
Piracy; and of those are called Performen[10]

Cap. III.

How they use to work at Sea.

Cap. IV.

Where and what times they use to be where they use to be where they must water, ballast, wood, trim their ships, and sell their goods.

Cap. V.

A means as well to prevent as suppress them.

Cap. I.

Daily experience proves it to be undoubtedly true, that English Pirates do first arm and horse themselves within your Highness' Dominions, as well England as Ireland, which the easier happens by reason that there are divers places (and chiefly such as are not capable of great shipping), that have no command,[11] as also by the negligence of the Owners of such small Ships, that having no force to defend them keep ill watch, and leave their Sails aboard; wherein those Officers cannot be excused, that do not discreetly look into the disposition and resorts of such seamen as either are within, or near their Harbors. So that it is commonly seen, that a very few, though but to the number of 10 or 12, do easily get out, and being assured of more Company wheresoever they shall touch upon the Coast, (by reason that the common sort of seamen are so generally necessitous and discontented) they make no doubt but when they have somewhat increased their number, to better their Ship by going into the Trade of Brittany[12] where they meet continually with small Frenchmen, Pinks,[13] and Brawmes[14] of Hoorn,[15] which being slightly manned are easily surprised. These commonly go well, and are of good burthen, as between 180 and 200 Ton; and then by the countenance of such a ship well manned they quickly overbear any small Ship with a few great Ordnance, and so by little and little reinforce themselves, to be able to encounter with a good Ship. But if they chance to put out of the North part of these Coasts, then they fit themselves in the North Seas. And to give your Highness a particular instance and taste how these men may and do easily embark themselves: When small Pinks and little vessels do stop below Gravesend, in Tilbury Hope, or against Queenborough, the wind being westerly, they may, with one or two wherries[16] in the night, go aboard and enter them, and put to sea before a wind, so that they cannot be stayed or prevented. In this manner, or the like, for the most part they begin both in England and Ireland; and although these things happen more often in England than Ireland, by reason there is more plenty of Ports and Shipping, as also more abundance of Seamen, yet in proportion Ireland doth much exceed it, for it may be well called the Nursery and Storehouse of Pirates, in regard of the general good entertainment they receive there; supply of victuals and men which continually repair thither out of England to meet with Pirates.[17] As also, for that they have as good or rather better intelligence where your Majesty's Ships are, than contrariwise they shall have of the Pirates. In regard of the benefit the Country receives by the one, and the prejudice, or incumber as they count it, of the other. Unto which must also be added the conveniency of the place, being that the South, the West, and the North Coasts, are so full of places and Harbors without command, that a Pirate being of any reasonable force, may do what he listeth. Besides that, many of that Nation are scarce so well reduced to any civil jurisdiction, as to make a conscience of trading with them.

Myself saw the experience of these things, for being in the North-west, where few Pirates come, and not understanding but hoping of your Highness' gracious Pardon, being for my safety bound to stand off to Sea, till I might hear a happy answer from my friends, to whom I then sent into England, I had near 60 new men come into me, and received letters from the Southwards that here were divers expected, that I would touch in those parts to take them in. And generally a Pirate may in all those parts trim his Ships, without affront from the Country, although it be in such places as they may well, either surprise or disappoint them, as also victual themselves in this manner.[18]

The Country people will not openly bring their victuals, nor in audience of any seem to harken to any such motion, yet privately with the Captain will appoint where he shall in the night find so many Beeves[19] or other refreshments as he shall need, who (that he may seem to take this away perforce) must land some small shot, and fetch them; with like cleanly conveyance, and secrecy, he must land the goods or money in exchange, which by custom, they expect must be 2 or 3 times the value. In the same sort shall he have all kind of Munition, or ship's provision, if it be there to be had. I say not that this is done by open allowance, or toleration of the chief Governors and Commanders, yet I may well imagine by proportion of other things in these days there may be some connivance where there is a fellow-feeling.

Cap. II.

The common sort of seamen, even those that willingly and willfully put themselves into these courses, are greatly emboldened by reason of a received opinion and custom that is here for the most part used, that none but the Captain, Master, and it may be some few of the principal of the Company shall be put to death.[20] Now since ordinarily there is not any mean used betwixt death and liberty, to punish them, unless it be a little lazy imprisonment, which is rather a charge to your Highness, than any affliction to them, since their whole life for the most part is spent but in a running Prison, and for that it may be thought too much effusion of blood, to take away the lives of so many, as may perchance be found together in such an action, as also for that the State may hereafter want such men, who commonly are the most daring and serviceable in war of all those kind of people:[21] and on the contrary, to set them at liberty is but licensing them to enter into the same way again, for that the most part of them will never be reclaimed, as appears plainly by those who have been heretofore pardoned: me thinketh (under correction of your Majesty's better judgement) it were no ill policy for this State, to make them Slaves, in the nature of Galley-Slaves;[22] whereof though now we have no use, yet for guarding of the Coast, there might be vessels of great force contrived, far more serviceable than any we have, especially for the Summer-time, to go with Sail and Oars: and in the meantime, they might be employed to the advancement of many good works, with small charge to your Majesty, as about the Navy; scouring of barred Havens, which especially on the East coast are choked up, to the great prejudice of the whole Kingdom, and almost the utter impoverishing of the particular places, and Inhabitants there; repairing of your Highness' Castles and Forts on the Sea-Coast, which myself have since my coming, seen and perceived to be miserably ruined and decayed; and divers such like, which men of better judgement and design than myself would easily invent. And this course, as it may be a means to save many their Souls, by giving them a long time of Repentance, so would it terrify and deter them, more than the assurance of Death itself. Myself have seen them in fight, more willingly expose themselves to a present and certain death, than to a doubtful and long slavery. Other Christian Princes use this kind of punishment and so convert it to a public profit, amongst whom it is observable, that as many as make slaves of offenders, have not any Pirates of their Nation.[23]

Many Pirates, especially those who are in small ships, a few in number, and that have been out but a while, so that little notice is had of them, having gotten some purchase, do use to clear themselves, by running their Ships ashore, or else by sinking them; and so saving themselves in Boats, whereby they are the less noted, and that in some parts far from the places of their abodes, as also most distant from the Coast where they made purchase. In this course their opinion is that either they go clear, and then they have what they desire, or if they be taken it is but compounding with the Vice-Admirals or some under Officers who (because there is no man to give evidence against them, being that the parties injured may have no notice of their apprehending) may very colorably discharge them. And although this be many times used and that chiefly in Ireland, yet I know there are sufficient Laws, and institutions to prohibit and punish them. And therefore the error of this is nothing but abuse by the Officers, which by a strict and severe course taken by your Highness for the execution of Justice might easily be reformed.

By reason that your Highness did grant a Pardon to one Peter

Cason who betrayed the Concord of London, and one other to a Dutchman named Peeters, who took another Ship of London, with condition that they should give satisfaction to the English; they do generally assure themselves of a Pardon, if they can but take a good English Ship and be able to return or satisfy their losses. And to this they usually add, that if they can get £1000 or two, they doubt not but to find friends to get their Pardons for them. They have also a conceit that there must needs be wars with Spain within a few years, and then they think they shall have a general Pardon. Lastly they say, that if there be no hope of Pardon here, yet Leghorn and Villefranche are free for them, and thither they go.

How to reform the abuse of those privileges so contrary to civil society and common comers betwixt Christian States I know not, except either by treaty with them to abolish such ill customs, or by making the cause equal, by granting free Ports for offenders against them in like nature, or by granting Letters of Reprisal to such as by the protection of those places, have their goods unlawfully detained from them. One thing I have not found to be well observed by any man, and yet is a great occasion to encourage men both to continue, and enter into those actions, is the misunderstanding of such as are called Perforstmen, by which is commonly meant, such as are taken out of Ships at Sea, so that it is intended that they are taken away against their wills. But that your Highness may the better understand and judge of such men, I must report truly that when I have had near six or seven hundred men at one time, and for the most part all taken out of Ships, I know not that I had three Perforstmen, In all my Company, neither of all that I had at Sea, was any taken, but in this or the like sort. Having fetched up and commanded a Ship, some of the Merchants-men would come to me, or to some of my Captains and Officers, to tell me they were desirous to serve me, but they durst not seem willing, least they should lose their wages, which they had contracted for with their Merchants; as also that if by any occasion they should come home to their Country, or be taken by any other Princes, it would be a benefit to them, and no hurt to me, to have them esteemed Perforstmen. In which respect I being desirous to have men serve me willingly and cheerfully, would give them a note under my hand to that purpose, and send men aboard to seem to take them away perforce. These men by such slender attestations are rather welcomed home, than any way molested or troubled, unless by mischance some under officer of the Admiralty light upon them, and pillage them of their goods. The inconvenience and mischief whereof is this: that such men knowing themselves to be privileged are more violent, head-strong, and mutinous, than any of the old Crew, either to commit any outrage upon their own Countrymen, or exercise cruelty upon others, as also the most unwilling men to be reduced home, till they have struck up a hand, and then they apprehend the first occasion they can to get ashore in any your Majesty's Dominions, where concealing their wealth they offer themselves to the next officers or Justices, complaining of the injury they have received in being so long detained by force, and so they are commonly not molested but relieved.

The way in this case neither to punish the innocent, nor to let the guilty escape, is (in my conceit) to have all such committed, till a just proof may be made whether they have received shares or pillage of the goods or not, more than to supply their necessary wants and wearing clothes; if they have, they are then absolutely as willing and as guilty as is the Commander. For I never knew seamen so violently liberal, as to force men to receive money, nor any so courteous and so conscionable as to refuse what was offered them.

Cap. III.

In their working they usually do thus: a little before day they take in all their sails, and lie a-hull,[24] till they can make what ships are about them; and accordingly direct their course, so as they may seem to such ships as they see to be Merchantmen bound upon their course. If they be a fleet, then they disperse themselves a little before day, some league or thereabouts asunder, and seeing no ships do most commonly clap close by a wind to seem as Plyers.[25]

If any ships stand in after them, they heave out all the sail they can make, and hang out drags[26] to hinder their going, that so the other that stand with them might imagine they were afraid and yet they shall fetch them up.[27]

They keep their tops[28] continually manned, and have signs to each other when to chase, when to give over, where to meet, and how to know each other, if they see each other afar off. In Chase they seldom use any Ordnance, but desire as soon as they can, to come a board and board;[29] by which course he shall more dishearten the Merchant and spare his own men. They commonly show such colors[30] as are most proper to their Ships, which are for the most part Flemish bottoms, if they can get them, in regard that generally they go well, are roomy Ships, floaty,[31] and of small charge.

Cap. IV.

This part may seem somewhat tedious to your Highness In regard that I imagine your Majesty hath not been much used to the Sea, but I thought good to set it down, that it might serve a little to advise your Majesty (according to my small understanding) what directions to give in Commissions, if there should be any purpose to employ Ships for the suppressing of Pirates.

Within the Straits of Gibraltar, there is not any place for Pirates to resort to, but only Algiers and Tunis, where they may be fitted with all manner of provisions and to ride safely from the Christian forces; yet at Algiers their Ships are commonly betrayed from them and manned out by the Turks, after the proportion of 150 Turks to 20 English, yet the English in their persons are well used and duly paid their shares.[32] But at Tunis they are better people, and hold their words more justly, especially since Uzuff Dye commanded, who is now there, and a very just man of his word.

Those of Algiers do for the most part come without the Straits, or if they stay in the Straits, the lie either off Cape de Gata, Cape de Palos, or Cape San Martin, and seldom go lower towards the bottom. Going in of the Straits, they keep close a board the Barbary shore; but going out on the Christian. At Tetuan, the first town on the Barbary side going in, a Pirate may water well, have good refreshing, buy store of powder (which is for the most part brought in by English and Flemish Merchants) and sell their good well which is quickly landed and dispatched by reason of the Boats of the town, but here is no command but to ride upon their guard; they ride also in foul ground and must perforce put to Sea if the Levant come here; the people are very just and trusty.

At Tlemcen they may water, and ballast, sell goods, and have some refreshing, but the town is 30 miles into the Country, so that things are long a-coming and the Road very dangerous, being in the bottom of a deep Bay, Cape Falcon,[33] bearing North-east, and Cape Tres Forcas[34] beating West-north-west; the people here are very treacherous.

At Formentera[35] by Iviza[36] is water, wood, and ballast, but nothing else, being no inhabitants. They must shift Roads as the winds are either Easterly or Westerly, which they must do by putting through betwixt the Islands wherein the best of the channel is 3 fathoms[37] water, and they tide in 5 or 6.

At Cape De Gata[38] on the Christian shore they may water, but if they be discovered for Pirates they will be put off.

At Bona[39] and Bougie[40] which are under the command of those of Algiers, Pirates may be very well refreshed with victual, water, and bread, and also sell goods well, and these are good Roads for Pirates, but they dare not trade with any unless they bring with them the Letters of Algiers; here they may ride under command of the Fort, and the people are very just.

Those of Tunis seldom come out of the Straits, but for the most part do lie off of St. Peters[41] by Sardinia, or Cape Passaro[42] in Sicily, or betwixt Cape Angelo and Zante, yet here they are somewhat fearful of the Venetian Galligrosses,[43] or else betwixt Cape Salamon in Candy and Scarponto, for ships bound from the bottom, or Gozzo by Candy and seldom go any lower.

At St. Peters they may water and at Lampedusa, and generally in all the Greek Islands they shall have good quarter, and great store of Hogs, and they are good people especially at Milo.

At Rhodes and Cyprus if they bring the letters of Tunis or Algiers they shall be well used, but generally in all these places it is not safe trusting them.

At Tripoli in Barbary they shall be entertained and re-freshed, and ride in command; but these are dangerous people, and the entrance bad for ships of any burthen, so that few dare come thither.

Sowsey[44] is under the command of Tunis, and a good har-bor there. Men shall be well dealt withal that have the Letters of Tunis, and there they ride safe under a Castle.

Porto Farina[45] is 7 leagues from Cape Carthage, and there is very good watering, and a good place to careen in, being Land-locked, yet the North-west winds are dangerous, coming in Perries[46] down the high hills; they can have nothing here with-out leave from Tunis but water.

Tunis is but an open Road, and the Castle cannot warrant the ships; it is a good Road all over the Bay in 5, 6, and 7 fathom, so that one or two Ships of force may keep them all in, where it is easy to fire all the Turks shipping in regard that when any Christian force comes in, they will all forsake their Ships and run ashore.

Algiers hath a mould[47] within which Ships ride and great store of singular good Ordnance, which commands the whole Road, which is very dangerous if the wind come Northerly, so that Ships cannot or dare not ride to keep them in. In Velez Malaga[48] there is no command, nor in Jabea-Roads,[49] and therefore they may take Ships at an Anchor. In Alicante[50] good Ships ride out far in the Road, and therefore there they may, the wind being landerly, take out a Ship, and in Cullera[51] they ride out of command.

Generally not any Pirates do stir in the Straits from the be-ginning or middest of May till towards the last of September, unless it be with their Galleys or Frigates, yet towards the mid-dest of August those of Algiers will go out of the Straits, if they meet with a set Levant.

I purpose not to trouble your Highness with the business of these Seas much, or the means to suppress Pirates here, for that they lie more commodious for the bordering Princes to defend and suppress; yet before I come out of the Straits I think it fit to acquaint your Highness what unequal terms we hold with those of Tunis and Algiers, for although we have Merchants, Factors, Ledgers,[52] there, and a free trade with them, yet at Sea they will take our Merchants; only if they do not fight, they will not make slaves of them, nor keep their Ships, but their goods they will. But I think that is rather in favor of themselves than in good will to us; for by that means the common sort of Mariners are not so willing to fight for the Merchant goods. Though this be a great injustice, yet I think it is necessary to hold quarter with them, for if we should have Wars with Spain, there is no place for our Merchants that trade that way to relieve themselves in any distress betwixt Sicily and Gibraltar so convenient as those places.

In all the Straits there is no any place to ground a Ship of any reasonable burthen, but they careen all, which is a mighty inconvenience to Pirates.

Without the Straits for the most part, all Pirates do resort to the coast of Spain and Portugal for purchase, and there according to the times of the year do lie off of one place or another; from the middest of February to the last of March, they commonly like South and South-south-west of Cape St. Maries, some 20 or 30 leagues off, for Indies men outward bound. And generally February, March, April, and May, they keep the coast of Spain, in which months those that look for Straits men homeward bound, like 20 Leagues off Cape St. Vincent west. Others that want victuals, lie some 15 Leagues off the Rock[53] or the Burlings of the Easterlings, which come full of victuals for the Spanish Fleet, and bring also good store of copper, linen, and wearing stuffs; and betwixt that height being 39 and 44[54] they are still in the way of Brazil men both outward and homeward bound, which commonly are going and coming all the year long. When they lie off this coast they use commonly to stand in all night, and off all day, if the wind be to the Northwards of the Worth-west, as for the most part on those coasts it is in those months either Northerly, or Easterly, and then they come within 3 or 4 Leagues of the shore, but if the wind be westerly, then they stand further off.

Some will bring Cape St. Vincent south-east and east-south-east, somewhat betwixt 8 and 16 Leagues, for men bound about the Cape for San Lucar, Cadiz, or the Straits, but gener-

ally all those must be good Ships, and stout men-of-war, in regard that they lie in the common rut of the King of Spain's
men-of-war. Other small men will it may be lie about the
North Cape, for small Gallego boats, and Burtons, which hall
the shore close aboard, especially if the wind be Easterly; some
who have the occasion to trim in Ireland in January and February will go to the Sound by the First of March, but there
they cannot stay long by reason of the King of Denmark's
Ships, but presently they return for Ireland, and trim, and so
some for the Coast of Spain.

[. . .]

At Lupo[55] they may get goats but nothing else.

In the Western Islands[56] they may water, on St. George's,[57]
on that side toward the Peak.[58] At Flores,[59] round about the Island, they may water, wood, and ballast, and the inhabitants
will not offer to molest them, but now they dare not trade with
Pirates as they were wont, by reason that the Governor of the
Terceiraes[60] hath punished them severely for it; yet at Corvo[61]
they will trade by stealth, and there they use very much.

On the bank of Newfoundland[62] they easily get bread, wine,
cider, and fish enough, with all necessaries for shipping.

In Newfoundland, if they be of good force, they will command all the land, in regard that the Fishermen will not stand
to each other, and so may a small man fit himself in divers
places of the Land, where there be but a few small Ships, yet
there are not many pretenders thither, in regard that the course
is very long, and the wind so very apt to be betwixt the west
and north-west, that unless they come by the middest of June,
they may (if they be not well fitted) be starved in the traverse.[63]
It hath been moved to the State many times to send Wafters[64]
to safeguard the Fishermen, but the best and cheapest way
were to command those of every harbor to fortify the place,
and to mount some few ordnance, which might easily be done
amongst so many men, especially in the beginning of the year
when they have little or nothing to do; yet I must confess that
2 or 3 Ships would do much good, though they cannot absolutely perform the service, in regard that the current sets so
strongly to the southward, and the wind for the most part be-

twixt the west and northwest, so that those that sail to the northward shall be to windward, and besides there are so many Ships coming and going that they shall not know which to chase, and the fog so great that they can have no long chase. In the out Isles of Scotland[65] and in divers places of the Main, they may trim well and in the Isles have any provision they have; but because we have little trade into those places, there be few that know them, and so for want of Pilots they seldom come thither.

Within St. George's Channel at Milford and the coast of Wales, they may trim, but because the coast and Channel are dangerous and that for the most part one of your Highness' ships is either at Milford or at Dublin, they use seldom thither unless it be some small nimble Ship.

I never was at Iceland[66] or Friesland, and therefore can say nothing on my own knowledge what they may there do; yet I have heard and judge it may be true, that there amongst the Fishermen, they may fit themselves with men and victuals. Yet this I know by experience of divers that I have met, who have been there, and by the necessity of their voyage, that all those that go for Iceland or Friesland must and do stop in Ireland, as they go back for the coast of Spain, to make clean their ships, and this place have I reserved for the last, in regard that it is most frequented by them, and therefore of most importance to be remembered, where besides that they have all commodities and conveniences that all other places do afford them, they have also good store of English, Scottish, and Irish wenches which resort unto them, and these are strong attractors to draw the common sort to them thither. I omit Rat Isle, Belle Isle, and diverse places on the Coast of Brittany, because they are selcome frequented, and my purpose (for brevity sake) is to speak of the most important and most used.

Cap. V.

These thing being thus known, it remains now to consider of a remedy for all these enormities, and which may be the best way so to handle the matter that those which are now out may be cut off, and those that are not yet may be prevented, which were both an honorable thing for the State, an acceptable thing to God, and a great benefit to all Christian Merchants.

First then to prevent their beginning, your Highness may do well to give special command to all officer of all Ports within your Highness' Dominions to enquire of the behavior of such Seafaring men as are there, and especially of such as have been Pirates, and to have such as live dissolutely without seeking honest employments put in good security for their behavior, or to be imprisoned. And in Ireland, because there is little or no shipping belonging to the Country, to command strictly that no seafaring man, especially that hath been a Pirate, shall come within 10 or 12 miles of the sea coast.

I know that there is such an order already,[67] and it is reasonable well observed in the South Coast, yet not so well (as I have heard) but that some have lately run away with Ships from thence, and in the West and North-west on my knowledge it hath not been, nor is not so; but me thinketh the best and surest way, and that which might much advance the wealth and glory of our State, were to devise some more universal employment than now we have, by which men of that spirit might not complain, as they now do, that they are forced for lack of convenient employment to enter into such unlawful courses. The proof of this is plain, for since your Highness' reign there have been more Pirates by ten for one, than were in the whole reign of the last Queen.[68]

There being now no voyage to speak of but Newfoundland, which they hold too toilsome, that of Newcastle which many hold too base, and the East Indies which most hold dangerous and tedious, and for your Highness' Ships the entertainment is so small, and the pay so bad that they hold it a kind of slavery to serve in them.[69] I speak of the private sailor not the officer. In this I must say to myself *Ne sutor ultra Crepidam*[70] and leave the project to your Highness' singular judgment, only I will remember this, that it is an ill policy, which provides more for punishing than preventing of offenders.

Next, to take away their hopes and encouragements, your Highness must put on a constant immutable resolution never to grant any Pardon, and for those that are or may be taken, to put them all to death, or make slaves of them, for if your Highness should ask me when those men would leave offending I might answer, as a wise Favorite did the late Queen, demanding when he would leave begging, he answered, when she would leave giving;[71] so say I, when your Highness leaves Pardoning. And in the little observation I could make in my small travels, I have noted those Countries best governed, where the Laws are most severely executed; as for instance in Tunis, where no offence is ever remitted, but strictly punished according to their customs and Laws. In 5 months together when I was coming and going I never heard of Murder, Robbery, or private Quarrel. Nay a Christian, which IS more than he can warrant himself in any part of Christendom, may on my knowledge travel 150 miles into the country, though he carry good store of money, and himself alone, and none will molest him. So likewise, in my Commonwealth of most uncivil and barbarous seamen (the common sort of seamen I mean), that are of all men the most uncivil and barbarous, I could never have subsisted as I did, if I had ever pardoned any notorious offence, though committed by my truest followers, by which constant severity I kept them all in a short time in so good obedience, and conformity, that for few years I never had any outrageous offence, but had them all aboard my ships in as good civility and order, as it could not have been much better in a Civil state; for questionless, as fear of punishment makes men doubtful to offend, so the hope of being pardoned makes them the apter to err.

[. . .]

Be slow in council, swift and determined in action.[72]

ALEXANDER O. EXQUEMELIN

West Indies

1684

Exquemelin was mentioned earlier, as the seaman accused by Henry Morgan of libel. Below is his account of how pirates organize their vessels. Some historians have argued that pirate ship organizations represented a proto-democracy, or even a utopian vision of shared authority that was otherwise unheard of in the early modern period. While that interpretation might be colored by a certain romanticism, it is true that the manner of organization that Exquemelin describes is much more egalitarian than that which a mariner might be expected to find on a merchantman, a navy vessel, or even in a rigid class hierarchy on land. For many people living in the 1600s, the promise of such self-determination might have been seductive indeed.

AFTER WHAT MANNER THE PIRATES ARM THEIR VESSELS, AND HOW THEY REGULATE THEIR VOYAGES[1]

Before the Pirates go out to Sea, they give notice unto every one, that goeth upon the voyage, of the day on which they ought precisely to embark. Intimating also unto them, their obligation of bringing each man in particular, so many pound of powder, and bullet, as they think necessary for that expedition. Being all come on board, they join together in Council, concerning what place they ought first to go unto, wherein to get provisions? Especially of flesh: seeing they scarce eat anything else. And of this the most common sort among them is Pork. The next food is Tortoises, which they use to salt a little. Sometimes they resolve to rob such, or such *Hogyards*; wherein the Spaniards often have a thousand heads of Swine together. They come unto these places in the dark of the night, and having beset the Keepers lodge, they force him to rise, and give them as many heads as they desire; threatening withal to kill him in case he disobeyeth their commands, or maketh any noise. Yea, these menaces are oftentimes, put in execution, without giving any quarter unto the miserable Swine keepers, or any other person, that endeavoureth to hinder their Robberies.

Having gotten provisions of flesh, sufficient for their Voyage, they return unto their Ship. Here their allowance, twice a day, unto every one, is as much as he can eat; without either weight, or measure. Neither doth the Steward of the Vessel give any greater proportion of flesh, or anything else unto the Captain, then unto the meanest Mariner. The ship being well victualled, they call another Council, to deliberate, towards what place they shall go, to seek their desperate fortunes? In this Council, likewise they agree upon certain Articles, which are put in writing, by way of bond, or obligation, the which every one is bound to observe, and all of them, or the chiefest, do set their hands unto. Herein they specify, and set down very distinctly, what sums of Money each particular person ought to have for that voyage. The fund, of all the payments, being the common stock, of what is gotten, by the whole expedition; for otherwise it is the same law among these people, as with other Pirates, *no prey, no pay*. In the first place, therefore they mention, how much the Captain ought to have for his Ship. Next the salary of the Carpenter, or Shipwright, who careened, mended, and rigged the Vessel. This commonly, amounteth unto one hundred, or an hundred and fifty pieces of eight; being according to the agreement, more or less. Afterwards for provisions and victualling, they draw out of the same common stock, about two hundred pieces of eight. Also a competent salary for the Surgeon, and his Chest of Medicaments, which usually is rated at two hundred, or two hundred and fifty pieces of eight. Lastly they stipulate in writing, what recompense or reward each one ought to have, that is either wounded, or maimed in his body, suffering the loss of any Limb,[2] by that voyage. Thus they order for the loss of a right Arm, six hundred pieces of eight, or six slaves: For the loss of a left Arm, five hundred pieces of eight, or five slaves: For a right leg, five hundred pieces of eight, or five slaves: For the left leg, four hundred pieces of eight, or four slaves: For an eye, one hundred pieces of eight, or one slave: For a Finger of the hand, the same reward, as for the eye. All which sums of Money, as I have said before, are taken out of the capital sum, or common stock, of what is gotten by their Piracy. For a very exact, and equal, dividend, is made of the remainder, among them all. Yet herein they have also regard unto qualities, and places. Thus the Captain, or chief Commander, is allotted five, or six portions to what the ordinary Seamen have. The Masters-Mate, only two: And other Officers proportionable to their employ. After whom they draw equal parts from the highest, even to the lowest Mariner; the boys not being omitted. For even these draw half a share; by reason, that when they happen to take a better Vessel, than their own, it is the duty of the Boys, to set fire unto the Ship or boat, wherein they are, and then retire unto the prize, which they have taken.

They observe among themselves, very good orders. For in the prizes they take, it is severely prohibited, unto everyone to usurp anything in particular, unto themselves. Hence all they take, is equally divided, according to what hath been said before. Yea, they make a solemn Oath to each other, not to abscond, or conceal the least thing they find amongst the prey. If afterwards any one is found unfaithful, and that hath contravened the said oath, immediately he is separated, and turned out of the society. Among themselves they are very civil and charitable to each other. Insomuch, that if any wanteth what another hath, with great liberality, they give it one to another. As soon as these Pirates have taken any Prize of Ship, or Boat, the first thing they endeavour is to set on shore the prisoners; detaining only some few for their own help, and service. Unto whom also they give their liberty, after the space of two or three years. They put in very frequently for refreshment, at one Island, or another. But more especially into those which lie on the Southern side of the Isle of Cuba. Here they careen their vessels, and in the meanwhile, some of them go to hunt, others to cruise upon the Seas, in Canoes, seeking their fortune. Many times they take the poor Fishermen of Tortoises, and carrying them to their habitations, they make them work so long, as the Pirates are pleased.

HENRY "LONG BEN" AVERY/EVERY

The *Fancy*

Atlantic and Indian Oceans

1690s

The story of Henry Avery shows the extent to which the romance of piracy has overwritten the true history of violence and brutality that would lead men like him to live a life like this. On the one hand it has all the sweeping elements of romance one most dreams of in a pirate story: diamonds, treasure, Mughal princesses, tropical islands, and adventure on the high seas stretching around the world, from Boston to the Caribbean to Madagascar. But it is also a story of singular horrors: child abuse, rape, enslavement, cheating, mistrust, and violence.

Henry Avery, sometimes spelled Every, was born probably around 1659, and, according to one crew-member deposition after his capture, in 1696 Avery was about forty years old, with a mother living near Plymouth and a wife working as a periwig seller.[1] After some time in the Royal Navy, he also engaged in the transatlantic slave trade between Guinea and Bermuda. His nickname "Long Ben" is of vague antecedent, though it's suggested it derived from an alias he occasionally used of "Benjamin Bridgeman."

Avery was serving as the first mate on a warship

called the Charles II *when the crew, restless after too long at anchor off the coast of Spain while waiting to be given a letter of marque, or to be paid, mutinied and elected Avery their captain. In 1695, Avery led what has been called the most profitable act of piracy in the Golden Age, when his ship, renamed the* Fancy, *attacked a convoy of Grand Mughal vessels in the Red Sea returning from their annual pilgrimage to Mecca. One of the large trading dhows, the* Ganj-i-Sawai, *was heavily laden with treasure for the pilgrimage including gold coins, silk, precious stones, and Chinese export porcelain, valued by one contemporary historian at about $98 million in 2022 money.*[2]

This single act of piracy shattered the fragile relationship between England and the Mughal Empire, in part because of the money but arguably also because of the sexual violence that attended the raid. However, we will also see that Avery was no stranger to sexual violence—his life before turning to piracy was brutal, as will be amply demonstrated in the following excerpt.

The English Privy Council joined together with the East India Company to levy a bounty on Avery's head, making him in some respect the subject of the first-ever global manhunt. But they never got him.

After 1696, Avery is no longer findable in the records. Some sources theorize that he was among the first pirates to set up a kind of pirate utopia on the tropical island of St. Mary's, off the coast of Madagascar—the following account makes that case. Most historians believe he died somewhere between 1699 and 1714, but nobody knows for sure.

They also don't know what happened to his Mughal treasure, though some of Avery's crew certainly sought refuge in the North American colonies. In 2014, coins from the Ganj-i-Sawai *were found at*

Sweet Berry Farm in Middletown, Rhode Island, and others have appeared in Massachusetts, Connecticut, and North Carolina.[3]

In another twist of fact versus myth, Avery became a figure of widespread fascination after his disappearance, and his actions were often lionized, or romanticized, as justifiable rebellion by working-class men against unfair usage by those in power over them. News of his exploits would have been widespread when the subsequent Golden Age pirates discussed in part II were all children.

THE LIFE OF CAPT. AVERY[4]

He was the son of John Avery, a victualler, near Plymouth, who, in a few years, was known as opulent in his purse, as in his body, by []ing 2 for 1; and when he had so done, drinking most of the liquor himself. By which means, and having a handsome wife, who knew her business as well as if she had been brought up to it from a child, as indeed she mostly was, her mother keeping the house before she married Mr. Avery, they become very rich soon, and able to give credit to a whole ships crew upon their tickets, which in those days were sold for less than half the value.

Having but one child, which was the captain, they at first resolved to bring him up a scholar, that he might advance the dignity of the family; but instead of learning his book, he was taught bawdy, and could swear to every point in the compass, which was a very diverting scene for the boatswain[5] and his crew, who were drinking in the kitchen, and had just received a man, short allowance money, on board the *Revenge,* every farthing of which they spent before they left the house: and it is hard to say whether the mother or the child gave them the most diversion, the one being as free with her tail, as the other with his tongue. But as soon as their money was spent, they had all like to have been confined by the landlady for a riot, as she called it. So they were soon glad to go off, and he thought himself happiest that could get soonest aboard. And indeed it had been happy for them if they had, for the ship was unmoor'd and gone to sea; which put the boatswain and his crew a swearing in ear[ly?] [rest]. Not knowing what to do, they returned to their landlady, Mrs. Avery; but she shut them out of doors, calling them a parcel of beggarly rascals, swearing if they would not go from the door she would send for a constable; and notwithstanding all the tears and entreaties of her son, who was then six years of age, she could not be prevailed on to let them in; so they were forced to stroll about the streets that night, and in the morning espying the ship at anchor (being driven back by contrary winds), they resolved to make the best of their way on board: but, on their way, who should they meet but young Avery, who no sooner saw them, but he cry'd after them. Zounds,[6] said the boatswain, let's take the young dog aboard, and the bitch his mother shall be glad to adjust the reckoning more to our satisfaction, before she shall have her son. This being agreed upon, and the boy as willing as they, they stepped into the boat, and in about an hour's time reached the ship, which they had no sooner got into, than they were brought before the captain, who being in want of hands, contented himself with bidden 'em all go to their business; for the wind turned about, and there was occasion for all hand to get the ship out. All this time young Avery was at the boatswain's heels, and was observed to swear two oaths to the boatswains' one; and the captain hearing him, enquired who had brought that young bastard aboard. The boatswain replied, he did; but he thought the boy's mother, who was his landlady, was born to be a curse to him; for he took him up in jest, but swore, he fear'd he should be obliged to keep him in earnest.

When the hurry was a little over, the captain ordered the boy to be brought to his cabin, with whom he had not talked long, but he took a fancy to him, telling him, if he would be a good boy, he should live with him, he being a great lover of children, would often divert himself by talking to the boy, till at length he took such a fancy to him, that he ordered him a little hammock in his cabin, and none so great as the captain and his boy Avery, which had like to have proved very fatal to him; for Avery one night observing the captain very drunk with some passengers on board bound to Carolina, got a lighted match, and had like to have blown up the ship, had not the gunner happened accidentally to follow him into the store room; which made the captain ever after shy of his new acquaintance.[7] Avery after being well whipped, and ordered down into the hold, where he remained till they arrived at Carolina, which happened in four or five days after; and then the boy was given to a merchant, who taking a fancy to him, put him to school. But he making little progress in his learning, and committing many unlucky tricks, the merchant, in about three years, shipt him off to his friends in Plymouth, on board the *Nonesuch*; where he was no sooner arrived, but his mother was overjoy'd with the sight of her son, his father being dead a month before his arrival.

> [. . . The mother dies, and after a time, Avery has to fend for himself, committing petty theft for years before going again to sea, where, "in time, he became as famous for robbing as Cromwell for rebellion.". . .]

He entered himself on board the *Duke*, Capt. Gibson commander, being one of the two ships of 24 guns and 100 men, which were fitted out by the merchants of Bristol, for the service of Spain: which they had no sooner done, but they were ordered by their agents to Bristol to sail to the Groin[8] to receive their orders. On board one of these ships Avery entered himself; being at that time about twenty years old. He had not been long aboard, before he observed the captain to be much addicted to drunkenness. He endeavored to spirit up not only his own ship's crew, but having given the word to part of the other ship's crew, the conspirators gave the signal, at which the Dutchess's long-boat appeared, which was the name of the other ship. The conspirators hailing her, were asked by the men in the boat, is your drunken boatswain aboard? Which was the word agreed upon: to whom Avery answered, all is safe. Upon which 20 lusty fellows came aboard and joined them; which was no sooner done, than they secured the hatches, and went to work, putting to sea without any disorder, altho' there were several ships in the bay, amongst which was a frigate of 44 guns.

The captain by this time being awakened, by the noise of the conspirators working the ship, he rung the bell, enquiring what the devil was the matter. Avery and some of the crew replied, Nothing: damn ye, what are you mutinous in your cups? Can't you lie down to sleep, and be quiet! No, says the captain, I am sure something is the matter with the ship: does she drive? What weather is it? Is it a storm? Pox on you, saith Avery, cannot you be quiet, which you are quiet: I tell you all is well, we are at sea, with a fair wind and good weather. At sea! Said the captain, that can't be. Be not frighted, answered Avery, and I'll tell you: you must note I am now captain of this ship; nay you must turn out for this is my cabin, and I am bound to Madagascar, to make my own fortune, as well as my companions.

The captain being more terrified than ever, did not know what to say, which Avery perceiving, bid him have a good heart: for, said he, if you will join me, and these brave fellows my companions, in time you may get some post under me: if not, step into the boat, and get about your business. The captain was glad to hear this; but yet began to expostulate with them upon the injustice of their doings. Damn you, said Avery, what do I care; every man for himself and God for us all.

Come, come, captain, if you will go, get you gone, and the devil go with you: the long-boat waits for you, and if there be any more cowards in the ship, you may all go together. These words so affrighted the whole crew, that there was not above nine or ten of them that durst venture, who made the best of their way to shore, and thought themselves well off.

The captain was no sooner gone, than they called a council, who all agreed to own Avery for their captain; which he accepted of with all the humility imaginable, excusing himself on account of his inexperience at sea. But he did it so artfully, that it the more confirmed them in their choice. Gentlemen, said he, what we have done we must live or die by; let us all be hearty, and of one mind, and I don't question but we shall make our fortunes in a little time. I propose that we should sail first to Madagascar where we may settle at correspondence, in order to secure our retreats, whenever we think fit to lie by. To which they all agreed. But hold, said Avery, it is necessary that we make some orders among us for the better governing of the ship's crew. These were in a few days drawn up by the ship's clerk. Avery promising them vast things, they all came into them at last, altho' the denying them women aboard when very much against the grain of many of them. When they arrived at Madagascar, they saw a ship lying at the N. E. part of the island, which the men had run away with from New England, and seeing Avery, supposed he had been sent after them to take them; but he soon undeceived them, and promised them protection; and therefore they resolved to sail together. In the whole company there was not above ten that pretended to any skill in navigation; for Avery himself could neither write, nor very well read, he being chosen captain, purely for his courage and contrivance. In the latitude of Descada,[9] one of the islands, they took two other sloops, which supplied them with provisions, and then they agreed to proceed for the West Indies; and coming to Barbados, they fell in with a ship for London, with 12 guns, from which they took some cloaths[10] and money, 10 barrels of powder, and 10 casks of beef; with five of their men, and then let her go. From thence they went to St. Domingo, and watered: there they met with six Englishmen, who willingly entered with Avery. He staid not long, before he sailed to the Granada island to clean his ships; which being known to the French colony, the governor of Martinico[11] sent four sloops well manned after them. But they staid not long there, making the best of their way to Newfoundland, and entered the harbor of Trepassi,[12] with black colors, drums beating, and trumpets sounding. It is impossible to relate the havoc they made there, burning all before them. When they left Newfoundland, they sailed for the West-Indies, and from thence to the island Delcada,[13] it being judged the most convenient place at that time of the year, to meet with a rich booty.

From thence they steered toward the Arabian coast, near the

river Indus, where spying a sail they gave her chase: at their
near approach she hoisted Mogul colors, and seemed as if she
would stand upon her defense whilst Avery contented himself
to cannonade her at a distance; which made many of his men
begin to mutiny, damning him for a coward. But Avery knew
better; and commanding the sloops to attack her, one on her
bow, and the rest on her quarter, clapt her on board; upon
which she struck her colors, and yielded. Aboard her was one
of the Mogul's own daughters, with several persons of distinc-
tion; who were carrying rich offerings of jewels, and other
valuable presents, to Mecca. Which booty was the more considerable, because those people always travel with great mag-
nificence, having all their slaves and attendants with them,
besides jewels, and great sums of money to defray their expenses.
But Avery, not content with this, ravished the princess, and
used other beastly actions to the ladies of her retinue: then
taking her into his own ship, he made the best of his way to
Madagascar, where he had a child by her, which died in its in
fancy, and she soon after broke her heart. Her father the Great
Mogul[14] no sooner heard of it, than he threatened all Europe
with revenge; and when he found they were Englishmen that
had defiled his daughter, and robbed him, he swore to send a
mighty army, to extirpate, with fire and sword, all the English
from their settlements on the Indian coasts. This gave no small
uneasiness to the India Company at London: and tho' they
protested their innocence, and that it was done contrary to the
laws of England, as well as nations, yet it took up no small
time, as well as expense, to pacify him;[15] which could never
have been done, had they not promised to fit out a fleet to retake his daughter, and refund him the damage he sustained.

In the meantime Avery was making the best of his way to
Madagascar with the princess and his booty; intending to
make that place the repository of his riches, and to build a fortification to defend himself against anything that might happen, well knowing he should bring all Europe upon his back
for what he had done; and that, if he could not defend himself,
he must expect no mercy.

But first, he considered that it was necessary to secure the money, which yet was aboard the sloops; and therefore he sent a message to each of the captains, desiring to speak with them, in order to hold a council, to consider what was to be done next for their future preservation. They no sooner came on board, than he begun to harangue them in his tarpaulin[16] oratory with their bravery and courage, introducing them into his cabin, where he had got a barrel of flip[17] ready made for their entertainment. After he found them a little merry, Captains and heroes, said he, you all know how lucky this expedition has been, which if we take due care of we have all made our fortune, without running any more hazards at sea. Let us make the best of our way to Madagascar, where we have riches enough to establish a colony, and build a fortification for our defense. You are not insensible what we have done against the Mogul's ship will alarm all the world, therefore, my brave boys, let us run no risks; let us secure what we have got, in case of a storm or separation. As for my ship, it is of sufficient force and power to defend itself against any surprise. Wherefore, if you shall think fit to put all the chests on board my ship, you shall every one seal them up with your own seals, till we arrive at the N. E. part of Madagascar, the place agreed to rendezvous at. To this they all agreed, being, by this time, overloaded with liquor. But it happened very luckily for Avery, when the chests were got aboard, none of the captains had got any other signet[18] than a tobacco-pipe, and one of them his wife's thimble, which he took from her by mistake at parting. Avery now grew weary of his guests, thinking with himself how he should keep all the treasure, in the midst of so many concerned in it. But being resolved to bite the biters, he feigned himself sick, and seemed to fall into a swoon. Zounds, said one of the guests, we have killed our commodore; let us be gone, lest the whole ship's crew arise and knock us on the head. Which they all did, so that Avery soon become master of their all, without any possibility of their ever being able to call him to account for it afterwards.

Avery now had nothing to do, but to secure the men in his own ship to stand by him: this he easily did, by telling them they had nothing to fear, the treasure being now in their own hands, and that if they would stand by him, he did not doubt but to order it so, as not only to cheat the ships crews of their parts, but also to make them subservient to them in their new intended settlement. By this time they came in sight of Madagascar, where they espy'd two sloops that had put in for refreshment, viz. George Dew, and Capt. Thomas Tew, from Bermudas, who had both turned pirates. This happened very luckily for Avery, for having secured the men and sloops, he strengthened his alliance, and was thereby prepared against any thing the others could offer.

As fast as they got ashore, Avery put them to work upon his new fortification, and if any of them began to talk of a division of the treasure, he told them, they had not time at present. So much influence he had over the common seamen, that when two of the mates began only to murmur, they were both hung up at the mast to frighten others from the like attempts. He had no sooner got his fortification in some order, than he began to form a society, and made several degrees of officers under him, as if he had been a sovereign; always preferring those he judged most in his interest. And for the malecontents, he took care to keep them under due obedience. So that in a few years it became the rendezvous of all the pirates in the world; and Avery thought himself not only in a condition to keep in subjection the petty kings that inhabited the island, but also to make alliance with foreign powers; which latter he often attempted, but could never bring it about.

He suffered no ship to go out without his passport, and when it returned, he had the tenths of all the prizes, so that he became so great, that the petty kings of the island sued for his protection, and yearly paid him contribution, which was commonly their daughters and young virgins, to be given unto his subjects.

You must understand that the natives are a sort of negroes, who have long hair, and are not of so beautiful a complexion as those of Guiney, and they have many princes, who are continually making war upon one another. When Avery first settled among them, his protection was very much courted by every one of these kings; and whosoever paid him best he always joined with, they being sure to be victorious. So that in a

little time Avery and his men became so terrible to the negroes, that if they saw but a file of white men among their enemies when they were going to engage, they would run away
faster than they would from the devil.

Avery had every now and then the horrors and dread of an
awakened conscience; and being sensible of the vast treasure
he had in jewels, which he could no ways dispose of in Europe,
because he could settle no correspondence there, but in piracy
and robbery, he made several underhand offers to some men in
power in England, of very large sums, some say to the amount
of the national debt, to be permitted to come home. Yet, tho'
the government at that time had very great need of money, his
proposals could no way be complied with, in justice and honor
to our nation, as well as equity and friendship to the Mogul,
with whom our East India company carries on a considerable
trade. Avery now because so tyrannical, that his government
became troublesome to his neighbors, and uneasy to his people, he grew wanton in cruelty; causing every [day] 2 or 3 of
his associates to be put to some cruel [. . .] or other, upon any
slight pretense, or for [perver]sion. But he soon found that fear
or his power would not secure him against a surprise; or his
men began to separate themselves amongst the negroes, and
teach them the use of fire-arms, very often, to one another.
This made Avery bethink himself of a retreat, judging it more
honorable to run the hazard of being hanged in his native
country, than to be cut to pieces by his own subjects, which he
found would unavoidably happen, if he continued much longer among them. He discovered his design to some intimate
friends, with whom he privately shipped himself in a small
sloop, taking the treasure he had left, and his jewels, with him,
to seek his fortune afresh.

In this condition, he and his small company embarked. They
touched at several parts of America, where, in some unsus-
pected places they ventured ashore. At length they arrived at
Boston in New-England, where he had some thoughts of settling; but finding that place not convenient for him, because
most of his wealth lay in diamonds; he resolved with those few
companions that were left to make the best of his way to Ire-

land. Many of his companions deserted him in New-England, contenting themselves with that little dividend he gave them, and not knowing anything of the diamonds he had about him.

In their voyage to Ireland, they sailed north about, and put into one of the northern ports of that kingdom, where they disposed of their sloop, and separated themselves as soon as they landed, Avery going to Cork, and his companions to Dublin, where they staid till K[ing] William's pardon[19] was published, which they all accepted, and pleased too. But Avery being now left alone to the wide world, was in several doubts what he should do with himself; sometimes resolving to expose them to sale there: but believing that nobody knew the value of them in that country, at length he resolved to go to Bristol, where he fancied he might find some friend or other, if not for his sake, yet for their own interest, whom he might entrust them with. But there the same dread seized him as in Ireland, and he was afraid of his own shadow: and so he departed from thence, and travelled into Devonshire; and as soon as he came to Biddiford,[20] he sent to an old acquaintance of his father's to come to him, to whom he communicated his whole secret, and desired his advice how he might dispose of his effects; who advised him (after several ways and means had been proposed) to put them into the hands of a merchant, as the safest way; and withal assured him, that he was very well acquainted with an eminent merchant in whom he might put confidence that he would not betray him, as well as that he would bring him a good return for his diamonds (if he gave him a commission to sell them), and all for a little profit. To which Avery, readily agreeing, returned him a thousand thanks, and promising him a large gratuity for his good will and kindness, desired him to go to the merchant, and fathom him, & if he thought it proper, to let him into the secret. This his friend consented to; and brought the merchant along with him to Avery, at Biddiford, who gave him all the assurances imaginable of his honor and integrity. Upon which Avery delivered him his diamonds, and some vessels of gold; and the merchant, in return, let him have what money he had about him, promising him any further supplies he should have occasion for.

[. . . Avery, according to this somewhat spurious account,
changes his name to Johnson, is cheated by the diamond
merchant, and loses all his money. He eventually falls ill
and dies, being buried in the churchyard at Bideford. "He
died the tenth day of June, in the first year of the reign of
King George I," or 1714, a somewhat ignominious end for
such a notorious pirate, if indeed his end it was. . . .]

I think it not improper under this head to return to Madagascar, and inquire what became of the pirates whom Avery
left behind him in the [island], who by this time had settled all
over the country, taking two or three wives apiece from among
the most beautiful of the negro women.

Their slaves they employed in fishing, hunting, and planting
of rice; and to the others they gave protection, on account of a
tribute they yearly brought them of the best of the produce of
the country; so that they were become so powerful that they
began to divide in separate parts of the island. But they used
their power so like tyrants, that the negroes conspired together
to rid themselves of their new masters in one night: which they
had certainly done, had not a negro woman discovered their
design. However this made them more cautious of the negroes
for the time to come; and finding their power along would not
secure them from a surprise, they endeavored to set the negroes together by the ears, whilst they stood by, looking on as
neuters. . . . And when this would not do, they endeavored to
spirit up private quarrels among them, till they killed one another; teaching them how to surprise their adversaries, and lent
them guns to dispatch them with, being sure the murderers
would fly to them. . . . By these, and such like arts, the bodies were
greatly multiplied, so that they began to divide at greater dis-
tances, and made choice of places over-run with wood, and
lying near waters, digging deep ditches round their houses. . . .

Thus they lived, in fear of the negroes, as much as they were
in fear of them, at the time that Capt. Rogers went to Madagascar in the *Delicia* to buy slaves, in order to sell them to the
Dutch at Batavia, where he met with the pirates, who, at that
time had been upon the island near thirty years, having a mot-

ley generation of children and grand-children among them, who, upon their first seeing him, supposed him to be a man of war sent to take them, and upon that account they fled into their holes and caves, but when they found his men came ashore without any acts of hostility, and that their business was to trade with the negroes, they came out attended like princes: only they had nothing to cover them, but the skins of beasts untanned, without shoes or stockings.

However, they soon changed their raiment, and for the slaves they sold, got good cloaths and other necessaries; which having put upon their backs they ventured on board the *Delicia*, a ship of 40 guns, getting soon acquainted with the men, where they seemed to be very curious in examining the ship; which they afterwards owned was to try if it was practical to surprise her in the night. But it seems the captain was aware of them, and kept so strong a watch that they found it was in vain to attempt it: and therefore they thought to inveigle some of the men ashore in order to persuade them to seize the captain & the rest of the men, and, upon a signal from on board the ship, they would be ready and come to their assistance; promising to them great profits by going a pirating with them, not doubting with such a ship they should be able to take any vessel at sea. But Captain Rogers prevented it, for, as luck would have it, observing too great and intimacy between them and some of his men, he would not suffer them for the future so much as to talk together, but sent an officer to treat them with them about their slaves.

Before he sailed away, they confessed all: so that he left them as he found them, rogues from the very beginning, only with fewer slaves than they had. One of these great men, I remember, told me, he had been a waterman, upon the river Thames, in England, where having killed a man, he made the best of his way for the West-Indies, and was one of them that run away with the sloop from thence. And I further observed, that there was not one amongst them all that could read or write: But these wretches being now most of them, dead or destroyed, I do not think it worth my while to give the ready any more trouble about them.

WILLIAM KIDD

Adventure Galley

Madagascar and New York

1695–1701

William Kidd was a Scotsman, born in Greenock in approximately 1645, with a Presbyterian minister for a father. He served in the crew on several ships throughout the Caribbean, and finally rose to become captain of a twenty-gun ship called Blessed William.[1] *Rather surprisingly for a man who would become a notorious pirate, he married, settled on Pearl Street in what would become New York City, and developed a close business relationship with the influential Scottish émigré Robert Livingston. Through Livingston's business connections Kidd linked up with Richard Coote, Earl of Bellomont, who agreed to back Kidd in a privateering commission to hunt pirates who were raiding English trading ports in the Indian Ocean. The syndicate would fund the ship, Kidd would captain, and all the investors would divide the spoils of whatever Kidd was able to seize from the sea raiders who were installed on St. Mary's Island off the coast of Madagascar.*

Kidd's commission came through in 1696, and the ship Adventure Galley, *of 287 tons and thirty-four guns, became his command. He enlisted a crew of around 100 sailors who agreed they would be paid only if they claimed prizes, be they French or pirate. But when Kidd's expedition arrived in the Indian*

Ocean, they found no prizes to take. His crew—
many of them ex-pirates themselves—became rest-
less and hungry. In 1698, in desperation, Kidd and
his crew took the Quedah Merchant, *a four-hundred-*
ton ship traveling from Surat in India and bound for
the Spice Islands loaded with textiles, opium, sugar,
and saltpeter.[2] *The cargo belonged to the Mughal,*
but the Quedah Merchant *flew a French flag and had*
an English captain. Kidd approached under French
colors—a maritime subterfuge—and the captain
tried to convince Kidd that his French pass should
make him exempt from attack. Kidd seized the cargo
anyway, sold it, and then raided down the Indian
Ocean, attacking Portuguese ships and, most infa-
mously, English East Indiamen—turning to the very
sort of piracy he had been commissioned to root out.
The Adventure Galley *was abandoned leaking and*
irreparable in St. Mary's harbor, off the southeast
coast of Madagascar, and Kidd continued his infa-
mous adventures in the former Quedah Merchant,
rechristened the Adventure Prize.

London, 21
December, 1699[3]

You have press'd me very often, and with much earnestness, to
give you a Relation of the Business of Captain Kidd, which you
say has for a great while, been the principal Subject of
discourse in the Kingdom where you are, and where our Friend
the Earl of Bellomont has the Honor to be a Peer; and you have
repeated it often, that the Common respect we have for him
exacts it from me.

[. . .]

It is well known that for several Years two very pernicious
things have been growing in our American Colonies; an
unlawful Trade, in fraud of the acts of Navigation and the
Plantations, infinitely prejudicial to England, and the cursed

practice of Piracy, utterly destructive of all Commerce. Many
were insensibly drawn into these ill Courses by Observing what
Excessive Wealth the Offenders gain'd in a short time, and with
what Impunity they Offended. For some Governors, having
found a way to share in the project, were obliged not only to
Connive at but protect the Criminals. During the late War[4]
these Evils increased exceedingly, either because Men's
thoughts being engaged nearer home, there was not leisure, nor
a possibility to look strictly after what was doing in those
Remote parts, or for some other reason. Tho it must be own'd
that officers were Employ'd by the Commissioners of the
Customs to inquire into the irregular Trade, and Orders were
frequently repeated to the Governors of Plantations, and to the
Squadrons and Men of War which were sent to the West-
Indies, to use their best diligence to Suppress Pirates. But it was
easy for them to avoid Squadrons, and not difficult to keep out
of the way of the Men of War, who were sent for particular
purposes, and were appointed to certain Stations which they
could not leave, and consequently could not pursue Rovers to
any purpose; who thereby growing bold did not only Commit
Spoils on the Coasts of America, but went beyond the Cape of
Good Hope, and Robb'd in the East-Indies and at the Entrance
to the Red Sea.

[. . .]

As soon as it was known that the Earl of Bellomont was
design'd for Governor, all Persons who had Concerns in
New-York made their Applications to him. Amongst others
Col. Robert Livingston, a Man of considerable Estate and a
fair Reputation, who had several Employments in that
Province, had frequent access to him, as well upon the account
of the public affairs there, as of several matters which he had
then depending before the Council and at the Treasury. The
Earl taking occasion to mention to his Gentleman the Scandal
which lay upon New-York in respect to the Encouragement and
Retreat which Pirates found there: Col. Livingston confess'd
there was too much ground for the Complaint, and that if some
Speedy and effectual Course were not taken to Suppress those

Enormities, so many persons would be drawn into the guilt, that it would become exceeding difficult to master them.

When he came again to wait on the Earl, he took notice of the Zeal the Earl had express'd at their last Conversation for putting a Stop to that Piratical Trade, since which time he said, he had spoke with one Captain William Kidd, lately come from New-York in a Sloop of his own upon the account of Trade, who told him that he knew most of the principal Men who had been ab[r]oad Roving, and divers who were lately gone out; and likewise had some knowledg[e] of the Places where they usually made their Rendezvous, and that he would undertake to Seize most of them, in case he might be Employ'd in one of the King's Ships, a good Sailer of about 30 Guns, and might have 150 Men. He said that tho the Pirates were many in number, yet they had at that time no Ships of considerable force. Livingston affirm'd that Kidd was a bold and honest Man, and he believed fitter than any other to be Employ'd on that occasion.

[. . .]

Col. Livingston, finding no hopes of any thing to be done this Way, did propose to the Earl, that if Persons of Consideration might be Induced to Join in the Expense of Buying and fitting Out a proper Ship, he had such an Opinion of Kidd's Capacity and good Meaning, and so great a desire that some Stop might be put to the Piracies, that he would be one of the Undertakers: And that He and Kidd would be at a 5th part of the Charge. Livingston affirm'd to the E[arl] that Kidd was a settled Inhabitant at New-York, Lived regularly, had a Competent Estate of his own, and had Married at New-York a Wife with a Considerable Fortune,[5] by whom he had a Child. Adding withal, that Kidd's good behavior might be depended upon with assurance, because if he did otherwise than as his Duty would Oblige him, he had no Place to go to, for he had acted such things against the French since the War, that he durst never trust himself to them. And as a further Evidence, how much he Confided in Kidd's Integrity, Livingston offer'd to become bound with him to the E[arl] for his Faithfull Execution of his Commission and safe bringing back of the Vessel.

[. . .]

Kidd had a Commission from the Admiralty dated the 10th of December 1695, as a Private Man of War, but that Impowered him only to act against the French. He had another Commission under the Great Seal, dated the 26 of January 1695, to the Effect following. That whereas Informations had been given to the King, that . . . other of his Majesty's Subjects had associated themselves with many wicked persons and committed Great Piracies in the parts of America and elsewhere, in violation of the Law of Nations, to the discouragement of Trade, and to the Dishonor of his Royal Authority, in case any of his Subjects guilty of such detestable Enormities should go Unpunish'd: His Majesty did there give Power to Captain Kidd, Commander of the *Adventure Galley*, and to the Commander of that Ship for the time being, to Apprehend and Seize the Persons above named, and all other Pirates whom he should meet with on the Coast of America, or other Seas, with their Ships and Goods; and in Case of Resistance to Fight with and compel them to yield, and to bring them to a legal Trial, in order to suffer the Punishment of the Law.

[. . . *The ship sailed from London in February 1695, not reaching Plymouth until April. The crew were all Englishmen, but virtually all of them had been subject to impressment. . . .*]

There was no Account of Kidd of his Proceedings for a great while. But some of the Crew of one Every,[6] who had run away with the Ship called the *Charles the 2d* and committed several Piracies, being taken, Letters were sent in the latter End of August, 1696, from the Privy Council to all the Plantations, taking notice of the Piracies Committed by the *Charles the 2d*, and requiring the Governors, to Issue out Proclamations for securing Every, and as many as could be found of his Accomplices, and Commanding them to do their Utmost to

Seize all other Pirates who had gone from several of the Plantations. About the same time the Lords Justices having Ordered a Letter brought to them, (wherein One of the Persons concerned in Every's Piracy offered to come in as a Witness, if he might have a Pardon), to be sent to the East-India Company, to know if they wanted Evidence. The Company took occasion to present a Petition, in which they said they had Witnesses enough, but desired that all Gold, Silver or Jewels, which had been or should be Seized with Pirates, should not be disposed of, but put into the Company's Possession, to be preserved for the use of the Proprietors in India.

[. . .]

About August 1698, the East-India Company inform'd the Lords Justices that they had receiv'd some Intelligence from their Factories in the East-Indies, that Captain Kidd had Committed several acts of Piracy; particularly in seizing a Moor's Ship called the *Quedah Merchant*. The Lords Justices immediately Ordered the Secretary of State to send Circular Letters to the Governors of all the Plantations in America, to give Notice of this News, and to Order them in the strictest manner to look after and Seize Kidd, in order that he might be Prosecuted with the utmost Rigor.

[. . .]

The first News of Kidd's return into the American Seas was by a Letter from the President and Council of Nevis to the Secretary of State, Dated the 18 of May, 1699, which gave Notice that he had been seen in a Genouese[7] Vessel very Leaky, that he was in distress for Provisions, and had touch'd at two or three Places to seek for Succor, and that they had sent the *Queenborough* Man of War, which then attended that Government, in pursuit of him.

The next Advice given of him was from Captain Quare, Judge of the Admiralty Court of Pensilvania,[8] who gave Notice that Kidd had been in Delaware Bay with a Sloop and about Forty Men in her, and that divers People had been on Board and supply'd him.

Afterwards . . . Kidd Sail'd into the Sound of New York, and set Goods on Shore at several Places there, and after went to

Rhode Island, from whence he sent one Emmot to the E[arl] of Bellomont at Boston, who told him, that Kidd had left a Moorish Ship, which he took in India call'd the *Quedah Merchant*, in a Creek on the Coast of Hispaniola, with Goods in her to a great Value. That he was come thither to make his Terms in a Sloop, which had on Board Goods to the Value of 10,000 pounds and was able to make his Innocence appear by many Witnesses.

[. . .]

In a few days Kidd return'd an Answer fill'd with Protestations of his Innocence, and on the first of June, 1699, landed at Boston with his Sloop, and was Examined before the Earl, and the Council of that Province.

[. . .]

Therefore on the 6th of June 1699, he [Earl of Bellomont] caused Kidd to be Seized and Committed close Prisoner with divers of his Crew, and at the same time caused the Cargo to be taken into the Possession of several Persons appointed by the council for that purpose, the Earl being determined to touch none of the effects himself, not rake one step, with respect to Kidd, but in Concurrence with the Council.

[. . . The letter then goes on to offer an account of Kidd's doings after he left England . . .]

He sailed from Plimouth[9] to New York, and in his way took a French Prize. From thence he Sail'd to the Maderas,[10] then to Bonavista[11] and St. Jage,[12] and proceeded to Madagascar, and from thence (touching at several Places) he Cruis'd at the Entrance of the Red-Sea, but effected nothing.

After he Sail'd to Calicut,[13] and about 1698, took a Ship of about 150 Tons, whereof the Master and 3 or 4 Seamen were Dutch, the rest Moors, and Carried her to Madagascar.

He Sail'd from thence again, and about 5 Weeks after took the *Quedah Merchant*, of the Burden of 400 Tons. The Master was one Wright, an Englishman. She had on Board 2 Dutch Mates and a French Gunner; the Crew were Moors, in all about 90 persons.

The Ship he Carried to St. Mary's near Madagascar, and there he shared the Goods with his Crew, who were about 151, reserving 40 shares for his own part. When this was done, 90 of his Crew left him, and went on Board the *Motha* Frigate, an East-India Company's Ship, which had turn'd Pirate, and then lay there.

Kidd and the Rest of his Men burnt the *Adventure Galley*, and having prevail'd with some others who were then at St. Mary's, to go along with them, they went on Board the *Quedah Merchant*, and Sailed for the West-Indies.

Being denied Succor at Anguilla and St. Thomas, he Sail'd to Mona,[14] lying between Porto Rico and Hispaniola, and there by the means of one Bolton, on which he Laded part of his Goods, and left the *Quedah Merchant* with the rest of the Goods, in trust with Bolton, and 17 or 18 Men in her. In this Sloop he touch'd at divers places where he distributed divers Bales of Goods, and at last came to Boston, where he was taken.

[. . . In New England at that time piracy was not punishable by death, and the people were thought to be friendly to pirates. So Kidd was extradited for trial back to London, where he was hanged in 1701.]

There's an amusing postscript to this story of Captain Kidd, as we also consider the relationship between history and myth. Kidd achieved a singular mythic stature, especially due to rumors of his activities along the East Coast of the United States. In 1895, a Kidd enthusiast named Franklin H. Head privately published a pamphlet rather cheekily entitled "Studies in Early American History: A Notable Lawsuit," which is excerpted below.[15]

Upon the rocky shore near of the residence of Mr. Olmsted,[16] as at the extreme south end of the island,[17] is a cave, the opening of which is upon the sea. The cave is about ten feet wide and high, of irregular shape, and extends back into the rock formation some twenty-five feet. . . . In 1892, Mr. Olmsted observed upon the rock at the inner end of the cave some marks or indentations, something in the form of a rude cross, which seemed to him possibly of artificial origin. [. . .] Mr. Olmsted one day suggested to his family, when in the cave, that as stories of Captain Kidd's buried treasures had sometimes located such treasures upon the Maine coast, they should dig at the place below the cross for such hidden wealth.

[. . . They dig in the sand and find in the clay a rusted out impression of a box pressed in the clay substrate, which for which they make a plaster cast. The fact that they would have to do this in between the tides, meaning a matter of only a couple of hours, already suggests this story is a fable, but it gets even better. Just wait.]

[. . .] Various questions presented themselves regarding this theory. Had the box contained the long-lost treasures of Captain Kidd? If so, to whom did the box and its contents belong? Mr. William M. Evarts, to whom Mr. Olmsted applied for an opinion as to the legal phase of this question, after careful examination of the evidence, gave his views, in substance, as follows:

1. That Captain Kidd, in the year 1700, had acquired, by pillage, vast treasures of gold and gems, which he somewhere concealed prior to his execution in 1701.

2. That if such treasure was concealed upon Deer Isle, that island was the absolute property, at that time, of Cotton Mather Olmsted;[18] for while the record title to the island bore date in President Washington's administration in 1794, yet this . . . was in affirmation of the title made in 1699 . . . and that Frederick Law Olmsted, by inheritance and purchase, had acquired all the rights originally held by his ancestor in that part of the island where the treasure was concealed.

3. That, as owner of such real estate, the treasure would belong to him, as affixed to the land, as against the whole world,

except possibly the lineal descendants of Captain Kidd, if any there were.

[. . . The pamphlet goes on to suggest that a fur trapper improbably named Jacques Cartier had found the box in 1801 and sold it for five thousand dollars to John Jacob Astor.[19] *It then posits that Frederick Law Olmsted accessed Astor's bank records from that period, proving that Astor traveled to London and sold a vast quantity of Spanish gold and jewels to a jeweler named Roderick Streeter for almost $495,000, and for two subsequent years in amounts totaling over a million dollars.]*

. . . The facts gathered thus far enabled Mr. Olmsted to formulate a theory in substance as follows: that Jacques Cartier had found the box containing the buried treasures of Captain Kidd; that he had taken it to New York and delivered it to Mr. Astor; that Mr. Astor had bought the contents of the box, or his interest in them, for the cheque of five thousand dollars; that he had taken the contents to England, and had, from their sale, realized the vast sums paid him by Mr. Streeter.

[. . . The pamphlet goes on to speculate what Astor might have done with the telltale iron box. Was it kept by the family as a relic? Was it sold for scrap?]

. . . Mr. Olmstead learned that the last house in which the original John Jacob Astor had lived had been torn down in the year 1893, to be replaced by a superb modern building, and that the old building had been sold to a well-known house-wrecking firm for an insignificant sum, as the material was worth but little above the cost of tearing down and removal. . . .

[. . . Then, the pamphlet says, Olmsted took out an ad in the New York Tribune, *saying that an iron box had been sold by mistake in 1893 and offering terms for its removal. Further beggaring the imagination, the box is returned to*

him and has the initials "W. K." on the lid. The story gets even more ludicrous with Kidd slipping his wife with a number in code in the thirty minutes they were allowed to speak before his execution, the code being "44106818," which later supposedly proved to be the latitude of Deer Island, the location of the supposed treasure. There is some further intrigue surrounding a pair of pearl bracelets supposedly stolen by Kidd from a Lady Dunsmore, the matching pair of which appear in possession of the current Lady Dunsmore when the originals appear among a lot of jewelry offered for sale by John Jacob Astor. The pamphlet concludes its fantastical "case" with the following argument.]

1. Captain Kidd had sailed along the Maine coast shortly before his arrest, and an iron box, marked with his initials, was afterward taken from the cave upon the land of Mr. Olmsted, and this box afterward came into Mr. Astor's possession.

2. Jacques Cartier had camped for many years, while employed by Mr. Astor, immediately adjoining the cave where the box was concealed, and his rapid increase in wealth and that of Mr. Astor were simultaneous.

3. Mr. Astor's great wealth came from the sale, through Mr. Streeter, of ancient Spanish and French gold, and of gems, some of which were proved to have been a part of the spoils of Captain Kidd, which made it reasonable presumption that all of such property was of the same character.

4. Captain Kidd was known to have captured and somewhere concealed gold and gems of vast value, and the card given his wife just before his execution, indicated by a plausible reading, the cave upon Mr. Olmsted's land as the place of concealment.

5. The family of Captain Kidd had long been extinct, and no one could successfully contest with Mr. Olmsted the ownership of the property concealed upon his land.

. . . Should the judgment upon the trial be in favor of Mr. Olmstead, or even against him upon some technical ground, it would, in either event, be a great boon to the people along our Atlantic seaboard, in that it will reveal the actual fate of the Kidd treasures. The publicity upon this point will stop the ceaseless and fruitless expenditure of money in digging for such hidden wealth, as well as the exactions of clairvoyants, Indian spiritual mediums, rappers, professional ghosts, and witch-hazel experts, who have yearly preyed upon the credulity of their victims in locating the Kidd deposits.

THOMAS TEW

The *Amity*

Rhode Island and Madagascar

1690s

What is a pirate? Is it anyone who breaks the law when on the sea? Is it anyone who acts in his own interest rather than on behalf of a government, syndicate, or boss? And how do we tell the difference? Thomas Tew was one of the pirates Henry Avery came upon at St. Mary's Island, the pirate nest off Madagascar, but he wound up there after having been retained as essentially a soldier of fortune. Tew was tasked by the Royal African Company, an English slave-trading corporation founded in 1660 and led by the Duke of York, brother of Charles II, with overthrowing the French slave-trading powers on an island off modern-day Senegal, and with traveling up the River Gambia in the interest of furthering Stuart control over the capture and sale of enslaved people. An Englishman himself, like many Golden Age pirates, Tew was originally from Rhode Island, then an English colony, but set off on his pirate career from a home base on Bermuda, where he moved in 1691. He used his ship the Amity[1] to rake in millions in prize money, gold, silver, ivory, gemstones, and silks.[2] On his second pirating excursion in 1695, Tew attacked a Mughal convoy of twenty-five ships, and Tew himself was killed, causing his crew to surrender.

Another worthy side note: the archive is cagey on revealing pirates of color. In 1694 a biracial enslaved man, described by turns as "very tall" and "remarkable," who went by the name of Calico Jack, liberated himself from a plantation on the Pocantico River in New York, eventually making his way along Long Island Sound as far as Stratford, Connecticut. Frederick Philipse, the plantation owner who was trying to capture Jack and drag him back, felt convinced that Jack's maritime knowledge and good use of languages—he spoke Dutch as well as English— caused him to enlist on a privateer outfitting at Newport to raid in the Red Sea, one of which might have been under the command of Thomas Tew. Years later Philipse instructed his captains that if they ever put in at Madagascar, they should inquire after Jack and either capture or try to persuade him to return.[3]

Tew has been rumored to be one of the founders of Libertalia, a probably apocryphal free utopian or anarchist settlement established by pirates and outlaws in Madagascar.

There they met with several of their Countrymen, the Crew of a Privateer Sloop which was commanded by Captain Thomas Tew; and since it will be but a short Digression, we will give an Account how they came here.[4]

Captain George Dew and Captain Thomas Tew, having received Commissions from the then Governor of Bermudas, to sail directly for the River Gambia in Africa; there, with the Advice and Assistance of the Agents of the Royal Africas Company, to attempt the taking of the French Factory at Goerie,[5] lying upon that Coast. In a few Days after they sailed out, Dew in a violent Storm, not only sprung his Mast, but lost

Sight of his Consort; Dew therefore returned back to refit, and Tew instead of proceeding on his Voyage, made for the Cape of Good Hope, and doubling the said Cape, shaped his Course for the Straits of Babel Mandel, being the Entrance into the Red Sea. Here he came up with a large Ship, richly laden, bound from the Indies to Arabia, with three hundred Soldiers on Board, besides Seamen; yet Tew had the Hardiness to board her, and soon carried her; and, 'tis said, by this Prize, his Men shared near three thousand Pounds a Piece: They had Intelligence from the Prisoners, or five other rich Ships to pass that Way, which Tew would have attacked, tho' they were very strong, if he had not been over-ruled by the Quarter-Master and others.— This differing in Opinion created some ill Blood amongst them, so that they resolved to break up pyrating, and no Place was so fit to receive them as Madagascar; hither they steered, resolving to live on Shore and enjoy what they got.

As for Tew himself, he with a few others in a short Time went off to Rhode Island, from whence he made his Peace.

THE GOLDEN AGE

THE PROCLAMATION PARDONING PIRATES

1717, September 5.

BY THE KING
A PROCLAMATION
FOR SUPPRESSING OF PIRATES[1]

George R.

Whereas We have received Information, That several Persons, Subjects of Great Britain, have, since the Twenty fourth Day of June, in the Year of our Lord One thousand seven hundred and fifteen, committed divers Piracies and Robberies upon the High Seas in the West-Indies, or adjoining to Our Plantations, which hath, and may Occasion great Damage to the Merchants of Great Britain, and others, Trading into those Parts; And though We have appointed such a Force as We Judge sufficient for Suppressing the said Piracies: Yet the more effectually to put an End to the same, We have thought fit, by and with the Advice of our Privy-Council, to Issue this Our Royal Proclamation; And We do hereby Promise and Declare, That in case any of the said Pirates shall, on or before the Fifth Day of September, in the Year of our Lord One thousand seven hundred and eighteen,[2] Surrender him or themselves to One of Our Principal Secretaries of State in Great Britain or Ireland, or to any Governor or Deputy-Governor of any of Our Plantations or Dominions beyond the Seas, every such Pirate and Pirates, so Surrendering him or themselves, as aforesaid, shall have Our Gracious Pardon of and for such his or their Piracy or Piracies, by him or them Committed before the Fifth Day of January next ensuing. And We do hereby strictly Charge and Command all Our Admirals,

Captains, and other Officers at Sea, and all Our Governors and Commanders of any Forts, Castles, or other Places in Our Plantations, and all other Our Officers Civil and Military, to Seize and Take such of the Pirates who shall refuse or neglect to Surrender themselves accordingly. And We do hereby further Declare, That in case any Person or Persons, on or after the Sixth Day of September, One thousand seven hundred and eighteen, shall Discover or Seize, or cause or procure to be Discovered or Seized, any One or more of the said Pirates, so neglecting of refusing to Surrender themselves, as aforesaid, so as they may be brought to Justice, and Convicted of the said Offence, such Person or Persons, so making such Discovery or Seizure, or causing or procuring such Discover or Seizure to be made, shall have and receive as a Reward for the same, viz. For every Commander of any Pirate-Ship or Vessel the Sum of One hundred Pounds; For every Lieutenant, Master, Boatswain, Carpenter, and Gunner, the Sum of Forty Pounds; For every Inferior Officer the Sum of Thirty Pounds; And for every Private Man the Sum of Twenty Pounds. And if any Person or Persons, belonging to, and being Part of the Crew of any such Pirate-Ship or Vessel, shall, on or after the said Sixth Day of September, One thousand seven hundred and eighteen, Seize and Deliver, or cause to be Seized or Delivered, any Commander or Commanders of such Pirate-Ship or Vessel, so as that he or they be brought to Justice, and convicted of the said Offence, such Person or Persons, as a Reward for the same, shall receive for every such Commander the Sum of Two hundred Pounds; which said Sums the Lord Treasures, or the Commissioners of Our Treasury for the time being, are hereby required and directed to Pay accordingly.

Given at Our Court at Hampton-Court,
the Fifth Day of September, 1717. In the Fourth Year of Our Reign.

GOD SAVE THE KING

London, Printed by John Baskett,
Printer to the Kings most Excellent Majesty,
And by the Assigns of Thomas Newcomb,
and Henry Hills, deceas'd 1717.

HOWELL DAVIS

The *Cadogan*

Caribbean and West Africa

1718–19

*Howell Davis's piratical career was furious and short,
which was much more the norm for Golden Age pirates than the sedate, wealthy retirements of Henry
Morgan and his ilk. He was Welsh, born around
1690. He was in service on a slave ship called the*
Cadogan *when it was seized by the pirate Edward
England, and Davis decided to turn pirate along
with him. They sailed in convoy for the slave mar-
kets in Brazil, but on the way, his crew mutinied—
no honor among thieves. Eventually Davis landed in
the notorious pirate nest New Providence, in the Bahamas. After some time in the Caribbean, he sailed
for the Cape Verde Islands, joining up with some
other pirates and at one time holding as prisoner
Bartholomew Roberts, who would go on to be
known as "Black Bart" and be an even more famous
pirate than Davis. Davis was especially cunning in
his use of trickery and deception, as outlined in the
following excerpt.*

THE LIFE OF CAPTAIN DAVIS;
WITH AN ACCOUNT OF HIS
SURPRISING THE FORT AT GAMBIA[1]

Davis was born in Monmouthshire, and, from a boy, trained to the sea. His last voyage from England was in the sloop *Cadogan* from Bristol, in the character of chief mate. This vessel was captured by the pirate England, upon the Guinea coast,[2] whose companions plundered the crew, and murdered the captain, as is related in England's life.

Upon the death of Captain Skinner, Davis pretended that he was urged by England[3] to become a pirate, but that he resolutely refused. He added, that England, pleased with his conduct, had made him captain in room of Skinner, giving him a sealed paper, which he was not to open until he was in a certain latitude, and then expressly to follow the given directions. When he arrived in the appointed place, he collected the whole crew, and solemnly read his sealed instructions, which contained a generous grant of the ship and all her stores to Davis and his crew, requesting them to go to Brazil, and dispose of the cargo to the best advantage, and make an equal division of the money.

Davis then commanded the crew to signify whether they were inclined to follow that mode of life, when, to his astonishment and chagrin, the majority positively refused. Then, in a transport of rage, he desired them to go where they would.

Knowing that part of the cargo was consigned to merchants in Barbados, they directed their course to that place. When arrived there, they informed the merchants of the unfortunate death of Skinner, and of the proposal which had been made to them. Davis was accordingly seized, and committed to prison, but he having never been in the pirate service, nothing could be proved to condemn him, and he was discharged without a trial. Convinced that he could never hope for employment in that quarter after this detection, he went to the island of Providence,[4] which he knew to be a rendezvous for pirates. Upon his arrival there, he was grievously disappointed, because the pirates who frequented that place had just accepted of his majesty's pardon, and had surrendered.

Captain Rodgers having equipped two sloops for trade, Davis obtained employment in one of these, called the *Buck*. They were laden with European goods to a considerable value, which they were to sell or exchange with the French and Spanish. They first touched at the island of Martinique, belonging to the French, and Davis knowing that many of the men were formerly in the pirate service, enticed them to seize the master,[5] and to run off with the sloop. When they had effected their purpose, they hailed the other ship, in which they knew that there were many hands ripe for rebellion, and coming to, the greater part joined Davis. Those who did not choose to adhere to them were allowed to remain in the other sloop, and continue their course, after Davis had pillaged her of what things he pleased.

In full possession of the vessel and stores and goods, a large bowl of punch was made; under its exhilarating influence, it was proposed to choose a commander, and to form their future mode of policy. The election was soon over, and a large majority of legal votes were in favor of Davis, and no scrutiny demanded, Davis was declared duly elected. He then drew up a code of laws, to which he himself swore, and required the same bond of alliance from all the rest of the crew. He then addressed the men in a short and appropriate speech, the substance of which was, a proclamation of war with the whole world.

They next consulted, what part would be most convenient to clean the vessel, and it was resolved to repair to Coxon's Hole,[6] at the east end of the island of Cuba, where they could remain in perfect security, as the entrance was so narrow that one ship could keep out a hundred.

They, however, had no small difficulty in cleaning their vessel, as there was no carpenter among them. They performed that laborious task in the best manner they could, and then made to the north side of Hispaniola. The first sail they met with was a French ship of twelve guns, which they captured;

and while they were plundering her, another appeared in view. Enquiring of the Frenchmen, they learned that she was a ship of twenty-four guns and sixty [men]. Davis proposed to his crew to attack her, assuring them that she would prove a rich prize. This appeared to the crew such a hazardous enterprise, that they were rather adverse to the measure. But he acquainted them that he had conceived a stratagem that he was confident would succeed; they might, therefore, safely leave the matter to his management. He then commenced chase, and ordered his prize to do the same. Being a better sailer, he soon came up with the enemy, and showed his black colors. With no small surprise at his insolence in coming so near them, they commanded him to strike. He replied, that he was disposed to give them employment until his companion came up, who was able to contend with them; meanwhile assuring them that, if they did not strike to him, it would most certainly fare the worse for them: then giving them a broadside, he received the same in return.

When the other pirate ship drew near, they, according to the directions of Davis, appeared upon deck in white shirts, which making an appearance of numbers, the Frenchman was intimidated, and struck. Davis ordered the captain with twenty of his men to come on board, and they were all put in irons except the captain. He then dispatched four of his men to the other ship, and calling aloud to them, desired that his compliments should be given to the captain, with a request to send a sufficient number of hands to go on board their new prize, to see what they had got in her. At the same time, he gave them a written paper with their proper instructions, even to nail up the small guns, to take out all the arms and powder, and to go every man on board the new prize. When his men were on board her, he ordered the greater part of the prisoners to be removed into the empty vessels, and by this means secured himself from any attempt to recover their ship.

During three days, these three vessels sailed in company, but finding that his late prize was a heavy sailer, he emptied her of everything that he stood in need of, and then restored her to the captain with all his men. The French captain was so much enraged at being thus miserably deceived, that, upon the discovery of the stratagem, he would have thrown himself overboard, had not his men prevented him.

Captain Davis then formed the resolution of parting with the other prize-ship also, and soon afterwards steered northward, and took a Spanish sloop. He next directed his course towards the western islands, and from Cape de Verd islands cast anchor at St. Nicholas,[7] and hoisted English colors. The Portuguese supposed that he was a privateer, and Davis going on shore was hospitably received, and they traded with him for such articles as they found most advantageous. He remained here five weeks, and he and half of his crew visited the principal town of the island. Davis, from his appearing in the dress of a gentleman, was greatly caressed by the Portuguese, and nothing was spared to entertain and render him and his men happy. Having amused themselves during a week, they returned to the ship, and allowed the other half of the crew to visit the capital, and enjoy themselves in like manner. Upon their return, they cleaned their ship and put to sea, but four of the men were so captivated with the ladies and the luxuries of the place, that they remained in the island, and one of them married and settled there.

Davis now sailed for Bonavista, and perceiving nothing in that harbor steered for the Isle of May.[8] Arrived there, he found several vessels in the harbor, and plundered them of whatever he found necessary. He also received a considerable reinforcement of men, the greater part of whom entered willingly into the piratical service. He likewise made free with one of the ships, equipped her for his own purpose, and called her the *King James*. Davis next proceeded to St. Jago to take in water. Davis, with some others going on shore to seek water, the governor came to inquire who they were, and expressed his suspicion of their being pirates. Upon this, Davis seemed highly affronted, and expressed his displeasure in the most polite but determined manner. He, however, hastened on board, informed his men, and suggested the possibility of surprising the fort during the night. Accordingly, all his men being well armed, they advanced to the assault; and, from the carelessness of the guards, they were in the garrison before the inhabitants were alarmed. Upon the discovery of their danger, they took shelter in the governor's house, and fortified it against the pirates: but the latter throwing in some grando[9] shells, ruined the furniture, and killed several people.

The alarm was circulated in the morning, and the country assembled to attack them; but, unwilling to stand a siege, the pirates dismounted the guns, pillaged the fort, and fled to their ships.

When at sea, they mustered their hands, and found that they were seventy strong. They then consulted among themselves what course they should steer, and were divided in opinion; but by a majority it was carried to sail for Gambia, on the coast of Guinea. Of this opinion was the captain, who having been employed in that trade,[10] was acquainted with the coast; and informed his companions, that there was always a large quantity of money deposited in that castle, and he was confident, if the matter was entrusted to him, he should successfully storm that fort. From their experience of his former prudence and courage, they cheerfully submitted to his direction, in the full assurance of success.

Arrived at Gambia, he ordered all his men below, except just so many as were necessary to work the vessel, that those from the fort, seeing so few hands, might have no suspicion that she was any other than a trading vessel: He then ran under the fort and cast anchor, and having ordered out the boat, manned with six men indifferently dressed, he, with the master and doctor, dressed themselves like gentlemen, in order that the one party might look like foremastmen,[11] and the other like merchants. In rowing ashore, he instructed his men what to say if any questions were put to them by the garrison.

On reaching land, the party was conducted by a file of musqueteers[12] into the fort, and kindly received by the governor, who enquired what they were, and whence they came? They replied, that they were from Liverpool, and bound for the river Senegal, to trade for gum and elephants teeth; but that they were chased on that coast by two French men-of-war, and narrowly escaped being taken. "We were now disposed," continued Davis, "to make the best of our voyage, and would willingly trade here for slaves." The governor then inquired what were the principal articles of their cargo. They replied, that they were iron and plate, which were necessary articles in that place. The governor then said, that he would give them slaves for all their cargo; and asked if they had any European liquor on board. They answered, that they had a little for their own use, but that he should have a hamper of it. He then treated them with the greatest civility, and desired them all to dine with him. Davis answered, that as he was commander of the vessel, it would be necessary for him to go down to see if she were properly moored, and to give some other directions; but that these gentlemen might stay, and he would return before dinner, and bring the hamper with him.

While in the fort, his eyes were keenly employed to discover the position of the arms, and how the fort might most successfully be surprised. He discovered that there was a sentry standing near a guard-house, in which there were a quantity of arms heaped up in a corner, and that a considerable number of small arms were in the governor's hall. When he went on board, he ordered some hands onboard a sloop lying at anchor, lest, hearing any bustle they should come to the aid of the castle; then desiring his men to avoid too much liquor, and to be ready when he should hoist the flag from the walls, to come to his assistance, he proceeded to the castle.

Having taken these precautions and formed these arrangements, he ordered every man who was to accompany him to arm himself with two pair of pistols, which he himself also did, concealed under their clothes. He then directed them to go into the guard-room, and fall into conversation, and immediately upon his firing a pistol out of the governor's window, to shut the men up, and secure the arms in the guard-room.

When Davis arrived, dinner not being ready, the governor proposed that they should pass the time in making a bowl of punch. Davis's boatswain attending him, had an opportunity of visiting all parts of the house, and observing their strength. He whispered his intelligence to his master, who being surrounded by his own friends, and seeing the governor unattended

by any of his retinue, presented a pistol to the breast of the latter, informing him that he was a dead man, unless he should
surrender the fort and all its riches. The governor, thus taken
by surprise, was compelled to submit; for Davis took down all
the pistols that hung in the hall, and loaded them. He then
fired his pistol out of the window. His men flew like lions, presented their pistols to the soldiers, and while some carried out
the arms, the rest secured the military, and shut them all up
in the guard-house, placing a guard on the door. Then one of
them struck the union flag on the top of the castle, which the
men from the vessel perceiving, rushed to the combat, and in
an instant were in possession of the castle, without tumult or
bloodshed.

Davis then harangued the soldiers, many of whom enlisted
with him; and those who declined, he put on board the small
ships, and to prevent the necessity of a guard, or the possibility
of escape, carried off the sails, rigging and cables.

That day being spent in feasting and rejoicing, the castle sa-
luting the ship, and the ship the castle, on the day following
they proceeded to examine the contents of their prize. They,
however, were greatly disappointed in their expectations, a
large sum of money having been sent off a few days before. But
they found money to the amount of about two thousand
pounds in gold, and many valuable articles of different kinds.
They carried on board their vessel whatever they deemed useful, gave several articles to the captain and crew of the small
vessel, and allowed them to depart, while they dismounted the
guns, and demolished the fortifications.

After doing all the mischief that their vicious minds could
possibly devise, they weighed anchor; but in the meantime,
perceiving a sail bearing towards them with all possible speed,
they hastened to prepare for her reception, and made towards
her. Upon her near approach they discovered that she was a
French pirate of fourteen guns and sixty-four men, the one
half French, and the other half negroes.

The Frenchman was in high expectation of a rich prize, but
when he came nearer, he suspected, from the number of her
guns and men, that she was a small English man-of-war; he

determined, notwithstanding, upon the bold attempt of boarding her, and immediately fired a gun, and hoisted his black colors: Davis immediately returned the compliment. The Frenchman
was highly gratified at this discovery; both hoisted out their
boats, and congratulated each other. Mutual civilities and
good offices passed, and the French captain proposed to Davis
to sail down the coast with him, in order to look out for a better ship, assuring him that the very first that could be captured
should be his, as he was always willing to encourage an industrious brother.

They first touched at Sierra Leone, where they espied a large
vessel, and Davis being the swifter sailer, came first up with
him. He was not a little surprised that she did not endeavor to
make off, and began to suspect her strength. When he came
alongside of her, she fired a whole broadside, and hoisted black
colors. Davis did the same, and fired a gun to leeward.[13] The
satisfaction of these brothers in iniquity was mutual, at having
thus acquired so much additional strength and ability to undertake more formidable adventures. Two days were devoted
to mirth and song, and upon the third, Davis and Cochlyn, the
captain of the new confederate, agreed to go in the French pirate ship to attack the fort. When they approached, the men in
the fort, apprehensive of their character and intentions, fired
all the guns upon them at once. The ship returned the fire, and
afforded employment until the other two ships arrived, when
the men in the fort seeing such a number on board, lost courage, and abandoned the fort to the mercy of the robbers.

They took possession, remained there seven weeks, and
cleaned their vessels. They then called a council of war, to deliberate concerning future undertakings, when it was resolved
to sail down the coast in company; and, for the greater regu-
larity and grandeur, Davis was chosen Commodore. That dangerous enemy, strong drink, had well nigh, however, sown the
seeds of discord among these affectionate brethren. But Davis,
alike prepared for council or for war, addressed them to the
following purport: "Hear ye, you Cochlyn and La Boise,
(which was the name of the French captain) I find, by strengthening you, I have put a rod into your hands to whip myself;

but I am still able to deal with you both: however, since we met in love, let us part in love; for I find that three of a trade can never agree long together." Upon this, the other two went on board of their respective ships, and steered different courses.

Davis held down the coast, and reaching Cape Appolonia he captured three vessels, two English and one Scottish, plundered them, and allowed them to proceed. In five days after he met with a Dutchman of thirty guns and ninety men. She gave Davis a broadside, and killed nine of his men; a desperate engagement ensued, which continued from one o'clock at noon until nine next morning, when the Dutchman struck. Davis equipped her for the pirate service, and called her The *Rover*. With his two ships he sailed for the bay of Anamaboa, which he entered about noon, and took several vessels which were there waiting to take in negroes, gold, and elephants' teeth. Davis made a present of one of these vessels to the Dutch captain and his crew, and allowed them to go in quest of their fortune. When the fort had intelligence that they were pirates, they fired at them, but without any effect; Davis fired also, and hoisted the black colors, but deemed it prudent to depart.

The next day after he left Anamaboa, the man at the masthead discovered a sail. It may be proper to inform our readers, that, according to the laws of pirates, the man who first discovers a vessel, is entitled to the best pair of pistols in the ship, and such is the honor attached to these, that a pair of them has been known to sell for thirty pounds.

Davis pursued that vessel, which, being between him and the shore, labored hard to run aground. Davis perceiving this, got between her and the land, and fired a broadside at her, when she immediately struck. She proved to be a very rich prize, having on board the Governor of Acra,[14] with all his substance, going to Holland. There was in money to the amount of fifteen thousand pounds, besides large quantity of merchant goods, and other valuable articles.

Before they reached the Isle of Princes,[15] the *St. James* sprang a leak, so that the men and the valuable articles were removed into Davis's own ship. When he came in sight of the fort he hoisted English colors. The Portuguese, seeing a large ship

sailing towards the shore, sent a sloop to discover her character and destination. Davis informed them, that he was an English man-of-war, sent out in search of some pirates which
they had heard were in this quarter. Upon this, he was piloted
into the port, and anchored below the guns at the fort. The
governor was happy to have Englishmen in his harbor; and to
do honor to Davis, sent down a file of musqueteers to escort
him into the fort, while Davis, the more to cover his design,
ordered nine men, according to the custom of the English, to
row him on shore.

Davis also took the opportunity of cleaning and preparing
all things for renewing his operations. He, however, could not
contentedly leave the fort, without receiving some of the riches
of the island. He formed a scheme to accomplish his purpose,
and communicated the same to his men. He design was to
make the governor a present of a few negroes in return for his
kindness; then to invite him, with a few of the principal men
and friars belonging to the island, to dine on board his ship,
and secure them all in irons, until each of them should give a
large ransom. They were accordingly invited, and very readily
consented to go: and deeming themselves honored by his attention, all that were invited, would certainly have gone on
board. Fortunately however, for them, a negro, who was privy
to the horrible plan of Davis, swam on shore during the night,
and gave information of the danger to the governor.

The governor occupied the whole night in strengthening the
defenses and posting the men in the most advantageous places.
Soon after daybreak, the pirates, with Captain Davis at their
head were discovered landing from the boats; and quickly
marched across the open space toward the fort. A brisk fire
was opened upon them from the fort, which they returned in a
spirited manner. At length, a hand grenade, thrown from the
wooden veranda of the fort killed three of the pirates; but several of the Portuguese were killed. The veranda of the fort
being of wood and very dry, it was set fire to by the pirates.
This was a great advantage to the attacking party, who could
now distinguish those in the fort without their being so clearly
seen themselves; but at this moment Captain Davis fell, mortally

wounded by a musket ball in his belly.[16] The fall of their chief, and the determined resistance of those in the fort, checked the impetuosity of the assailants. They hesitated, and at last retreated, bearing away with them their wounded commander. The Portuguese cheered, and led on by the governor, now became the assailants. Still the pirates' retreat was orderly; they fired and retired rank behind rank successively. They kept the Portuguese at bay until they had arrived at the boats, when a charge was made and a severe conflict ensued. But the pirates had lost too many men; and without their Captain, felt dispirited. As they lifted Davis into the boat in his dying agonies he fired his pistols at his pursuers. They now pulled with all their might to escape from the muskets of the Portuguese, who followed them along the banks of the river, annoying them in their retreat to the vessel. And those on board, who expected to hoist in treasure had to receive naught but their wounded comrades and dead commander.

CHRISTOPHER "BILLY ONE-HAND" CONDENT/CONDON

The *Flying Dragon*

Nassau and St. Mary's

1718–20

Even for a period of time in which spellings of proper names still often varied widely, the true identity of Christopher Condent is hard to pin down. His surname is sometimes spelled Condon, Connor, or Congdon, and his first name could be anything from Christopher to William to Edward. After fleeing the Bahamas ahead of the governor pledging to rid the islands of pirates, Condent raided off the Cape Verde islands and then down to Brazil, then across the Atlantic to the coast of Ghana, eventually ending up at the notorious pirate nest St. Mary's, off Madagascar. Over the course of his career, he amassed a crew of almost five hundred people, including many pirates of color who knew the Indian Ocean. Eventually, despite the brutality illustrated in the ensuing selection, Condent was able to negotiate a pardon for himself and supposedly ended his days a rich merchant in St. Malo, France.

At one time it was rumored that the wreck of the Flying *(sometimes given as* Fiery*)* Dragon *had been*

located in the harbor of St. Mary's, but that assump-
tion was ultimately disproven.

THE ADVENTURES OF
CAPTAIN CONDENT[1]

CAPTAIN CONDENT was a Plymouth man born, but we are
as yet ignorant of the motives and time of his first turning pirate. He was one of those who thought fit to retire from Providence, on Governor Rogers' arrival at that island, in a sloop
belonging to Mr. Simpson, of New York, a Jew merchant, of
which sloop he was then quartermaster. Soon after they left
the island, an accident happened on board, which put the
whole crew into consternation. They had among them an Indian man, whom some of them had beaten; in revenge, he got
most of the arms forward into the hold, and designed to blow
up the sloop; upon which, some advised scuttling the deck,
and throwing grenade shells down, but Condent said that was
too tedious and dangerous, since the fellow might fire through
the deck and kill several of them. He, therefore, taking a pistol
in one hand, and his cutlass in the other, leaped into the hold.
The Indian discharged a piece at him, which broke his arm;
but, however, he ran up and shot the Indian. When he was
dead, the crew hacked him to pieces, and the gunner, ripping
up his belly and tearing out his heart, broiled and eat it.

After this, they took a merchantman called the *Duke of
York*; and some disputes arising among the pirates, the captain, and one half of the company, went on board the prize;
the other half, who continued in the sloop, chose Condent captain. He shaped his course for the Cape-de Verd Islands, and
in his way took a merchant ship from Madeira, laden with
wine, and bound for the West Indies, which he plundered and
let go; then coming to the Isle of May, one of the said islands,
he took the whole salt fleet, consisting of about 20 sail. Wanting a boom,[2] he took out the mainmast of one of these ships to
supply the want. Here he took upon himself the administration of justice, inquiring into the manner of the commanders'

behavior to their men, and those against whom complaint was made, he whipped and pickled.[3] He took what provision and other necessaries he wanted, and having augmented his company by volunteers and forced men, he left the ships and sailed to St. Jago, where he took a Dutch ship, which had formerly been a privateer. This proved also an easy prize, for he fired but one broadside, and clapping her on board, carried her without resistance, for the captain and several men were killed, and some wounded by his great shot.

The ship proving for his purpose, he gave her the name of the *Flying Dragon*, went on board with his crew, and made a present of his sloop to a mate of an English prize, whom he had forced with him. From hence he stood away for the coast of Brazil, and in his cruise took several Portuguese ships, which he plundered and let go.

After these he fell in with the *Wright* galley, Capt. John Spelt, commander, hired by the South Sea company, to go to the coast of Angola for slaves, and thence to Buenos Ayres. This ship he detained a considerable time, and the captain being his townsman, treated him very civilly. A few days after he took Spelt, he made prize of a Portuguese, laden with bale goods and stores. He rigged the *Wright* galley anew, and put on board of her some of the goods. Soon after he had discharged the Portuguese, he met with a Dutch East Indiaman of 28 guns, whose captain was killed the first broadside, and took her with little resistance, for he had hoisted the pirate's colors on board Spelt's ship.

He now, with three sail, steered for the island of Ferdinando, where he hove down and cleaned the *Flying Dragon*. Having careened, he put 11 Dutchmen on board Capt. Spelt, to make amends for the hands he had forced from him, and sent him away, making him a present of the goods he had taken from the Portuguese ship. When he sailed himself, he ordered the Dutch to stay at Ferdinando 24 hours after his departure; threatening, if he did not comply, to sink his ship, if he fell a second time into his hands, and to put all the company to the sword. He then stood for the coast of Brazil, where he met a Portuguese man of war of 70 guns, which he came up with. The Portuguese hailed him, and he answered, from London, bound to Buenos Ayres. The Portuguese manned his shrouds[4] and cheered him, when Condent fired a broadside, and a smart engagement ensued for the space of three glasses;[5] but Condent finding himself over matched, made the best of his way, and being the best sailer, got off.

A few days after, he took a vessel of the same nation, who gave an account that he had killed above forty men in the Guarda del Costa, beside a number wounded. He kept along the coast to the southward, and took a French ship of 18 guns, laden with wine and brandy, bound for the South Sea, which he carried with him into the River of Platte.[6] He sent some of his men ashore to kill some wild cattle, but they were taken by the crew of a Spanish man-of-war. On their examination before the captain, they said they were two Guinea ships, with slaves belonging to the South Sea company, and on this story were allowed to return to their boats. Here five of his forced men ran away with his canoe; he plundered the French ship, cut her adrift, and she was stranded. He proceeded along the Brazil coast, and hearing a pirate ship was lost upon it, and the pirates imprisoned, he used all the Portuguese who fell into his hands, who were many, very barbarously, cutting off their ears and noses; and as his master was a papist, when they took a priest, they made him say mass at the mainmast, and would afterwards get on his back and ride him about the decks, or else load and drive him like a beast. He from this went to the Guinea coast, and took Capt. Hill, in the *Indian Queen.*

In Luengo Bay he saw two ships at anchor, one a Dutchman of 44 guns, the other an English ship, called the *Fame*, Capt. Bowen, commander. They both cut and ran ashore; the *Fame* was lost, but the Dutch ship the pirate got off and took with him. When he was at sea again, he discharged Captain Hill, and stood away for the East Indies. Near the Cape he took an Ostend East-Indiaman, of which Mr. Nash, a noted merchant of London, was supercargo. Soon after he took a Dutch East-Indiaman, discharged the Ostender, and made for Madagascar. At the Isle of St. Mary, he met with some of Capt. Halsey's crew, whom he took on board with other stragglers, and shaped his course for the East-Indies, and in the way, at the island of Johanna, took, in company with two other pirates he met at St. Mary's, the *Cassandra* East-Indiaman, commanded by Capt. James Macraigh. He continued his course for the East-Indies, where he made a very great booty; and returning, touched at the island of Mascarenhas, where he met with a Portuguese ship of 70 guns, with the viceroy of Goa on board. This ship he made prize of, and hearing she had money on board, they would allow of no ransom, but carried her to the coast of Zanguebar,[7] where there was a Dutch fortification, which they took and plundered, razed the fort, and carried off several men voluntarily. From hence they stood for St. Mary's, where they shared their booty, broke up their company, and settled among the natives. Here a snow[8] came from Bristol, which they obliged to carry a petition to the governor of Mascarenhas for a pardon, though they paid the master very generously. The governor returned answer he would take them into protection if they would destroy their ships, which they agreed to, and accordingly sunk the *Flying Dragon*, &c. Condent and some others went to Mascarenhas, where Condent married the governor's sister-in-law, and remained some time; but, as I have been credibly informed, he is since come to France, settled at St. Maloes, and drives a considerable trade as a merchant.

EDWARD "NED" LOW

The *Fancy*

Boston and the Caribbean

1720–23

*Lots of men turned to piracy during the Age of
Sail, whether out of desperation or desire. Many
of them, in the course of their careers, committed
acts of barbarity that would shock our cushioned
twenty-first-century sensibilities. But few were as
brutal as Ned Low. Most of the details of his life appear in the following excerpt, with no need to restate
them here. Another view of Ned Low comes later,
from Philip Ashton, a fisherman from Marblehead,
Massachusetts, who was captured and taken prisoner when Low seized the fishing fleet on the Grand
Banks in 1722. Ashton refused to sign the articles
that would put him in league with the pirates, and
paid for it with whippings, beatings, and repeated
threats of death before he made a daring escape to
Roatán, where he was marooned.*

*Ned Low's notorious cruelties—including murder
and mutilation, at one point slicing off a man's lips
and then feeding them to him—were useful, insofar
as they stoked fear into the hearts of his victims, giving them a reason to surrender and make themselves
agreeable to his desires. But it's also possible that he
enjoyed it.*

*The end of Low's life remains a mystery, but one
account that seems persuasive, given the picture we*

can draw of his character, holds that he was set adrift
without provisions after his crew mutinied aboard a
vessel called the Merry Christmas, *brought about by*
Low's capricious murder of a crewmember while he
was asleep. The Pirates Own Book *suggests that he*
was rescued from this dire condition, put on trial in
Martinique, and hanged in 1724.

Unlike most of the other pirates explored here,
there is some evidence that Low used his own ver-
sions of the Jolly Roger black flag, the most notori-
ous one being a bloodred skeleton on a black field.

THE LIFE OF CAPTAIN EDWARD LOW[1]

This ferocious villain was born in Westminster, and received
an education similar to that of the common people in England.
He was by nature a pirate; for even when very young he raised
contributions among the boys of Westminster, and if they declined compliance, a battle was the result. When he advanced
a step farther in life, he began to exert his ingenuity at low
games, and cheating all in his power; and those who pretended
to maintain their own right, he was ready to call to the field of
combat.

He went to sea in company with his brother, and continued
with him for three or four years. Going over to America, he
wrought in a rigging-house at Boston for some time. He then
came home to see his mother in England, returned to Boston,
and continued for some years longer at the same business. But
being of a quarrelsome temper, he differed with his master,
and went on board a sloop bound for the Bay of Honduras.

While there, he had the command of a boat employed in
bringing logwood to the ship. In that boat there were twelve
men well armed, to be prepared for the Spaniards, from whom
the wood was taken by force. It happened one day that the
boat came to the ship just a little before dinner was ready, and
Low desired that they might dine before they returned. The
captain, however, ordered them a bottle of rum, and requested

them to take another trip, as no time was to be lost. The crew
were enraged, particularly Low, who took up a loaded musket
and fired at the captain, but missing him, another man was
shot, and they ran off with the boat. The next day they took a
small vessel, went on board her, hoisted a black flag, and declared war with the whole world.

In their rovings, Low met with Lowther,[2] who proposed
that he should join him, and thus promote their mutual advantage. Having captured a brigantine,[3] Low, with forty more,
went on board her; and leaving Lowther, they went to seek
their own fortune. Their first adventure was the capture of a
vessel belonging to Amboy, out of which they took the provisions, and allowed her to proceed. On the same day they took
a sloop, plundered her, and permitted her to depart. The sloop
went into Black Island,[4] and sent intelligence to the governor
that Low was on the coast. Two small vessels were immediately fitted out, but, before their arrival, Low was beyond their
reach. After this narrow escape, Low went into port to procure water and fresh provisions; and then renewed his search
of plunder. He next sailed into the harbor of Port Rosemary,[5]
where were thirteen ships, but none of them of any great
strength. Low hoisted the black flag, assuring them that if they
made any resistance they should have no quarter; and man-
ning their boat, the pirates took possession of every one of
them, which they plundered and converted to their own use.
They then put on board a schooner[6] ten guns and fifty men,
named her the *Fancy*, and Low himself went on board of her,
while Charles Harris was constituted captain of the brigantine. They also constrained a few of the men to join them, and
sign their articles.

After an unsuccessful pursuit of two sloops from Boston,
they steered for the Leeward Islands, but in their way were
overtaken by a terrible hurricane. The search for plunder gave
place to the most vigorous exertion to save themselves. On
board the brigantine, all hands were at work both day and
night; they were under the necessity of throwing overboard six
of her guns, and all the weighty provisions. In the storm, the

two vessels were separated, and it was some time before they again saw each other.

After the storm, Low went into a small island west of the Carribbees, refitted his vessels, and got provisions for them in exchange of goods. As soon as the brigantine was ready for sea, they went on a cruise until the *Fancy* should be prepared, and during that cruise, met with a vessel which had lost all her masts in the storm, which they plundered of goods to the value of 1000 and returned to the island. When the *Fancy* was ready to sail, a council was held what course they should next steer. They followed the advice of the captain, who thought it not safe to cruise any longer to the leeward, lest they should fall in with any of the men-of-war that cruised upon that coast, so they sailed for the Azores.

The good fortune of Low was now singular; in his way thither he captured a French ship of 34 guns, and carried her along with him. Then entering St. Michael's roads, he captured seven sail, threatening with instant death all who dared to oppose him. Thus, by inspiring terror, without firing a single gun, he became master of all that property. Being in want of water and fresh provisions, Low sent to the governor demanding a supply, upon condition of releasing the ships he had taken, otherwise he would commit them to the flames. The request was instantly complied with, and six of the vessels were restored. But a French vessel being among them, they emptied her of guns and all her men, except the cook, who, they said, being a greasy fellow, would fry well; they accordingly bound the unfortunate man to the mast, and set the ship on fire.

The next who fell in their way was Captain Carter, in the *Wright* galley; who, because he showed some inclination to defend himself, was cut and mangled in a barbarous manner. There were also two Portuguese friars, whom they tied to the foremast, and several times let them down before they were dead,[7] merely to gratify their own ferocious dispositions. Meanwhile, another Portuguese, beholding this cruel scene, expressed some sorrow in his countenance, upon which one of the wretches said he did not like his looks, and so giving him a stroke across the body with his cutlass, he fell upon the spot. Another of the miscreants, aiming a blow at a prisoner, missed his aim, and struck Low upon the under jaw. The surgeon was called, and stitched up the wound; but Low finding fault with the operation, the surgeon gave him a blow which broke all the stiches, and left him to sew them himself. After he had plundered this vessel, some of them were for burning her, as they had done the Frenchman; but instead of that, they cut her cables, rigging, and sails to pieces, and sent her adrift to the mercy of the waves.

They next sailed for the island of Madeira, and took up a fishing boat with two old men and a boy. They detained one of them, and sent the other on shore with a flag of truce, requesting the governor to send them a boat of water, else they would hang the other man at the yard arm. The water was sent, and the man dismissed.

They next sailed for the Canary Islands, and there took several vessels; and being informed that two small galleys were daily expected, the sloop was manned and sent in quest of them. They, however, missing their prey, and being in great want of provision, went into St. Michael's in the character of traders, and being discovered, were apprehended, and the whole crew conducted to the castle, and treated according to their merits.

Meanwhile, Low's ship was overset upon the careen and lost,[8] so that, having only the *Fancy* schooner remaining, they all, to the number of a hundred, went on board her, and set sail in search of new spoils. They soon met a rich Portuguese vessel, and after some resistance captured her. Low tortured the men to constrain them to inform him where they had hid their treasures. He accordingly discovered that, during the chase, the captain had hung a bag with eleven thousand moidores[9] out of the cabin window, and that, when they were taken, he had cut the rope, and allowed it to fall into the sea. Upon this intelligence, Low raved and stormed like a fury, ordered the captain's lips to be cut off and broiled before his eyes, then murdered him and all his crew.

After this bloody action, the miscreants steered northward,

and in their course seized several vessels, one of which they burned, and plundering the rest, allowed them to proceed. Having cleaned in one of the islands, they then sailed for the bay of Honduras. They met a Spaniard coming out of the bay, which had captured five Englishmen and a pink, plundered them, and brought away the masters prisoners. Low hoisted Spanish colors, but, when he came near, hung out the black flag, and the Spaniard was seized without resistance. Upon finding the masters of the English vessels in the hold, and seeing English goods on board, a consultation was held, when it was determined to put all the Spaniards to the sword. This was scarcely resolved upon, when they commenced with every species of weapons to massacre every man, and some flying from their merciless hands into the waves, a canoe was sent in pursuit of those who endeavored to swim on shore. They next plundered the Spanish vessel, restored the English masters to their respective vessels, and set the Spaniard on fire.

Low's next cruise was between the Leeward Islands and the mainland, where, in a continued course of prosperity, he successively captured no less than nineteen ships of different sizes, and in general treated their crews with a barbarity unequalled even among pirates. But it happened that the *Greyhound*, of twenty guns and one hundred and twenty men, was cruising upon that coast. Informed of the mischief these miscreants had done, the *Greyhound* went in search of them. Supposing they had discovered a prize, Low and his crew pursued them, and the *Greyhound*, allowing them to run after her until all things were ready to engage, turned upon the two sloops.

One of these sloops was called the *Fancy*, and commanded by Low himself, and the other the *Ranger*, commanded by Harris;[10] both hoisted their piratical colors, and fired each a gun. When the *Greyhound* came within musket shot, she hauled up her mainsail, and clapped close upon a wind, to keep the pirates from running to leeward, and then engaged. But when the rogues found whom they had to deal with, they edged away under the man-of-war's stern, and the *Greyhound* standing after them, they made a running fight for about two hours; but little wind happening,[11] the sloops gained from her,

by the help of their oars; upon which the *Greyhound* left off
firing, turned all hands to her own oars, and at three in the afternoon came up with them. The pirates hauled upon a wind to
receive the man-of-war, and the fight was immediately renewed,
with a brisk fire on both sides, till the *Ranger's* mainyard[12] was
shot down. Under these circumstances, Low abandoned her to
the enemy, and fled.

The conduct of Low was surprising in this adventure, because his reputed courage and boldness had hitherto so possessed the minds of all people, that he became a terror even to
his own men; but his behavior throughout this whole action
showed him to be a base cowardly villain; for had Low's sloop
fought half so briskly as Harris' had done (as they were under
a solemn oath to do,) the man-of-war, in the opinion of some
present, could never have hurt them. Nothing, however, could
lessen the fury, or reform the manners, of that obdurate crew.
Their narrow escape had no good effect upon them, and with
redoubled violence they renewed their depredations and cruelties. The next vessel they captured, was eighty miles from
land. They used the master with the most wanton cruelty,[13]
then shot him dead, and forced the crew into the boat with a
compass, a little water, and a few biscuits, and left them to the
mercy of the waves; they, however, beyond all expectation, got
safe to shore.

Low proceeded in his villainous career with too fatal success. Unsatisfied with satiating their avarice and walking the
common path of wickedness, those inhuman wretches, like to
Satan himself, made mischief their sport, cruelty their delight,
and the ruin and murder of their fellow men their constant
employment. Of all the piratical crews belonging to the English nation, none ever equaled Low in barbarity. Their mirth
and their anger had the same effect. They murdered a man
from good humor, as well as from anger and passion. Their ferocious disposition seemed only to delight in cries, groans, and
lamentations. One day Low having captured Captain Graves,
a Virginia man, took a bowl of punch in his hand, and said,
"Captain, here's half this to you." The poor gentleman was
too much touched with his misfortunes to be in a humor for

drinking, he therefore modestly excused himself. Upon this Low cocked and presented a pistol in the one hand, and his bowl in the other, saying, "Either take the one or the other."

Low next captured a vessel called the *Christmas*, mounted her with thirty-four guns, went on board her himself, assumed the title of admiral, and hoisted the black flag. His next prize was a brigantine half manned with Portuguese, and half with English. The former he hanged, and the latter he thrust into their boat and dismissed, while he set fire to the vessel. The success of Low was unequalled, as well as his cruelty; and during a long period he continued to pursue his wicked course with impunity.

All wickedness comes to an end and Low's crew at last rose against him and he was thrown into a boat without provisions and abandoned to his fate. This was because Low murdered the quartermaster while he lay asleep. Not long after he was cast adrift a French vessel happened along and took him into Martinico, and after a quick trial by the authorities he received short shift on a gallows erected for his benefit.

STEDE "GENTLEMAN PIRATE" BONNET

Sloop *Revenge*

Barbados and North Carolina

1717–18

Perhaps you have met Stede Bonnet, if you have seen the HBO comedy series Our Flag Means Death *(2022). He was unusual, in that unlike Ned Low or his ilk, Bonnet had ample opportunity to do literally anything else with his life. He was a reasonably well-off landowner, with a plantation on Barbados inherited from his father. So why would he make such a dangerous choice?*

Perhaps Bonnet was a thrill seeker. Maybe he was a dilettante rich boy, thinking his money could buy him the kind of authenticity and adventure that a coddled shoreside slaveholding life otherwise lacked. After all, unlike most pirates who got their start with a mutiny or seizure under extreme circumstances, Bonnet kitted out his own ship and crew with his own money, with an express purpose of going pirating. Perhaps as a boy he had been steeped in the romantic-seeming exploits of the generation of pirates that came before him, which were well documented in newspapers, broadsides, and folklore that Bonnet, as a small child on an English-colonized Caribbean island, would have certainly heard.

Or perhaps he just preferred the company of men.

The following excerpt poses this question, in a roundabout way. Puzzling over why a man of wealth, influence, and education (Ned Low, in contrast, was illiterate and spent his boyhood as a petty thief) would choose such a hazardous mode of living, particularly given that he had no maritime training or experience, it suggests that the choice stemmed from a "disorder of the mind." More particularly, the excerpt specifies that Bonnet's mental problem, whatever it might have been, was "occasioned by some discomforts he found in a married state."

Now, in the 1710s, plenty of discomforts could be found in a married state. Maybe he had syphilis. Perhaps he suffered from erectile dysfunction. Or maybe he preferred not to be with a woman at all. One prominent scholar of gay history, albeit not writing about the eighteenth century, makes the case that one reason for the longstanding association between sailors and gay sex in popular culture stems from the possibility that men who prefer the company of other men might naturally gravitate to careers or circumstances in which men live together in close quarters, without women.[1] Of course, for most people in the eighteenth century, the idea of wielding any choice over one's mode of self-support was almost preposterous, especially in the age of slavery and impressment. But, crucially, Stede Bonnet was that rare man in the eighteenth-century Atlantic world: a man with choice. Further, his sexual behavior, once he embarked on a life of piracy, stands in marked contrast to that of his closest pirate confederate Edward Teach, better known as Blackbeard, as we will see shortly.

Was Stede Bonnet gay? Not in the way that we typically use the word today. But your editor thinks there is a persuasive case to be made that, for lack of a better, more historically contingent term, he probably was.

OF MAJOR STEDE BONNET
AND HIS CREW[2]

The Major was a Gentleman of good Reputation in the Island of Barbadoes, was Master of a plentiful Fortune, and had the Advantage of a liberal Education. He had the least Temptation of any Man to follow such a Course of Life, from the Condition of his Circumstances. It was very surprising to everyone, to hear of the Major's Enterprise, in the Island where he liv'd; and as he was generally esteem'd and honored, before he broke out into open Acts of Piracy, so he was afterwards rather pity'd than condemned, by those that were acquainted with him, believing that his Humor of going a pirating, proceeded from a Disorder in his Mind, which had been but too visible in him, some Time before this wicked Undertaking; and which is said to have been occasioned by some Discomforts he found in a married State; be that as it will, the Major was but ill qualify'd for the Business, as not understanding maritime Affairs.

However, he fitted out a Sloop with ten Guns and 70 Men, entirely at his own Expense, and in the Night-Time sailed from Barbadoes. He called his Sloop the *Revenge*; his first Cruise was off the Capes of Virginia, where he took several Ships, and plundered them of their Provisions, Cloaths, Money, Ammunition, &c. in particular the *Anne*, Captain Montgomery, from Glasgow; the *Turbet* from Barbadoes, which for Country sake, after they had taken out the principal Part of the Lading, the Pirate Crew set her on Fire; the *Endeavour*, Captain Scot, from Bristol, and the *Young* from Leith. From hence they went to New-York, and off the East End of Long-Island, took a Sloop bound for the West-Indies, after which they stood in and landed some Men at Gardner's Island, but in a peaceable Manner, and bought Provisions for the Company's Use, which they paid for, and so went off again without Molestation.

Some Time after, which was in August 1717, Bonnet came off the Bar of South-Carolina, and took a Sloop and a Brigantine bound in; the Sloop belonged to Barbadoes, Joseph Palmer Master, laden with Rum, Sugar and Negroes; and the Brigantine came from New-England, Thomas Porter Master, whom they plundered, and then dismiss'd; but they sailed away with the Sloop, and at an Inlet in North-Carolina careened by her, and then set her on Fire.

After the Sloop had cleaned, they put to Sea, but came to no Resolution what Course to take; the Crew were divided in their Opinions, some being for one Thing, and some another, so that nothing but Confusion seem'd to attend all their Schemes.

The Major was no Sailor as was said before, and therefore had been obliged to yield to many Things that were imposed on him, during their Undertaking, for want of a competent Knowledge in maritime Affairs; at length happening to fall in Company with another Pirate one Edward Teach, (who for his remarkable black ugly Beard, was more commonly called Black-Beard). This Fellow was a good Sailor, but a most cruel hardened Villain, bold and daring to the last Degree, and would not stick at the perpetrating the most abominable Wickedness imaginable; for which he was made Chief of that execrable Gang, that it might be said that his Post was not unduly filled, Black-Beard being truly the Superior in Roguery, of all the Company, as has been already related.

To him Bonnet's Crew joined in Consortship, and Bonnet himself was laid aside, notwithstanding the Sloop was his own; he went aboard Black-Beard's Ship, not concerning himself with any of their Affairs, where he continued till she was lost in Topsail Inlet,[3] and one Richards was appointed Captain in his Room. The Major now saw his Folly, but could not help himself, which made him Melancholy; he reflected upon his past Course of Life, and was confounded with Shame, when he thought upon what he had done; His Behavior was taken Notice of by the other Pirates, who liked him never the better for it; and he often declared to some of them, that he would gladly leave off that Way of Living, being fully tired of it; but he should be ashamed to see the Face of any English Man again; therefore if he could get to Spain or Portugal, where he might be undiscovered, he would spend the Remainder of his Days in Either of those Countries, otherwise he must continue with them as long as he lived.

When Black-Beard lost his Ship at Topsail Inlet, and surrendered to the King's Proclamation, Bonnet reaffirmed the Command of his own Sloop, *Revenge*, goes directly away to Bath-Town in North-Carolina, surrenders likewise to the King's Pardon, and receives a Certificate. The War was now broke out between the Triple Allies and Spain;[4] so Major Bonnet gets a Clearance for his Sloop at North-Carolina, to go to the Island of St. Thomas, with a Design (at least it was pretended so) to get the Emperor's Commission, to go a Privateering upon the Spaniards. When Bonnet came back to Topsail Inlet, he found that Teach and his Gang were gone, and that they had taken all the Money, small Arts and Effects of Value out of the great Ship, and set ashore on a small sandy Island above a League from the Main, seventeen Men, no doubt with a Design they should perish, there being no Inhabitant, or Provisions to subsist withal, nor any Boat or Materials to build to make any kind of Launch or Vessel, to escape from that desolate Place: They remained there two Nights and one Day, without Subsistence, or the least Prospect of any, expecting nothing else but a lingering Death; when to their inexpressible Comfort, they saw Redemption at Hand: for Major Bonnet happening to get Intelligence of their being there, by two of the Pirates who had escaped Teach's Cruelty, and had got to a poor little Village at the upper End of the Harbor, sent his Boat to make Discovery of the Truth of the Matter, which the poor Wretches seeing, made a signal to them, and they were all brought on Board Bonnet's Sloop.

Major Bonnet told all his Company, that he would take a Commission to go against the Spaniards, and to that End, was going to St. Thomas's therefore if they would go with him, they should be welcome; whereupon they all consented, but as the Sloop was preparing to sail, a Bom-Boat,[5] that brought Apples and Sider to sell to the Sloop's Men, informed them, that Captain Teach lay at Ocricock Inlet,[6] with only 18 or 20 Hands. Bonnet, who bore him a mortal Hatred for some Insults offered him, went immediately in pursuit of Black-Beard, but it happened too late, for his missed of him there, and after four Days Cruise, hearing no father News of him, they steered their Course towards Virginia.

In the Month of July, these Adventurers came off the Capes, and meting with a Pink with a Stock of Provisions on Board, which they happened to be in Want of, they took out of her ten or twelve Barrels of Pork, and about 400 Weight of Bread; but because they would not have this set down to the Account of Piracy, they gave them eight or ten Casks of Rice, and an old Cable, in lieu thereof.

Two Days afterwards they chased a Sloop of Sixty Ton, and took her two Leagues off of Cape Henry; they were so happy here as to get a Supply of Liquor to their Victuals, for they brought from her two Hogsheads[7] of Rum, and as many of Mo[l?]osses, which, it seems, they had need of, tho' they had not ready Money to purchase them: What Security they intended to give, I can't tell, but Bonnet sent eight Men to take Care of the Prize Sloop, who, perhaps, not caring to make Use of those accusotm'd Freedoms, took the first Opportunity to go off with her, and Bonnet (who was pleased to have himself called Captain Thomas,) saw them no more.

After this, the Major threw off all Restraint, and though he had just before received his Majesty's Mercy, in the Name of Stede Bonnet, he relaps'd in good Earnest into his old Vocation, by the Name of Captain Thomas,[8] and recommenced a down-right Pirate, by taking the plundering all the Vessels he met with: He took off Cape Henry, two Ships from Virginia, bound to Glasgow, out of which they had very little besides an hundred Weight of Tobacco. The next Day they took a small Sloop bound from Virginia to Bermudas, which supply'd them with twenty Barrels of Pork, some Bacon, and they gave her in return, two Barrels of Rice, and a Hogshead of Molossus;[9] out of this Sloop two Men enter'd voluntarily. The next they took was another Virginia Man, bound to Glasgow, out of which they had nothing of Value, save only a few Combs, Pins and Needles, and gave her instead thereof, a Barrel of Pork, and two Barrels of Bread.

From Virginia they sailed to Philadelphia, and in the Latitude of 38 North, they took a Schooner, coming from North-Carolina, bound to Boston, they had out of her only two Dozen Calf-Skins, to make Covers for Guns, and two of their

Hands, and detained her some Days. All this was but small Game, and seem'd as if they design'd only to make Provision for their Sloop against they arrived at St. Thomas's; for they hitherto had dealt favorably with all that were so unhappy as to fall into their Hands; but those that came after, fared not so well, for in the Latitude of 32, off of Delaware River, near Philadelphia, they took two Snows bound for Bristol, out of whom they got some Money, besides Goods, perhaps to the Value of 15 Pounds; at the same Time they took a Sloop of sixty Tons bound from Philadelphia to Barbadoes which after taking some Goods out, they dismissed along with the Snows.

The 29th Day of July, Captain Thomas took a Sloop of 50 Tons, six or seven Leagues off Delaware Bar, bound from Philadelphia to Barbadoes, Thomas Read Master, loaden with Provisions, which they kept and put four or five of their Hands on Board her. The last Day of July, they took another Sloop of 60 Tons, commanded by Peter Mainwaring, bound from Antigua to Philadelphia, which they likewise kept with all the Cargo, consisting chiefly of Rum, Molosses, Sugar, Cotton, Indigo, and about 25 Pound in Money, valued in all to 500 Pound.

The last Day of July, our Rovers with the Vessels last taken, left Delaware Bay, and sailed to Cape Fear River, where they staid too long for their Safety, for the Pirate Sloop which they now new named the *Royal James*, proved very leaky, so that they were obliged to remain here almost two Month, to refit and repair their Vessel: They took in this River a small Shallop,[10] which they ripped up to mend the Sloop, and retarded the further Prosecution of their Voyage, as before mentioned, till the New came to Carolina, of a Pirate Sloop's being there to careen with her Prizes.

[. . . The governor of South Carolina equips two sloops to get rid of the pirates. . . .]

. . . The *Henry* with 8 Guns and 70 Men, commanded by Captain John Masters, and the *Sea Nymph*, with 8 Guns and 60 Men, commanded by Captain Fayrer Hall, both under the entire Direction and Command of the aforesaid Colonel [William] Rhat, who, on the 14th of September, went on Board the *Henry*, and, with the other Sloop, sailed from Charles-Town to Swillivants Island,[11] to put themselves in order for the Cruise. Just then arrived a small Ship from Antigua, one Cock Master, with an Account, that in Sight of the Bar he was taken and plundered by one Charles Vane, a Pirate, in a Brigantine of 12 Guns and 90 Men; and who had also taken two other Vessels bound in there, one a small Sloop, Captain Dill Master, from Barbadoes; the other a Brigantine, Captain Thomson Master, from Guiney, with ninety odd Negroes, which they took out of the Vessel, and put on Board another Sloop then under the Command of one Yeats, his Consort, with 25 Men. This prov'd fortunate to the Owners of the Guiney Man, for Yeats having often attempted to quit this Course of Life, took an Opportunity in the Night, to leave Vane and run into North-Edisto River, to the Southward of Charles-Town, and surrendered to the Majesty's Pardon. The Owners got their Negroes,[12] and Yeats and his Men and Certificates given them from the Government.

[. . .]

On the 26th following, in the Evening, the Colonel with his small Squadron, entered the River,[13] and saw, over a Point of Land, three Sloops at an Anchor, which were Major Bonnet and his Prizes; but it happened that in going up the River, the Pilot[14] run the Colonel's Sloops aground, and was dark before they were on Float,[15] which hindered their getting up that Night. The Pirates soon discovered the Sloops, but not knowing who they were, or upon what Design they came into that River, they manned three Canoes, and sent them down to take them, but they quickly found their Mistake, and returned to the Sloop, with the unwelcome News. Major Bonnet made Preparations that Night for engaging, and took all the Men out of the Prizes. He shewed Captain Manwaring, one of his Prisoners, a Letter, he had just wrote, which he declared he would send to the Governor of Carolina; the Letter was to this Effect, viz. That if the Sloops, which then appeared, were sent out against him, by the said Governor, and he should get clear off, that he would burn and destroy all Ships or Vessels going in or coming out of South-Carolina. The next Morning they got under Sail, and came down the River, designing only a running Fight. Colonel Rhet's Sloops got likewise under Sail, and stood by him, getting upon each Quarter of the Pirate, with Intent to board him; which he perceiving, edged in towards the Shore, and being warmly engaged, their Sloop ran a-ground: The Carolina Sloops being in the same shoal Water, were in the same Circumstances; the *Henry*, in which Colonel Rhet was, grounded within Pistol shot of the Pirate, and on his Bow; the other Sloop grounded right a-head of him, and almost out of Gun-Shot, which made her of little Service to the Colonel, while they lay a-ground.

At this Time the Pirate had a considerable Advantage; for their Sloop, after she was a-ground, lifted from Colonel Rhet's, by which Means they were all covered, and the Colonel's Sloop lifting the same Way, his Men were much exposed; notwithstanding which, they kept a brisk Fire the whole Time they lay thus a-ground, which was near five Hours. The Pirates made a Wiff in their bloody Flag, and beckoned several Times with their Hats in Derision to the Colonel's Men, to come on Board, which they answered with Cheerful Huzza's, and said, that they would speak with them by and by; which accordingly happened, for the Colonel's Sloop being first a float, he got into deeper Water, and after mending the Sloop's Rigging, which was much shattered in the Engagement, they stood for the Pirate, to give the finishing Stroke, and designed to go directly on Board him; which he prevented, by sending a Flag of Truce, and after some Time capitulating, they surrendered themselves Prisoners. The Colonel took Possession of the Sloop, and was extremely pleased to find that Captain Thomas, who commanded her, was the individual Person of Major Stede Bonnet, who had done them the Honor several Times to visit their own Coast of Carolina.

There were killed in this Action, on Board the *Henry*, ten Men, and fourteen wounded; on Board the *Sea Nymph*, two killed and four wounded. The Officers and Sailors in both Sloops behaved themselves with the greatest Bravery; and had not they Sloops so unluckily run aground, they had taken the

Pirate with much less loss of Men; but as the designed to get by them, and to make a running Fight, the Carolina Sloops were obliged to keep near him, to prevent his getting away. Of the Pirates there were seven killed and five wounded, two of which died soon after of their Wounds. Colonel Rhet weigh'd the 30th of September, from Cape Fear River, and arrived at Charles-Town the 3rd of October, to the great Joy of the whole Province of Carolina.

Bonnet and his Crew, two Days after, were put ashore, and there not being a public Prison, the Pirates were kept at the Watch-House, under a Guard of Militia; but Major Bonnet was committed into the Custody of the Marshal, at his House; and in a few Days after, David Hariot the Master, and Ignatius Pell the Boatswain, who were designed for Evidences against the other Pirates, were removed from the rest of the Crew, to the said Marshal's House, and every Night two Sentinels set about the said House; but whether thro' any Corruption, or want of Care in guarding the Prisoners I can't say; but on the 24th of October, the Major and Hariot made their Escape, the Boatswain refusing to go along with them. This made a great Noise in the Province, and People were open in their Resentments, of the reflecting on the Governor, and others in the Magistracy, as tho' they had been brib'd, for conniving at their Escape.

[. . .]

Bonnet stood to the Northward, in a small Vessel, but wanting Necessaries, and the Weather being bad, he was forced back, and so return'd with his Canoe, to Swillivants Island, near Charles-Town, to fetch Supplies; but there being some Information sent to the Governor, he sent for Colonel Rhet, and desired him to go in pursuit of Bonnet; and accordingly gave him a Commission for that Purpose; Wherefore the Colonel, with proper Craft, and some Men, went away that Night for Swillivant's Island, and, after a very diligent Search, discovered Bonnet and Hariot together; the Colonel's Men fired upon them, and killed Hariot upon the Spot, and wounded one Negro and an Indian. Bonnet submitted, and surrender'd himself; and the next Morning, being November the 6th, was brought by Colonel Rhet to Charles-Town, and, by the Governor's Warrant, was committed into safe Custody, in order for his being brought to his Trial.

On the 28th of October, 1718, a Court of Vice-Admiralty was held at Charles-Town, in South-Carolina, and, by several Adjournments, continued to Wednesday, the 12th of November following for the Trial of the Pirates taken in a Sloop formerly called the *Revenge*, but afterwards the *Royal James*, before Nicholas Trot, Esq; Judge of the Vice-Admiralty, and Chief Justice of the said Province of South-Carolina, and other Assistant Judges.

> [. . . *Without going into a full list of the men indicted with Bonnet, or reproducing the indictments as Johnson does here, it's interesting to note where they came from. Bonnet himself was from Barbados, but many others were from Jamaica, Aberdeen, Glasgow, Guernsey, London, Dublin, Charleston, North Carolina, Bristol, "Bath-Town" North Carolina, one from Newcastle-Upon-Tyne, and one from Antigua. However, often they were described as "late of," suggesting the shifting nature of sailor's ties to the ports where they touch land.*]

All the Prisoners arraigned, pleaded Not Guilty, and put themselves upon their Trials. . . . The Prisoners made little or no Defense, every one pretending only that they were taken off a Maroon Shore, and were shipped with Major Bonnet to go to St. Thomas's; but being out at Sea, and wanting Provisions, they were obliged to do what they did by others; and so did Major Bonnet himself, pretend that 'twas Force, not Inclination, that occasioned what had happened. However, the Facts being plainly proved, and that they had all shared ten or eleven Pounds a Man . . . they were all . . . found Guilty. The Judge made a very grave Speech to them, setting forth the Enormity of their Crimes, the Condition they were now in, and the Nature and Necessity of an unfeigned Repentance; and then recommended them to the Ministers of the Province, for more ample Directions, to fit them for Eternity, for (concluded he) the Priest's Lips shall keep Knowledge, and you shall seek the Law at their Mouths; for they are the Messengers of the Lord. Mal. II:17.[16] And the Ambassadors of Christ, and unto them is committed the World [or Doctrine] of Reconciliation, 2 Cor. V. 19. 20.[17] And then pronounced Sentence of Death upon them.

> [. . . *Bonnet's crew were hanged on November 8 "at the White-Point near Charles-Town."*]

As for the Captain, his Escape protracted his Fate, and spun out his Life a few Days longer, for he was try'd the 19th, and being found Guilty, received Sentence in like Manner as the former; before which Judge Trot, made a most excellent Speech to him, rather somewhat too long to be taken into our History, yet I could not tell how to pass by so good and useful a Piece of Instruction, not knowing whose Hands this Book may happen to fall into.

> [. . . *The speech is indeed long and pious, taking him to account for his sins of piracy and also murder, at least eighteen that they know of. The speech includes many biblical justifications for his sentence of death. It also makes note of Bonnet's status as a "Gentleman that have had the Advantage of a liberal Education, and being generally esteemed a Man of Letters," who should understand the necessity of repentance. It concludes with his sentencing.*]

That you, the said Stede Bonnet, shall go from hence to the Place from whence you came, and from thence to the Place of Execution, where you shall be hanged by the Neck till you are dead.

And the God of infinite Mercy be merciful to your Soul.

EDWARD "BLACKBEARD" TEACH

The *Queen Anne's Revenge*

Carolinas

1716–18

Two distinctive aspects of Blackbeard's story come to mind to introduce him: race and rape. We've encountered glancing references to pirates of color so far before this, to be sure, not least of whom was the possible self-liberating member of Thomas Tew's crew, or the "ninety Moors" pirating under William Kidd. While there aren't as yet any records of pirate captains of color, we have seen any number of nameless "negroes" and "Indians" fleeing to harbors under cover of night, murdered, captured, and in many cases joining along in piracy for their own advantage. Namelessness by itself isn't all that significant, as pirate crew's names in general tended only to make it into the archive out of trial transcripts and indictments; the vast majority of people who went out on the account remain anonymous. Though pirates of color are hard to see in the archive, they are definitely there. And true to form, when Edward "Blackbeard" Teach fought to his death in Ocracoke Inlet in 1718, five out of the eighteen men in the crew, fighting and bloodthirsty right alongside him, were men of color, including one who had to be forc-

ibly stopped from blowing up the gunpowder maga-
zine in revenge.[1]

Blackbeard got his name from the distinctive char-
acter of his facial hair, which the third edition of A
General History of the Pyrates *describes as follows:*
"This Beard was black, which he suffered to grow of
an extravagant Length; as to breadth, it came up to
his Eyes; he was accustomed to twist it with Rib-
bons, in small Tails, after the Manner of our Rami-
lies Wiggs,[2] *and turn them about his Ears: In Time*
of Action, he wore a Sling over his Shoulders, with
three brace of Pistols, hanging in Holsters like Ban-
daliers; and stuck lighted Matches under his Hat,
which appearing on each Side of his Face, his Eyes
naturally looking fierce and wild, made him alto-
gether such a Figure, that Imagination cannot form
an Idea of a Fury, from Hell, to look more frightful."

And frightful he was, because another marked as-
pect of Blackbeard's character is that he was a rapist.
Of course there's no shortage of rape in pirate litera-
ture and lore, but Blackbeard seemed to have a defi-
nite taste for it, judging from the outsize role it seems
to play in contemporary accounts of him. There's a
lot of rape in this excerpt. Be forewarned.

Intriguingly, the excerpt also dangles the suggestion
of collusion between legitimate colonial American
leaders and traders and their illegitimate counterparts,
as after his defeat correspondence between Teach
and Governor Eden, as well as some traders out of
New York, was found on board.

OF CAPTAIN TEACH,
ALIAS BLACK-BEARD[3]

Edward Teach was a Bristol Man born, but had sailed some
Time out of Jamaica in Privateers, in the late French War; yet

tho' he had often distinguished himself for his uncommon Boldness and personal courage, he was never raised to any Command, till he went a-pirating, which I think was at the latter End of the Year 1716, when Captain Benjamin Hornigold[4] put him into a Sloop that he had made Prize of, and with whom he continued to Consortship till a little while before Hornigold surrendered.

In the Spring of the Year 1717, Teach and Hornigold sailed from Providence,[5] for the Main of America, and took in the Way a Billop from the Havana with 120 Barrels of Flower,[6] as also a Sloop from Bermuda, Thurber Master, from whom they took only some Gallons of Wine, and then let him go; and a Ship from Madera to South-Carolina, out of which they got Plunder to a considerable Value.

After cleaning on the Coast of Virginia, they returned to the West-Indies, and in the Latitude of 24, made Prize of a large French Guiney Man, bound to Martinico, which by Hornigold's Consent, Teach went aboard of as Captain, and took a Cruise in her; Hornigold returned with his Sloop to Providence, where, at the Arrival of Captain Rogers, the Governor, he surrendered to Mercy, pursuant to the King's Proclamation.

Aboard of this Guiney Man Teach mounted 40 Guns, and named her the *Queen Ann's Revenge*; and cruising near the Island of St. Vincent, took a large Ship, called the *Great Allen*, Christopher Taylor Commander; the Pirates plundered her of what they though[t] fit, put all the Men ashore upon the Island above mentioned, and then set Fire to the Ship.

A few Days after, Teach fell in with the *Scarborough* Man of War, of 30 Guns, who engaged him for some Hours; but she finding the Pirate well mann'd, and having tried her strength, gave over the Engagement, and returned to Barbadoes, the Place of her Station; and Teach sailed towards the Spanish America.

In his Way he met with a Pirate Sloop of ten Guns, commanded by one Major Bonnet, lately a Gentleman of good Reputation and Estate in the Island of Barbadoes, whom he joined; but in a few Days after, Teach, finding that Bonnet knew nothing of a maritime Life, with the Consent of his own

Men, put in another Captain, one Richards, to Command Bonnet's Sloop, and took the Major on board his own Ship, telling him, that as he had not been used to the Fatigues and Care of such a Post, it would be better for him to decline it, and live easy and at his Pleasure, in such a Ship as his, where he should not be obliged to perform Duty, but follow his own Inclinations.

At Turniff, ten Leagues short of the Bay of Honduras, the Pirates took in fresh Water, and while they were at an Anchor there, they saw a Sloop coming in, whereupon, Richards in the Sloop called the *Revenge*, slipped his Cable, and run out to meet her, who upon seeing the black Flag hoisted, struck his Sail and came to, under the Stern of Teach the Commodore. She was called the *Adventure*, from Jamaica, David Harriot Master. They took him and his Men on board the great Ship, and sent a Number of other Hands with Israel Hands, Master of Teach's Ship, to Man the Sloop for the piratical Account.

The 9th of April, they weighed from Turniff,[7] having lain there about a Week, and sailed to the Bay, where they found a Ship and four Sloops, three of the latter belonged to Jonathan Bernard, of Jamaica, and the other to Captain James; the Ship was of Boston, called the *Protestant Caesar*, Captain Wyar Commander. Teach hoisted his Black Colors, and fired a Gun, upon which Captain Wyar and all his Men, left their Ship, and got ashore in their Boat. Teach's Quarter-Master, and eight of his Crew, took Possession of Wyar's Ship, and Richards secured all the Sloops, one of which they burnt out of sight to the Owner; the *Protestant Caesar* they also burnt, after they had plundered her, because she belonged to Boston, where some Men had been hanged for Piracy; and the three Sloops belonging to Bernard they let go.

From hence the Rovers sailed to Turkill,[8] and then to the Grand Caimanes, a small Island about thirty Leagues to the Westward of Jamaica, where they took a small Turtler, and so to the Havana, and from thence to the Bahama Wrecks, and from the Bahama Wrecks, they sailed to Carolina, taking a Brigantine and two Sloops in their Way, where they lay off the Bar of Charles-Town[9] for five or six Days. They took here a

Ship as she was coming out, bound for London, commanded by Robert Clark, with some Passengers on Board for England; the next Day they took another Vessel coming out of Charles-Town, and also two Pinks coming into Charles-Town; likewise a Brigantine with 14 Negroes aboard; all which being done in the Face of the Town, struck a great Terror to the whole Province of Carolina, having just before been visited by Vane,[10] another notorious Pirate, that they abandoned themselves to Despair, being in no Condition to resist their Force. They were eight Sail in the Harbor, ready for the Sea, but none dared to venture out, it being almost impossible to escape their Hands. The inward bound Vessels were under the same unhappy Dilemma, so that the Trade of this Place was totally interrupted: What made these Misfortunes heavier to them, was a long expensive War, the Colony had had with the Natives, which was but just ended when these Robbers infested them.

Teach detained all the Ships and Prisoners, and, being in want of Medicines, resolves to demand a Chest from the Government of the Province; accordingly Richards, the Captain of the *Revenge* Sloop, with two or three more Pirates, were sent up along with Mr. Marks, one of the Prisoners, whom they had taken in Clark's Ship, and very insolently made their Demands, threatening, that if they did not send immediately the Chest of Medicines, and let the Pirate-Ambassadors return, without offering any Violence to their Persons, they would murder all their Prisoners, send up their Heads to the Governor, and set the Ships they had taken on Fire.

Whilst Mr. Marks was making Application to the Council, Richards, and the rest of the Pirates, walk'd the Streets publicly, in the Sight of all People, who were fired with the utmost Indignation, looking upon them as Robbers and Murderers, and particularly as the Authors of their Wrongs and Oppressions, but durst not so much as think of executing their Revenge, for fear of bringing more Calamities upon themselves, and so they were forced to let the Villains pass with Impunity. The Government were not long in deliberating upon the Message, tho' 'twas the greatest Affront that could have been put upon them; yet for the saving so many Men's Lives . . . they comply'd with the Necessity, and sent aboard a Chest, valued at between 3[00] and 400 pounds. And the Pirates went back safe to their Ships.

Black-beard, (for so Teach was generally called, as we shall hereafter shew) as soon as he had received the Medicines and his Brother Rogues, let go the Ships and the Prisoners; having first taken out of them in Gold and Silver, about 1500 pounds Sterling, besides Provisions and other Matters.

From the Bar of Charles-Town, they sailed to North-Carolina; Captain Teach in the Ship, which they called the *Man of War*, Captain Richards and Captain Hands in the Sloops, which they termed Privateers, and another Sloop serving them as a tender. Teach began now to think of breaking up the Company, and securing the Money and the best of the Effects for himself, and some others of his Companions he had most Friendship for, and to cheat the rest: Accordingly, on Pretense of running into Topsail Inlet to clean, he grounded his Ship, and then, as if it had been done undesignedly, and by Accident; he orders Hands's Sloop to come to his Assistance, and get him off again, which he endeavoring to do, ran the Sloop on Shore near the other, and so were both lost. This done, Teach goes into the Tender Sloop, with forty Hands, and leaves the *Revenge* there; then takes seventeen others and Maroons them upon a small sandy Island, about a League from the Main, where there was neither Bird, Beast, or Herb for their Subsistence, and where they must have perished if Major Bonnet had not two Days after taken them off.

Teach goes up to the Governor of North-Carolina, with about twenty of his Men, surrender to his Majesty's Proclamation, and receive Certificates thereof, from his Excellency; but it did not appear that their submitting to this Pardon was from any Reformation of Manners, but only to wait a more favorable Opportunity to play the same Game over again; which he soon after effected, with great Security to himself, and with much better Prospect of Success having in this Time cultivated a very good understanding with Charles Eden, Esq, the Governor above mentioned.

The first Piece of Service this kind Governor did to Blackbeard, was, to give him a Right to the Vessel which he had taken, when he was a pirating in the great Ship called the *Queen Ann's Revenge*; for which purpose, a Court of Vice-Admiralty was held at Bath-Town; and, tho' Teach had never any Commission in his Life, and the Sloop belonging to the English Merchants, and taken in Time of Peace; yet was she condemned as a Prize taken from the Spaniards, by the said Teach. These Proceedings shew that Governors are but Men.

Before he sailed upon his Adventures, he marry'd a young Creature of about sixteen Years of Age, the Governor performing the Ceremony. As it is a Custom to marry here by a Priest, so it is there by a Magistrate; and this, I have been informed, made Teach's fourteenth Wife, whereof, about a dozen might be still living. His Behavior in this State, was something extraordinary; for while his Sloop lay in Okerecock Inlet, and he ashore at a Plantation, where his Wife lived, with whom after he had lain all Night, it was his Custom to invite five or six of his brutal Companions to come ashore, and he would force her to prostitute her self to them all, one after another, before his Face.

[. . . *Teach sails in June 1718 and near Bermuda takes a French ship bound for Martinique and splits the proceeds with the governor of North Carolina, pretending he took it legitimately as a privateer. The governor's share was sixty hogsheads of sugar. To cover it up, the governor gives Teach permission to burn the ship to the waterline.*]

Captain Teach, alias Black-beard, passed three or four Months in the River, sometimes lying at Anchor in the Coves, at other Times sailing from one Inlet to another, trading with such Sloops as he met, for the Plunder he had taken, and would often give them Presents for Stores and Provisions took from them; that is, when he happened to be in a giving Humor; at other Times he made bold with them, and took what he liked, without saying, by your Leave, knowing well, they dared not send him a Bill for the Payment. He often diverted himself with going ashore among the Planters, where he reveled Night and Day: By these he was well received, but whether out of

Love or Fear, I cannot say; sometimes he used them courteously enough, and made them Presents of Rum and Sugar, in Recompence of what he took from them; but, as for Liberties (which 'tis said) he and his Companions often took with the Wives and Daughters of the Planters, I cannot take upon me to say, whether he paid them *ad Valorem*,[11] or no. At other Time he carried it in a lordly Manner towards them, and would lay some of them under Contribution; nay, he often proceeded to bully the Governor, not, that I can discover the least Cause of Quarrel betwixt them, but it seemed only to be done, to shew he dared do it.

The Sloops trading up and down this River, being so frequently pillaged by Black-beard, consulted with the Traders, and some of the best of the Planters, what Course to take; they saw plainly it would be in vain to make any Application to the Governor of North-Carolina, to whom it properly belonged to find some Redress; so that if they could not be relieved from some other Quarter, Black-beard would be like to reign with Impunity, therefore, with as much Secrecy as possible, they sent a Deputation to Virginia, to lay the Affair before the Governor of that Colony, and to solicit an armed Force from the Men of War lying there, to take or destroy this Pirate.

[. . . Virginia's governor in Williamsburg enlists two captains of men of war to take some sloops in search of Blackbeard. They also publish a proclamation offering rich rewards for anyone who takes or destroys a pirate. Teach now has a one-hundred-pound bounty on his head, with lesser monetary rewards for lower-ranking pirate officers like quartermaster or boatswain, or forty pounds for a commander of less renown than Blackbeard. It's published November 24, 1718.]

The 17th of November, 1718, the Lieutenant sail'd from Kicquetan,[12] in James River in Virginia, and, the 21st in the Evening, came to the Mouth of Okerecock Inlet, where he got Sight of the Pirate. This Expedition was made with all imaginable Secrecy, and the Officer manag'd with all the Prudence that was necessary, stopping all Boats and Vessels he met with, in the River, from going up, and thereby preventing any Intelligence from reaching Black-beard, and receiving at the same time an Account from them all, of the Place where the Pirate was lurking; but notwithstanding this Caution, Black-beard had Information of the Design, from his Excellency of the Province; and his Secretary, Mr. Knight, wrote him a Letter, particularly concerning it, intimating, That he had sent him four of his Men, which were all he could meet with, in our about Town, and so bid him be upon his Guard. These Men belonged to Black-beard, and were sent from Bath-Town to Okerecock Inlet, where the Sloop lay, which is about 20 Leagues.

[. . .]

When he had prepared for Battle, he set down and spent the Night in drinking with the Master of a trading Sloop, who, 'twas thought, had more Business with Teach, than he should have had.

Lieutenant Maynard came to an Anchor, for the Place being shoal, and the Channel intricate, there was no getting in, where Teach lay, that Night; but in the Morning he weighed, and sent his Boat a-head of the Sloops to sound; and coming within Gun-Shot of the Pirate, received his Fire; whereupon Maynard hoisted the King's Colors, and stood directly towards him, with the best Way that his Sails and Oars could made. Black-beard cut his Cable, and endeavored to make a running Fight, keeping a continual Fire at his Enemies, with his Guns; Mr. Maynard not having any, kept a constant Fire with small Arms, while some of his Men labored at their Oars. In a little Time Teach's Sloop ran a-ground, and Mr. Maynard's drawing more Water[13] than that of the Pirate, he could not come near him; so he anchored within half Gun-Shot of the Enemy, and, in order to lighten his Vessel, that he might run him aboard,[14] the Lieutenant ordered all his Ballast to be thrown over-board, and all the Water to be staved,[15] and then weigh'd and stood for him; upon which Black-beard hail'd him in this rude Manner: Damn you for Villains, who are you? And, for whence came you? The Lieutenant made him Answer, You may see by our Colors we are no Pirates. Black-beard bid him send his Boat on Board, that he might see who he was; but Mr. Maynard reply'd thus: I cannot spare my Boat, but I will come aboard of you as soon as I can, with my Sloop. Upon this, Black-beard took a Glass of Liquor, and drank to him with these Words: Damnation seize my Soul if I give you Quarters, or take any from you. In Answer to which, Mr. Maynard told him, The he expected no Quarters from him, nor should he give him any.

By this time Black-beard's Sloops fleeted,[16] as Mr. May-nard's Sloops were rowing towards him, which being not above a Foot high in the Waste,[17] and consequently the Men all exposed, as they came near together, (there being hitherto little or no Execution done, on either Side,) the Pirate fired a Broadside, charged with all Manner of small Shot.[18]

A fatal Stroke to them! The Sloop the Lieutenant was in, having twenty Men killed and wounded, and the other Sloop nine: This could not be help'd, for there being no Wind, they were oblig'd to keep to their Oars, otherwise the Pirate would have got away from him, which, it seems, the Lieutenant was resolute to prevent.

After this unlucky Blow, Black-beard's Sloop fell Broadside to the Shore; Mr. Maynard's other Sloop, which was called the *Ranger*, fell a-stern, being, for the present, disabled; so the Lieu-tenant finding his own Sloop had Way, and would soon be on Board of Teach, he ordered all his Men down, for fear of an-other Broadside, which must have been their Destruction, and the loss of their Expedition. Mr. Maynard was the only Person that kept the Deck, except the Man at the Helm, whom he di-rected to lie down snug, and the Men in the Hold were ordered to get their Pistols and their Swords ready for close fighting, and to come up at his Command; in order to which, two Lad-ders were placed in the Hatch-Way for the more Expedition. When the Lieutenant's Sloop boarded the other, Captain Teach's Men threw in several new fashioned sort of Grenadoes, viz. Café Bottles fill'd with Powder, and small Shot, Slugs, and Pieces of Lead or Iron, with a quick Match in the Mouth of it, which being lighted without Side, presently runs into the Bottle to the Powder, and as it is instantly thrown on Board, generally does great Execution, besides putting all the Crew into a Confusion; but by good Providence, they had not that Effect here; the Men being in the Hold, and Black-beard seeing few or no Hands aboard, told his Men, That they were all Knock'd on the Head, except three or four; and therefore, says he, let's jump on Board, and cut them to Pieces.

Whereupon, under the Smoke of one of the Bottles just mentioned, Black-beard enters with fourteen Men, over the Bows of Maynard's Sloop, and were not seen by him till the Air cleared; however, he just then gave a Signal to his Men, who all rose in an Instant, and attack'd the Pirates with as much Bravery as ever was done upon such an Occasion: Black-beard and the Lieutenant fired the first Pistol at each other, by which the Pirate received a Wound, and then engaged with Swords, till the Lieutenant's unluckily broke, and stepping back to cock a Pistol, Black-beard, with his Cutlass, was striking at that Instant, that one of Maynard's Men gave him a terrible Wound in the Neck and Throat, by which the Lieutenant came off with a small Cut over his Fingers.

They were now closely and warmly engaged, the Lieutenant and twelve Men, against Black-beard and fourteen, till the Sea was tinctur'd with Blood round the Vessel; Black-beard received a Shot into his Body from the Pistol that Lieutenant Maynard discharg'd, yet he stood his Ground, and fought with great Fury, till he received five and twenty Wounds, and five of them by Shot. At length, as he was cocking another Pistol, having fired several before, he fell down dead; by which Time eight more out of the fourteen dropp'd, and all the rest, much wounded, jump'd overboard, and call'd out for Quarters, which was granted, tho' it was only prolonging their Lives for a few Days. The Sloop *Ranger* came up, and attack'd the Men that remain'd in Black-beard's Sloop, with equal Bravery, till they likewise cry'd for Quarters.

Here was an End of that courageous Brute, who might have pass'd in the World for a Hero, had he been employ'd in a good Cause; his Destruction, which was of such Consequence to the Plantations, was entirely owning to the Conduct and Bravery of Lieutenant Maynard and his Men, who might have destoy'd him with much less Loss, had they had a Vessel with great Guns; but they were obliged to use small Vessels, because the Holes and Places he lurk'd in, would not admit of others of great Draught; and it was no small Difficulty for this Gentleman to get to him, having grounded his Vessel, at least, a hundred time, in getting up the River, besides other Discouragements, enough to have turn'd back any Gentleman without Dishonor, who was less resolute and bold than this Lieutenant. The Broadside that did so much Mischief before they boarded, in all Probability saved the rest from Destruction; for before that Teach had little or no Hopes of escaping, and therefore had posted a resolute Fellow, a Negro, whom he had bred up, with a lighted Match,[19] in the Powder-Room, with Commands to blow up, when he should give him Orders, which was as soon as the Lieutenant and his Men could have entered, that so he might have destoy'd his Conquerors: and when the Negro found how it went with Black-beard, he could hardly be persuaded from the rash Action, by two Prisoners that were then in the Hold of the Sloop.

[. . .]

The Lieutenant caused Black-beard's Head to be severed from his Body, and hung up at the Bolt-sprit End, then he sailed to Bath-Town, to get Relief for his wounded Men.

BARTHOLOMEW
"BLACK BART" ROBERTS

The *Royal Fortune*

Atlantic

1719–26

If measured in terms of raw numbers of vessels cap-
tured, Bartholomew Roberts could qualify as the
most successful pirate of the Golden Age, capturing
over four hundred vessels before his death in battle.[1]
He looked the part of a pirate, enjoying dressing in
scarlet breeches with a flamingo plume in his hat.
But he was generally more modest in his habits, im-
patient with drunkenness to a degree unusual in sail-
ors in general, much less pirates in particular. He
was reportedly more fond of tea. He was kinder on
average than Ned Low and his ilk, but not as kind as
others. His nickname derives from the darkness of
his complexion, though he was Welsh.

He got his start in piracy when the Guineaman on
which he was serving as second mate was captured
by Howell Davis, who appears previously. When
Davis died Roberts was elected his successor by the
popular acclaim of the crew.

In more recent popular culture, Black Bart is ar-
guably another source for "the Dread Pirate Rob-
erts" in The Princess Bride. *He also gets name-checked*
in Robert Louis Stevenson's Treasure Island *as the*

captain of the doctor who amputated Long John Sil-
ver's leg.

CAPT. ROBERTS AND HIS CREW[2]

Bartholomew Roberts left London in November 1719, and went second mate on board the *Princess*, Capt. Plumb, commander, which arrived at Guiney in February following, where, taking on slaves for the West Indies, he was taken by Howell Davis. At first he was very averse to piracy, but afterwards he changed his mind, and what he did not like as a private man, he was fond of as a commander. After Davis's death the ship's crew found themselves under a necessity of choosing another captain; upon which, after some debates, Roberts was chosen; who willingly accepted thereof. After this they resolved to revenge Davis's death, he being well beloved among them; and in order to do it about 30 men were landed to make an attempt upon the fort, headed by one Kennedy, a bold daring fellow, who marched up directly under the fire of the ship's guns, and went into the fort without opposition, the Portuguese deserting it at their approach; which having set on fire, and thrown all the gun in it down into the sea, they retreated to their ship, and not thinking this sufficient revenge for the loss of their captain, would have burnt the town, had not Roberts prevented it.

The governors of Barbadoes and Martinico hearing that Roberts was on their coasts, sent a man of war in pursuit of him. This so provoked him, that he hoisted his own figure portrayed, standing upon two skulls, and underneath the letters A. B. H. and A. M. H. signifying thereby a Barbadean's and a Martinian's head.[3] At Dominico, the next island they touched at, they took a Dutch interloper of 19 guns, and 70 men, which made some defense till many of the men were killed, and then struck. With this prize he went down to Guadalupe, and took a French fly boat loaden with sugar. From thence he went to Monay, another island, thinking to clean, but finding the sea

run too high for his design, he went to the North part of Hispaniola, where, in the gulf of Surinam, he cleaned the ship and
the brigantine.

Some time after, while they were drunk, Harry Glasby, a reserved sober man, master of the *Royal Fortune*, having two
more with him, moved off with out bidding them farewell; but
being soon missed, detachment was presently sent after him,
which brought him back with his companions, who were immediately brought to trial. When they were all ready, the captain in the chair, they were called up into the steerage, where a
large bowl of rum punch was placed upon the table, pipes and
tobacco being ready, the trial came on, & the indictment was
read. The letter of the law of their own making, being strong
against them, they were about to pronounce sentence; when,
after taking the other cup, the prisoners pleaded for an arrest
of judgment; but their crimes being so very great the court
would not admit of it. Immediately up starts Valentine Sturdy-
back,[4] saying, he something to offer to the court on behalf of
one of the prisoners, whom he swore he knew to be as honest
a man as ever a one of them: his name was Glasby. By God,
says he, he shall not die, damn me if he do. Upon which he
pulled out a pistol, presenting it to the breast of one of the
judges, who seeing his argument so well supported moved that
Glasby might be acquitted, which they all agreed to, allowing
it to be law. But the other prisoners were condemned, & all the
favor shown them was, that they should choose four out of the
company to shoot them; which was done accordingly. Then
burning their own ship, they manned Norton's brigantine,
sending the master away in a Dutch interloper not dissatisfied.

With the *Royal Fortune* and the brigantine, which they
named the *Good Fortune*, they made towards Deseada, where
they met with Capt. Hall, richly laden for Jamaica, whom they
plundered and carried to Bermudas. Then returning to the
West Indies, they daily met with some prize or other, most
French, which stored them with plenty of provisions; after
which they began to think of something worth their aim, accordingly proceeding again for the coast of Guinay, where
they thought to buy gold dust very cheap. In their passage they

took many ships, some of which they burnt, & others they restored, according as the master pleased or displeased them.

About 400 leagues from the coast of Africa, the brigantine,
in a dark night, left them. This brings me back to an accident
that happened in the West Indies, which had like to have ruined all, and was the occasion of the brigantine going off.

Capt. Roberts being insulted by John Popple, he killed him
on the spot; which was resented by many of his crew, particularly by one Ralph Brag, who died afterwards in the Martha
Sea, he cursing Roberts for killing his comrade. So saying, he
ought to be served the same sauce. Roberts hearing thereof,
ran to him in his passion, with his sword in his hand, and run
into the body, who, notwithstanding his wound, fell upon
Roberts & beat him to his heart's content, which put the whole
ship's crew in an uproar, some being for the captain and others
against him. However the tumult was at length appeased by
the quartermaster; and as the majority were of opinion that
the dignity of the captain ought to be supported, especially on
board, they sentenced Brag to receive two lashes from every
one of the crew. But Brag being bent on revenge, he, with several of his comrades, conspired with Anstis, captain of the
brigantine, who was also a malcontent on account of Robert's
naughty carriage towards him. So in a little time, Brag & his
consort go on board captain Anstis, on pretense of making
him a visit, when, consulting with the crew, they found the
majority were for leaving Roberts, & for giving a soft farewell,
as they call it that night; which they all did with one consent.
But Roberts proceeded to windward, nigh Senegal, which is
monopolized by the French, who keep cruisers to hinder the
interloping trade: two of which having got fight of Roberts, &
supposing him to be one of them, chased with all the sail they
could make to get up with him, but their hopes deceived them;
for upon hoisting the Jolly Roger, the name they gave the flag,
their French hearts failed them, and they surrendered without
resistance. With them he went to Sierraleon, and called one of
them *Ranger*, the other he made a storeship to clean by. Afterwards he went to Old Calabar[5] to clean their ships, where they
divided the fruits of their labors, & drank & drove care away.

There they took Capt. Lowe, and two or three Bristol ships. But the negroes here did not prove so kind to them as they expected, refusing to trade with them after they knew they were pirates. This did but exasperate the pirates, who sent 40 men ashore under their cannon to drive the negroes into the woods, against whom the negroes drew out a body of 2000 men; but having three or four men killed, they retired; on which the pirates set fire to the town, & then returned to their ships, with which they sailed for Cape Lopez[6] to water, and at Anna Bonna[7] took aboard fresh provisions, and then sailed to the coast again.

This was their last and fatal expedition. For falling down as low as Cape [L?]ahon, they took a ship named the *King Solomon*, and a trading vessel. They being to the leeward of the *King Solomon* at Cape Apolonia, & the wind and the current against her, they sent their long boat with men to take her, which rowed to the *King Solomon* with a great deal of cheerfulness. Capt. Trahern prepared to receive them, firing at them as they came under his stern, which they returned with a volley. Then he asked his men whether they would stand by him, saying, it was a shame to lose the company's ship without one blow. But Philips, his boatswain, laying down his arms in the king's name, (as he called it) called out to the boat for quarters: by whose example all the rest surrendered, and they lost the ship.

The *Swallow* and *Weymouth* men of war left Sierraleon the 28th of May, and, having received Mr. Baldwin's letters, went in pursuit of the pirates; and meeting with a Dutch ship, enquired of him if he had heard any thing of Roberts in those seas. He answered that he had just been at Cape Lopez, & had seen no ship there. However they beat up for the cape, and on the 5th at dawning, were surprised with the noise of a gun from Cape Lopez bay, where they discovered three ships at anchor, which they concluded was Roberts and his consorts: but the *Swallow* being to windward was obliged to sheer off,[8] which the pirates interpreting fear, righted the French *Ranger*, ordering her to chase out in all haste. The *Swallow*, finding they had mistaken her design, kept off to sea, as if she had really been afraid; on which, in a little time, the pirates drew near enough to fire their chase guns, hoisting their black flag, thinking her to be a Portuguese, when on a sudden they saw her bring to, and fire at a distance. Being now at their wits end, their main-top mast coming down by a shot, after two hours firing they grew sick of the play, struck their colors, and called out for quarters, having 10 men killed and twenty wounded, without the loss of one of the king's men.

While the *Swallow* was sending her boats to fetch the prisoners, half a dozen of the most desperate thought to blow themselves up, but having too small a quantity of powder left, it only burnt them in a frightful manner.

They secured the prisoners with shackles and pinions, but the ship was so disabled that they thought of setting her on fire: but she having the wounded men on board, they repaired her rigging and sent her into Princes.[9]

On the 9th the *Swallow* gained the cape again, & saw the *Royal Fortune* standing into the bay, with the *Neptune*, Capt. Hill, of London. On the 10th the man of war bore away to round the cape. Roberts's crew discerning their masts over land, went out and told him; but he took no notice of it, and his men almost as little. As the *Swallow* approach'd nigher, some of them swore it was a man of war coming to take them all, at whom Roberts swore, calling them a parcel of cowardly rascals: but as she came nearer, being perfectly convinced, he slip'd his cable[10] and got under sail, ordering his men to arms, swearing it was a bite, but be it as it will, says he, I will get clear or die.

Roberts in the engagement made a noble figure, dressed in a rich crimson damask waistcoat & breeches, a red feather in his hat, a gold chain round his neck, with a diamond cross hanging to it, a sword in his [. . . Much of the rest of this paragraph is illegible, sadly, as Roberts clearly has a serious sense of style].

Roberts was a tall man about 40, born at Neweybag, in Lembrokeshire,[11] of good natural parts & personal bravery. He was used to say, A short life and a merry one shall by my motto; yet among all his vile actions he never forced any into the service.

When Roberts was dead the men neglected all means of defense; and their main mast being shot by the board, they called for quarters. The *Swallow* kept aloof while the boat passed and repassed for the prisoners, some of the desperadoes swearing they would blow up the ship. She had 40 guns and 160 men, 13 of whom were killed without any loss to the *Swallow*. There was found in the [ ] 2000 pounds in gold dust, besides many other rich things.

SAMUEL "BLACK SAM" BELLAMY

Whydah

Bahamas and Cape Cod

1717

Whydah *is known today as one of the most famous pirate ships ever to have been actually located and excavated after its sinking off Cape Cod. It was a three-hundred-ton galley, which by the 1700s was a term that meant a ship built to maximize speed rather than cargo space. This was because the* Whydah *was designed as a slave transport ship, and so speed across the Atlantic was grimly paramount to its purpose. Built in England, the* Whydah *sailed for the Gold Coast of Ghana, to the slave market in a town also called Whydah (Ouidah), in present-day Benin, and then made the passage to Jamaica to sell the people on board. In February 1717,* Whydah *began the journey back to England with a rich cargo of sugar, indigo, quinine, silver, and gold, passing through the Bahamas.[1] The Bahamas, of course, were a notorious haunt for pirates, and Sam Bellamy was there, lying in wait.*

Sam Bellamy, called "Black Sam" around Cape Cod because he preferred to wear his dark hair pulled back in a ponytail rather than a wig, was another English sailor turned pirate operating in the Atlantic world, though only for one eventful year.

He was born in Devon and began his career at sea in the Royal Navy. Eventually he landed in Cape Cod, had a sordid love affair, and, funnily enough, left to go looking for sunken treasure off Florida in 1716 before turning to a life of piracy, at different points serving with Benjamin Hornigold and with Blackbeard. Bellamy enjoyed a reputation for mercy toward the people on the vessels he took, and fancied himself something of a Robin Hood figure. He took Whydah *in the spring of 1717. Two months later, the galley was driven onto the shore at Wellfleet in a nor'easter, taking silver, gold, cannons, and 144 pirates down with it, including Samuel Bellamy. A few survivors made it to shore, only to stand trial for their crimes; their trial description follows.*

In 1984, the Whydah *wreck was discovered off the coast of Cape Cod, buried under a thick layer of sand and scattered across several miles. The ship's bell was found in 1985, which bore its name, and proved the identity of the wreck. Among the pirates lost was a boy named John King, who had been a passenger with his mother on a ship taken by Bellamy, and who demanded to join the crew and go pirating.[2] In 2006, the* Boston Globe *reported that the archaeologists working on the wreck had discovered a black leather boy's shoe, with a white silk stocking and a fibula inside—all that remained of Bellamy's pirate crew.[3]*

. . . Before the PIRACY on the Atlantic, by reason of whom Sailing is now dangerous, arrive to any thing like what we have seen on the Mediterranean, the British Crown, Equips a Squadron of Men of War for the Extirpation. And, May our Glorious GOD give success until the Enterprise.[4]

In the mean time, what the Compassion of our GOD has done for New-England, in the Inflictions of His Justice on an horrid crew of PIRATES, which made a [.isre?] unto our Coast, has had in it some Occurrences, the Relation whereof may be worthy to be Preserved and Published.

About the latter end of April, there came upon the Coast a Ship called, The *Whido*, whereof one Bellamy was Commander: A Pirate Ship, of about 190 Men, and 23 Guns. These Pirates, after many other Depredations, took a Vessel which had Wines aboard; and [put?] Seven of their Crew on Board, with Orders to Steer after the *Whido*. The seven Pirates being pretty free with the Liquor, got so Drunk, that the Captive who had the Steering of the Vessel, took the opportunity of the Night, now to run her ashore, on the backside of Eastham.

A Storm was now raised and raging; and the *Whido* ignorantly following the Light of her Stranded Prize, perished in a Shipwreck, and the whole Crew were every one of them drowned, except only one Englishman, and one Indian, that were left on Shore Alive.

It is credibly affirmed, That when these Barbarous Wretches, perceived that their Ship was breaking under them, and that they must Swim for their Lives, they horribly Murdered all their Prisoners (whereof they had a great Number) aboard; But they should appear as Witnesses against them.[5] The doleful Cries heard unto the Shore, a little before they Sank; and the Bloody Wounds found in the Bodies afterwards thrown ashore; were two great Confirmations of this Report.

Alas! How far the Wickedness of Men may carry them!

The Good People of the Cape, saw a Marvelous Deliverance, in the Time of Tide, when these Monsters perished. Had it not been Just as it was, they had reach'd the Shore alive; and have made their way thro' the Blood of the Inhabitants, which Lived between Eastham, and the Hook of the Cape, where they would there have met with Vessels to have served them, in a Return to the Trade, which they had hitherto been upon.

The Delivered People said, Blessed be the Lord, who hath not given us as a Prey to their Teeth!

After some waiting for Direction, His Excellency, Colonel SHUTE, the Governor of New-England, received such Orders, that the Trial of the Pirates, who had not been drowned, might be proceeded in.

Accordingly on Tuesday, October 22 1717 there was held at Boston, a Special Court of Admiralty (according to the Act of Parliament) for the Trial of

Simon Vanvoort, who was Born at New-York.
John Brown, Born in Jamaica.
Thomas Baker, Born at Flushing in Holland.
Henrick Quinter, Born in Amsterdam.
Peter Cornelius Hooff, Born in Sweden.
John Shuan, Born at Nants In France.
And T. S. Born at Boston in England.

The Last was Cleared; But the other Six, after a very fair Trial, were found Guilty, and received Sentence of Death.
[. . .]
On Friday, P.M. Novemb. 15. Came on the Execution of these Miserable.

What may now be offer'd, is, A Recollection of several Passages, which occurr'd in Discourse with the Prisoners, while they walked from the Prison, to the Place of Execution.

Minister: Your determined Hour is now arriv'd. You Cry in the Destruction which GOD this Afternoon brings upon you. I am come to help you what I can, that your Cry may turn to some Good Account. How do you find your Heart now disposed?

Baker: Oh! I am in a dreadful Condition! Lord JESUS, Dear JESUS, Look upon me!

[. . . Several pages of Puritan remonstrations of the pirate sinners follow this.]

Minister: But I wish, that you, and all your miserable Companions here, were more sensible of the Crime, for which you are presently to be chased from among the Living.

Robbery and Piracy! You felt the Light of GOD in your own
Soul, condemning you for it, while you were committing of it.
All Nations agree, to treat your Tribe, as the Common Enemies of Mankind, and Extirpate them out of the World. Besides all this, and the Miseries you brought on many good
people, in their Disappointed Voyages, I am told, that some
were Kill'd in your subduing of them. You are Murderers!
Their Blood cries up to Heaven against you. And so does the
Blood of the poor Captives; & Fourscore, I hear, that were
drown'd, when the *Whido* was Lost in the Storm, which cast
you on Shore.

V.V: We were Forced Men.

Min[ister]: Forced! No; There is no man who can say, He is
Forced unto any Sin against the Glorious GOD. Forced! No;
You had better have Suffered anything, than [to have] Sinn'd
as you have done. Better have died a Martyr by the cruel Hands
of your Brethren, than have become one of their Brethren.

Of, If I should allow that you were at first a Forced Man,
what were you Anon; when you came upon the Coast of Cape
Cod? Were not you one of those, who came Armed Aboard
the Prize, wherein you were Lost? When the Mate so managed
the Tack, that you Lost the Sight of the *Whidau*, and you
might have Escaped easily from your Masters into our Arms,
did not you Curse the Mate, and Compel him with a thousand
Menages, to Recover the Sight of your Ship? After your Shipwreck, did you fly into our Arms like men Escaped out of
Prison? Or, did not you Endeavour still such a flight from us,
as might Enable you to Return unto the Trade you were now
used unto? Is this the Conduct of a Forced Man?

[. . . *For several more pages, the minister recriminates
each sinner, each of whom begs forgiveness and owns up to
his sins.*]

A Supplication, that GOD would Sanctify the horrible Spec-
tacle unto the vast Crowd of Spectators now assembled; and
Effectually Caution them to Shun the Paths of the Destroyer.

Especially, the Young People; That they might Betimes give

themselves up to the Conduct of their SAVIOR; Lest their Disobedience provoke Him, to Leave them in the Hands of the
Destroyer.

And a Supplication for our Sea-faring People; That they may
more generally Turn and Live unto GOD; That they may not
fall into the Hands of Pirates; That such as are fallen into their
Hands, may not fall into their Ways; That the poor Captives
may with Cries to GOD that shall pierce the Heavens, procure
His Good Providence to work for their Deliverance; And, That
the Pirates now infesting the Seas, may have a Remarkable
Blast from Heaven following of them; the Sea-monsters, of all
the most cruel, be Extinguished; and that the Methods now
taking by the British Crown for the Suppression of these Mis-
chiefs may be prospered.

On the Scaffold, as the Last Minute come on, several of the
Malefactors, discovered a great Consternation.

Baker and Hoof appeared very distinguishingly Penitent.

But Brown, behaved himself at such a rate, as one would
hardly imagine that any *Compos Mentis*,[6] could have done so.
He broke out into furious Expressions, which had in them too
much of the Language he had been used unto.[7] Then he fell to
Reading of Prayers, not very pertinently chosen. At length he
made a Short Speech, which every body trembled at; Advising
Sailors, to beware of all wicked Living, such as his own had
been; especially to beware of falling into the Hands of the Pirates: But if they did, and were forced to join with them, then,
to have a care whom they kept, and whom they let go, and
what Countries they come into.

In such amazing Terms did he make his Exit! With such
Madness, Go to the Dead!

The rest said Little, only Vanvoorst, having (with Baker)
Sung a Dutch Psalm, Exhorted Young Persons to Lead a Life
of Religion, and keep the Sabbath, and carry it well to their
Parents.

Behold, Reader, The End of Piracy!

WILLIAM SNELGRAVE

Sierra Leone

1719–21

William Snelgrave was not himself a pirate. He was a sea captain, slave trader, and ivory trader working along the African coast. In 1734 he published an account justifying and defending the slave trade, which also gives an account of his capture by pirate captain Thomas Cocklyn.[1] He also crossed paths with Howell Davis, who reportedly apologized for the violent treatment meted out by Cocklyn.

[. . . They sail March 10, 1718/19 to the River "Sieraleon," arriving April 1, 1719.]

We met with nothing remarkable in our Passage, except, that near the Canary Islands, we were chased by a Ship whom we judged to be a Sallec-Rover;[2] but our Ship outsailing her, they soon gave over the Chase.

There were, at the time of our unfortunate Arrival in the above mentioned River, three Pirate Ships, who had then taken ten English Ships in that place. As it is necessary for illustrating this Story, to give an Account how these three Ships came to meet there, I must observe, That the first of them which arrived in the River, was called the *Rising Sun*, one Cocklyn Commander, who had not with him above 25 Men. These having been with one Captain Moody, a famous Pirate, some Months before, in a Brigantine, which sailed very well, and took the *Rising Sun*, they were marooned by him, (as they call it) that is forced on board that Ship, and deprived of their share of the Plunder, taken formerly by the Brigantine. These People being obliged to go away in her, with little Provision and Ammunition, chose Cocklyn for their Commander, and made for the River Sieraleon; where arriving, they surprised in his Sloop, one Segnor Joseph, a black Gentleman, who had been formerly in England, and was a Person of good account in this Country. This Man's Ransom procured the Pirates a sufficient supply of Provision and Ammunition. Moreover, several Bristol and other Ships arriving soon after, were likewise taken; and many of their People entering with the Pirates, they had, when I fell into their hands, near 80 Men in all.

The Crew of the Brigantine, who, with their Captain Moody, had thus forced their Companions away in the *Rising Sun*, soon after repenting of that Action, it bred great Discontents among them; so that they quarreled with their Captain and some others, whom they thought the chief Promoters of it; and at last forced him, with twelve others, into an open Boat, which they had taken a few days before, from the Spaniards of the Canary Islands; and as they never were heard of afterwards, doubtless they perished in the Ocean. After this, they chose one Le Boufe a Frenchman for their Commander, who carried them to the River Sieraleon, where they arrived about a Month after their parting with the *Rising Sun*.

At the first Appearance, of this Brigantine, Cocklyn and his Crew were under a great Surprise; but when they understood how Moody and some others had been served by them, they cheerfully joined their Brethren in Iniquity.

On the same day also arrived on Captain Davis, who had been pirating in a Sloop, and had taken a large Ship at the Cape de Verd Islands. He coming into Sieraleon with her, it put the other two Pirates into some fear, believing at first it was a Man of War: But upon discovering her black Flag at the Main-top-mast-head, which Pirate Ships usually hoist to terrify Merchant-Men; they were easy in their Minds, and a little time after, saluted one another with their Cannon.

This Davis was a generous Man, and kept his Crew, which consisted of near 150 Men, in good order; neither had he consorted or agreed to join with the others, when I was taken by Cocklyn; which proved a great Misfortune to me, as will appear afterwards. For I found Cocklyn and his Crew, to be a set of the basest and most cruel Villains that ever were. And indeed they told me, after I was taken, "That they chose him for their Commander, on account of his Brutality and Ignorance; having resolved never to have again a Gentleman-like Commander, as, they said, Moody was."

Upon mentioning this, I think it necessary to observe in this place, that the Captain of a Pirate Ship, is chiefly chosen to fight the Vessels they may meet with. Besides him, they choose another principal Officer, whom they call Quarter-master, who has the general Inspection of all Affairs, and often controls the Captain's Orders: This Person is also to be the first Man in boarding any Ship they shall attack; or go in the Boat on any desperate Enterprise. Besides the Captain and Quarter-master, the Pirates had all other Officer as it usual on board Men of War.

I come now to give an account how I was taken by them. The day that I made the Land, when I was within three Leagues of the River's Mouth, it became calm in the afternoon. Seeing a Smoke on Shore, I sent for my first Mate Mr. Simon Jones, who had been formerly at Sieraleon, where I had not; "bidding him take the Pinnace,[3] and go where the Smoke was, to enquire of the Natives, how Affairs stood up the River." But he replied, "it would be to little purpose, for no People lived there: As to the Smoke we saw, he believed it might be made by some Travelers who were roasting of Oysters on the Shore; and would be gone before he could get a Mile from the Ship. Moreover, as Night drew on, it would be difficult for him to find the Ship again." Thinking this answer reasonable, I did not press him further; tho' I understood afterwards, there was a Town where the Smoke appeared. But I did not then in the least suspect Mr. Jones would have proved such a Villain as he did afterwards.

About five a Clock in the Afternoon, a small Breeze arising from the Sea, and the Tide of Flood[4] setting strong, we stood for the River's Mouth. At Sun-setting we perceived a Ship at

Anchor, a great way up the River; which was the Pirate that took us soon after. The other two Pirate Ships, with their Prizes, were hid from our sight by a Point of Land.

It becoming calm about seven a Clock, and growing dark, we anchor'd in the River's Mouth; soon after which I went to Supper, with the Officers that usually eat with me. About eight a Clock the Officer of the Watch upon Deck, sent me word, "He heard the rowing of a Boat." Whereupon we all immediately went upon Deck; and the night being very dark, I ordered Lanthorns and Candles to be got ready, supposing the Boat might come from the Shore with some white Gentlemen, that lived there as free Merchants; or else from the Ship we had seen up the River a little while before we came to an Anchor. I ordered also, by way of Precaution, the first Mate to go into the Steerage, to put all things in order, and to send me forthwith twenty Men on the Quarter-deck with fire Arms and Cutlases, which I thought he went about.

As it was dark, I could not yet see the Boat, but heard the noise of the rowing very plain: Whereupon I ordered the second Mate to hail the Boat, to which the People in it answered, "They belonged to the *Two Friends*, Captain Eliot of Barbadoes." At this, one of the Officers who stood by me, said, "He knew the Captain very well, and that he commanded a Vessel of that name." I replied, "It might be so; but I would not trust any Boat in such a place," and ordered him to hasten the first Mate, with the People and Arms upon Deck, as I had just before ordered. By this time our Lanthorns and Candles were brought up, and I ordered the Boat to be hailed again: To which the People in it answered, "They were from America:" And at the same time fired a volley of small Shot at the Ship, tho' they were then above Pistol shot from us; which showed the Boldness of these Villains: For there was in the Boat only twelve of them, as I understood afterwards, who knew nothing of the Strength of our Ship; which was indeed considerable, we having 16 Guns, and 45 Men on board. But as they told me after we were taken, "They judged we were a small Vessel of little force. Moreover, they depended on the same good fortune as in the other Ships they had taken; having met with no resistance: For the People were generally glad of an opportunity of entering with them:" Which last was but too true.

When they first began to fire, I called aloud to the first Mate, to fire at the Boat out of the Steerage Port-holes; which not being done, and the people I had ordered upon Deck with small Arms not appearing, I was extremely surprised; and the more, when an Officer came and told me, "The People would not take Arms." I went thereupon down into the Steerage, where I saw a great many of them looking at one another. Little thinking that my first Mate had prevented them from taking Arms, I asked them with some Roughness, "Why they had not obeyed my Orders?" Calling upon some brisk Fellows by name, that had gone a former Voyage with me, to defend the Ship; saying "It would be the greatest Reproach in the World to us all, if we should be taken by a Boat." Some of them replied, "They would have taken Arms, but the Chest they were kept in could not be found." The reason of which will be related hereafter.

By this time the Boat was along the Ship's Side, and there being no body to oppose them, the Pirates immediately boarded us; and coming on the Quarter-deck, fired their Pieces several times down into the Steerage, and shot a Sailor in the Reins, of which Wound he died afterwards. They likewise threw several Granado-shells, which burst amongst us, so that 'tis a great wonder several of us were not killed by them, or by their Shot.

At last some of our People bethought themselves to call out for Quarter; which the Pirates granting, the Quarter-master came down into the Steerage, enquiring, "Where the Captain was?" I told him, "I had been so till now." Upon that he asked me, "How I durst order my People to fire at their Boat out of the Steerage? Saying, that they had heard me repeat it several times." I answered, "I thought it my Duty to defend the Ship, if my People would have fought." Upon that he presented a Pistol to my Breast, which I had but just time to parry before it went off; so that the Bullet past between my Side and Arm. The Rogue finding he had not shot me, he turned the But-end of the Pistol, and gave me such a Blow on the Head as stunned me; so that I fell upon my Knees; but immediately recovering my self, I forthwith jumped out of the Steerage upon the Quarter-deck, where the Pirate Boatswain was.

He was a bloody Villain, having a few days before killed a poor Sailor, because he did not do something so soon as he had ordered him. This cruel Monster was asking some of my People, "Where their Captain was." So at my coming upon Deck, one of them, pointing at me, said, "There he is." Tho' the night was very dark, yet there being four Lanthorns with Candles, he had full fight of me: Whereupon lifting up his broad Sword, he swore, "No Quarter should be given to any Captain that offered to defend his Ship," aiming at the same time a full stroke at my Head. To avoid it I stooped so low, that the Quarter-deck Rail received the Blow; and was cut in at least an inch deep: Which happily saved my Head from being cleft asunder: And the Sword breaking at the same time, with the force of the Blow on the Rail, it prevented his cutting me to pieces.

By good Fortune his Pistols, that hung at his Girdle, were all discharged; otherwise he would doubtless have shot me. But he took one of them, and with the But-end endeavored to beat out my Brains, which some of my People that were then on the Quarter-deck observing, cried out aloud "For God's sake don't kill our Captain, for we never were with a better Man." This turned the Rage of him and two other Pirates on my People, and saved my Life: But they cruelly used my poor Men, cutting and beating them unmercifully. One of them had his Chin almost cut off; and another received such a Wound on his Head, that he fell on the Deck as dead; but afterwards, by the care of our Surgeon he recovered.

All this happen'd in a few Minutes, and the Quarter-master then coming up, ordered the Pirates to tie our People's Hands, and told me, "That when they boarded us, they let their Boat go adrift, and that I must send an Officer, with some of my People in our Boat to look for theirs." Whereupon my first Mate, Mr. Simon Jones, who stood by, offered to go: And the Quarter-master telling him, "He must return quickly, otherwise he should judge that they were run away with the Boat, in order to go on Shore; and if they did so he would cut me to pieces:" Mr. Jones replied, "He would not stay above a quarter of an Hour, but return whether he found the Boat or not." Happily for me he soon found her, and returned (tho' it was very dark) in less time than he had promised.

Then the Quarter-master took me by the hand, and told me, "My Life was safe provided none of my People complained against me." I replied, "I was sure none of them could."

The Pirates next, loaded all their small Arms, and fired several Volleys for Joy they had taken us: Which their Comrades on board their Ship hearing, it being then very near us, tho' we could not see it for the darkness of the Night, they concluded we had made Resistance, and destroyed their People.

It will be proper to observe here, that soon after we had anchored in the Mouth of the River Sieraleon, it became calm; and the Tide of Ebb beginning to come down, the Pirates cut their Cable, and let their Ship drive down with the Tide towards us, from the place where we had seen her at anchor; having sometime before sent their Boat against the Tide of Flood, to discover us. The Ship being by that means come near us, and seeing our Lights, without asking any Questions, gave us a Broad-side with their great Guns; verily believing we had destroyed their Boat and People. This put the Pirates on board us into Confusion, which I observing, asked the Quartermaster, "Why he did not call them with the speaking Trumpet, and tell their Ship they had taken us?" Upon that he asked me angrily, "Whether I was afraid of going to the Devil by a great Shot? For, as to his part, he hoped he should be sent to Hell one of these days by a Cannon Ball." I answered, "I hoped that would not be my Road." However, he followed my Advice, and informed their Ship, "They had taken a brave Prize, with all manner of good Liquors and fresh Provisions on board."

Just after this, Cocklyn, the Pirate Captain, ordered them to dress a quantity of these Victuals; so they took many Geese, Turkeys, Fowls and Ducks, making our People cut their Heads off, and pull the great Feathers out of their Wings: But they would not stay till the other Feathers were pick'd off. All these

they put into our great Furnace, which would boil Victuals for
500 Negroes, together with several Westphalia Hams, and a
large Sow with Pig, which they only bowelled, leaving the
Hair on. This strange medley filled the Furnace, and the Cook
was ordered to boil them out of Hand.

As soon as the Pirate-ship had done firing, I asked the
Quarter-master's leave, for our Surgeon to dress my poor People that had been wounded; and I likewise went into the Steerage, to have my Arm dress'd, it being very much bruised by the
Blow given me by the Pirate-Boatswain. Just after that, a person came to me from the Quarter-master, desiring to know,
"What a Clock it was by my Watch?" Which judging to be a
civil way of demanding it, I sent it him immediately: desiring
the Messenger to tell him, it was a very good going Gold
Watch. When it was delivered to the Quarter-master, he held it
up by the Chain, and presently laid it down on the Deck, giving it a kick with his Foot; saying, "I was a pretty Foot-ball:"
On which, one of the Pirates caught it up, saying, "He would
put it in the common Chest to be sold at the Mast."

JOHN UPTON

Perry galley

Aruba

1725

Not much is known about John Upton beyond the biographical notes in this passage, but in general, we find a picture of a mariner who spent most of his career in the Royal Navy, eventually driven by debt to the merchant marine, then to immigrate to Canada, and finally to piracy. In some respects, Upton's life is a snapshot picture of downward mobility, beginning as he was relatively well educated and securely employed before his circumstances changed around him. This account effectively provides two views on Upton: his own, in which he claimed that he became a pirate only by force, and the account of one of his crewmates, who gave a rather different version when Upton was finally brought to trial.

THE LIFE OF JOHN UPTON, A PIRATE; INCLUDING ALSO THE HISTORY OF THAT SORT OF PEOPLE, PARTICULARLY THE CREW UNDER CAPTAIN COOPER, IN THE *NIGHT RAMBLER*[1]

No laws in any civilized nations are more severe than those against piracy, nor are they less severely executed, and the criminals who suffer by them are usually the least pitied, or

rather the most detested of all who come to die an ignominious death by the sentence of the Law. Of old they were styled
hostes humani generis,[2] and the oldest systems we have of
particular institutions have treated them with a rigor suitable
to their offence. With respect to those who fall into the hands
of British justice, it must be remarked that they usually plead
as an excuse for what they have done their being forced into
pirates' service, and as it is well known that numbers are really
forced into crimes they detest, so the lenience of our judicators
generally admit whatever proofs are probable in such a case.
But where the contrary appears, and the acts of piracy plainly
arise from the wicked dispositions of the offenders, the Royal
Mercy is less frequently extended to them than to any other
sort of criminal whatever.

As to the prisoner of whom we are to speak, John Upton
was born at Deptford, of very honest parents who gave him
such an education as fitted their station, and that in which
they intended to breed him. When grown up to be a sturdy
youth, they put him out apprentice to a waterman, with whom
he served out his time faithfully, and with a good character.
Afterwards he went to sea and served for twenty-eight years
together on board a man-of-war, in the posts of either boatswain or quartermaster. Near the place of his birth he married
a woman, took a house and lived very respectably with her
during the whole course of her life, but she dying while he was
at sea, and finding at his return that his deceased wife had run
him greatly in debt, clamors coming from every quarter, and
several writs being issued out against him, he quitted the service in the man-of-war, and went immediately in a merchantman to Newfoundland. There by agreement he was discharged
from the ship and entered himself for eighteen pounds *per
annum* into the service of a planter in that country in order to
serve him in fishing and furring, the chief trade of that place;
for Newfoundland abounding with excellent harbors, there is
no country in the world which affords so large and so plentiful a fishery as this does. However its climate renders it less
desirable, it being extremely hot in the summer and as in-
tensely cold in the winter, when the wild beasts roam about in

great numbers, and furnish thereby an opportunity to the inhabitants of gaining considerably by falling them, and selling
their furs.

Upton having served his year out was discharged from his
master, and going to New England, he there, in the month of
July, 1725, shipped himself on board the *Perry* merchantman
bound for Barbadoes. The ship was livred[3] and loaded again,
the captain designing them to sail for England, whereupon Upton
desired leave to go on board his Majesty's ship *Lynn*, Captain
Cooper. But Captain King absolutely refusing to discharge
him in order thereto, on the ninth of November, 1725, he
sailed in the aforesaid vessel for England.

On the twelfth of the same month, off Dominica, they were
attacked by a pirate sloop called the *Night Rambler*, under the
command of one Cooper.[4] The pirate immediately ordered the
captain of the *Perry* galley to come on board his ship, which
he and four of his men did, and the pirate immediately sent
some of his crew on board the *Perry* galley, who effectually
made themselves masters thereof, and as Upton said, used him
and the rest of the persons they found on board with great in-
humanity and baseness, a thing very common amongst those
wretches. Upton also insisted that as to himself, one of the pirate's crew ran up to him as soon as they came on board and
with a cutlass in his hand, said with an oath, *You old son of a
bitch, I know you and you shall go along with us or I'll cut
out your liver*, and thereupon fell to beating him fore and aft
the deck with his cutlass.

The same evening he was carried on board the pirate sloop,
where, according to his journal, three of the pirates attacked
him; one with a pistol levelled at his forehead demanded
whether he would sign their articles, another with a pistol at
his right ear, swore that if he did not they would blow out his
brains, while a third held a couple of forks at his breast, and
terrified him with the continual apprehensions of having them
stabbed into him. Whereupon he told them that he had four
young infants in England, to whom he thought it his duty to
return, and therefore begged to be excused as having reason to
decline their service, as well as a natural dislike to their pro-

ceedings. Upon which, he said, he called his captain to take notice that he did not enter voluntarily amongst them. Upon this the pirate said they found out a way to satisfy themselves by signing for him, and this, he constantly averred, was the method of his being taken into the crew of the *Night Rambler*, where he insisted he did nothing but as he was commanded, received no share in the plunder, but lived wholly on the ship's allowance, being treated in all respect as one whom force and not choice had brought amongst them.

But to return to the *Perry* galley, which the pirates carried to the Island of Aruba, a maroon or uninhabited island, or rather sand bank, where they sat the crew ashore and left them for seventeen days without any provision, except that the surgeon of the pirate now and then brought them something in his pocket by stealth. On the tenth of December the pirates saw a sail which proved to be a Dutch sloop, which they took, and on board this Upton and two others who had been forced as well as himself were put, from whence as he said, they made their escape. After abundance of misfortunes and many extraordinary adventures, he got on board his Majesty's ship *Nottingham*, commanded by Captain Charles Cotterel, where he served for two years in the quality of quartermaster. He was then taken up and charged with piracy, upon which he was indicted at an Admiralty sessions held in the month of May, 1729, when the evidence at his trial appeared so strong that after a short stay the jury found him guilty.

But his case having been very differently represented, I fancy my readers will not be displeased if I give them an exact account of the proofs produced against him.

The first witness who was called on the part of the Crown was Mr. Dimmock, who had been chief mate on board the *Perry* galley, and he deposed in the following terms:

"On the twelfth of November, 1725, we sailed from Barbadoes on the *Perry* galley bound for England. On the 14th, about noon, we were taken by the *Night Rambler*, pirate sloop, one Cooper commander. Our captain and four men were ordered on board the pirate sloop, part of the pirate's crew coming also on board the *Perry*. Wherein they no sooner entered, but the prisoner at the bar said, *Lads, are ye come? I'm glad to see ye; I have been looking out for ye for a great while.* Whereupon the pirates saluted him very particularly, calling him by his name, and the prisoner was as busy as any of the rest in plundering and stripping the ship on board of which he had served, and the rest who belonged to it, the very next day after being made boatswain of the pirate. The same day I was carried on board the pirate sloop, tied to the gears and received two hundred lashes with a cat o' nine tails which the prisoner Upton had made for that purpose; after which they pickled me, and the prisoner Upton stabbed me in the head near my ear with a knife, insomuch that I could not lay my head upon a pillow for fourteen days, but was forced to support it upon my hand against the table; and when some of the pirate's crew asked me how I did, upon my answering that I was as bad as a man could be and live, the prisoner, Upton, said D——n him, give him a second reward."

It was also further deposed by the same gentleman that at the island of Aruba, the prisoner was very busy in stripping the *Perry* galley of the most useful and valuable parts of her rigging, carrying them on board the pirate, and making use of them there. He had also in his custody several things of value, and particularly wearing apparel, belonging to one Mr. Furnell, a passenger belonging to the said *Perry* galley; and when it was debated amongst the pirates, and afterwards put to the vote, whether the crew of the said galley should have their vessel again or no, John Upton was not only against them, but also proposed burning the said vessel, and tying the captain and mate to one of the masts in order to their being burnt too.

Mr. Eaton, the second mate of the ship, was the next witness called. He confirmed all that had been sworn by Mr. Dimmock, adding that the day they were taken the pirates asked if he would consent to sign their articles, which he refused. Whereupon they put a rope about his neck, and hoisted him up to the yard's arm, so that he totally lost his senses. He recovered them by some of the pirate's crew pricking him in the fleshy parts of his body, while others beat him with the flat of their swords. As soon as they perceived he was a little come to himself they put the former question to him, whether he would sign their articles. He answered, No, a second time. One of the crew thereupon snatched up a pistol, and swore he would shoot him through the head; but another of them said, No, d——n him, that's too honorable a death; he shall be hanged. Upon this they pulled him up by the rope again, and treated him with many other indignities, and at last in the captain's cabin, pulled a cap over his eyes and clapped a pistol to his head; then he expected nothing but immediate death, a person having almost jabbed his eye out with the muzzle of the pistol, but at last they did let him go. He swore, also, that when the pirates' articles were presented to him to sign, he saw there the name of John Upton, he being well acquainted with his hand.

Mr. Furnell, a passenger in the ship, was the third evidence against the prisoner. He deposed to the same effect with the other two, adding that John Upton was more cruel and barbarous to them than any of the other pirates, insomuch that when they were marooned, and under the greatest necessities for food, Upton said, D——n them, let them be starved, and was the most active of all the rest in taking the goods, and whatever he could lay his hands on out of the *Perry* galley.

In his defense the prisoner would fain have suggested that what the witnesses had sworn against him was chiefly occasioned by a malicious spleen they had against him. He asserted that he was forced by the pirates to become one of their number and was so far from concerned with them voluntarily that he proposed to the mate, after they were taken, to regain the ship, urging that there were but thirteen of the pirates on board, and they all drunk, and no less than nine of their own men left there who were all sober; that the mate's heart failed him, and instead of complying with his motion, said, This is a dangerous thing to speak of; if it should come to the pirates' ears we shall be all murdered, and therefore entreated the prisoner not to speak of it any more. The mate denied every syllable of this, and so the prisoner's assertions did not weigh at all with the jury. After they had brought in their verdict, Mr. Upton said to those who swore against him, Lord! What have you three done?

Under sentence of death he behaved himself with much courage, and yet with great penitence. He denied part of the charge, viz., that he was willingly one of the pirates, but as to the other facts, he confessed them with very little alteration. He averred that the course of his life had been very wicked and debauched, for which he expressed much sorrow, and to the day of his death behaved himself with all outward mark of true repentance. At the place of execution, he was asked whether he had not advised the burning of the *Perry* galley, with Captain King and the chief mate on board. He averred that he did not in any shape whatsoever either propose or agree to an act of such a sort. Then, after some private devotions, he submitted to his sentence, and was turned off on the 16th day of May, 1729, being then about fifty years of age.

RICHARD LUNTLY

The *Eagle*

Barbados

1720

We don't often get a firsthand account of a pirate on his way to the gallows, but here is one such account.[1]

. . . So Gentlemen I shall go away upon my Discourse of the Rest of the Voyage, which my short Time will not me allow to lay down every particular saying of their whole Actions of the Voyage in my Time, I cannot pretend to say it, what was done before, you would think, or at last I should Count myself unwise, to lay down any of the Passages that was before, but to the Truth as I shall say, and so parting with those other two Pirates Ship, after having gone down the Coast with this *Offender* Ship, whom I have given you an Account of before, and Davis thought her more fit for his Design, Sailing with her in Company along the Coast, until he came to a Place, called, the Bite or Old-cally bar upon the Coast of Guiney, where they came to an Anchor, and consulted whether they should keep both Ships, and after having passed their Approbation they consented for to quit with the *King James*, and take to the other Ship *Offender*, thinking she was better for their Design then the *King James* was, and so Davis consented to quit the Ship, the *King James*, and Davis and his Crew with all the forced Men to put them on Board of the *Offender*, which they after named the *Royal-Rover*, which is as I believe remaining upon the Sea to this Time, which is the Man that we ever came to got clear of, but having made the hard Attempt as we have done, in taking one of their Prizes away from them, and made our Escape from them, taking all their Treasure away from them, that some of them had got for several Years in that Practice, and after having, Davis parted with the Ship *King James*, in the Bite of Old-cally bar, upon the Coast of Guiney, and left her riding at an Anchor in this Place, forced with the rest of Davis[2] Crew, compelled us that were forced Men to go on Board of the *Rover*, or suffer immediate Death, while they were on Board of the *Rover*, they concluded for to Sail for an Island, called, Princess,[3] belonging to the part of the King of Portugal, and whose Inhabitants dwells there, it is an Island which lies upon, or were the Latitude of those as I shall Mention, the Island Saint Thome,[4] which lies in or upon the Equinobial,[5] or upon the Meridian Line, which is the Place that parts the North from the South, and after Sailed and came to this Island Princess.

Captain Davis would go on Shore, acquainting the Governor of the said Island that he was a King's Ship belonging to England, which for some Time was entertained accordingly till some Passages happened between Davis & the Governor, about some Reasoning why a King's Ship should not be supplied there, as well in their Wants as in Britain, the Governor taking some Resentment at his Discourse, made it his Business to prepare for him the next Morning in Order to Receive him with all Friendship; but to his Misfortune they received him & those that were with him in a very Barbarous Manner, which was about the Number of Twelve People, and he and eight more they killed in a very Barbarous Manner, and afterward Davis was killed, they parted from thence, and Sailed away to another Island in the Latitude two Degrees South, who was inhabited by Negroes, where there is good Eatables, such as, Cabrito, or Goat in Abundance, and likewise Hog in Abundance, Yams and Potato, in which they made those Natives supply them with as much fresh Stock as supplied us to the Coast of

Brazil, and after being supplied at this island, Sailed away
from this Place for an other Island, near the Coast of Brazil,
called, Ferdenando, which lies in the Latitude five Degrees
South, which not inhabited, by any Creature, there is several
Islands of them which lies all in a Cluster, but all Barren and
Destitute, they thought to got Water there, which at length
they found a small Place that yielded some Water, but it being
the dry Time, that Way they made a Shift for to fill about nine
Buts[6] of Water, and careened the Ship and departed that Island
and then ranged along the Coast Brazil as low as the Place,
called, Bahia, or the Bay of all Saints, went as near as they
could see their Forts and Shipping, lying in that Place, there
cruised for about a Fortnight or there away, of and one in that
Bay, but they could not get any Things there, but two Indians
that was Fishing for their Fathers, and gave Captain Roberts
an Account that the Fleet was Sailed two Days before he came
to Cruise there, which made him very Mad, but they told him
there was another Fleet to Sail in a very short Time, so he concluded with his Crew to strike away in Latitude of about 23
Deg. 35 Mm. South, and then for to Talk and stand away for
the Northward as they did, and met with the Portuguese Fleet,
that those two Indians had given Captain Roberts an Account
of, they Lite[?] of this Fleet of a Place, called, Pernabocko,
which lyeth to Northward off Cape Augustine in the Latitude
of about 7 Deg. 25 Min. South, where Captain Roberts finding
them to be all great Ships, excepting three, which he made it
his Business to take one of the small Ships without firing of a
Gun; and afterwards made the Captain of the Ship tell him,
which was the best Ship, and had the most Money on Board,
and so the Captain told him, it was such a Ship which proved
to be the Vice Admiral of the Fleet, which Roberts came along
side off immediately, and the other thinking he was a French
Gollone-haile, and asked him where he was Bound, and Roberts told him on Board of him, and told him come, which immediately Roberts clapped his four Top-sails aback, and fell
on Board of him, and lashed all along side of his Ship, and
then he entered his Men, and in Half an Hour carried her, putting all the men of the great ship into the small one, and turned

the small Ship away, and kept the great Ship to himself, their Fleet consisting in Number 48 Sail, then all about when they found their Vice Admiral was taken, some of them Run away till the other Men of War came up, and then they joined and gave Chase, which they had as good sent a Cow after an Hare, and to Captain Roberts and his Quarter-Master with the rest of his Crew, concluded to go to a Place called, Ciana[7] in the West-Indies, where they were, and sitting of their two Ships, with a Sloop in Company, which they had taken some Days before belonging to Rhode Island, which they fitted upon Speed and Mounted 10 Guns, besides several others small Swivel Guns, so lying in this Place, and fitting both their Ships for to go, and lie in Latitude of Barbados, and Cruise there all Winter, and take as many Ships with Provision and Men as they should have Occasion for to proceed for the East Indies; and we that were forced Men, were compelled by the Force of Arms to do Things that our Conscience thought to be Unlawful, we were one Night consulting to Run away with the Sloop, and make the best of our Way to the West Indies; there happened one of the Pirates to over-hear us, and went and told Captain Roberts of it, and his Quarter-Master, and immediately all Hands were called up to know what they should do with us, some of them was for shooting of us, other some not, and so they consented to put us away upon a Desolate Island, Especially, we that was first, which was Richard Jones and myself, and William Fenton, they happened to see a Sail, which upon Captain Roberts and about 40 more of his Crew went away, in Order to take the said Vessel, but returned not that Night, next Day his Quarter-Master went and fitted both Ships, and Sailed in Order to Lite of Captain Roberts, but could not find him, so they gave the Portuguese Ship unto him that was Captain of the Sloop, and told him where Roberts was, and bid him to follow them to the Latitude of Barbados, and there they should find them there, and after in a short Time afterwards took this Vessel in which we came to Britain in, and in hopes to get Justice, knowing very well that if we had found any Justice you could not have brought us to an untimely End. But GOD forgive you all, & I shall indeed, for I think I have made an happy Exchange. I shall say no more upon this Respect, but shall Praise my GOD for all Things, and shall conclude with this Saying, LORD be Merciful to me a poor Sinner.

RICHARD LUNTLY.
Written with my own Hand the 9th Day of January 1721.

EDINBURGH, Printed by Robert Brown in Forrester's-Wynd. 1721.

ANNE BONNY
AND
MARY READE

Port Royal, Jamaica

1720–21

*Every ship had boys on board, be it a Royal Navy
ship or even a pirate ship, as in the case of the unfortunate boy whose fibula was found in the wreck of
the* Whydah. *But in these two famous instances, the
boys on board "Calico" Jack Rackham's pirate ship
weren't boys at all. Anne Bonny and Mary Reade,
however improbably, both ended up disguised as
men in the same pirate crew, each wending a different path toward a life of piracy. Both wound up
being put on trial, and both "pleaded their bellies,"
as pregnant women would not, as a rule, be taken to
the place of execution until after they had been delivered.*

*Jack Rackham, who was Anne Bonny's lover,
came into his piratical career after succeeding Charles
Vane on the* Ranger. *Like many of the pirates in this
account he accepted the King's Pardon, and attempted to make a life for himself in Nassau. There
he met Anne Bonny, who joined him when he resumed his life as a sea robber. On that cruise Mary
Reade also shipped, in disguise. Their careers were
short-lived, however; Calico Jack was caught in
1720, tried in Port Royal, sentenced to death by
hanging, and his body was then gibbeted (hung in*

*chains) at the entrance to Port Royal on a small
rocky island now known as Rackham's Cay.*

*But enough about Calico Jack. Let's get to the
women who actually made him worth talking about.*

THE LIFE OF MARY READ[1]

Now we are to being a History full of surprising Turns and
Adventures; I mean, that of Mary Read and Anne Bonny, alias
Bonn, which were the true Names of these two Pirates; the
odd Incidents of their rambling Lives are such, that some may
be tempted to think the whole Story no better than a Novel or
Romance; but since it is supported by many thousand Witnesses, I mean the People of Jamaica, who were present at
their Trials, and heard the Story of their Lives, upon the first
discovery of their Sex; the Truth of it can be no more con-
tested, than that there were such Men in the World, as Roberts
and Black-beard, who were Pirates.

Mary Read was born in England, her Mother was married
young, to a Man who used the Sea, who going a Voyage soon
after their Marriage, left her with Child, which Child proved
to be a Boy. As to the Husband, whether he was cast away, or
died in the Voyage, Mary Read could not tell; but however, he
never returned more; nevertheless, the Mother, who was young
and airy, met with an Accident, which has often happened to
Women who are young, and do not take a great deal of Care;
which was, she soon proved with Child again, without a Husband to Father it, but how, or by whom, none but her self
could tell, for she carried a pretty good Reputation among her
Neighbors. Finding her Burthen grow, in order to conceal her
Shame, she takes a formal Leave of her Husband's Relations,
giving out, that she went to live with some Friends of her own
in the Country: Accordingly she went away, and carried with
her young Son, at this Time, not a Year old: Soon after her Departure her Son died, but Providence in Return, was pleased to
give her a Girl in his Room, of which she was safely delivered,
in her Retreat, and this was our Mary Read.

Here the Mother liv'd three or four Years, till what Money she had was almost gone; then she thought of returning to London, and considering that her Husband's Mother was in some Circumstances, she did not doubt but to prevail upon her, to provide for the Child, if she could but pass it upon her for the same, but the changing a Girl into a Boy, seem'd a difficult Piece of Work, and how to deceive an experience old Woman, in such a Point, was altogether as impossible; however, she ventured to dress it up as a Boy, brought it to Town, and presented it to her Mother in Law, as her Husband's Son; the old Woman would have taken it, to have bred it up, but the Mother pretended it would break her Heart, to part with it, so it was greed betwixt them, that the Child should live with the Mother, and the supposed Grandmother should allow a Crown a Week for its Maintenance.

Thus the Mother gained her Point, she bred up her Daughter as a Boy, and when she grew up to some Sense, she thought proper to let her into the Secret of her Birth, to induce her to conceal her Sex. It happen'd that the Grandmother died, by which Means the Subsistence that came from that Quarter, ceased, and they were more and more reduced in their Circumstances; wherefore she was obliged to pay her Daughter out, to wait on a French Lady, as a Foot-boy, being now thirteen Years of Age: Here she did not live long, for growing bold and strong, and having also a roving Mind, she entered her self on Board a Man of War, where she served some Time, then quitted it, when over into Flanders, and carried Arms in a Regiment of Foot, as a Cadet; and tho' upon all Actions, she behaved herself with a great deal of Bravery, yet she could not get a Commission, they being generally bought and sold; therefore she quitted the Service, and took on it a Regiment of Horse; she behaved so well in several Engagements, that she got the Esteem of all of Officers; but her Comrade who was a Fleming, happening to be a handsome young Fellow, she falls in Love with him, and from that Time, grew a little more negligent in her Duty, so that, it seems, Mars and Venus could not be served at the same Time; her Arms and Accoutrements which were always kept in that best Order, were quite neglected: 'tis true, when her Comrade was ordered out upon a Party, she used to go without being commanded, and frequently run herself into Danger, where she had no Business, only to be near him; the rest of the Troopers little suspecting the secret Cause which moved her to this Behavior, fancied her to be mad, and her Comrade himself could not account for this strange Alteration in her, but Love is ingenious, and as they lay in the same Tent, and were constantly together, she found a Way of letting him discover her Sex, without appearing that it was done with Design.

He was much surprised at what he found out, and not a little pleased, taking it for granted, that he should have a Mistress solely to himself, which is an unusual Thing in a Camp, since there is scarce one of those Campaign Ladies, that is ever true to a Troop or Company; so that he thought of nothing but gratifying his Passions with very little Ceremony; but he found himself strangely mistaken, for she proved very reserved and modest, and resisted all his Temptations, and at the same Time was so obliging and insinuating in her Carriage, that she quite changed his Purpose, so far from thinking of making her his Mistress, he now courted her for a Wife.

This was the utmost Wish of her Heart, in short, they exchanged Promises, and when the Campaign was over, and the Regiment marched into Winter Quarters, they bought Woman's apparel for her, with such Money as they could make up betwixt them, and were publicly married.

The Story of two Troopers marrying each other, made a great Noise, so that several Officers were drawn by Curiosity to assist at the Ceremony, and they agreed among themselves that every one of them should make a small Present to the Bride towards House-keeping, in Consideration of her having been their fellow Soldier. Thus being set up, they seemed to have a Desire of quitting the Service, and settling in the World; the Adventure of their Love and Marriage had gained them so much Favor, that they easily obtained their Discharge, and they immediately set up an Eating House or Ordinary, which was the Sign of the Three Horse-Shoes, near the Castle of

Breda,[2] when they soon run into a good Trade, a great many Officers eating with them constantly.

But this Happiness lasted not long, for the Husband soon died, and the Peace of Reswick being concluded, there was no Resort of Officers to Breda as usual; so that the Widow having little or no Trade, was forced to give up House-keeping, and her Substance being by Degrees quite spent, she again assumes her Man's Apparel, and going into Holland, there takes on in a Regiment of Foot quarter'd in one of the Frontier Towns; Here she did not remain long, there was no likelihood of Preferment in Time of Peace, therefore she took a Resolution of seeking her Fortune another Way and withdrawing from the Regiment, ships her self on Board of a Vessel bound for the West-Indies.

It happen'd this Ship was taken by English Pirates, and Mary Read was the only English Person on Board, they kept her amongst them, and having plundered the Ship, let it go again; after allowing this Trade for some time, the King's proclamation came out, and was publish'd in all part of the West-Indies, for pardoning such Pirates, who should voluntarily surrender themselves by a certain Day therein mentioned. The Crew of Mary Read took the Benefit of this Proclamation, and having surrender'd, liv'd quietly on Shore; but Money beginning to grow short, and hearing that Captain Woods Rogers, Governor of the Island of Providence, was fitting out some Privateers to cruise against the Spaniards, she with several others embark'd for that Island, in order to go upon the privateering Account, being resolved to make her fortune one way or other.

These Privateers were no sooner sail'd out, but the Crews of some of them, who had been pardoned, rose against their Commanders, and turned themselves to their old Trade: In this Number was Mary Read. It is true, she often declared, that the Life of a Pirate was what she always abhor'd, and went into it only upon Compulsion, both this Time, and before, intending to quit it, whenever fair Opportunity should offer itself; yet some of the Evidence against her, upon her Trial, who were forced Men, and had sailed with her, deposed upon Oath, that in Times of Action, no Person amongst them were more resolute, or ready to board or undertake any Thing that was hazardous, as she and Anne Bonny; and particularly at the time they were attack'd and taken, when they came to close Quarters, none kept the Deck except Mary Read and Anne Bonny, and one more; upon which, she, Mary Read, called to those under Deck, to come up and fight like Men, and finding they did not stir, fired her Arms down the Hold amongst them, killing one, and wounding others.

This was part of the Evidence against her, which she denied; which, whether true or no, thus much is certain, that she did not want Bravery, nor indeed was she less remarkable for her Modesty according to her Notions of Virtue: Her Sex was not so much as suspected by any Person on Board till Anne Bonny, who was not altogether so reserved in point of Chastity, took a particular liking to her; in short, Anne Bonny took her for a handsome young Fellow, and for some Reasons best known herself, first discovered her Sex to Mary Read; Mary Read knowing what she would be at, and being very sensible of her own Incapacity that Way, was forced to come to a right Understanding with her and so to the great Disappointment of Anne Bonny she let her know she was a Woman also; but this Intimacy so disturb'd Captain Rackham, who was the Lover and Gallant of Anne Bonny, that he grew furiously jealous, so that he told Anny Bonny, he would cut her new Lover's Throat, therefore, to quiet him, she let him into the Secret also.

Captain Rackham, (as he was enjoined,) kept the Thing a Secret from all the Ship's Company, yet notwithstanding all her Cunning and Reserve, Love found her out in this Disguise, and hinder'd her from forgetting her Sex. In their Cruise they took a great Number of Ships belonging to Jamaica and other Parts of the West-Indies, bound to and from England; and whenever they meet any good Artist, or other Person that might be of any great Use to their Company, if he was not willing to enter, it was their Custom to keep him by Force. Among these was a young Fellow of a most engaging Behavior, or, at least, he was so in the Eyes of Mary Read, who became so smitten with his Person and Address, that she could neither rest Night or Day; but as there is nothing more ingenious than Love, it was no hard Matter for her, who had before been practiced in these Wiles, to find a Way to let him discover her Sex: She first insinuated her self into his liking, by talking against the Life of a Pirate, which he was altogether averse to, so they became Mess-Mates and strict Companions: When she found he had a Friendship for her, as a Man, she suffered the Discovery to be made, by carelessly shewing her Breasts, which were very White.

The young Fellow, who was made of Flesh and Blood, had his Curiosity and Desire so rais'd by this Sight, that he never ceased importuning her, till she confessed what she was. Now begins the scene of Love; as he had a Liking and Esteem for her, under her supposed Character it was now turn'd into Fondness and Desire; her Passion was no less violent than his, and perhaps she express'd it, but one of the most generous Actions that ever Love inspired. It happened this young Fellow had a Quarrel with one of the Pirates, and their Ship when lying at an Anchor, near one of the Islands, they had appointed to go ashore and fight, according to the Custom of the Pirates: Mary Read, was to the last Degree uneasy and anxious, for the fate of her Lover; she would not have had him refuse the Challenge, because, she could not bear the Thoughts of his being branded with Cowardice; on the other side, she dreaded the Event, and apprehended the Fellow might be too hard for him: When Love once enters into the Breast of one who has any Sparks of Generosity, it stirs the heart up to the most noble Actions; in this Dilemma, she shew'd, that she fear'd more for his Life than she did for her own; for she took a Resolution of quarreling with this Fellow herself, and having challenged him ashore, she appointed the Time two Hours sooner than that when he was to meet her Lover, where she fought him at Sword and Pistol, and killed him upon the Spot.

It is true, she had fought before, when she had been insulted by some of those Fellows, but now it was altogether in her Lover's Cause, she stood as it were betwixt him and Death, as if she could not live without him. If he had no regard for her before, this Action would have found him to her forever; but there was no Occasion for Ties and Obligations, his Inclination towards her was sufficient; in fine, they applied their Troth to each other, which Mary Read said, she look'd upon to be as good a Marriage, in Conscience, as if it had been done by a Minister in Church; and to this was owing her great Belly, which she pleaded to save her Life.

She declared she had never committed Adultery for Fornication with any Man, she commended the Justice of the Court, before which she was tried, for distinguishing the Nature of their Crimes; her Husband, as she call'd him, with several others, being acquitted; and being ask'd, who he was? She would not tell, but, said he was an honest Man, and had no Inclination to such Practices, and that they had both resolved to leave the Pirates the first Opportunity, and apply themselves to some honest Livelihood.

It is not doubt, but many had Compassion for her, yet the Court could not avoid finding her Guilty; for among other Things, one of the Evidences against her, deposed, that being taken by Rackham, and detain'd some Time on Board, he fell accidentally into Discourse with Mary Read, whom he taking for a young Man, ask'd her, what Pleasure she could have in being concerned with such Enterprises, where her Life was continually in Danger, by Fire or Sword; and not only so, but she must be sure of dying an ignominious Death, if she should be taken alive?— She answer'd, that as to hanging, she thought it no great Hardship, for, where it not for that, every cowardly Fellow would turn Pirate, and so infest the Seas, that Men of Courage must starve:— That if it was put to the Choice of the Pirates, they would not have the punishment less than Death, the Fear of which, kept some dastardly Rogues honest; that many of those who are now cheating the Widows and Orphans, and oppressing their poor Neighbors, who have no Money to obtain Justice, would then rob at Sea, and the Ocean would be crowded with Rogues, like the Land, and no Merchant would venture out; so that the Trade, in a little Time, would not be worth following.

Being found quick with Child,[3] as has been observed, her

Execution was respited, and it is possible she would have found Favor, but she was seize'd with a violet Fever, soon after her Trial, of which she died in Prison.

THE LIFE OF ANNE BONNY

As we have been more particular in the Lives of these two Women, than those of other Pirates, it is incumbent on us, as a faithful Historian, to begin with their Birth. Anne Bonny was born at a Town near Cork, in the Kingdom of Ireland, her Father an Attorney at Law, but Anne was not one of his legitimate Issue, which seems to cross an old Proverb, which says, that Bastards have the best luck. Her Father was a Married Man and his Wife having been brought to Bed, contracted an Illness in her lying in,[4] and in order to recover her Health, she was advised to remove to Change of Air; the Place she chose, was a few Miles distance from her Dwelling, where her Husband's Mother liv'd. Here she sojourn'd some Time, her Husband staying at Home, to follow his Affairs. The Servant-Maid, whom she left to look after the House, and attend the Family, being a handsome young Woman, was courted by a young Man of the same Town, who was a Tanner; this Tanner used to take his Opportunities, when the Family was out of the Way, of coming to pursue his Courtship; and being with the Maid on Day as she was employ'd in the Household Business, not having the Fear of God before his Eyes, he takes his Opportunity, when her Back was turned, of whipping three Silver Spoons into his Pocket. The Maid soon miss'd the Spoons, and knowing that no Body had been in the Room, but herself and the young Man, since she saw them last, she charged him with taking them; he very stiffly denied it upon which she grew outrageous, and threatened to go to a Constable, in order to carry him before Justice of the Peace: These Menaces frighten'd him out of his Wits, well knowing he could not stand Search; wherefore he endeavoured to pacify her by desiring her to examine the Drawers and other Placed, and perhaps she might find them; in this time slips into another

Room, where the Maid usually lay, and puts the Spoons betwixt the Sheets and then makes his Escape by the back Door,
concluding she must find them, when she went to Bed and so
next Day he might pretend he did it only to frighten her, and
the Thing might be laugh'd for a Jest.

> [. . . *The mistress eventually returns and finds the spoons*
> *in the maid's bed and concludes they weren't found be-*
> *cause the maid had been sleeping with her husband while*
> *she was gone. The mistress becomes inflamed with jeal-*
> *ousy.*]

The Mistress, that every Thing might look to be done without Design, lies that Night in the Maid's Bed, little dreaming
of what an Adventure it would produce: After she had been a
Bed some Time, thinking on what had pass'd, for Jealousy
kept her awake, she heard some Body enter the Room; at first
she apprehended it to be Thieves, and was so fright'ned, she
had not Courage enough to call out; but when she heard these
Words, Mary, are you awake? She knew it to be her Husband's
Voice; then her Fright was over, yet she made no Answer, least
he should find her out, if she spoke, therefore she resolved to
counterfeit Sleep, and take what followed.

The Husband came to Bed, and that Night play'd the vigorous Lover; but one Thing spoil'd the Diversion on the Wife's
Side, which was, the Reflection that it was not design'd for her;
however she was very passive, and bore it like a Christian.
Early before Day, she stole out of Bed, leaving him asleep, and
went to her Mother in Law, telling her what had passed, not
forgetting how he had used her, as taking her for the Maid; the
Husband also stole out, not thinking it convenient to be catch'd
in that Room; in the mean Time, the Revenge of the Mistress
was strongly against the Maid, and without considering, that
to her she ow'd the Diversion of the Night before, and that one
good Turn should deserve another; she sent for a Constable,
and charge her with stealing the Spoons: The Maid's Trunk
was broke open, and the Spoons found, upon which she was

carried before a Justice of the Peace, and by him committed to Gaol.

The Husband loiter'd about till twelve a Clock at Noon, then comes Home, pretended he was just come to Town; as soon as he heard what had passed, in Relation to the Maid, he fell into a great Passion with his Wife; this set the Thing into a greater Flame, the Mother takes the Wife's Part against her own Son, insomuch that the Quarrel increasing, the Mother and Wife took Horse immediately, and went back to the Mother's House, and the Husband and Wife never bedded together after.

The Maid lay a long Time in the Prison, it being near half a Year to the Assizes; but before it happened, it was discovered she was with Child; when she was arraign'd at the Bar, she was discharged for want of Evidence; the Wife's Conscience touch'd her, and as she did not believe the Maid Guilty of any Theft, except that of Love, she did not appear against her; soon after her Acquittal, she was delivered of a Girl.

[... *The mistress has twins, a boy and a girl, and the mother dies, leaving money for the mistress and the twins. The husband brings the maid's daughter to come live with him, pretending it is a boy that he has taken in to train as a clerk. Then he loses his competence from his wife, takes the maid to live with him publicly, and when his fortunes collapse, they all set out from Cork to travel to Carolina.*]

. . . His Maid, who passed for his Wife, happened to die, after which his Daughter, our Anne Bonny, now grown up, kept his House.

She was of a fierce and courageous Temper, wherefore, when she lay under Condemnation, several Stories were reported of her, much to her Disadvantage, as that she had kill'd an English Servant-Maid once in her Passion with a Cake-Knife, while she look'd after her Father's House; but upon further Enquiry, I found this Story to be groundless: It was certain she was so robust, that once, when a young Fellow would have lain with her, against her Will, she beat him so, that he lay ill of it a considerable Time.

While she lived with her Father, she was look'd upon as one that would be a good Fortune, wherefore it was thought her Father expected a good Match for her; but she spoilt all, for without his Consent, she marries a young Fellow, who belonged to the Sea, and was not worth a Groat;[5] which provoked her Father to such a Degree, that he turned her out of Doors, upon which the young Fellow, who married her, finding himself disappointed in his Expectation, shipped himself and Wife, for the Island of Providence,[6] expecting Employment there.

Here she became acquainted with Rackham the Pirate, who making Courtship to her, soon found Means of withdrawing her Affections from her Husband, so that she consented to elope from him, and go to Sea with Rackham in Men's Cloaths: She was as good as her Word, and after she had been at Sea some Time, she proved with Child, and beginning to grow big, Rackham landed her on the Island of Cuba; and recommending her there to some Friends of his, they took Care of her, till she was brought to Bed: When she was up and well again, he sent for her to bear him Company.

The King's Proclamation being out, for pardoning of Pirates, he took the Benefit of it, and surrendered; afterwards being sent upon the privateering Account, he returned to his old trade, as has been already hinted in the Story of Mary Read. In all these Expeditions, Anne Bonny bore him Company, and when any Business was to be done in their Way, no Body was more forward or courageous than she, and particularly when they were taken; she and Mary Read, with one more, were all the Persons that durst keep the Deck, as has been before hinted. Her Father was known to a great many Gentlemen, Planters of Jamaica, who had dealt with him, and among whom he had a good Reputation; and some of them, who had been in Carolina, remember'd to have seen her in his House; wherefore they were inclined to shew her Favor, but the Action of leaving her Husband was an ugly Circum-

stance against her. The Day that Rackham was executed, by
special Favor, he was admitted to see her; but all the Comfort
she gave him, was, that she was sorry to see him there, but if
he had fought like a Man, he need not have been hang'd like
a Dog.

She was continued in Prison, to the Time of her lying in, and
afterwards, reprieved from Time to Time; but what is become
of her since, we cannot tell; only this we know, that she was
not executed.

JOHN PHILIPS

The *Squirrel*

Annisquam, Cape Ann

1724

Here's an account of a piratical attack on a New England fishing boat and a punishment meted out to the pirate responsible.[1]

The sloop *Squirrel*, commanded by Skipper Andrew Haraden, sailed out of Annisquam harbor, Cape Ann,[2] on the morning of April 14th, 1724, bound eastward on a fishing voyage. She was newly built. In fact, the owner and skipper were both so anxious to see her on her way to the banks that they didn't wait for all the deck-work to be completed before she sailed and so the necessary tools were taken along with the intensions of finishing the work before Cape Sable[3] was reached. As the sloop made outward into Ipswich Bay two or three sails were in sight, among them a sloop, off but a point or two more to the north, so that early in the afternoon when the vessels were both off the Isles of Shoals, the stranger was only a gunshot distant.

Skipper Haraden was looking her over when suddenly a puff of smoke broke out of a swivel on her rail and the ball struck the water less than a hundred feet in front of the *Squirrel*'s bow. Just after the gun was fired the sloop ran up a black flag and soon the Annisquam fisherman was headed into the wind[4] and her skipper was getting into a boat in answer to a command that came across the water from the pirate. When he reached her deck, Haraden found that the pirates was commanded by Capt. John Philips who was well-known from the captures he had made among the fishing fleets the year before. He was then on his way north after spending a pleasant winter in the warm waters of the West Indies and on the way up the coast had made numerous captures.

When Captain Philips found that he had taken a newly built vessel, with lines that suggested speed, he decided to take her over and the next day the guns, ammunition and stores were transferred to the *Squirrel* and the fishermen were ordered aboard the other sloop and left to shift for themselves; but Skipper Haraden was forcibly detained.

Haraden soon found that about half of the men with Philips had been forced like himself and were only waiting for a chance to escape and one of them, Edward Cheeseman, a ship carpenter, "broke his mind" to Haraden not long after the vessels separated. It developed that various plans had already been cautiously discussed by several of the captured men and now that another bold man was aboard and an extra broadax and adz used to complete the carpenter work on the *Squirrel* were about the deck, the time seemed ripe to rise and capture the vessel. John Filmore, a fisherman who had been captured by Philips while off the Newfoundland coast and previous fall, was active in abetting Cheeseman in the proposal to rise. . . .

Several of the men on the *Squirrel* were for surprising the pirates at night but as the sailing master, John Nutt, was a man of great strength and courage, it was pointed out that it would be dangerous to attack him without firearms. Cheeseman, who had taken the lead in proposing the capture of the vessel, was resolutely in favor of making the attack by daylight as less likely to end in confusion or mistake. He also volunteered to make way with the long-armed Nutt. The plan agreed upon called for a united assault at noon on April 17th, while the carpenter's tools lay about the deck, Cheeseman, the ship-carpenter, having his tools there also. When the time arrived, Cheeseman brought out his brandy bottle and took a dram with the rest, drinking to the boatswain and the sailing master and "To their next merry meeting." He then took a turn about the deck with Nutt, asking what he thought of the weather and the like. Meanwhile, Filmore took up a broadax and whirling it around on its point as though at play, winked at Cheeseman to let him know that all was ready. He at once seized Nutt by the collar and putting the other hand between his legs and holding hard he tossed him over the side of the vessel. Nutt, taken by surprise, had only time to grasp Cheeseman's coat sleeve and say "Lord, have mercy upon me! What are you trying to do, carpenter?" Cheeseman replied that it was an unnecessary question "For, Master, you are a dead man," and striking him on the arm, Nutt lost his hold and fell into the sea and never spoke again.

By this time the boatswain was dead, for as soon as Filmore saw the master going over the rail he raised his broadax and gave the boatswain a slash that divided his head clear to his neck. Nutt's cry and the noise of the scuffle brought the captain on deck to be met by a blow from a mallet in the hands of Cheeseman, which broke his jaw-bone but didn't knock him down. Haraden then made for the captain with a carpenter's adz which Sparks, the gunner, attempted to prevent and for his pains was tripped up by Cheeseman and tumbled into the hands of Charles Ivemay, another of the conspirators, who, aided by two Frenchmen, instantly tossed him overboard. Meanwhile, Haraden had smashed the captain over the head with the adz and ended his piratical career for all time. Cheeseman lost no time and jumped from the deck into the hold and was about to beat out the brains of John Rose Archer, the quartermaster, and already had got in two or three blows with his mallet when Harry Giles, a young seaman, came down after him and cried out that Archer's life should be spared as evidence of their own innocence so that it might not afterwards appear that the attack on the pirates had been made with the intent of seizing their plunder. Cheeseman saw the force of this advice and so Archer was spared and secured with ropes as were three others who were below when the attack was made on deck and who surrendered when the found out what had happened.

Captain Haraden now took command of the *Squirrel* and altered her course from Newfoundland to Annisquam which was reached on April 24th. As they came into the harbor they prepared to fire a swivel to announce their arrival to the village, but in some way the gun was prematurely discharged and a French doctor on board, a forced man, was instantly killed. Tradition, still lingering on the Cape, affirms that the head of Philips was hanging at the sloop's mast-head when she arrived in Annisquam[5] and there is an island in Annisquam River, known as Hangman's Island, which received its name from some connection with this event. . . . It is possible, however, that Captain Haraden may have brought back one or more bodies of the dead pirates, as trophies, and these bodies may have been placed on gibbets erected on what is now Hangman's Island.

PHILIP ASHTON

Marblehead, Massachusetts, and Roatán

1725

Philip Ashton was a nineteen-year-old fisherman from the town of Marblehead in Massachusetts, a place that is still known for its sailors. Ashton's remarkable experience is primarily known as a survivalist tale, as he lived for sixteen months alone on an island off the coast of Ecuador, and upon his safe return told his story in the eighteenth-century equivalent of a bestselling adventure tale. But Ashton became a castaway by choice after having been kidnapped by pirates off the coast of Nova Scotia. Here is his account of life among the pirates led by Ned Low at the tail end of the Golden Age.[1]

UPON Friday, June 15th. 1722. After I had been out for some time in the Schooner *Milton*, upon the Fishing grounds, off Cape Sable Shore, among others, I came to Sail in Company with Nicholas Merritt, in a Shallop, and stood in for Port Rossaway, designing to Harbor there, till the Sabbath was over; where we Arrived about Four of the Clock in the Afternoon. When we came into the Harbor, where several of our Fishing Vessels had arrived before us, we spy'd among them a Brigantine, which we supposed to have been an Inward bound Vessel, from the West Indies, and had no apprehensions of any Danger from her; but by that time we had been at Anchor two or three Hours, a Boat from the Brigantine, with Four hands, came along side of us, and the Men Jumpt in upon our Deck, without our suspecting anything but that they were Friends, come on board to visit, or inquire what News; till they drew their Cutlasses and Pistols from under their Clothes, and Cock'd the one and Brandish'd the other, and began to Curse & Swear at us, and demanded a Surrender of our Selves and Vessel to them. It was too late for us to rectify our Mistake, and think of Freeing ourselves from their power: for however we might have been able, (being Five of us and a Boy) to have kept them at a Distance, had we known who they were, before they had boarded us; yet now we had our Arms to seek, and being in no Capacity to make any Resistance, were necessitated to submit ourselves to their will and pleasure. In this manner they surprised Nicholas Merritt, and 12 or 13 other Fishing Vessels this Evening.

When the Boat went off from our Vessel, they carried me on board the Brigantine, and who should it prove but the Infamous Ned Low, the Pirate, with about 42 Hands, 2 Great Guns, and 4 Swivel Guns. You may easily imagine how I look'd, and felt, when too late to prevent it, I found myself fallen into the hands of such a mad, roaring, mischievous Crew; yet I hoped, that they would not force me away with them, and I purposed to endure any hardship among them patiently, rather than turn Pirate with them.

Low presently sent for me Aft, and according to the Pirates usual Custom, and in their proper Dialect, asked me, If I would sign their Articles, and go along with them. I told him, No; I could by no means consent to go with them, I should be glad if he would give me my Liberty, and put me on board any Vessel, or set me on shore there. For indeed my dislike of their Company and Actions, my concern for my Parents, and my fears of being found in such bad Company, made me dread the thoughts of being carried away by them; so that I had not the least Inclination to continue with them.

Upon my utter Refusal to join and go with them, I was thrust down into the Hold, which I found to be a safe retreat for me several times afterwards. By that time I had been in the

Hold a few Hours, they had completed the taking the several Vessels that were in the Harbor, and the Examining of the Men; and the next Day I was fetched up with some others that were there, and about 30 or 40 of us were put on board a Schooner belonging to Mr. Orne of Marblehead, which the Pirates made use of for a sort of a Prison, upon the present occasion; where we were all confined unarm'd, with an armed Guard over us, till the Sultan's pleasure should be further known.

The next Lord's Day about Noon, one of the Quarter Masters, John Russel by Name, came on board the Schooner, and took six of us, (Nicholas Merritt, Joseph Libbre, Lawrence Fabins, and myself, all of Marblehead, the Eldest of us, if I mistake not, under 21 Years of Age, with two others) and carried us on board the Brigantine; where we were called upon the Quarter Deck, and Low came up to us with Pistol in hand, and with a full mouth demanded, Are any of you Married Men? This short and unexpected Question, and the sight of the Pistol, struck us all dumb, and not a Man of us dared to speak a word, for fear there should have been a design in it, which we were not able to see thro[ugh.] Our Silence kindled our new Master into a Flame, who could not bear it, that so many Beardless Boys should deny him an Answer to so plain a Question; and therefore in a Rage, he Cock'd his Pistol, and clapt it to my Head, and cried out, You D-g! why don't you Answer me? and Swore vehemently, he would shoot me thro' the Head, if I did not tell him immediately, whether I was Married or no.

I was sufficiently frightened at the fierceness of the Man, and the boldness of his threatening, but rather than lose my Life for so trifling a matter, I e'en ventured at length to tell him, I was not Married, as loud as I dar'd to speak it; and so said the rest of my Companions. Upon this he seemed something pacified, and turned away from us.

It seems his design was to take no Married Man away with him, how young soever he might be, which I often wondered at; till after I had been with him some considerable time, and could observe in him an uneasiness in the sentiments of his Mind, and the workings of his passions towards a young Child he had at Boston (his Wife being Dead, as I learned, some small time before he turned Pirate) which upon every lucid interval from Reveling and Drink he would express a great tenderness for, insomuch that I have seen him sit down and weep plentifully upon the mentioning of it; and then I concluded, that probably the Reason of his taking none but Single Men was, that he might have none with him under the Influence of such powerful attractives, as a Wife & Children, lest they should grow uneasy in his Service, and have an Inclination to Desert him, and return home for the sake of their Families.

Low presently came up to us again, and asked the Old Question, Whether we would Sign their Articles, and go along with them? We all told him No; we could not; so we were dismissed. But within a little while we were call'd to him Singly, and then it was demanded of me, with Sternness and Threats, whether I would Join with them? I still persisted in the Denial; which thro' the assistance of Heaven, I was resolved to do, tho' he shot me. And as I understood, all my Six Companions, who were called in their turns, still refused to go with him.

Then I was led down into the Steerage, by one of the Quartermasters, and there I was assaulted with Temptations of another kind, in hopes to win me over to become one of them; a number of them got about me, and instead of Hissing, shook their Rattles, and treated me with abundance of Respect and Kindness, in their way; they did all they could to sooth my Sorrows, and set before me the strong Allurement of the Vast [illegible] they should gain, and what Mighty Men they designed to be and would fain have me to join with them, and share in their Spoils; and to make all go down the more Glib, they greatly Importuned me to Drink with them, nor doubting but this wile would sufficiently entangle me, and so they should prevail with me to do that in my Cups,[2] which they perceived they could not bring me to while I was Sober: but all their fair and plausible Carriage, their proffered Kindness, and airy notions of Riches, had not the Effect upon me which they desired; and I had no Inclination to drown my Sorrows with my Senses in their Inebriating Bowls, and so refused their Drink, as well as their Proposals.

After this I was brought upon Deck again, and Low came up to me, with his Pistol Cock'd, and clap'd it to my Head, and said to me, You D-g you! if you will not sign our Articles, and go along with me, I'll shoot you thro' the Head; and uttered his Threats with his utmost Fierceness, and with the usual Flashes of Swearing and Cursing. I told him, That I was in his hands, and be might do with me what be pleased, but I could not be willing to go with him: and then I earnestly beg'd of him, with many Tears, and used all the Arguments I could think of to persuade him, not to carry me away; but he was deaf to my Cries, and unmoved by all I could say to him; and told me, I was an Impudent D-g, and Swore, I should go with him whether I would or no. So I found all my Cries, and Entreaties were in vain, and there was no help for it, go with them I must, and as I understood, they set mine, and my Townsmen's Names down in their Book, tho' against our Consent. And I desire to mention it with due Acknowledgments to GOD, who withheld me, that neither their promises, nor their threatenings, nor blows could move me to a willingness to Join with them in their pernicious ways.

Upon Tuesday, June 19th. they changed their Vessel, and took for their Privateer, as they call'd it, a Schooner belonging to Mr. Joseph Dolliber of Marblehead, being new, clean, and a good Sailer, and shipped all their hands on board her, and put the Prisoners, such as they designed to send home, on board the Brigantine, with one—who was her Master, and ordered them for Boston.

When I saw the Captives were likely to be sent Home, I thought I would make one attempt more to obtain my Freedom, and accordingly Nicholas Merritt, my Townsman and Kinsman, went along with me to Low, and we fell upon our knees, and with utmost Importunity besought him to let us go Home in the Brigantine, among the rest of the Captives: but he immediately called for his Pistols, and told us we should not go, and Swore bitterly, if either of us offered to stir, he would shoot us down.

Thus all attempts to be delivered out of the hands of unreasonable Men (if they may be called Men) were hitherto unsuccessful; and I had the melancholy prospect of seeing the Brigantine sail away with the most of us that were taken at Port-Rossaway, but myself, and three Townsmen mentioned, and four Isle of Shoal-men detained on board the Schooner, in the worst of Captivity, without any present likelihood of Escaping.

And yet before the Brigantine sailed, an opportunity presented, that gave me some hopes that I might get away from them; for some of Low's people, who had been on shore at Port-Rossaway to get water, had left a Dog belonging to him behind them; and Low observing the Dog ashore howling to come off, order'd some hands to take the Boat and fetch him. Two Young Men, John Holman, and Benjamin Ashton, both of Marblehead, readily Jumpt into the Boat, and I (who pretty well knew their Inclination to be rid of such Company, & was exceedingly desirous myself to be freed from my present Station, and thought if I could but once set foot on shore, they should have good luck to get me on board again) was getting over the side into the Boat; but Quarter Master Russel spy'd me, and caught hold on my Shoulder, and drew me in board, and with a Curse told me, Two was eno', I should not go. The two Young Men had more sense and virtue than to come off to them again, so that after some time of waiting, they found they were deprived of their Men, their Boat, and their Dog; and they could not go after them.

When they saw what a trick was play'd them, the Quarter Master came up to me Cursing and Swearing, that I knew of their design to Run away, and intended to have been one of them; but tho' it would have been an unspeakable pleasure to me to have been with them, yet I was forced to tell him, I knew not of their design; and indeed I did not, tho' I had good reason to suspect what would be the event of their going. This did not pacify the Quarter-Master, who with outrageous Cursing and Swearing clapt his Pistol to my Head, and snap'd it; but it miss'd Fire: this enraged him the more; and he repeated the snapping of his Pistol at my Head three times, and it as often miss'd Fire; upon which he held it over-board, and snap'd it the fourth time, and then it went off very readily. (Thus did GOD mercifully quench the violence of the Fire, that was meant to destroy me!) The Quarter-Master upon this, in the utmost fury, drew his Cutlass, and fell upon me with it, but I leap'd down into the Hold, and got among a Crowd that was there, and so escaped the further effects of his madness and rage. Thus, tho' GOD suffered me not to gain my wished-for Freedom, yet he wonderfully preserved me from Death.

All hopes of obtaining Deliverance were now past and gone; the Brigantine and Fishing Vessels were upon their way homeward, the Boat was ashore, and not likely to come off again; I could see no possible way of Escape; and who can express the concern and Agony I was in, to see myself, a Young Lad not 20 Years Old, carried forcibly from my Parents, whom I had so much reason to value for the tenderness I knew they had for me, & to whom my being among Pirates would be as a Sword in their Bowels, and the Anguishes of Death to them; confined to such Company as I could not but have an exceeding great abhorrence of; in Danger of being poisoned in my morals, by Living among them, and of falling a Sacrifice to Justice, if ever I should be taken with them. I had no way left for my Comfort, but earnestly to commit myself and my cause to GOD, and wait upon Him for Deliverance in his own time and way; and in the mean while firmly to resolve, thro' Divine Assistance, that nothing should ever bring me to a willingness to Join with them, or share in their Spoils.

I soon found that any Death was preferable to being link'd with such a vile Crew of Miscreants, to whom it was a sport to do Mischief; where prodigious Drinking, monstrous Cursing and Swearing, hideous Blasphemies, and open defiance of Heaven, and contempt of Hell itself, was the constant Employment, unless when Sleep something abated the Noise and Revelings.

Thus Confined, the best course I could take, was to keep out of the way, down in the Hold, or wherever I could be most free from their perpetual Din; and fixedly purpose with myself, that the first time I had an opportunity to set my Foot on shore, let it be in what part of the World it would, it should prove (if possible) my taking a final leave of Low and Company.

I would remark it now also (that I might not interrupt the Story with it afterwards) that while I was on board Low, they used once a Week, or Fortnight, as the Evil Spirit moved them, to bring me under Examination, and a new demand my Signing their Articles, and Joining with them; but Blessed be GOD, I was enabled to persist in a constant refusal to become one of them, tho' I was thrashed with Sword or Cane, as often as I denied them; the fury of which I had no way to avoid, but by Jumping down into the Hold, where for a while I was safe. I look'd upon myself, for a long while, but as a Dead Man among them, and expected every Day of Examination would prove the last of my Life, till I learned from some of them, that it was one of their Articles, Not to Draw Blood, or take away the Life of any Man, after they had given him Quarter, unless he was to be punished as a Criminal; and this emboldened me afterwards, so that I was not so much afraid to deny them, seeing my Life was given me for a Prey.

This Tuesday, towards Evening, Low and Company came to sail in the Schooner, formerly called the *Mary*, now the *Fancy*, and made off for Newfoundland; and here they met with such an Adventure, as had like to have proved fatal to them. They fell in with the Mouth of St. John's Harbor.[3] in a Fog, before they knew where they were; when the Fog clearing up a little, they spy'd a large Ship riding at Anchor in the Harbor, but could not discern what she was, by reason of the thickness of the Air, and concluded she was a Fish trader; this they look'd upon as a Boon Prize for them, and thought they should be wonderfully well accommodated with a good Ship under Foot, and if she proved but a good Sailer, would greatly further their Roving Designs, and render them a Match for almost anything they could meet with, so that they need not fear being taken.

Accordingly they came to a Resolution to go in and take her; and imagining it was best doing it by Stratagem, they concluded to put all their Hands, but Six or Seven, down in the

Hold, and make a show as if they were a Fishing Vessel, and so run up alongside of her, and surprise her, and bring her off; and great was their Joy at the distant prospect how cleverly they should catch her. They began to put their designs in Execution, stowed away their Hands, leaving but a few upon Deck, and made Sail in order to seize the Prey; when there comes along a small Fisher-Boat, from out the Harbor and hailed them, and asked them, from whence they were? They told them, from Barbadoes, and were laden with [illegible] and Sugar; then they asked the Fisherman, What large Ship that was in the Harbor? who told them it was a large Man of War.

The very Name of a Man of War struck them all up in a Heap, [stopped?] their Mirth, their fair Hopes, and promising Design of having a good Ship at Command; and left they should catch a [mor?]tar, they thought it their wisest and safest way, instead of going into the Harbor, to be gone as fast as they could; and accordingly they stretched away farther Eastward, and put into a small Harbor, called Carboneur, about 15 Leagues distance; where they went on Shore, took the Place, and destroyed the Houses, but hurt none of the People; as they told me, for I was not suffered to go ashore with them.

The next Day they made off for the Grand Bank, where they took seven or eight Vessels, and among them a French Banker, a Ship of about 350 Tons, and 2 Guns; this they carried off with them, and stood away for St. Michaels.

Off of St. Michael, they took a large Portuguese Pink, laden with Wheat, coming out of the Road, which I was told was formerly call'd the *Rose*-Frigate.[4] She struck to the Schooner, fearing the large Ship that was coming down to them; tho' all [illegible] had been no Match for her, if the Portuguese had made a good Resistance. This Pink they soon observed to be a much better Sailer than their French Banker, which went heavily; and therefore they threw the greatest part of the Wheat over board, reserving only eno' to Ballast the Vessel for the present, and took what they wanted out of the Banker, and then Bu[?] her, and sent the most of the Portuguese away in a large Launch they had taken.

Now they made the Pink, which Mounted 14 Guns, their

Commodore, and with this and the Schooner Sailed from St. Michaels, to the Canaries, where off of Tenerife they gave Chase to a Sloop, which got under the Command of the Fortress, and so escaped falling into their Hands; but stretching along to the Western end of the Island, they came up with a Fishing Boat, and being in want of Water, made them Pilot them into a small Harbor, where they went ashore and got a supply.

After they had Watered, they Sailed away for Cape de Verde Islands, and upon making the Isle of May, they descry'd a Sloop, which they took, and it proved to be a Bristol-man, one Pa[?] or Pier Master; this Sloop they designed for a Tender, and put on board her my Kinsman Nicholas Merritt, with 8 or 9 hands more, and Sailed away for Bonavista, with a design to careen their Vessels.

In their Passage to Bonavista, the Sloop wronged both the Pink and the Schooner; which the Hands on board observing, being mostly Forced Men, or such as were weary of their Employment, upon the Fifth of September. Ran away with her and made their Escape.

When they came to Bonavista, they [illegible] down the Schooner, and careen'd her, and then the Pink; and here they gave the Wheat, which they had kept to Ballast the Pink with, to the Portuguese, and took other Ballast.

After they had cleaned and fitted their Vessels, they steered away for St. Nicholas, to get better Water: and here as I was told, 7 or 8 hands out of the Pink went ashore a Fowling,[5] but never came off more among which I suppose Lawrence Fabins was one, and what became of them I never could hear to this Day. Then they put out to Sea, and stood away for the Coast of Brazil hoping to meet with Richer Prizes than they had yet takes; in the Passage thither, they made a Ship, which they gave chase [illegible], but could not come up with; and when they came upon the Coast, it had like to have proved a sad Coast to them For the Trade-Winds blowing exceeding hard at South East, they fell in upon the Northern part of the Coast, near 200 Leagues to the Leeward of where they designed; and here we were all in exceeding great Danger, and for Five Days and Nights together, hourly feared when we should be swallowed up by the violence of the Wind and Sea, or [e?]nded upon some of the Shoals, that lay many Leagues off from Land. In this time of Extremity, the Poor Wretches had nowhere to go for Help! For they were at open Defiance with their Maker, & they could have but little comfort in the thoughts of their Agreement with Hell; such mighty Hectors[6] as they were, in a clear Sky and a fair Gale, yet a fierce Wind and a boisterous Sea sunk their Spirits to a Cowardly dejection, and they evidently feared the Almighty, whom before they defied, lest He was come to Torment them before their expected Time; and tho' they were so habituated to Cursing and Swearing, that the Dismal Prospect of Death, & this of so long Continuance, could not Correct the Language of most of them, yet you might plainly see the inward Horror and Anguish of their Minds, visible in their Countenances, and like Men amazed, or starting out of Sleep in a fright, I could hear them ever now and then, cry out, Oh! I wish I were at Home.

When the Fierceness of the Weather was over, and they had recovered their Spirits, by the help of a little N[?]tes, they bore away to the West Indies, and made the three Islands call'd the Triangles, lying off the Main about 40 Leagues to the Eastward of Surinam. Here they went in and careened their Vessels again; and it had like to have proved a fatal Scouring to them.

For as they hove down the Pink, Low had ordered so many hands upon the Shrouds, and Yards, to throw her Bottom out of Water, that it threw her Ports, which were open, under Water; and the Water flow'd in with such freedom that it presently overset her. Low and the Doctor were in the Cabin together, and as soon as he perceived the Water to gush in upon him, he bolted out at one of the Stern-Ports, which the Doctor also attempted, but the Sea rushed so violently into the Port by that time, as to force him back into the Cabin, upon which Low nimbly run his Arm into the Port, and caught hold of his Shoulder and drew him out, and so saved him. The Vessel pitched her Masts to the Ground, in about 6 Fathom Water, and turn'd her Keel out of Water; but as her Hull filled, it sunk, and by the help of her Yard-Arms, which I suppose bore upon the Ground, her Masts were raised something out of Water: the Men that were upon her Shrouds and Yards, got upon her Hull, when that was uppermost, and then upon her Top-Masts and Shrouds, when they were raised again. I (who with other light Lads were sent up to the Main-Top-Gallant[7] Yard) was very difficultly put to it to save my Life, being but a poor Swimmer; for the Boat which picked the Men up, refused to take me in, & I was put upon making the best of my way to the Buoy, which with much ado I recovered, and it being large I stayed myself by it, till the Boat came along close by it, and then I called to them to take me in; but they being full of Men still refused me; and I did not know but they meant to leave me to perish there; but the Boat making way a head very slowly because of her deep load, and Joseph Libbre calling to me to put off from the Buoy and Swim to them, I e'en ventured it, and he took me by the hand and drew me in board. They lost two Men by this Accident, viz. John Bell, and one they called Zana Gourdon. The Men that were on board the Schooner were busy a mending the Sails, under an Awning so they knew nothing of what had happened to the Pink, till the Boat full of Men came along side of them, tho' they were but about Gun-Shot off, and We made a great out-cry; and therefore they sent not their Boat to help take up the Men.

And now Low and his Gang, having lost their Frigate, and with her the greatest part of their [food?] and Water, were again reduced to their Schooner as their only Privateer, and in her they put to Sea, and were brought to very great straits for want of Water; for they could not get a supply at the Triangles, and when they hoped to furnish themselves at Tobago, the Current set so strong, & the Season was so Calm,[8] that they could not recover the Harbor, so they were forced to stand away for Grand Grenada, a French Island about 18 Leagues to the Westward of Tabago, which they gained, after they had been at the hardship of half a pint of Water a Man for Sixteen Days together.

Here the French came on board, and Low having put all his Men down, but a sufficient number to Sail the Vessel, told them upon their Enquiry, Whence he was, that he was come from Barbadoes, and had lost his Water, and was oblig'd to put in for a recruit; the poor People not suspecting him for a Pirate, readily suffered him to send his Men ashore and fetch off a supply. But the Frenchmen afterwards suspecting he was a Smuggling Trader, thought to have made a Boon Prize of him, and the next day fitted out a large Rhode-Island built Sloop of 70 Tuns, with 4 Guns mounted, and about 30 Hands, with design to have taken him. Low was apprehensive of no danger from them, till they came close alongside of him and plainly discovered their design, by their Number and Actions, and then he called up his hands upon Deck, and having about 90 Hands on board, & 8 Guns mounted, the Sloop and Frenchmen fell an easy prey to him, and he made a Privateer of her.

After this they cruised for some time thro' the West Indies, in which excursion they took 7 or 8 Sail of Vessels, chiefly Sloops; at length they came to Santa Cruz, where they took two Sloops more, & then came to Anchor off the Island.

While they lay at Anchor here, it came into Low's Head, that he wanted a Doctor's Chest, & in order to procure one, he put four of the Frenchmen on board one of the Sloops, which he had just now taken, & sent them away to St. Thomas's, about 12 Leagues off where the Sloops belonged, with the promise, that if they would presently send him off a good Doctors Chest, for what he sent to purchase it with, they should have their Men & Vessels again, but if not, he would kill all the Men & burn the Vessels. The poor People in Compassion to their Neighbors, & to preserve their Interest, readily complied with his Demands; so that in little more than 24 Hours the four Frenchmen returned with what they went for, & then according to promise, they & their Sloops were Dismissed.

From Santa Cruz they Sailed till they made Curacao, in which Passage they gave Chase to two Sloops that outsailed them & got clear; then they Ranged the Coast of New Spain, and made Carthagena, & about mid-way between Carthagena and Port-Abella, they descry'd two tall Ships, which proved to be the *Mermaid* Man of War, & a large Guinea-Man. Low was now in the Rhode-Island Sloop, & one Farrington Spriggs a Quarter-Master, was Commander of the Schooner, where I still was. For some time they made Sail after the two Ships, till they came so near that they could plainly see the Man of War's large range of Teeth, & then they turned Tail to, and made the best of their way from them; upon which the Man of War gave them Chase & overhauled them apace. And now I confess I was in as great terror as ever I had been yet, for I concluded we should be taken, & I could expect no other but to Die for Companies sake; so true is what Solomon tells us, a Companions of Fools shall be destroyed. But the Pirates finding the Man of War to overhaul them, separated, & Low stood out to Sea, & Spriggs stood in for the Shore. The Man of War observing the Sloop to be the larger Vessel much, and fullest of Men, threw out all the Sail she could, & stood after her, and was in a fair way of coming up with her presently: But it happened there was one Man on board the Sloop, that knew of a Shoal Ground thereabouts, who directed Low to run over it; he did so; and the Man of War who had now so forereached him as to sling a Shot over him, in the close pursuit ran a Ground upon the Shoal, and so Low and Company escaped Hanging for this time.

Spriggs, who was in the Schooner, when he saw the Danger they were in of being taken, upon the Man of War's outsailing them, was afraid of falling into the hands of Justice; to prevent which, he, and one of his Chief Companions, took their pistols, and laid them down by them, and solemnly Swore to each other, and pledg'd the Oath in a Bumper of Liquor, that if they saw there was at last no possibility of Escaping, but that they should be taken, they would set Foot to Foot, and Shoot one another, to Escape Justice and the Halter. As if Divine Justice were not as inexorable as Human!

But, as I said, he stood in for the Shore, and made into Pickeroon Bay, about 18 Leagues from Carthagena, and so got out of the reach of Danger. By this means the Sloop and Schooner were parted; and Spriggs made Sail towards the Bay of Honduras, and came to Anchor in a small Island called Utilla,[9] about 7 or 8 Leagues to Leeward of Roatan, whereby the help of a small Sloop, he had taken the Day before, he hauled down, and cleaned the Schooner.

While Spriggs lay at Utilla, there was an Opportunity presented, which gave occasion to several of us to form a design,
of making our Escape out of the Pirates Company; for having
lost Low, and being but weak handed, Spriggs had determined
to go thro' the Gulf, and come upon the Coast of New-
England, to increase his Company, and supply himself with
Provision; whereupon a Number of us had entered into a Combination, to take the first fair advantage, to Subdue our Masters, and Free ourselves. There were in all about 22 Men on
board the Schooner, and 8 of us were in the Plot, which was,
That when we should come upon the Coast of New-England,
we would take the opportunity when the Crew had sufficiently
dozed themselves with Drink, and had got found a Sleep, to
secure them under the Hatches, and bring the Vessel and Company in, and throw ourselves upon the Mercy of the Government.

But it pleased GOD to disappoint our Design. The Day that
they came to Sail out of Utilla, after they had been parted
from Low about five Weeks, they discovered a large Sloop,
which bore down upon them. Spriggs, who knew not the
Sloop, but imagined it might be a Spanish Privateer, full of
Men, being but weak handed himself, made the best of his
way from her. The Sloop greatly overhauled the Schooner
Low, who knew the Schooner, & thought that since they had
been separated, she might have fallen into the hands of honest
Men, fired upon her, & struck her the first Shot. Spriggs, seeing the Sloop fuller of Men than ordinary, (for Low had been
to Honduras, & had taken a Sloop, & brought off several Bay-
men, & was now become an Hundred strong) & [illegible] still
ignorant of his old Mate, refused to bring to, but continued to
make off; and resolved if they came up with him, to fight them
the best he could. Thus the Harpies had like to have fallen foul
of one another. But Low hoisting his Pirate Colors, discovered
who he was; and then, hideous was the noisy joy among the
Piratical Crew, on all sides, accompanied with Firing, & Carousing, at the finding their Old Master, & Companions, &
their narrow Escape: and so the design of Cruising upon the
Coast of New-England came to nothing. A good Providence it

was to my dear Country, that it did so; unless we could have timely succeeded in our design to surprise them.

Yet it had like to have proved a fatal Providence to those of us that had a hand in the Plot; for tho' our design of surprising Spriggs and Company, when we should come upon the Coast of New-England, was carried with as much secrecy as was possible, (we hardly daring to trust one another, and mentioning it always with utmost privacy, and not plainly, but in distant hints) yet now that Low appeared, Spriggs had got an account of it some way or other; and full of Resentment and Rage he goes aboard Low, and acquaints him with what he called our Treacherous design, and says all he can to provoke him to Revenge the Mischief upon us, and earnestly urged that we might be shot. But GOD who has the Hearts of all Men in His own Hands, and turns them as He pleases, so over ruled, that Low turned it off with a Laugh, and said he did not know, but if it had been his own case, as it was ours, he should have done so himself; and all that Spriggs could say was not able to stir up his Resentments, and procure any heavy Sentence upon us.

Thus Low's merry Air saved us at that time; for had he lisped a Word in compliance with what Spriggs urged, we had surely some of us, if not all, have been lost. Upon this he comes on board the Schooner again, heated with Drink, but more chased in his own Mind, that he could not have his Will of us, and swore & tore like a Mad man, crying out that four of as ought to go forward, & [illegible] and to me in particular he said, You D-g, Ashton, deserve to be hang'd up at the Yards-Arm, for designing to cut us off. I told him, I had no design of hurting any man on board, but if they would let me go away quietly I should be glad. This matter made a very great noise on board for several Hours, but at length the Fire was quenched, and thro' the Goodness of GOD, I Escaped being consumed by the violence of the Flame.

The next Day, Low ordered all into Roatan Harbor to clean, and here it was that thro' the Favor of GOD to me, I first gained Deliverance out of the Pirates hands; tho' it was a long while before my Deliverance was perfected, in a return to my Country, and Friends; as you will see in the Sequel.

Roatan Harbor, as all about the Gulf of Honduras, is full of small Islands, which go by the General Name of the Keys. When we had got in here, Low and some of his Chief Men had got ashore upon one of these small Islands, which they called Port-Royal Key, where they made them Booths, and were Carousing, Drinking, and Fighting, while the two Sloops, the Rhode-Island, and that which Low brought with him from the Ray were cleaning. As for the Schooner, he leaded her with the Logwood which the Sloop brought from the Bay, & gave her, according to promise, to one John Blaze, and put four men along with him in her, and when they came to Sail from this Place, sent them away upon their own account, and what became of them I know not.

Upon Saturday the 9th of March, 1723, the Cooper with Six hands in the Long-Boat were going ashore at the Watering place to fill their Casks; as he came along by the Schooner I called to him and asked him, if he were going ashore? he told me Yes; then I asked him, if he would take me along with him; he seemed to hesitate at the first; but I urged that I had never been on shore yet, since I first came on board, and I thought it very hard that I should be so closely confined, when everyone else had the Liberty of going ashore at several times, as there was occasion. At length he took me in, imagining, I suppose, that there would be no danger of my Running away in so desolate uninhabited a Place, as that was.

I went into the Boat with only an Ozenbrigs Frock[10] and Trousers on, and a Mill'd Cap upon my Head, having neither Shirt, Shoes, nor Stockings, nor anything else about me; whereas, had I been aware of such an Opportunity, but one quarter of an Hour before, I could have provided myself something better. However thought I, if I can but once get footing on Terra Firma, tho' in never so bad Circumstances, I shall count it a happy Deliverance; for I was resolved, come what would, never to come on board again.

Low had often told me (upon my asking him to send me away in some of the Vessels, which he dismissed after he had taken them) that I should go home when he did, and not before, and Swore that I should never set foot on shore till he did.

But the time for Deliverance was now come. GOD had ordered it that Low and Spriggs, and almost all the Commanding Officers, were ashore upon an Island distinct from Roatan where the Watering place was; He presented me in sight, when the Long Boat came by, (the only opportunity I could have had) He had moved the Cooper to take me into the Boat, and under such Circumstances as rendered me least liable to Suspicion; and so I got ashore.

When we came first to Land, I was very Active in helping to get the Cask out of the Boat, & Rowing them up to the Watering place; then I lay down at the Fountain & took a hearty Draught of the Cool Water; & anon, I gradually strol'd along the Beach, picking up Stones & Shells, & looking about me; when I had got about Musket Shot off from them (tho' they had taken no Arms along with them in the Boat) I began to make up to the Edge of the Woods; when the Cooper spying me, call'd after me, & asked me where I was going; I told him I was going to get some Coco-Nuts, for there were some Coco-Nut Trees just before me. So soon as I had recovered the Woods, and lost sight of them, I betook myself to my Heels, & ran as fast as the thickness of the Bushes, and my naked Feet would let me. I bent my Course, not directly from them, but rather up behind them, which I continued till I had got a considerable way into the Woods, & yet not so far from them but that I could hear their talk, when they spake anything loud; and here I lay close in a very great Thicket, being well assured, if they should take the pains to hunt after me never so carefully they would not be able to find me.

WILLIAM FLY

The *Fame's Revenge*

Jamaica and Boston

1726

William Fly's career as a pirate was also short and
sweet, or rather bitter—begun in a mutiny and ended
gibbeted in chains on Nix's Mate, an island at the
mouth of Boston harbor. Unlike many of his compa-
triots who were brought to trial, however, Fly stead-
fastly refused to bow to the ministers' exhortations
to express regret over the course of his life and the
coming damnation of his soul. On the contrary:
Fly's dying words were warnings to sailing masters
to treat their men well or risk a mutiny themselves.

A REMARKABLE RELATION OF A COCKATRICE CRUSH'D IN THE EGG[1]

A Vessel of that sort which they call, a Snow, belonging to certain Merchants in Bristol, and commanded by John Green, of that City, sailed from Jamaica, some time in April, 1726, bound for Guinea. The Boatswain, William Fly, having before concerted with some aboard, (in a way of Revenge, they said, for Bad Usage) the Destruction of the Master and the Mate, and the proper Consequences, on May 27. about One a Clock in the Morning, he, with one Alexander Mitchel, went into the Cabin, and seizing on the Master, held his Hands, while Mitchel wounded him. Then they hauled him up; who perceiving their Intention to throw him overboard, beg'd, For the Lord's sake, don't throw me overboard; For if you do, you throw me into Hell immediately. But Fly bid him say, Lord, Have Mercy on my Soul! And when he seized the Mainsheets[2] with his Hand, to prolong his Time, the merciless Monsters, with a Cooper's Broad-axe, cut off his Hand, and threw him over-board. While this was a doing, one Samuel Cole, presently assisted with Mitchel and one Winthrop, secured the Mate, whose Name was Thomas Jenkins, and brought him upon Deck, telling him, that he should go after the Master. Accordingly, having first cut him down the Shoulder with a Broad-axe, they threw him over, just before the Main Shrouds. After he was thrown over, he cried out unto the Doctor, For the Lord's sake, to fling him a Rope. But Fly soon secured the Doctor, and put him in Irons; and confined the Gunner also and the Carpenter, who were not for their Turn.

Two Days after this, they met one of the Ships, that came out in Company with Green, and hailing them, ask'd, How Captain Green did. They answered, Very well! At your Service! But upon consulting, whether they had best attack that Ship, they left her, in Consideration, That they had not Hands enough to Man her. So, they bore away for North-Carolina; Where, off Cape Hatteras Bar, on June 3. there lay a Sloop at Anchor, whereof the Commander was one whose Name is Fulker. Some of the Sloop's Hands went aboard Fly, who was now become the Captain of the Snow, supposing them to want a Pilot. Fly commanded Fulker aboard, and informed him, They were Gentlemen of Fortune; and let him know, that they must have the Sloop, if it sailed better than the Snow. The contrary Winds rendering the Sloop unable to be brought off, our New Captain fell into a great Passion, and swore he would burn her, and bringing Fulker to the Gears,[3] (who it seems, unadvisedly provoked them) inflicted a severe Scourging upon him. The Boats Crew, could not bring the Sloop any further than the Bar, but there she bilged[4] and sank: and the Pirates endeavored then to set her on Fire, but could not make the Fire to take. Fulker and his Men, and his Passengers, were detained Prisoners by Fly; But on June 5. they sailed from thence; and on the Day following they saw a Ship commanded by one whose Name is Gale, bound from Barbados to Virginia. They could not come up with Gale till the next Morning; when they hoisted their Black Flag, and fired several Guns at the Ship; and there being little Wind. Gale struck; and Fly made the Men his Prisoners; but robbed the Ship only of several Sails, and some Clothes and small Arms; and after a Captivity of Two Days released them; at the same time giving Fulker, and one of his Passengers, and a Servant, and Green's Doctor, their Liberty.

However they forcibly detained one William Atkinson, who had been Commander of a Brigantine, but left her for a Passage home in Fulker, bound then for Boston: And who had often declared, That if the Pirates ever took him, he would humor them, till he could see his first Opportunity to rise upon them. They wanted him to be their Pilot, for the Coast of New-England; which they told him he should be, or, They would blow his Brains out. It seems, they forgot, how bad a Coast New-England has been for Pirates to come upon! Off of Delaware Bay, they met a Sloop commanded by one Harris bound from New-York to Pennsylvania, having about Fifty Scotch-Irish Passengers aboard; which upon their hoisting of their Black Flag Surrendered unto them. After they had a little ransacked the Vessel, and kept her twenty four Hours, they forced a Lusty Blade,[5] one James Benbrook, from her, and so dismissed her. Fly bore away for Martha's Vineyard, pretending to Water there, and so away for Guinea; But the Pilot purposely missed the port, (whereat Fly was very angry,) and on June 23. bearing Eastward, they met with a Fishing Schooner, on Browns Bank; from which upon Fly's hoisting his Black Flag, and threatening to sink her, the Master came aboard them, & Fly told him, he must have the Schooner, unless he could inform him, where to get a better Sailor. About Noon, they saw some other Schooners; and Fly sent that Schooner with seven hands after them. Fly (who had now entirely sold himself to the God of Ekron),[6] and Three other Pirates, whereof one (Samuel Cole aforesaid, was in Irons upon Suspicion of Mutiny, remained aboard the Snow; and fifteen others that had been taken by him; namely, Fulker's Mate, a couple of his Boys, Green's Gunner and Carpenter, five of Gale's Men, Benbrook, Three Fishermen belonging to the Schooner, and our Atkinson. While the Pirates were gone upon their chase, there appeared in Sight several other Fishing-Vessels; and Atkinson by telling Fly what he saw, drew him forward, from his two Loaden Guns, and Sword, which he had with him; and while Fly sat on the Windlass with his Prospective-Glass, Benbrook and Walker, (who had been Fulker's Mate) upon the Direction from Atkinson, secured Fly, and put him in Irons; and Atkinson struck another of the Pirates; and with the Help of the Carpenter, soon confined the other Two. Thus they made themselves Masters of the Snow; the rest of the Prisoners all the while standing unactive, not being made acquainted with the Design, which was now managing for their Deliverance.

On June 28. the Happy Captors brought in their New Captives; having taken them Captives, whose Captives they were. So, The Triumphing of the wicked, was but for a moment.

And, the Special Court of Admiralty which the Act of Parliament has ordered for the Trial of Pirates, [Whereof the chief Judge, was the Honorable WILLIAM DUMMER Esq. the Lieutenant Governor, and Commander in Chief, of the Massachusetts-Province,] quickly tried these Four Pirates, and after plain and full Conviction, on July 3, passed the just Sentence of Death upon them; namely, upon William Fly, the upstart Captain, who was a Young man, about Seven and twenty years of old; Henry Greenville, a married Man about forty seven years of Age; Samuel Cole, about Thirty seven years of Age, having a Wife and seven Children; And, George Condick, a Youth of Twenty, or thereabouts.

They were now cast into a place, Where, besides the prayers, which abundance of Godly Christians made for them, That in the Destruction of the Flesh their Spirit might be Saved, great pains were taken, by the Ministers of City, to dispose them for a Return unto God.

[. . .]

A Conference, with the Pirates. July 6. M. stands for Minister. P. P. for Pirates.

[. . .]

M. It is a most hideous Article in the Heap of Guilt lying on you, that an Horrible Murder is charged upon you; There is a cry of Blood going up to Heaven against you.

P. P. [Under all the marks of Confusion.] Fly said, I can't charge myself with Murder. I did not strike and wound the Master or Mate! It was Mitchel did it!—

The rest said, There was a Murder; and whatever Mitchel and this Man did, we were aiding and assisting to it. And it is the dreadfulest of all the Things we have to think of.

M. Fly, I am astonished at your stupidity. I cannot understand you. I am sure, you don't understand yourself. I shall be better able, another time to reason with you.

Fly said, It is very strange another should know more of me, than I do of myself. There are False Oaths taken against me.

[. . .]

M. Thus, I have in a few words given you the Sum of the Matter; which I hope, you will Think over, when I am departed from you. For one Conference, thus much may be Enough, if you will try when I am withdrawn, to go over the Way of Life that has been set before you.

I will at this Time add only this One Remark. If you come to the Repentance that is unto Salvation, it will appear, in Dispositions, that will be the Reverse of Those, which have pushed you on, to the Sins Repented of. I'll Illustrate it, with Two Instances.

First, That which pushed you on to Robberies and Piracies, was an Immoderate, Inordinate, Irregular Desire of Worldly Possessions. Now, if you Repent, you will have a Disposition patiently to bear any Wants and Straits, that GOD may order for you; and rather suffer any Poverty and all sorts of Difficulties, than Sin, or do any Unlawful Thing, to gain the World. In this point how do you find yourselves disposed?

Fly,—Be sure, I have nothing more to Expect from the World.

Co. and, Gr: We hope, we should never do as we have done.

M. Secondly, That which has pushed you on to Murders, as well as Robberies and Piracies, was an Hatred of your Brother,

'Tis what you have carried on to the last Extremity, A most Finished Hatred; Now if you Repent, you will have a Disposition full of Benignity; Good will towards Men, will sweeten your Minds; You will have an Hearty Love to your Neighbor. You will Wish well to everyone, whose Welfare, is Consistent with the public Safety.

Now, shall I Enquire after this point also; How you find yourselves disposed in it? Say—Fly particularly, Do you say; Are there any in the world, which you don't wish well to.

Fly. Yes; There is one Man, that I don't, and I can't wish well to! It is a Vain Thing to lie, If I should say, that I forgive that Man, and that I wish him well, I should lie against my Conscience, and add Sin to Sin.

M. Alas, Man, Thou dost add Sin to Sin. To bear Malice against your Neighbor, or be unable wish him well, though' it be not a Lie, yet it is as great a Sin as a Lie. But you must part with all Sin, if you would find the Mercy and have the Comfort of a Penitent. The Great GOD has over and over again required you to put away all Malice, and lay aside all Malice. Yea, the SON of GOD, the True witness, who delivereth Souls, has expressly told you, That if you do not Forgive, you shall not be forgiven. I hope, the Lords-Prayer is not forgotten with you. Our Lord has taught us to pray, Forgive us as we forgive. I hope, you pray according to that Prayer.

Fly. Yes, I do!—But for all that, I cannot Forgive that Man. GOD Almighty Revenge me on him!—'Tis a Vain thing—I won't die with a Lie in my mouth.

[. . .]

A Second Conference. July 9.

[. . .]

M. And now, Fly; I hope, you are come to a Better Frame, than what I lately left you in.

F. I am where I was.

M. I am sorry for it. What? Is not your Heart yet prevailed withal, to let the Leaven of Malice be purged out of it? Can't you die, wishing well to every one?

F. 'Tis a Vain Thing to dissemble. No; I can't. There are those, that I can't Forgive.

M. But you must; and you must Resign your Heart up to your SAVIOUR, that by the Influences and Assistances of His Grace, you may.

F. But I can't.—And I won't go out of the World, with a lie in my mouth.

M. What Criminal and prodigious Nonsense are you guilty of!—And yet you'll go out of the World, with what is as Bad in your Heart; Even with Murder there, You will go out of the World, in a plain Rebellion against a Command of GOD our SAVIOUR, the Glorious One, who is the Judge of the World; whose Judgment-Seat you must appear before.

Has not the Great GOD our SAVIOUR, Expressly commanded you, To forgive, even the greatest of Enemies and of Injuries; and set before you an admirable and most Imitable Example of doing so? Dare you to Die, persisting in a plain and a known Disobedience to Him? Can you imagine, that He will be the Author of an Eternal Salvation for you, if you flatly refuse to Obey Him? O Vain Imagination! O Vile Imagination!

And I pray what, have you to say of the Government?

F. GOD Reward them according to their Deserts.

[. . .]

M. [. . .] I will pass from This, to another Matter, wherein I hope to see some Relentings begun upon you. Your Murders, your Cruel and Bloody Murders!—

F. I can't Charge myself,—I shan't own myself Guilty of any Murder,—Our Captain and his Mate used us Barbarously. We poor Men can't have Justice done us. There is nothing said to our Commanders, let them never so much abuse us, and use us like Dogs. But the poor Sailors—

M. What's this, to clearing you of the horrid Murders you stand convicted of?

F. I never Struck, either of the Persons!

M. You held the Captains Hands down, while Mitchel struck him:

F. No, 'Twas to Save him from the strokes.

M. And haul him out of the Cabin, and throw him overboard!

But who plotted the Revolution aboard the Ship? a Day or Two before! What was your Intention about the Captain and the Mate, when you should seize them? Why did you carry Mitchel, with his Broad-Axe into the Cabin? Who threw the Captain and the Mate overboard?

If Mitchel was the only Murderer, why did you not seize him, and reserve him for Justice? Were the Murders, any other than one Article, in the Complicated Plot of Piracy, which you were now upon? Every step that any one of you all, took in the Piracy you have been prosecuting, involved you all in the Murders, which the Piracy begun withal?

And, who was it that gave the Ghostly Advice to the Captain, how to make Sufficient Preparation for the Eternal World? I hope, you now think, a more preparation to be Necessary. [. . .]

THE EXECUTION

AND now, speedily, that is to say, On Tuesday, the Sentence against the Evil Works of these Men, must be executed. One of the Four, namely, Condick, was Reprieved. As for Fly, he had been all along, a most uncommon and amazing Instance of Impenitency and Stupidity, and what Spectacles of Obduration the Wicked will be, when they have by a course of Wickedness under and against Warnings, provoked the GOD of Heaven to withhold His Influences from them. The Sullen and Raging Mood, into which he fell, upon his being first Imprisoned, caused him to break forth into furious Execrations, and Blasphemies too hideous to be mentioned; and not eat one morsel of anything, but subsist only upon a little Drinking, for almost all the remaining part of his Life. He declined appearing in the Public Assemblies, on the Lords-day, with the other Prisoners, to be under the appointed means of Grace, because, forsooth, he would not have the Mob to gaze upon him. He seemed all along ambitious to have it said, That he died a brave fellow. He passed along to the place of Execution, with a

Nosegay in his hand, and making his Complements, where he thought he saw occasion. Arriving there, he nimbly mounted the Stage, and would fain have put on a Smiling Aspect. He reproached the Hangman, for not understanding his Trade, and with his own Hands rectified matters, to render all things more Convenient and Effectual.

When he was called upon, to Speak what he should judge proper to be spoken on that sad occasion, at least for the Warning of Survivors, he only said, That he would advise the Masters of Vessels to carry it well to their Men, lest they should be put upon doing as he had done.

At the same time, he declared his obstinate Refusal, to Forgive the Person that had been the Instrument of bringing him to Justice. When the Necessity of that Charity was urgently pressed upon him; and advantage taken from a Recital of the Lords-Prayer used among the Devotions of the Criminals on the present Occasion, to urge it; he still persisted in his Unrelenting Frame; and an Expression of that Importance was in the last words, he Expired withal. But it was observed and is affirmed, by some Spectators, that in the Midst of all his affected Bravery, a very sensible Trembling attended him; His hands and his Knees were plainly seen to Tremble.—And so we must leave him for the Judgment to come.

The other Two, Cole and Greenville, had much greater Signs of Repentance upon them. They made their Prayers, and seemed continually praying, and much affected. They desired the Spectators to take Warning by them. And they mentioned Profane Swearing and Cursing, with Drunkenness and Sabbath-breaking, as Crimes which were now particularly grievous to them. They also justified the Court, as well as acknowledged the Justice of the Glorious GOD, in the Punishment they were now brought unto.

A Minister present having made a Pertinent and Pathetic Prayer, the Officer, willing that all that was possible might be done for their good, after some time, asked them, whether they would have another Prayer. Fly did not accept the offer, but said, If the other Two be Ready, I am! However, the other

Two desiring it, another such prayer was made by another Minister; and after that, another by a Third; with which they joined attentively. (while Fly looked about him unconcerned.)

Then the Execution was finished; And Fly's Carcass hanged in Chains, on an Island, at the Entrance into Boston-Harbor.

FANNY CAMPBELL

Lynn, Massachusetts, and Cuba

1775

Though her story takes place on a journey from Lynn, Massachusetts, to piratical exploits in Cuba, and her fame was so extensive that her face is often found on pieces of scrimshaw for decades into the nineteenth century, Fanny Campbell, female pirate captain, was fictional. She was the heroine of a best-selling novel published in 1844, written by "Lieutenant Murray," a pseudonym for Maturin Murray Ballou.[1] In the story, Fanny disguises herself as a man to rescue her lover, who has been taken prisoner by pirates, and becomes a noble privateer in service to the American revolutionary cause. As in so many examples of pirate truth and pirate fiction building upon and reinforcing each other, Fanny reportedly inspired a woman named Sarah Emma Edmonds to disguise herself as a man and fight on the side of the Union in the American Civil War, and in the 1870s a captain's wife named Maud Buckley obtained her own license to captain on Lake Michigan a triple-masted schooner that she named the Fanny Campbell.

Fanny managed to blush even through the deep tinge of brown that bronzed her handsome cheek. And when does a female look more interesting than when betraying the modest color of virtue. It is a rainbow from the heart showing it to be unvitiated by the evil and bitterness of the world.

"Shall I wear these to the end of the voyage?" asked Fanny.

"Ask no privilege of me," said Lovell, "you are still master and commander here, and will, I hope, continue so."

"I, too, have thought it best—indeed absolutely necessary that I should continue my disguise until our arrival in port."

"It is, certainly," said Lovell. "But tell me, Fanny, how you possibly could have attained the knowledge you have displayed in this emergency? For I am free to confess you have sailed this brig as well, and commanded these turbulent fellows, as I could have done it with years of experience."

"I'll tell thee, William. Soon after your departure from home, my heart being on the sea, I made almost every trip out with my father, for the whole season, until I understood fully the management of the schooner, which, you remember, was half a brig in its rig. I read, too, every nautical work I could procure, from love alone of the sea, where I knew you were, but never in my most romantic moments did I imagine that these acquirements would be of the service to me which they have proved. Of our kind friend Rev. Mr. Livingston, of Boston, I learned navigation, practically too, for you know he was for many years a seaman. Since then, experience and good fortune have done the rest."

"Thou has been a most apt scholar."

"Say rather a willing one, William."

"I may say both, and say truly."

"Stubborn as ever," said Fanny, playfully.

"But why have you kept concealed from me these four days?"

"I have confined myself below so much of the time to enable you to find yourself fairly at liberty before you should know that it was your Fanny who has released you, backed by a generous and active crew. I believed it best for many reasons and thought I should be happier to do so. I shall now appear as heretofore upon deck, and you shall see how willing and apt these fellows are. Would you believe it, William? They love me, I really believe, though I have put on a severity at times," and here Fanny scowled as fiercely as she might, by way of explanation.

"How could they help loving thee, Fanny?" said Lovell, pressing her fondly in his arms and impressing a kiss upon her lips.

"There, that will do," said she, gently unclasping his embrace, "you must not abate one iota in your respect or distance, William, while on deck, and before the people, or we may have another mutiny; be careful you address me as Captain Channing, don"t be forgetful."

"I'll remember, trust me."

The two then proceeded to the quarter-deck, Lovell paying the customary respect to his commanding officer.

"Sail ho!" shouted the look-out, with the long drawl peculiar to the hail.

"Where away?" promptly demanded the captain.

William Lovell could not disguise his nervousness lest Fanny should betray herself; now that he knew the secret of her disguise he feared that it might be disclosed at any moment. But there was nothing wanting; she was perfect even in all the minutiae of sea parlance.

"Two points on the starboard bow," answered the look out.

Fanny taking a glass, coolly surveyed the stranger for several minutes.

"English, I think," she observed to Lovell, referring to the stranger.

"I make her out so," was the reply.

"It remains to be seen whether we are to run or fight," said Captain Channing, (for so we will continue to call Fanny, who was still the same to the crew,) "It must be a fast vessel that the Constance cannot spare a topsail to."

The two vessels neared each other fast, and it was soon evident that the stranger was an English vessel of some five hundred tons, and consequently much larger than the *Constance*. That she was an armed vessel too, was soon quite evident, for suddenly a cloud of smoke burst from her bows, and anon the dull heavy report of a cannon came down across the water to the brig.

"Show them that pine tree, Mr. Lovell, that's what they want."[2]

"Ay, ay, sir," said the mate, promptly obeying the order.

But no sooner had the flag of the colonial Congress reached

its station aloft and expanded to the breeze, than the report of another gun came booming heavily over the sea from the stranger, and this time also a shot; but the ball fell far short of the brig and her consort, throwing a jet of spray aloft as it struck the sea and sunk into its depths.

The captain and the first mate conversed together earnestly for a few moments, when the captain turning towards the crew with a countenance beaming with spirit, said:

"Clear away the long-tom, and prepare for action!"

A dozen willing hands promptly executed the order, and the mate soon took his station by the gun to superintend its management, but not until he had in an under tone urged Fanny to leave the deck and secure herself below.

"What! Skulk below?" said Fanny, "No no, I have seen this game before."

"That's the talk," said Terrence Moony, as the order was given to clear away the gun. "Jist give me that crisscross flag of England to look at for an enemy and I'll fight all day, grub time and all. Arrah yes, ye blockheads," said he stripping himself to his shirt and trowsers to work at the gun. Terrence loved the English about as well as his satanic majesty affects holy water, and no more, believe us.

JOSE "GASPARILLA" GASPAR

Florida

1782

Since 1904 the city of Tampa, Florida, has hosted a "Gasparilla Pirate Festival" in honor of one of the many semi-mythical corsairs who raided in the Gulf of Mexico at the end of the eighteenth and the beginning of the nineteenth century. This account of Gasparilla, on the one hand, feels too vague to be credible, being riddled as it is with sexual licentiousness, Spanish royalty, and vague ship names, dates, and places.[1] But exist Gaspar did. His checkered career ended around 1820, at a time when would-be privateers sought ever-more-questionable commissions from newly independent or rebelling Spanish colonial holdings in Latin America to raid shipping under a sheen of legitimacy. Gaspar sailed a ship called the Jupiter *out of Saint-Barthélemy in the British West Indies under a supposed commission from Uruguay, plundering a Yankee ship named* Orleans *on August 19.[2] By the following October the USS* Grampus *had ended his piratical career, but Gasparilla's campaign marks a moment when the history of piracy and the myth of piracy begin to become entwined.*

His name was Jose Gaspar (Gasparilla meaning Gaspar, the outlaw). He stood high in the graces of the Spanish Court, so high indeed that he filched the crown jewels. Jose was also an of-

ficer of high standing in the naval affairs of the Spaniards. Some
records give him the honor of being what we would call an admiral. His theft discovered, he deserted his wife and children,
gathered together a nice lot of cut-throats, stole the prize vessel of the Spanish fleet, and escaped. This happened in the year
1782. A price was declared upon his head, and, it is stated,
when Gasparilla heard this decree, he swore eternal vengeance
upon all Spaniards in general, and commenced to destroy the
commerce of Spain.

The Gulf of Mexico at that time being a rendezvous for pirate fleets, Gaspar settled in Charlotte Harbor and built upon
the shores of what his now called Turtle Bay twelve houses,
where, under guard, his female captives were placed, all male
prisoners being killed when captured. The buildings were constructed of palmetto logs, and arranged in a semi-circle close
to the water's edge.

About one hundred yards further inland the burying ground
was discovered several years ago, containing not only the
bones of his men, but the skeletons of his murdered women
captives. Many a touching story has been unearthed when the
ghostly remains were uncovered—stories of great strong men
who died in the fight, of women who died to save their honor,
and of nobility we even find a trace, but these are only traditions, and the story of "The Little Spanish Princess," as told
by old Panther Key John Gomez, we will relate later on.

Close to Turtle Bay lies the little Isle of Cayopelean.[3] Upon
this island stood a burial mound fifty feet high and four hundred feet in circumference at the base, built centuries earlier, it
is thought, by the Mound Builders of a prehistoric race.[4] Exca-
vations in this mound have produced ornaments of gold and
silver, together with hundreds of human skeletons. On its summit Gasparilla constructed an observation tower, where always a grim sentinel was stationed and looked across the
warm, smiling waters of the Gulf for a victim.

The present Isle of Gasparilla the pirate named for himself.
Taking the best of everything when a capture was made, he
chose the best of the island in Charlotte Harbor for his own
secret haunts. It is said that Jose was saluted the King of the

Pirates, and his home on Gasparilla Island was regal in its fittings.

Some writers have said that Gasparilla joined Pierre LaFitte,[5] the famous French pirate, while others have stated on good authority that LaFitte joined Gasparilla's band, contributing a boat and thirty men.

While taking the census of 1900 two gentlemen stopped at Panther Key[6] and spent the night with John Gomez. The race of the old buccaneer was nearly run, but all through that night he told a story of piracy that could scarce be believed, yet it was a dying man that was clearing his soul before his Maker. He told of the looting of ships, the massacre of innocents, and last of all, when his life had nearly passed, he told the story of "The Little Spanish Princess," whose name he did not remember. He told where the body would be found, and a sketch was prepared under his direction, and in recent years in the exact location as described the skeleton of a beheaded woman was found. This is the story.

In the early days of the year 1801 a princess of Spain sailed in great state for Mexico. While in that country she was royally entertained by its Ruler, and to show her appreciation to the Mexican people she prevailed upon the nobles to allow her to take eleven of Mexico's fairest daughters away with her to be educated in Spanish customs. A treasure of much gold, bound in chests of copper, it is said, was in cargo. When about forty miles from what is now Boca Grande, Gasparilla engaged them in combat, killed the crew, took the gold, and carried away as captives the princess and the eleven Mexican girls. The princess he kept for himself, the maids were divided among his men. The little Spanish princess spurned the one-time favorite of the King, and Gasparilla swore that if she did not return of her own free will the affections lavished upon her, she would be beheaded, and the story goes the threat of Gaspar was fulfilled. Far away from her native land, alone on a tropical isle, the little princess still lies in the lonely bed made for her by Gasparilla. The night birds sing in the dusk and lull her spirit to rest in the evening, and the moon throws kindly shadows o'er the spot where royalty sleeps.

From members of Gaspar's crew many a strange story has drifted down concerning him, his traits, his ways, his passions. He was polished in his manners and a great lover of fashionable clothes; fearless in fight, and at all times cruel in his nature. Concerning women he was fanatical, and his houses were always filled with captives. It is stated beauty was essential with him. He kept for himself a certain number of picked beauties, but so fickle was his nature that when an additional capture was made and a new face appealed to him, one of his old loves must forfeit her life to make room for the new favorite. That this was true there is no doubt, as the graveyard of Gasparilla tells its own terrible story.

In 1819 the United States, having obtained, under the Louisiana Purchase in 1803, the states bordering on the Gulf, made war upon the robber bands. On Sanibel Island[7] a conference was held by all the pirates, and with the exception of Gasparilla, Baker, Caesar, and old King John, all sailed away, to be heard of no more.

Nearly two years later, the war on piracy becoming too severe, Jose and his crew agreed to divide their wealth, which was then estimated at thirty million dollars, to give up piracy, and live as honest men the rest of their lives. This was decided upon and plans made accordingly.

In the spring of 1822, while getting together his treasure for division, which at that time was hidden in six separate hiding places, he sited what appeared to be a large English merchantman just off Boca Grande Pass. It is said his greedy eyes lit with pleasure at the thoughts of just one more victim ere his piratical days were over. Closely following the shore-line of the Gulf, he slipped into Charlotte Harbor through what is now known as Little Gasparilla Pass, crept around Gasparilla Island, and gathered together his crew. Great excitement received when the plan were unfolded. The band of eighty men was divided into two parts, he commanding thirty-five men, LaFitte thirty-five, while ten were left in charge of the camp. At about four in the afternoon Gasparilla and his men dashed through the Boca Grande Pass for the English prize; fast overtaking the fleeing ship, the black flag was hoisted, and his men stood ready with the grappling hooks, but suddenly the English flag floated down and the Stars and Stripes pulled in place; in a moment guns were uncovered on deck, and Gasparilla, realizing that he was in a trap, turned to flee. His boat, disabled by the shots from the war vessel and capture staring him in the face, he wrapped a piece of anchor chain around his waist and jumped into the sea. His age at his death was about sixty-five. His crew was hanged at the yardarms, with the exception of the cabin boy and the ten men left in charge of the captives, they having escaped to the mainland. Panther Key John was in this gang. The cabin-boy was carried to New Orleans, where he remained in prison ten years.

THE
NINETEENTH
CENTURY

FIRST BARBARY WAR

Algeria, Tunis, Tripoli

1801–05

*When is piracy not piracy? The First Barbary War
was in some respects the first international incident
that the newly formed United States had to deal
with, and the rhetoric of "piracy" was deployed to
justify military action, but the Barbary pirates weren't
pirates in exactly the same way as we have been
defining it, if we define a pirate as an extralegal
independent operator seeking to make his own fortune. In 1785 Thomas Jefferson, then Secretary of
State, received a plaintive letter from a mariner
named Richard O'Brien (the spelling of his name
varies in the correspondence), describing his ship
being seized by Algerian raiders, who kept all the
sailors aboard as slaves. O'Brien begged Jefferson to
intercede on their behalf. But the Barbary pirates
were acting on the instructions of the deys of the
Barbary Coast. The deys expected tribute to be paid
by all European and American ships wanting to
trade in the Mediterranean. Was this so different,
crucially, from a decade old nation funding itself
primarily by levying port taxes? The deys held the
enslaved captives out of a desire to force tribute
and to maintain their influence and control as war-
lords. There was even some correspondence between Jefferson and other members of the cabinet,
wondering if O'Brien's letters were credible—after
all, what man imprisoned in blistering sun in Algeria
with only a blanket, forced to break rocks every day*

on a diet of gruel, crushed olives, and vinegar, has pen, ink, and paper and leisure enough to write Thomas Jefferson letters? But true it was, even if his correspondence served a dual purpose, of the city-states of the Barbary Coast reaching lucrative agreements with the new United States and of the United States ginning up a legitimate reason to establish a Navy that would come in handy for the coming hostilities with Great Britain.

There is, of course, a certain bitter irony to the sailors' appeal to Thomas Jefferson, himself a slaveowner.

From Richard
O'Bryen[1]
Algier august the
24th. 1785

Sir

We the Subjects of the United States of America Having the Misfortune of Being Captured off The Coast of Portugal the 24th. and 30th. of July By the Algerines, and Brought into this port Where we have Become Slaves, and Sent To the workhouses, Our Sufferings is Beyond Our Expressing or your Conception. Hoping your Honor will be pleased to represent Our Grievances to Congress. Hoping They will Take Such Measures as to tend to our speedy Redemption. Hoping you will Consider our Unfortunate Situation, and Make some provision for the Unfortunate Sufferers, Until we are redeemed, Being Stript of all our Cloaths and nothing to Exist on But two small Cakes of Bread per day, without any other Necessary of Life. Charles Logie Esqr. British Consul seeing our distressed Situation has taken us Three Masters of Vessels out of the Work Houses and has Given Security for us to the Dey of Algiers, King of Cruelties. My Crew Certainly will Starve if There is not Some Immediate Relief. It Being the Method of all Christian powers whose Subjects falls in the Hands of Those

Savages to Make Some provision for them, until they are redeemed, I should Esteem it a particular favor If you would be pleased to write to Mr. Logie, Consul here.

Ship *Dauphin*, Richd. OBryen Master, Belonging to Messrs. Mathew and Thomas Irwin & Co. Merchants of the City of Philadelphia Bound to Philadelphia from St. Ubes. Taken the 30th. July, out two Days.

Schooner *Maria*, Isiack Stevens Master, from Boston bound to Cadiz, Belonging to Messrs. Wm. Foster & Co. Merchants in Boston. Taken the 24th. July, Out 26 Days.

The Cruisers in This port are fitting out With all possible Expedition and I Am of That Opinion They will Take Most of Our Ships that will come for Europe. They will Cruise to The Northward of the Western Islands and towards the British Channel. The Sooner we Could put a stop to them the Better, they Valuing the Number of prizes they take, To the Sum for the Peace. The Spaniards Coming on terms with them, all other European Nations must. I hope we shall apply Before any more does, for they Must Be at war with Some.

I am very respectfully your most obedt. and very Humble Servant & Petitioner,

Richd. OBryen

"To the Honourable Plenipotentary of
The United States of America At Paris";
endorsed in an unidentified hand.

IV. REPORT ON AMERICAN CAPTIVES IN ALGIERS[2]

The Secretary of State, having had under Consideration the Situation of the Citizens of the United States in Captivity at Algiers, makes the following Report thereupon to the President of the United States.

When the House of Representatives, at their late Session,

were pleased to refer to the Secretary of State, the Petition of our Citizens in Captivity at Algiers, there still existed some Expectation that certain Measures, which had been employed to effect their Redemption, the Success of which depended on their Secrecy, might prove effectual.

Information received during the Recess of Congress, has so far weakened those Expectations as to make it now a Duty to lay before the President of the United States, a full Statement of what has been attempted for the Relief of these our suffering Citizens, as well before, as since he came into Office, that he may be enabled to decide what further is to be done.

On the 25th. of July 1785, the Schooner *Maria*, Captain Stevens, belonging to a Mr. Foster of Boston, was taken off Cape St. Vincents, by an Algerine Corsair: and five days afterwards, the Ship *Dauphin*, Captain Obrian, belonging to Messrs. Irwins of Philadelphia, was taken by another Algerine, about 50. Leagues Westward of Lisbon. These Vessels, with their Cargoes and Crews, twenty one Persons in Number, were carried into Algiers.

Congress had, some Time before, commissioned Ministers Plenipotentiary for entering into Treaties of Amity and Commerce with the Barbary Powers, and to send them proper Agents for preparing such Treaties. An Agent was accordingly appointed for Algiers, and his Instructions prepared, when the Ministers Plenipotentiary received Information of these Captures. Though the Ransom of Captives was not among the Objects expressed in their Commissions, because at their Dates the Case did not exist, yet they thought it their Duty to undertake that Ransom, fearing that the Captives might be sold and dispersed through the interior and distant Countries of Africa, if the previous Orders of Congress should be waited for. They therefore added a supplementary Instruction, to the Agent, to negociate their Ransom. But while acting thus without Authority, they thought themselves bound to offer a Price so moderate as not to be disapproved. They, therefore, restrained him to Two hundred Dollars a Man; which was something less than had been just before paid for about Three hundred French Captives, by the Mathurins, a religious Order of France, instituted in ancient Times for the Redemption of Christian Captives from the infidel Powers. On the Arrival of the Agent at Algiers, the Dey demanded Fifty nine thousand four hundred and ninety six Dollars for the Twenty one Captives, and could not be brought to abate but little from that Demand. The Agent, therefore, returned in 1786, without having effected either Peace or Ransom. In the Beginning of the next Year, 1787, the Minister Plenipotentiary of the United States at Paris procured an Interview with the General of the religious Order of Mathurins, before mentioned, to engage him to lend his Agency, at the Expence of the United States, for the Redemption of their captive Citizens. He proffered, at once, all the Services he could render, with the Liberality and the Zeal which distinguish his Character. He observed that he had Agents on the Spot, constantly employed in seeking out, and redeeming the Captives of their own Country; that these should act for us, as for themselves; that Nothing could be accepted for their Agency; and that he would only expect that the Price of Redemption should be ready on our Part, so as to cover the Engagement into which he should enter. He added that, by the Time all Expences were paid, their last Redemption had amounted to near Two thousand five hundred Livres a Man, and that he could by no Means flatter us that they could redeem our Captives as cheap as their own. The Pirates would take Advantage of it's being out of their ordinary Line. Still he was in Hopes they would not be much higher.

The Proposition was submitted to Congress, that is to say, in February 1787, and on the 19th. of September, in the same Year, their Minister Plenipotentiary at Paris, received their Orders to embrace the Offers of the Mathurins. This he immediately notified to the General, observing, however, that he did not desire him to enter into any Engagements, till a sufficient Sum to cover them should be actually deposited in Paris. The General wished that the whole might be kept rigorously secret, as, should the Barbarians suspect him to be acting for the

United States, they would demand such Sums as he could never agree to give, even with our Consent, because it would injure his future Purchases from them. He said he had Information from his Agent at Algiers, that our Captives received so liberal a daily Allowance as to evince that it came from a public Source. He recommended that this should be discontinued, engaging that he would have an allowance administered to them, much short, indeed, of what they had hitherto received, but such as was given to his own Countrymen, quite Sufficient for physical Necessaries, and more likely to prepare the Opinion that, as they were subsisted by his Charity, they were to be redeemed by it also.

These Ideas, suggested to him by the Danger of raising his Market, were approved by the Minister Plenipotentiary, because this being the first Instance of a Redemption by the United States, it would form a Precedent; because a high Price given by us, might induce these Pirates to abandon all other Nations in pursuit of Americans, whereas the contrary would take place, could our Price of Redemption be fixed at the lowest Point.

To destroy, therefore, every Expectation of a Redemption by the United States, the Bills of the Spanish Consul at Algiers, who had made the Kind Advances before spoken of, for the Sustenance of our Captives, were not answered. On the Contrary, a Hint was given that these Advances had better be discontinued, as it was not known that they would be reimbursed. It was necessary even to go further, and to suffer the Captives themselves and their Friends to believe, for a while that no Attention was paid to them, no Notice taken of their Letters. They are still under this Impression. It would have been unsafe to trust them with a Secret, the disclosure of which might forever prevent their Redemption, by raising the Demands of the Captors to Sums which a due Regard for our Seamen, still in Freedom, would forbid us to give. This was the most trying of all Circumstances, and drew from them the most afflicting Reproaches.

It was a Twelvemonth afterwards before the Money could be deposited in Paris, and the Negociation be actually put into Train. In the meantime the General had received Information from Algiers of a very considerable Change of Prices there. Within the last two or three Years the Spaniards, the Neapolitans, and the Russians had redeemed at exorbitant Sums. Slaves were become scarce, and would hardly be sold at any Price. Still he entered on the Business with an Assurance of doing the Best in his Power, and he was authorized to offer as far as Three thousand Livres or Five hundred and fifty five Dollars a Man. He wrote immediately to consult a confidential Agent at Marseilles, on the best Mode of carrying this Business into Effect; from whom he received the Answer hereto annexed.

Nothing further was known of his Progress or Prospects when the House of Representatives were pleased, at their last Session, to refer the Petition of our Captives at Algiers to the Secretary of State. The preceding Narrative shews that no Report could have then been made without risking the Object, of which some Hopes were still entertained. Later Advices, however, from the Chargé des Affaires of the United States, at Paris, inform us that these Measures, though not yet desperate, are not to be counted on. Besides the Exorbitance of Price, before feared, the late Transfer of the Lands and Revenues of the Clergy, in France, to the Public, by withdrawing the Means, seems to have suspended the Proceedings of the Mathurins in the Purposes of their Institution. It is Time, therefore, to look about for something more promising, without relinquishing, in the meanwhile, the Chance of Success through them. Endeavours to collect Information, which have been continued a considerable Time, as to the Ransoms which would probably be demanded from us, and those actually paid by other Nations, enable the Secretary of State to lay before the President the following short View, collected from original Papers now in his Possession, or from Information delivered to him personally.

Passing over the Ransoms of the Mathurins, which are kept far below the common Level, by special Circumstances;

In 1786, the Dey of Algiers demanded from our Agent 59,496 Dollars for 21 Captives, which was 2,833 Dollars a Man. The Agent flattered himself they could be ransomed for 1200 Dollars apiece. His Secretary informed us, at the same Time, that Spain had paid 1600 Dollars.

In 1787, the Russians redeemed at 1546 Dollars a Man.

In 1788, a well informed Inhabitant of Algiers, assured the Minister Plenipotentiary of the United States, at Paris, that no Nation had redeemed, since the Spanish Treaty, at less than from 250 to 300 Pounds sterling, the medium of which is 1237 Dollars. Captain Obrian, at the same Date, thinks we must pay 1800 Dollars, and mentions a Savoy Captain, just redeemed at 4074 Dollars.

In 1789, Mr. Logie, the English Consul at Algiers, informed a Person who wished to ransom one of our common Sailors, that he would cost from 450 to 500 Pounds Sterling, the Mean of which is 2137 Dollars. In December of the same Year, Captain Obrian thinks our Men will now cost 2920 Dollars each, though a Jew Merchant believes he could get them for 2264 Dollars.

In 1790, July 9th. a Mr. Simpson, of Gibraltar, who at some particular Request, had taken Pains to find for what Sum our Captives could be redeemed, finds that the Fourteen will cost 34,792 28/38 Dollars, which is 2485 Dollars a Man. At the same Date, one of them, a Scotch Boy, a common Mariner, was actually redeemed at 8,000 Livres, equal to 1481 Dollars, which is within 19 Dollars of the Price Simpson states for common Men: and the Chargé des Affaires of the United States at Paris is informed that the Whole may be redeemed at that Rate, adding Fifty per Cent on the Captains, which would bring it to 1571 Dollars a Man.

It is found then that the Prices are 1200. 1237. 1481. 1546. 1571. 1600. 1800. 2137. 2264, 2485. 2833. and 2920. Dollars a Man, not noticing that of 4074. Dollars, because it was for a Captain.

In 1786, there were 2200 Captives in Algiers, which in 1789 had been reduced by Death or Ransom to 655. Of ours six have died, and one has been ransomed by his Friends.

From these Facts and Opinions some Conjecture may be formed of the Terms on which the Liberty of our Citizens may be obtained.

But should it be thought better to repress Force by Force, another Expedient, for their Liberation, may perhaps offer. Captures made on the Enemy, may perhaps put us into Possession of some of their Mariners, and Exchange be substituted for Ransom. It is not, indeed, a fixed Usage with them to exchange Prisoners. It is rather their Custom to refuse it. However such Exchanges are sometimes effected, by allowing them more or less of Advantage. They have sometimes accepted of two Moors for a Christian, at others, they have refused five or six for one. Perhaps Turkish Captives may be Objects of greater Partiality with them, as their Government is entirely in the Hands of Turks, who are treated, in every Instance as a superior Order of Beings. Exchange, too, will be more practicable in our Case, as our Captives have not been sold to private Individuals, but are retained in the hands of the Government.

The Liberation of our Citizens has an intimate Connection with the Liberation of our Commerce in the Mediterranean, now under the Consideration of Congress. The Distresses of both proceed from the same Cause, and the Measures which shall be adopted for the Relief of the one, may very probably involve the Relief of the other.

Th: Jefferson Secretary of State
Dec. 28. 1790.

Enclosed with this was Simpson's "List of American Prisoners at Algiers 9th July 1790 with the sums demanded by the Regency for their ransom," reading as follows:

"Crew of the Ship *Dolphin* captured 30th July 1785.

Richard O Bryan	Captain	ransom demanded Zs	2000
Andrew Montgomery	Mate		1500
Jacob Tessanier	French passenger		2000
William Paterson	Seaman	(Keeps a Tavern)	1500
Philip Sloan	"		725
Peleg Lorin	"		725
John Robertson	"		725
James Hall	"		725

Crew of the Schooner *Mary* taken 25th July 1785.

Isaac Stephens	Captain		2000
Alexander Forsyth	Mate		1500
James Cathcart	Seaman	(Keeps a Tavern)	900
George Smith	"	(in the King's house)	725
John Gregory	"		725
James Hermit	"		725
		Algerine Sequines	16,475
	Duty on the above sum, 10 Pr. %		1647½
	Sundry gratifications to Officers of the Dey's household and Regency, equal to 171/6 Zs. each person		240⅛
	34,792. 28/38—Mexican dollars @ 38 Mozunas each are Zequins		18,362.5/6"

STERRET'S SEA FIGHT.[3]

Stand to your guns my hearts of oak,
Let no word on board be spoke,
Victory soon will crown the joke;
Be silent and be ready.
Ram down your guns and spunge them well,
Let us be sure the balls will tell,
The cannons' roar shall sound their knell;
Be steady boys, be steady.
Not yet, nor yet—reserve your fire,
Says brave Sterret—Fire!
And sink those Moorish Tripolines,
All were amaz'd who beheld the scenes.
A broadside my boys.
See the blood in purple tide,
Trickle down her batter'd side;
Wing'd with fate the bullets fly,
Conquer boys—or bravely die.
Be steady and defend your rights.
She's silent—huzza!
To Columbia's flag she strikes.

ZHENG YI SAO

South China Sea and Macau

1801–1810

In the first decades of the nineteenth century, the South China Sea became as much a hotbed of piracy as the Caribbean had been a hundred years before. From around 1775 through 1810, groups of internally organized pirates in competing fleets controlled the South China Sea. Whereas earlier waves of piracy in this region had been surreptitiously backed by Western governments for their own purposes, this period of Chinese piracy grew from, among other things, a rise in the standard of living that was unequally shared. Fishing and maritime communities along the Chinese coast suffered from low wages and economic pressures that were worsened by an unusual volume of natural disasters: crop failures, typhoons, and food shortages. At the same time, the Tay Son rebellion in nearby Vietnam provided patronage to organized pirate bands and contributed to the relative lawlessness on the waters.[1]

South China Sea pirates had their share of charismatic leaders, but perhaps the most celebrated of these was Zheng Yi Sao, who was the wife of the famous pirate Zheng Yi. She was born in 1775 in Guangdong and married in 1801. When Tay Son patronage for Chinese pirates ended around 1802, Zheng Yi and Zheng Yi Sao established an agreement that created the Guangdong Pirate Confederation, in which pirate fleets retained some autonomy, each raiding under their own colored banner. Zheng Yi and Zheng Yi Sao commanded the Red Banner fleet. When her husband was washed overboard in 1807, Zheng Yi Sao assumed sole control and rose to a position of prominence within the Guangdong Pirate Confederation. She negotiated a surrender to the Qing leadership in 1810 that enabled her and her husband's adopted son, who later become her lover, to retain control of a substantial portion of their fleet. She died in 1844.

The following perspective on the South China Sea pirates under Zheng Yi Sao's control was written by Richard Glasspoole, a mate on the British East India Company ship Marquis of Ely *who was taken prisoner by pirates of the Red Banner fleet in 1809 and lived among them as a captive for two months, awaiting his ransom.*

A BRIEF NARRATIVE OF MY CAPTIVITY AND TREATMENT AMONGST THE LADRONES[2,3]

On the 17th of September 1809, the Honourable Company's ship *Marquis of Ely* anchored under the Island of Sam Chow, in China, about twelve English miles from Macao, where I was ordered to proceed in one of our cutters to procure a pilot, and also to land the purser with the packet.[4] I left the ship at 5 p.m. with seven men under my command, well armed. It blew a fresh gale from the N. E. We arrived at Macao at 9 p.m., where I delivered the packet to Mr. Roberts, and sent the men with the boat's sails to sleep under the Company's Factory,[5] and left the boat in charge of one of the Compradore's[6] men; during the night the gale increased.—At half-past three in the morning I went to the beach, and found the boat on shore half-filled with water, in consequence of the man having left her. I called the people, and baled her out; found she was considerably damaged, and very leaky. At half-past 5 a.m., the ebb-tide make, we left Macao with vegetables for the ship.

One of the Compradore's men who spoke English went with us for the purpose of piloting the ship to Lintin, as the Mandarines, in consequence of a late disturbance at Macao, would not grant chops[7] for the regular pilots. I had every reason to expect the ship in the roads,[8] as she was preparing to get under weigh when we left her; but on our rounding Cabaretta-Point, we saw her five or six miles to leeward, under weigh, standing on the starboard-tack:[9] it was then blowing fresh at N. E. Bore up, and stood towards her; when about a cable's-length[10] to windward of her, she tacked; we hauled our wind[11] and stood after her. A hard squall then coming on, with a strong tide and heavy swell against us, we drifted fast to leeward, and the weather being hazy, we soon lost sight of the ship. Struck our masts, and endeavoured to pull;[12] finding our efforts useless, set a reefed foresail and mizen, and stood towards a country-ship[13] at anchor under the land to leeward of Cabaretta-Point, When within a quarter of a mile of her she weighed and made sail, leaving us in a very critical situation, having no anchor, and drifting bodily on the rock to leeward. Struck the masts: after four or five hours hard pulling, succeeded in clearing them.

[. . .]

Our situation was now truly distressing, night closing fast, with a threatening appearance, blowing fresh, with hard rain and a heavy sea; our boat very leaky, without a compass, anchor or provisions, and drifting fast on a lee-shore,[14] surrounded with dangerous rocks, and inhabited by the most barbarous pirates. I close-reefed my sails,[15] and kept tack and tack[16] 'till day-light, when we were happy to find we had drifted very little to leeward of our situation in the evening. The night was very dark, with constant hard squalls and heavy rain.

[. . .]

Wednesday the 20th at day-light, supposed the flood-tide making, weighed and stood over to the weather-land,[17] but found we were drifting fast to leeward. About ten o'clock perceived two Chinese boats steering for us. Bore up,[18] and stood towards them, and made signals to induce them to come

within hail; on nearing them, they bore up, and passed to leeward of the islands. The Chinese we had in the boat advised
me to follow them, and he would take us to Macao by the leeward passage. I expressed my fears of being taken by the
Ladrones. Our ammunition being wet, and the muskets rendered useless, we had nothing to defend ourselves with but
cutlasses, and in too distressed a situation to make much resistance with them, having been constantly wet, and eat nothing
but a few green oranges for three days.

As our present situation was a hopeless one, and the man assured me there was no fear of encountering any Ladrones, I
complied with his request, and stood in to leeward of the islands,[19] where we found the water much smoother, and apparently a direct passage to Macao. We continued pulling and
sailing all day. At six o'clock in the evening I discovered three
large boats at anchor in a bay to leeward. On seeing us they
weighed and made sail towards us. The Chinese said they were
Ladrones, and that if they captured us they would most certainly put us all to death! Finding they gained fast on us,
struck the masts, and pulled head to wind[20] for five or six
hours. The tide turning against us, anchored close under the
land to avoid being seen. Soon after we saw the boats pass us
to leeward.

Thursday the 21st, at day-light, the flood making, weighed
and pulled along shore in great spirits, expecting to be at
Macao in two or three hours, as by the Chinese account it was
not above six or seven miles distant.[21] After pulling a mile or
two perceived several people on shore, standing close to the
beach; they were armed with pikes and lances. I ordered the
interpreter to hail them, and ask the most direct passage to
Macao. They said if we came on shore they would inform us;
not liking their hostile appearance I did not think proper to
comply with the request. Saw a large fleet of boats at anchor
close under the opposite shore. Our interpreter said they were
fishing-boats, and that by going there we should not only get
provisions, but a pilot also to take us to Macao.

I bore up, and on nearing them perceived there were some
large vessels, very full of men, and mounted with several guns.

I hesitated to approach nearer; but the Chinese assuring me they were Mandarine junks[22] and salt-boats, we stood close to one of them, and asked the way to Macao? They gave no answer, but made some signs to us to go in shore. We passed on, and a large row-boat pulled after us; she soon came alongside, when about twenty savage-looking villains, who were stowed at the bottom of the boat, leaped on board us. They were armed with a short sword in each hand, one of which they laid on our necks, and the other pointed to our breasts, keeling their eyes fixed on their officer, waiting his signal to cut or desist. Seeing we were incapable of making any resistance, he sheathed his sword, and the others immediately followed his example. They then dragged us into their boat, and carried us on board one of their junks, with the most savage demonstrations of joy, and as we supposed, to torture and put us to a cruel death. When on board the junk, they searched all our pockets, took the handkerchiefs from our necks, and brought heavy chains to chain us to the guns.

At this time a boat came, and took me, with one of my men and the interpreter, on board the chief's vessel. I was then taken before the chief. He was seated on deck, in a large chair, dressed in purple silk, with a black turban on. He appeared to be about thirty years of age, a stout commanding-looking man. He took me by the coat, and drew me close to him; then questioned the interpreter very strictly, asking who we were, and what was our business in that part of the country. I told him to say we were Englishmen in distress, having been four days at sea without provisions. This he would not credit, but said we were bad men, and that he would put us all to death; and then ordered some men to put the interpreter to the torture until he confessed the truth.

Upon this occasion, a Ladrone, who had been once to England and spoke a few words of English, came to the chief, and told him we were really Englishmen, and that we had plenty of money, adding, that the buttons on my coat were gold. The chief then ordered us some coarse brown rice, of which we made a tolerable meal, having eat nothing for nearly four days, except a few green oranges. During our repast, a number of Ladrones crowded round us, examining our clothes and hair, and giving us every possible annoyance. Several of them brought swords, and laid them on our necks, making signs that they would soon take us on shore, and cut us in pieces, which I am sorry to say was the fate of some hundreds during my captivity.

JEAN LAFFITE

New Orleans, Barataria, and Galveston

1810–1821

The Golden Age of Piracy was largely a memory after the 1730s, due in part to the lessening of treasure exports from New Spain, the fracturing of colonial holdings in the Americas as different communities sought to self-govern, and changes in labor and economics in maritime communities. But in the Gulf of Mexico and into the Caribbean as the nineteenth century dawned, there were still pirates to be found. Much of their raiding was of the slave trade.

Jean Laffite is the most notorious pirate of the Gulf of Mexico, having establishments first in a smuggling outpost in the swamps of Louisiana outside the Balize, on an island called Grande-Terre in a small bay called Barataria, and later on the sandy barrier island of Galveston, Texas, now a sleepy beach community (except during spring break) about an hour's drive from Houston. Laffite's pirating enterprises were largely built on seizing slave ships and laundering the human cargo once the importation of slaves had been banned in the United States. The ensuing accounts offer snapshot pictures of the role that the newly ascendant United States Navy played in the policing of piracy as the century began.

Jean Laffite's antecedents are vague, but famously, when Governor Claiborne of Louisiana put a bounty on his head, he in turn offered one for Governor Claiborne. He attained a semi-mythic status in Texas and Louisiana, though it's worth noting, before we

get too romantic about him, that he made his pirati-
cal fortune by laundering black market enslaved
people over the Sabine into Louisiana to work on
sugarcane plantations, and he sold them for a dollar
a pound.

[Jean Laffite's] career is, naturally, shrouded in a good deal of
obscurity and uncertainty, but after much searching and trouble on the author's part, it was discovered that Lafitte was
born in France in 1780; some authorities giving St. Malo as
the place of his birth, others maintaining that he first saw the
light of day at Bordeaux . . . Lafitte is said to have gone to New
Orleans in 1807; and it is perfectly well known that about
1810–12 he was at the head of an organized and formidable
band of desperadoes, whose headquarters were on the island
of Grand Terre, in Barataria Bay, some thirty or forty miles
west of the mouth of the Mississippi.[1]
    Acting ostensibly under the flag of the republic of Cartha-
gena (or New Grenada), it was, however, perfectly well known
and admitted that these adventurers preyed practically on the
vessels of any nation. The bay of Barataria afforded a secure
retreat for their fleet of small craft; and their goods were smug-
gled into New Orleans by being conveyed in boats through an
intricate labyrinth of lakes, bayous and swamps, to a point
near the Mississippi river a little above the city. After various
ineffectual presentments and prosecutions before the civil tri-
bunals, an expedition was dispatched against the Baratarians
in 1814, under the command of Commodore Patterson. The
settlement on Grande Terre was captured, with all the vessels
that happened to be in port at the time; but Lafitte and his
comrades made their escape among the swamps and bayous of
the interior, from which they returned to the same rendezvous
and resumed operations as soon as Commodore Patterson's
forces had retired.

About the same time the British, then maturing their plans for a descent upon the southern coast of the United States, made overtures to Lafitte for the purpose of securing his co-operation in that enterprise. A brig-of-war was dispatched to Barataria, her commander bearing a letter from Commodore Percy, commanding the British naval forces in the Gulf of Mexico, and one from Colonel Nichols, then in command of the land forces on the coast of Florida, offering Lafitte 130,000 and a commission in the British navy, on condition of obtaining his services in conducting the contemplated expedition to New Orleans and distributing a certain proclamation to the inhabitants of Louisiana. Lafitte dissembled with the British officer, Capt. Lockyer, of the *Sophia*, who was the bearer of these tempting proposals, and asked for time to consider them.

Meantime he immediately wrote to Gov. Claiborne of Louisiana, enclosing the documents that had been handed him by Capt. Lockyer, informing the governor of the impending invasion, pointing out the importance of the position he occupied, and offering his services in defense of Louisiana, on the sole condition of pardon for himself and followers for the offences with which they stood charged. This amnesty would, of course, include in its provisions a brother of Jean Lafitte, who was then in prison in New Orleans under an indictment for piracy. After some hesitation on the part of the United States authorities, Lafitte's offer was accepted.

In connection with an officer of the U.S. corps of engineers, he was employed in fortifying the passes of Barataria bay, and rendered efficient service, in command of a party of his followers, in the battle of New Orleans, Jan. 8th, 1815. The subsequent career of Lafitte is involved in as much obscurity as his earlier life. A proclamation of President Madison confirmed the amnesty which had been granted by Governor Claiborne to all the Baratarians who had enlisted in the American service, though it does not appear that their chief ever received any further reward from the government. After the war Lafitte soon returned to his old pursuits, taking a privateer's commission, either, as formerly, from the government of New Grenada, or else from that of Mexico; and that, while thus engaged, he formed a settlement on the site of the present city of Galveston, which was broken up in 1821 by a naval force under the orders of Lieutenant, afterwards Commodore, Kearney.

It is quite possible, however, that his brother Pierre, who commanded one of his vessels, has been confounded with him. His death is attributed by different authorities to foundering at sea, to being burned with his vessel after capture by a Spanish man-of-war, and to wounds received in a desperate conflict with a British cruiser. There are yet other versions; while one account states that he returned to France and died among his relatives on the Garonne. In person Lafitte is represented as having been well-formed and handsome, about six feet two inches in height, with large hazel eyes and black hair. His appearance was totally unlike the popular idea of a pirate, his manners were polished and easy, though retiring; his address was winning and affable; his management of piracy entirely business-like, just as his influence over his followers was almost absolute.

The piratical establishment of Barrataria having been broken up and Lafitte not being content with leading an honest, peaceful life, procured some fast sailing vessels, and with a great number of his followers, proceeded to Galvezton Bay, in Texas, during the year 1819; where he received a commission from General Long; and had five vessels generally cruising and about 300 men.[2] Two open boats bearing commissions from General Humbert, of Galvezton, having robbed a plantation on the Marmento river, of negroes, money, &c. were captured in the Sabine river,[3] by the boats of the United States schooner *Lynx*. One of the men was hung by Lafitte, who dreaded the vengeance of the American government. The *Lynx* also captured one of his schooners, and her prize that had been for a length of time smuggling in the Carmento. One of his cruisers, named the *Jupiter*, returned safe to Galvezton after a short cruise with a valuable cargo, principally specie; she was the first vessel that sailed under the authority of Texas. The American government well knowing that where Lafitte was, piracy and smuggling would be the order of the day, sent a vessel of war to cruise in the Gulf of Mexico, and scour the coasts of Texas. Lafitte having been appointed governor of Galvezton and one of the cruisers being stationed off the port to watch his motions, it so annoyed him that he wrote the following letter to her commander, Lieutenant Madison.

"TO THE COMMANDANT OF THE AMERICAN CRUISER, OFF THE PORT OF GALVEZTON.

Sir-

I am convinced that you are a cruiser of the navy, ordered by your government. I have therefore deemed it proper to inquire into the cause of your lying before this port without communicating your intention. I shall by this message inform you, that the port of Galvezton belongs to and is in the possession of the republic of Texas,[4] and was made a port of entry the 9th October last. And whereas the supreme congress of said republic have thought proper to appoint me as governor of this place,[5] in consequence of which, if you have any demands on said government, or persons belonging to or residing in the same, you will please to send an officer with such demands, whom you may be assured will be treated with the greatest politeness, and receive every satisfaction required. But if you are ordered, or should attempt to enter this port in a hostile manner, my oath and duty to the government compels me to rebut your intentions at the expense of my life.

To prove to you my intentions towards the welfare and harmony of your government, I send enclosed the declaration of several prisoners, who were taken in custody yesterday, and by a court of inquiry appointed for that purpose, were found guilty of robbing the inhabitants of the United States of a number of slaves and specie. The gentleman bearing this

message will give you any reasonable information relating to
this place, that may be required.

Yours, &c.

J. LAFITTE.

About this time one Mitchell, who had formerly belonged to
Lafitte's gang, collected upwards of one hundred and fifty desperadoes and fortified himself on an island near Barrataria,
with several pieces of cannon; and swore that he and all his
comrades would perish within their trenches before they would
surrender to any man. Four of this gang having gone to New
Orleans on a frolic, information was given to the city watch,
and the house surrounded, when the whole four with cocked
pistols in both hands sallied out and marched through the
crowd which made way for them and no person dared to make
an attempt to arrest them.

The United States cutter, *Alabama*, on her way to the station off the mouth of the Mississippi, captured a piratical schooner belonging to Lafitte; she carried two guns and twenty-five
men, and was fitted out at New Orleans, and commanded by
one of Lafitte's lieutenants, named Le Page; the schooner had
a prize in company and being hailed by the cutter, poured into
her a volley of musketry; the cutter then opened upon the privateer and a smart action ensued which terminated in favor of
the cutter, which had four men wounded and two of them
dangerously; but the pirate had six men killed; both vessels
were captured and brought into the Bayou St. John.[6] An expedition was now sent to dislodge Mitchell and his comrades
from the island he had taken possession of; after coming to anchor, a summons was sent for him to surrender, which was answered by a brisk cannonade from his breastwork. The vessels
were warped close in shore; and the boats manned and sent on
shore whilst the vessels opened upon the pirates; the boat's
crews landed under a galling fire of grape shot and formed in
the most undaunted manner; and although a severe loss was

sustained they entered the breastwork at the point of the bayonet; after a desperate fight the pirates gave way, many were
taken prisoners, but Mitchell and the greatest part escaped to
the Cypress swamps where it was impossible to arrest them. A
large quantity of dry goods and specie together with other
booty was taken. Twenty of the pirates were taken and brought
to New Orleans, and tried before Judge Hall, of the Circuit
Court of the United States, sixteen were brought in guilty; and
after the Judge had finished pronouncing sentence of death
upon the hardened wretches, several of them cried out in open
court, *Murder—by God*.

Accounts of these transactions having reached Lafitte, he
plainly perceived there was a determination to sweep all his
cruisers from the sea; and a war of extermination appeared to
be waged against him. In a fit of desperation he procured a
large and fast sailing brigantine mounting sixteen guns and
having selected a crew of one hundred and sixty men he started
without any commission as a regular pirate determined to rob
all nations and neither to give or receive quarter. A British
sloop of war which was cruising in the Gulf of Mexico, having
heard that Lafitte himself was at sea, kept a sharp look out
from the mast head; when one morning as an officer was
sweeping the horizon with his glass he discovered a long dark
looking vessel low in the water, but having very tall masts,
with sails white as the driven snow. As the sloop of war had
the weather gage[7] of the pirate and could outsail her before the
wind, she set her studding sails and crowded every inch of can-
vass in chase; as soon as Lafitte ascertained the character of
his opponent, he ordered the awnings to be furled and set his
big squaresail and shot rapidly through the water; but as the
breeze freshened the sloop of war came up rapidly with the
pirate, who finding no chance of escaping, determined to sell
his life as dearly as possible; the guns were cast loose and the
shot handed up; and a fire opened upon the ship which killed
a number of men and carried away her foretopmast, but she
reserved her fire until within cable's distance of the pirate;
when she fired a general discharge from her broadside, and a
volley of small arms; the broadside was too much elevated to

hit the low hull of the brigantine,[8] but was not without effect; the foretopmast fell, the jaws of the main gaff were severed and a large proportion of the rigging came rattling down on deck; ten of the pirates were killed, but Lafitte remained unhurt. The sloop of war entered her men over the starboard bow and a terrific contest with pistols and cutlasses ensued; Lafitte received two wounds at this time which disabled him, a grape shot broke the bone of his right leg and he received a cut in the abdomen, but his crew fought like tigers and the deck was ancle deep with blood and gore; the captain of the boarders received such a tremendous blow on the head from the butt end of a musket, as stretched him senseless on the deck near Lafitte, who raised his dagger to stab him to the heart. But the tide of his existence was ebbing like a torrent, his brain was giddy, his aim faltered and the point descended in the Captain's right thigh; dragging away the blade with the last convulsive energy of a death struggle, he lacerated the wound. Again the reeking steel was upheld, and Lafitte placed his left hand near the Captain's heart, to make his aim more sure; again the dizziness of dissolution spread over his sight, down came the dagger into the captain's left thigh and Lafitte was a corpse.

The upper deck was cleared, and the boarders rushed below on the main deck to complete their conquest. Here the slaughter was dreadful, till the pirates called out for quarter, and the carnage ceased; all the pirates that surrendered were taken to Jamaica and tried before the Admiralty court where sixteen were condemned to die, six were subsequently pardoned and ten executed. Thus perished Lafitte,[9] a man superior in talent, in knowledge of his profession, in courage, and moreover in physical strength; but unfortunately his reckless career was marked with crimes of the darkest dye.

"He was the mildest manner'd man, That ever scuttled ship or cut a throat; With such true breeding of a gentleman, You never could discern his real thought. Pity he loved an adventurous life's variety, He was so great a loss to good society."

SCHOONER *JANE*

Gibraltar, Canary Islands, and Scotland

1821

*By the nineteenth century, accounts of piracy tend
to be linked less to one charismatic leader who seizes
a succession of ships and instead to a particular vessel that is either attacked or experiences a mutiny.
This is an account of the trial of two men, Peter
Heaman and Francois Gautiez, or Gautier, for mutiny and piracy of the schooner on which they were
both employed.*

*Part of the complaint includes a list of goods that
weren't cargo for profit, and which instead provides
an intimate glimpse of the everyday goods of a seaman at this time. "Three white muslin neckcloths,
marked T. J.," two muskets, a pistol, a silver watch
with the name "Wm Simpson, London" on the dial
plate, two pair cotton trousers, a striped cotton
waistcoat, a silk and worsted waistcoat, a buff colored "cassimere" waistcoat, a striped cotton jacket,
a green coat, a red-and-white muslin half handker-
chief, a blue watch coat; a book entitled (somewhat
ironically, given the circumstances)* Trial of Captain
Delano for Piracy. *A trunk with a canvas cover, a
trunk with a calfskin cover, two plain white linen
shirts, three pairs of short white cotton stockings, a
white flannel jacket, one and a half pair of white cotton sheets, a pair of white braces (a British term for
suspenders), and two coarse hand towels. One of the
accused, Peter, was the mate, and the other, Francois, was the cook.*

*Francois Gautiez was a Frenchman and spoke no
English. He was appointed an interpreter for the du-
ration of the trial, a French teacher living in Edinburgh. The two men who were imprisoned by the
mutineers, and who depose against them, were both
little more than kids, each nineteen and unmarried,
each having been at sea for around four years. One
of them had overheard the mate plotting to murder
the captain and take the money and had tried to tip
off the captain about it, which was why when the
mutiny unfolded, he was confined below and almost
lost his life. He was only spared after begging and
promising on the Bible that he would never speak
about what had happened.*

*In the end, the assize court at Edinburgh found
the two men guilty. But were they? Their lawyer
pointed out a number of inconsistencies in the account. And one of the men couldn't even speak English. Read the depositions and decide for yourself.*[1]

. . . IN SO FAR AS, the schooner or schooner brig,[2] *Jane* of
Gibraltar, of which Moses Levy, merchant in Gibraltar, was
owner, and Thomas Johnson was captain or master, having
sailed from Gibraltar for the port of Bahia, or some other port
in the Brazils, on the 19th day of May 1821 . . . having on
board specie to the amount of 38,180, or thereby, Spanish silver hard dollars, and two reals, of which 31,195 dollars or
thereby were shipped by Manoel of Manvel de Andrade Sylva,
residing in Gibraltar, and consigned . . . ; 6765 dollars, or
thereby, and two reals, were shipped by Manoel or Manvel
Nunes Chanto, merchant at Gibraltar, or by the company carrying on business in Gibraltar under the description or firm
of Barros & Chanto, of which company the said Manoel or
Manvel Nunes Chanto is a partner, and consigned . . . ; and

220 dollars, or thereby, were shipped by Joshua Levy, merchant in Gibraltar, and consigned; and having also on board 20 pipes or thereby of sweet oil; 34 bales of paper or thereby; 98 barrels of thereby of bees wax; 15 bags or thereby of aniseed; the said good being consigned . . . ; and having also on board a variety of other good and merchandise of different sorts belonging to person to the prosecutors unknown; the said specie and other cargo above mentioned being then in the lawful possession, or under the charge of the said Thomas Johnson, and being deliverable at the said port of Bahia; and they there said Peter Heaman and Francois Gautiez or Gautier, having, time aforesaid, sailed on board the said vessel *Jane*, while the said vessel was sailing in her course to the said port of Bahia, and in seven degrees, of thereby, north latitude, and five days sail, or thereby, to the west of the Canary Islands, or in some other part of the Atlantic ocean, between the Straits of Gibraltar and the said port of Bahia, to the prosecutors unknown, on the 7th day of June 1821 . . . wickedly and feloniously, and for the piratical purpose of seizing and taking possession of the said vessel, and of the said specie and other cargo above mentioned, on board the said vessel, both and each, or other of them, attack and assault the said Thomas Johnson, and did murder the said Thomas Johnson, by discharging musket loaded with ball, or other hard substance, at the head, or some part of the body of the said Thomas Johnson . . . and by savagely and cruelly beating the said Thomas Johnson with the butt end of a musket . . . in consequence whereof the said Thomas Johnson died immediately thereafter; and that the said Peter Heaman and Francois Gautiez . . . did . . . wickedly and feloniously attack and assault James Paterson, then a seaman on board the said vessel, and did murder the said James Paterson, by beating and wounding him with muskets. . . . And they . . . did thereafter throw, or cause to be thrown, the bodies . . . overboard into the sea; and they . . . did then confine Peter Smith and David Robertson Strachan, alias Robert Strachan, then seamen on board the said vessel, in the forecastle of the said vessel, by fastening down the hatchways or otherwise, and did attempt to suffocate the said two persons by

smoke, and did thereby succeed in terrifying the said Peter Smith and David Robertson Strachan . . . and did compel them to assist the said Peter Heaman and Francois Gautiez. . . . In their plan of seizing the said vessel, and the said specie and cargo on board thereof. . . . And did thereafter alter the course of destination of the said vessel, and did steer, or cause to be steered, the said vessel for the coast of Ireland, or of Scotland, for the purpose of enabling them . . . to appropriate to themselves the said specie and cargo which they had thus piratically and feloniously seized; and they . . . having arrived in the said vessel off the coast of the island of Lewis, in the county of Ross, on the 21st day of July 1821 . . . did then and there, nearly opposite to the point of Chickenhead, in the said island of Lewis. . . . Feloniously sink, or cast away the said vessel *Jane*, by boring, or causing to be bored, holes in the bottom of the said vessel . . . by which means the said vessel was lost and driven ashore on the coast the said island; and they . . . did, on the 22nd . . . land the said specie, or part thereof, and the said cargo . . . on the coast of the said island, near to Swordale, in the parish of Stornoway, in the county of Ross aforesaid, for the purpose of secreting and carrying off the same, when they . . . where [sic] apprehended. . . ."

Andrew Carmelier, aged 18, unmarried, a native of Malta, at sea for four years, serving as cabin boy, deposed:

That the deponent was awakened by the shot, and instantly went on deck: That the cabin was dark at the time; and that the shot seemed close to the deponent, he being near the captain's head, and it appeared to him that it was fired into the captain's bed: That when the deponent went upon deck, the first thing he saw was the mate striking Paterson: That they were then near the main hatchway; that the mate had a musket in his hand, with the butt end of which he was striking Paterson: That the deponent heard Paterson cry, but did not hear the mate say anything to him, nor had Paterson anything in his hand: . . . That Paterson fell beside the main-hatchway, under the boat which was them upon deck: . . . and when the captain came up, he said to the deponent "What is this? What is this?" That at this time the captain was holding his hand upon the right side of his head . . . that he saw some blood on the captain's head when he came upon deck: That the deponent told the captain . . . that he believed the mate was fighting with Paterson: That the cook was coming from forward, and caught the captain, and struck him with the butt end of a musket . . . That the captain cried, or groaned, after he had been struck by the mate and cook: That, after the captain had been knocked down, the mate went forward and called the people from the forecastle, to come upon deck. . . . That the bodies were hove overboard, and the body of Paterson was thrown overboard first, and Paterson appeared to be quite dead: That he was thrown over with his clothes on, and with a piece of iron tied to his foot. . . . That the deponent was ordered by the mate to assist in throwing the bodies overboard: That the deponent was crying at this time, and was not able to give much assistance, but had a hand in it . . . That some stones were tied to the captain's body . . . That the captain did not appear to be quite dead when he was thrown overboard . . . That after the captain was killed, the deponent said to the mate, "Don't kill me," where upon the mate answered, "Very well. Go forward."

Compeared[3] Roderick M'Iver, surveyor of the customs at Stornoway, aged about 46 years, who . . . depones, That he is surveyor of the customs at Stornoway: Recollects to have heard of a vessel, supposed to be a smuggler, being at anchor near Stornoway in the month of July last: That the deponent immediately dispatched four of his boatmen, to ascertain what the vessel was, and he himself soon after followed with his eldest son: That he did not find the vessel, but found a large boat, a fishing boat, on shore, and six men belonging to it, who had pitched a tent on shore: That the deponent spoke to one of these men, Peter Heaman, the panel, who stated that he was mate of the brig *Betsy*, of New York, loaded with tobacco and cotton, which had been lost off Barra head: That he said that captain and he had quarreled, and the captain had gone off in a boat with five men for Liverpool: That he, Heaman, and the rest of the crew had taken another boat, and had attempted to reach the main-land, but had been driven into the place where they then were; he added that the brig belonged to his father: That the deponent then proceeded to search five or six chests, some of them large chests, which were in their possession: That the first chest which was opened, and which Peter Smith claimed, contained clothes on the top, and a very large bag of dollars in the bottom: That the deponent searched and found dollars in all the other chests: That the deponent took a list of the names of the people as they gave them: That it rained so fast that the names were obliterated as soon as written, but the mate gave his name George Sadwell: That the deponent returned to Stornoway, leaving two boatmen in charge of these persons: That after the deponent and his eldest son, who had accompanied him, had gone about one hundred yards, a foreign boy, one of the persons whom he has mentioned, and whom he saw here, under examination this day, followed him and told him that the mate and the cook had murdered the master and a seaman of the name of Paterson, and had taken possession of the ship: That the deponent deferred questioning the boy further, till they reached the top of the cliff, which overhung the beach where the boat was, when the boy told him more particularly that the vessel belonged to Gibraltar . . . That the deponent sent back two of his boatmen with directions to keep all the country people that might come to the spot, and that if the seamen attempted to escape, that they should stave the boat, and tie the men with cords . . . That the Maltese boy informed the deponent there was a further quantity of dollars concealed in the hammocks of these persons, and a still greater quantity hid on the beach[4] . . . That the deponent proceeded to the shore . . . when he found the dollars concealed, precisely as had been described by the Maltese boy: That the total amount of the dollars found by the deponent, including those found in the chests, was thirty-one thousand, two hundred and eleven, as nearly as the deponent can recollect: That the mate said, on the night before, when

the deponent was searching the chests, that three thousand belonged to him of those dollars that were in the chests, and that
these in the chests might be about a fourth of the whole number; all which is truth as the deponent shall answer to God.

Compeered PETER HEAMAN, Mariner, late mate of the
schooner *Jane* of Gibraltar, aged 35 years, or thereby, declares,
That . . . the *Jane* was brig-rigged fore, and schooner-rigged
aft;[5] would carry from ninety to one hundred and twenty tons;
was commanded by Thomas Johnson, with whom the declarant agreed for serving in her as mate, . . . on the afternoon of
the 17th, commenced to take in the cargo, which consisted of
ten pipes[6] of sweet oil, thirty-five bales of stamped paper for
printing. On the 18th, took on board ten more pipes of sweet
oil, one hundred and twenty barrels of bees wax, fourteen
round jars of fine oil, three hundred oblong jars of olives, fourteen boxes of raisins, six eighteen gallon casks, one of about
nine and one of about seven gallons, all filled with Spanish
dollars, and contained in bags, containing one thousand and
some of them five hundred dollars each, stowed with saw-dust
in casks, and the whole quantity amounted to thirty-eight
thousand. . . . That on the 19th the vessel sailed from Gibraltar; and prior to sailing, two of the crew, viz. the cook Francois, and John Lawrence the Portuguese, took their clothes on
the deck, and wished to go on shore again, when the master
called them "damn'd fools," and said "they did not know
when to do themselves good;" and turning himself round,
said, "I mean to do some good for myself this voyage;" upon
which they agreed to go: . . . That from the time the vessel left
the port . . . there were frequent conversations among the crew
about the money, and how to come at it; and Paterson said, it
would be the best plan to make the master walk on shore on a
plank;[7] to which the Frenchman answered, it would be too
hard a death: That such conversations took place among the
whole crew, every meal-time and every watch-time, when they
had an opportunity: That the declarant has heard such conversations frequently himself, which were held partly in a jesting
manner; and they were left off for three or four days before the

6th day of June, on which day John Lawrence having displeased the captain in some seamanship, the captain seized a large marling-spoke,[8] and followed Lawrence, threatened to strike him, but did not do it; on which John Lawrence said to himself, in the hearing of the declarant, "You will not strike me with a marling-spoke bye and bye."

Declares, That the cook, who did not understand English, very often displeased the master in making the victuals ready; and frequently swore in French, and sometimes in Spanish, which displeased the master, who frequently upon such occasions threatened to blow the cook's brains out with a pistol. . . .

Declares, that about three or four of the morning of the 7th, the master came upon deck in his night-gown, with a loaded pistol, and mistaking Paterson, who was at the helm, for the Frenchman, blowed his brains out; and the Frenchman, who was forward in the vessel looking out, came aft to the captain; and the captain finding that it was not the Frenchman he had shot, began to strike him with the pistol, saying, he wished it was loaded for his sake . . . That in the meantime, the whole crew came upon deck, and the master having continued to beat the Frenchman, had got him down on the deck, the master himself having been down different times, and on which occasion the Frenchman's arm was broken: That the declarant thinks the crew all struck the master, and he saw them all over each other together in a cluster . . . That during this time the declarant kept the helm: That immediately thereafter, the whole crew came aft to the declarant, to consult with him what was best to be done, and the declarant gave his advice, that it was best to proceed on the voyage and say nothing about what had happened: That he did this to keep peace amongst them.

Declares, That John Lawrence advised to go to America with the vessel, as he knew something about the American coast, and to divide the money and destroy the vessel, but this was not agreed to. . . . Smith and Strachan proposed to go to the north of Scotland, where they could buy a boat and so get ashore, and scuttle the ship at sea, to which all agreed and so shaped their course towards England.

[. . . The deposition goes on the describe in technical detail how they went about scuttling the boat.]

Interrogated, Where the declarant gave orders to do these things?

Declares, That they were done by consultation among the whole crew; and the declarant did not give orders, except in working the vessel, to which order the crew frequently did not pay attention.

Verdict: guilty

Sentencing: "If the law of this country permitted a punishment great than death to be imposed in any case, that punishment would be inflicted upon you; but although barbarians sometimes are to be found upon our shores, there is nothing barbarous in our laws. . . . While I announce to you, therefore, the sentence of death, I have to intimate to you, at the same time, that this sentence will, in all human probability be forthwith put into execution. To the misguided and penitent offender the door of mercy is sometimes opened, but against the pirate and the murderer it will be for ever shut.

[. . . The sentencing went on, in technical legal language. They were to be "carried from the bar back to the tollbooth of Edinburgh, therein to be detained, and to be fed on bread and water only . . . until the second Wednesday of January next to come . . . and upon that day, betwixt the hours of nine o'clock in the morning and twelve o'clock noon, to be taken forth of the said tollbooth to the sands of Leith, within floodmark, and then and there to be hanged by the neck, upon a gibbet, by the hands of the common executioner, until they be dead, and their bodies thereafter to be delivered to Dr. Alexander Monro, professor of anatomy in the university of Edinburgh, to be by him publicly dissected and anatomized, in terms of the said act. And ordains all their heritable goods and gear to be escheat[9] and inbrought to his Majesty's use—WHICH IS PRONOUNCED FOR DOOM!"]

THE *DOVER*

Matanzas, Cuba

1822

The "plunder" seized by these Spanish pirates will not strike anyone as "treasure." Most piracy resulted in hauls like this, of raids of stores or cargo, and speaks more to desperation rather than romance.

Captain Sabins of the former reported that on January 16, 1822: "Pan of Matanzas, bearing S[outh], saw a boat coming to us from a small drogher,[1] which came out of Matanzas the night before us, with five Spaniards armed with long knives, pistols, cutlasses, etc.[2] When they got within hail, they fired a musket at us, cheered and came on board. They were the most villainous-looking rascals that anyone had probably ever beheld. They immediately drew their weapons, and after beating us severely with their cutlasses, drove us below. They then robbed us of all our clothes except what we had on, our watches, and everything of value. We were afterwards called up singly. Four men with drawn knives stood over the captain and threatened him if he did not give up his money they would kill all hands and burn the vessel. After robbing the people, they commenced plundering the brig. They broke open the hatches, made us get out our boat and carry their plunder to their vessel.

"They took from us a compass, five bags of coffee, a barrel of sugar, nearly all our provisions, our colors, rigging, and cooking utensils. They then ordered us to stand to the north, or they would overhaul us, murder the crew, and burn the vessel. We made sail, and shortly after were brought to by another boat of the same character, which fired into us, but left us upon being informed that we had been already robbed."

THE *PORPOISE*

Off Cuba

1822

By the 1820s, the United States Navy was playing a larger and larger role in policing the Caribbean against acts of piracy to protect American trade, as evidenced by the next two military accounts of pirate suppression.

United States
Schooner *Porpoise*,
Off North Coast of
Cuba,
20th January, 1822.[1]

Sir: Having completed the necessary equipments of this vessel at New Orleans, on the 7th inst[ant], and previously having given notice that I should sail from the Balize on the 10th, with convoy, I now have the honor to inform you that I proceeded to sea on the day appointed, with five sail under my protection. On the 15th, having seen the vessels bound to Havana and Matanzas safe to their destined ports, I made all sail to the westward, and on the following day boarded the brig *Bolina*, of Boston, Gorham, master, from whom I received the following information: That, on the day previous, his vessel was captured by pirates and robbed of every material they

could carry away with them, at the same time treating the crew
and himself with inhuman cruelty.

After supplying him from this vessel with what necessaries
he required, I made sail for the land, and early the following
morning (Saddle Hill, on the north coast of Cuba, then bearing
S. by E.), I dispatched our boats with 40 men, under command
of Lieutenant Curtis, in pursuit of these enemies of the human
race.

The boats, having crossed the reef, which here extends out a
considerable distance from the shore, very soon discovered,
chased and captured a piratical schooner, the crew of which
made their escape to the woods; Lieutenant Curtis very
judiciously manned the prize from our boats, and proceeded
about ten miles to leeward, where, it was understood, the
principal depot of these marauders was established. This he
fortunately discovered and attacked. A slight skirmish here
took place, but as our force advanced the opposition party
precipitately retreated. We then took possession and burnt and
destroyed their fleet, consisting of five vessels—one being a
beautiful new schooner, of about 60 tons, ready for the sea,
with the exception of her sails. We also took three prisoners;
the others fled to the woods.

In the affair just mentioned the officers of the expedition
state the enemy's loss to be severe. Only one man was wounded
in our boats; and it is worthy of remark that this man was one
of their own gang, then a prisoner in our possession, and
surrounded by our people.

The destruction of this place will, I trust, be of some service.
From information received by me, it was their principal depot,
from which they dispatched squadrons to Cape Antonio. These
returning loaded with plunder, it was transhipped to Havana in
vessels sent from here for that purpose. Stores and materials
were collected on the spot, not only for repairing, but building
vessels.

The prisoners now on board are recognized by a seaman in
my possession, who was one of the crew of the English ship
Alexander, of Greenock, lately burned by these pirates: and not
content with destroying the vessel, they inhumanly butchered

her unfortunate commander. The seaman in question I retain as an evidence in the case.

Lieutenant Curtis speaks in the highest terms of the gallantry and good conduct of Midshipmen Pinkney, Kingston and Morris, as also of Dr. Terrill, and every other officer and man employed in the expedition. Nothing could exceed their ardor in pursuit but their enthusiasm in attack; and both affording abundant proof that more would have been done had more been required.

I have manned one of the schooners taken, a very fine, fast-sailing vessel, and kept her with me. She will prove of great service in my further operations on this coast.

I cannot close this letter, sir, without naming to you Lieutenant Curtis, whose conduct, not only in the present instance, but in every other respect during the period he has been under my command, has merited my warm and decided approbation.

I have the honor to be, etc.,

James Ramage, Lieutenant Commanding.

Hon. Smith Thompson, Secretary of the Navy.

THE *ALLIGATOR*

Matanzas, Cuba

November 1822

The same year as the Porpoise, *and in the same waters off Cuba, the US schooner* Alligator *responded to a ransom request from a group of pirates that had taken an American brig and schooner captive.*

In November, 1822, the U. S. schooner *Alligator*, Lieutenant W. H. Allen, arriving at Matanzas, was informed that an American brig and schooner had been captured and were in possession of a large gang of pirates at a place about 45 miles east of Matanzas.[1] The master of the brig and mate of the schooner had been sent to the latter place to procure a ransom of $7000 for the two vessels, with the threat that their vessels would be destroyed and their crews severely dealt with in case of failure to bring the money.

The master and mate were taken on board the *Alligator*, which sailed immediately to the rescue. At daylight on November 9th she arrived near the bay, and hid behind intervening land, behind which they discovered a ship, two brigs and five schooners. One of the schooners, her deck black with men, was under way, and was immediately chased by the armed boats of the *Alligator*. The wind was light, and the schooner using her long sweeps,[2] endeavored to escape up the bay. When the *Alligator*'s boats arrived within hail, the schooner, with her bloody flag nailed to the mast, opened fire with a long brass eighteen-pound pivot gun and four smaller ones. Lieutenant Allen, Captain Freeman of the marines, and twelve men, were in the launch, far in advance of the other boats; pulling hard at the oars, they reached the pirate and took possession of her, after a desperate resistance which nothing but the most daring bravery could have overcome. The freebooters, all but one, escaped by taking to their boats and jumping overboard before the *Alligator*'s boats reached them. But in the meantime the gallant Allen fell, pierced by two musket balls.

The surgeon of the *Alligator*, in a letter to a friend published in many newspapers of the day, said: "Capt. Allen continued giving orders, and conversing with Mr. Dale and the rest of us, until a few minutes before his death, with a degree of cheerfulness that was little to be expected from a man in his condition. He said he wished his relatives and his country to know that he had fought well, and added that he died in peace and good will towards all the world, and hoped for his reward in the next . . .

[. . .] After the wounding of Allen, the second pirate schooner escaped, but another heavily-armed schooner, the ship and two more "fore and afters" were captured. Besides Lieutenant Allen, the *Alligator* lost four men killed and three wounded. The pirates lost fourteen killed and several by drowning; their best armed schooner carried a long 12-pounder, two 6-pounders, two 3-pounders, and two swivel guns. In all the three piratical schooners had 125 men and 14 guns. The *Alligator*'s boats' crews numbered about forty, armed with muskets, swords and pistols.

On November 19th, 1822, the *Alligator* was, unfortunately, lost on Carysford reef, a dangerous spot off the Florida coast, where many a fine ship before and since has come to grief. Her officers and crew were all saved.

THE *BELVIDERE*

Beverly, Massachusetts

1822

This volume skips over American privateers during the War of 1812, largely because privateering during that conflict was technically legal, and so not, strictly speaking, piracy, though the shifting nautical landscape of that conflict is a rich area of inquiry for maritime enthusiasts. Zachariah G. Lamson was one of the many American ship captains who found himself early in his career taking the risk to a run a blockade of his home port that was being enforced by his own country's navy, as the young United States endeavored to restrict maritime trade with both England and France until the conflict between those two nations was resolved. Lamson first went to sea as a cabin boy at sixteen, having advised his father that "the seafaring life was my constant wish to follow," as he noted some years later in an incomplete memoir. By twenty-one, he had risen to be master of schooners sailing between New England, the Caribbean, and New Orleans. The Belvidere *was his second command to be attacked by pirates. The first time, they robbed him blind. The second time, it was a different story.*

An account has already been published of an attack made by a piratical vessel upon the brig *Belvidere*, Capt. Lamson, of Beverly, on her passage from Port-au-Prince to New Orleans, and of the successful defense of the *Belvidere*. Capt. Lamson has arrived at the Balize,[1] and furnished the following particulars, which appear in the New Orleans papers.[2] He was hailed by the piratical Capt. and ordered on board his vessel. Capt. L. replied that he was coming, and after some delay, during which the crew of the *Belvidere* were preparing to defend themselves, the commander of the pirates came alongside in his boat and jumped on board the *Belvidere*. Capt. L. instantly shot him down with a musket, and a severe conflict ensued between the crew of the boat and that of the *Belvidere*, the issue of which was the total defeat of the pirates, with the loss of six of their number killed. One man of the *Belvidere* was mortally wounded.

"Capt. Lamson (who on a former voyage was robbed and shamefully abused[3] by pirates, and determined to resist any further attacks from them, had prepared his vessel and crew accordingly) is certainly entitled to great praise for his gallant and spirited conduct. A few such checks as this will as effectually prevent a repetition of the outrages perpetrated by these lawless sea-monsters as anything which our Seventy-fours[4] or Frigates can do."

"Extract from the log-book of the *Belvidere*, Capt. Lamson, arr. at New Orleans from Port-au-Prince."

May 2, fell in with a sch'r [schooner] and three launches, which gave chase; blowing heavy and being to windward, succeeded in getting from them the next day. At 10 AM made a sch. [schooner] on our larboard[5] bow, lying under mainsail and jib;[6] at 11, she was on our lee quarter, fired a shot, and coming up very fast, at 20 minutes past 11, gave us a second shot, and hoisted a red flag, with death's head and cross under it.

Finding I had a *hard character* to deal with, I prepared for him as well as we were able, and immediately brailed[7] up my topsails, hauled up my courses, clewed down top-gallant sails, hauled down jib, braced to the main-topsail,[8] and kept off two points,[9] fired a musket and hoisted colors—at 12, she came alongside, within 10 yards distance—hailed with '*God d—you, send your boat on board or I will murder all hands of you.*'

He had not discovered our gun at that time—I told him I would send her directly—he immediately gave me a whole volley of musketry and blunderbusses,[10] before I had answered him—our gun was pointed and cloth removed, and we commenced as smart a fire as possible with our 24 pound carronade, 4 muskets and 7 pistols, and on our first fire six of them were seen to fall, the captain among them, or leader, being the one that hailed me—he only discharged his long gun three times alongside, as our third shot broke his carriage,[11] and his gun fell into the lee scupper[12]—he then kept up as smart a fire as he was able with muskets and blunderbusses, and dropped near the stern, expecting to find more comfortable quarters, but there he got a most terrible cutting up from a brass 3 pounder, by which he was raked within 20 yards distance with a round and two bags of 40 musket balls each, which completely fixed him—I did not receive any fire from, nor even hear a word spoken on board of him, and in fact did not see any one on deck. His vessel holding such a wind and sailing so fast, she was soon clear of grapeshot range, and wore ship, when we counted 6 or 7 of them, which appeared to be all that was left; the captain I saw distinctly laid on deck. Our loss was one man killed, shot through the head; about 40 musket balls through the rudder case, tiller, skylight, companion way, our fore topsail halliards[13] shot away and our try-sail halliards cut in 3 pieces. The pirate was 36 to 40 tons; we counted 22 men when he came alongside; he had a brass 6 or 9 pounder amidships, and muskets and blunderbusses.

Z. G. LAMSON

THE *MARY*

Philadelphia

1822

This account, in contrast, is almost certainly fictional. Published in the American Monthly Magazine *in February 1824, it was ostensibly written by a man who was traveling from Philadelphia to New Orleans for his health. The degree of overwrittenness, the amount of money he was carrying, the way he claimed he was carrying it, and the gore that ensues suggest that the public hunger for dramatic stories of piracy required as much glamorous embellishment then as it does now. In reality, pirates weren't interested in torture for its own sake, or at least, when they were, it was unusual enough that their contemporaries remarked upon it. They were interested in stealing coffee, salted beef, wine, and shoes. Other clues that this account is wholly fictitious: the pirates even shoot the dog, and the narrator is the sole survivor, without any details about how he managed to be saved while passed out and lashed to the mast of a sinking ship.*

In the early part of June I sailed from Philadelphia in the schooner *Mary*, on a voyage to New Orleans.[1] My principal object in going round by sea was the restoration of my health, which had been for many months declining. Having some friends in New Orleans, whose commercial enterprises were conducted on an extensive scale, I was charged with the care of several sums of money in gold and silver, amounting altogether to nearly $18,000. This I communicated to the captain, and we concluded to secure it in the best manner our circumstances would admit. A plank was accordingly taken off the ribs of the schooner in my own cabin, and the money being deposited in the vacancy, the plank was nailed down in its original place, and the seams filled and tarred over. Being thus relieved from any apprehension that the money would be found upon us in case of an attack from pirates, my mind was somewhat easier. What other articles of value I could conveniently carry about with me, I did so.

I had also brought a quantity of banknotes to the amount of $15,000. Part of these I caused to be carefully sewed in the left lapel of my coat, supposing that in case of my being lost at sea, my coat, should my body be found, would still contain the most valuable of my effects. The balance was carefully quilted into my black silk cravat. Our crew consisted of the captain and four men, with a supply of livestock for the voyage, and a Newfoundland dog, valuable for his fidelity and sagacity. He had once saved his master from a watery grave, when he had been stunned and knocked overboard by a sudden shifting of the boom. I was the only passenger on board. Our voyage at first was prosperous, and time went rapidly. I felt my strength increase the longer I was at sea, and when we arrived off the southern coast of Florida my feelings were like those of another man.

It was towards the evening of the fourteenth day, two hours before sunset, that we espied a sail astern of us. As twilight came it neared us with astonishing rapidity. Night closed, and all around was impenetrable darkness. Now and then a gentle wave would break against our bow and sparkle for a moment, and at a distance behind us we could see the uneven glow of light, occasioned by the foaming of the strange vessel. The breeze that filled our canvas was gentle, though it was fresh.

We coursed our way steadily through the night, though once or twice the roaring of the waves increased so suddenly as to make us believe we had passed a breaker.

At the time it was unaccountable to me, but I now believe it to be occasioned by the schooner behind us, coming rather near in the darkness of the night. At midnight I went on deck. Nothing but an occasional sparkle was to be seen, and the ocean was undisturbed. Still it was a fearful and appalling darkness, and in spite of my endeavors I could not compose myself. At the windlass, on the forecastle, three of the sailors, like myself, unable to sleep, had collected for conversation. On joining them, I found our fears were mutual. They all kept their eyes steadily fixed upon the unknown vessel, as if anticipating some dreadful event. They informed me that they had put their arms in order and were determined to stand or die.

At this moment a flash of light, perhaps a musket burning priming, proceeded from the vessel in pursuit, and we saw distinctly that her deck was covered with men. My heart almost failed me. I had never been in battle, and knew not what it was. Day at length dawned, and setting all her canvas, our pursuer gained alarmingly upon us. It was evident that she had followed us the whole night, being unwilling to attack us in the dark. In a few minutes she fired a gun and came alongside. She was a pirate. Her boat was lowered, and about a dozen hideous-looking objects jumped in, with a commander at their head. The boat pushed off and was fast nearing us, as we arranged ourselves for giving her a broadside. Our whole stock of arms consisted of six muskets and an old swivel used as a signal gun, belonging to the *Mary*, and a pair of pistols of my own, which I carried in my belt. The pirate boat's crew were armed with muskets, pistols, swords, cutlasses, and knives; and when she came within her own length of us we fired five of our muskets and the swivel into her.

Her fire was scarcely half given when she filled and went down, with all her crew. At this success we were inclined to rejoice, but looking over the pirate schooner we observed her deck still swarming with the same description of horrid-looking wretches. A second boat's crew pushed off, with their muskets pointed directly at us the whole time. When they came within the same distance as the other, we fired, but with little, if any effect. The pirate immediately returned the fire, and with horrid cries jumped aboard us. Two of our brave crew were lying dead upon the deck, and the rest of us expected nothing better. French, Spanish and English were spoken indiscriminately and all at once. The most horrid imprecations were uttered against us, and threats that fancy cannot imagine.

A wretch whose black, shaggy whiskers covered nearly his whole face,[2] whose eyes were only seen at intervals from beneath his bushy eyebrows, and whose whole appearance was more that of a hell-hound than of a human being, approached me with a drawn cutlass in his hand. I drew one of my pistols and snapped it in his face, but it flashed in the pan,[3] and before I could draw the other, the pirate, with a brutality that would have disgraced a cannibal, struck me over the face with his cutlass and knocked me down. I was too much wounded to resist, and the blood ran in torrents from my forehead. In this situation the wretch seized me by the scalp, and thrusting his cutlass in my cravat cut it through completely. I felt the cold iron glide along my throat, and even now the very thought makes me shudder.

The worst idea I had ever formed of human cruelty seemed now realized, and I could see death staring me in the face. Without stopping to examine the cravat, he put it in his pocket, and in a voice of thunder exclaimed, "Levez vous"; I accordingly rose to my feet, and he pinioned my hands behind my back, led me to the vessel's bulwark, and asked another of the gang, in French, whether he should throw me overboard. At the recollection of that scene I am still staggered. I endeavored to call the prospects of eternity before me, but could think of nothing except the cold and quiverless apathy of the tomb. His infamous companion replied. "Il est trop bien habille, pour l'envoyer an diable,"[4] and led me to the foremast, where he tied me with my face to the stern of the vessel. The cords were drawn so tight around my arms and legs that my agony was excruciating. In this situation he left me.

On looking round, I found them all employed in plundering and ransacking everything we had. Over my left shoulder one of our sailors was strung up to the yardarm, and apparently in the last agonies of death: while before me our gallant captain was on his knees and begging for his life. The wretches were endeavoring to extort from him the secret of our money: but for a while he was firm and dauntless. Provoked at his obstinacy, they extended his arms and cut them off at the elbows. At this human nature gave way, and the injured man confessed the spot where we had concealed our specie. In a few moments it was aboard their own vessel. To revenge themselves on our unhappy captain, when they had satisfied themselves that nothing else was hidden, they spread a bed of oakum on the deck, and after soaking it through with turpentine, tied the captain on it, filled his mouth with the same combustibles, and set the whole on fire. The cries of the unfortunate man were heart-rending, and his agonies must have been unutterable, but they were soon over. All this I was compelled to witness. Heart sick with the sight, I once shut my eyes, but a musket discharged close to my ear was a warning sufficient to keep them open.

On casting my eyes towards the schooner's stern, I discovered that our boatswain had been nailed to the deck through his feet, and the body spiked through to the tiller. He was writhing in the last agonies of crucifixion. Our fifth comrade was out of sight during all this tragedy: in a few minutes, however, he was brought upon the deck blindfolded. He was then conducted to the muzzle of the swivel and commanded to kneel. The swivel was then fired off, and his head was dreadfully wounded by the discharge. In a moment after it was agonizing to behold his torments and convulsions—language is too feeble to describe them; I have seen men hung upon the gibbet, but their death is like sinking in slumber when compared with his.

Excited with the scene of human butchery, one of those wretches fired his pistol at the captain's dog; the ball struck his shoulder and disabled him; he finished him by shooting him again, and at last by cutting out his tongue! At this last hell-engendered act my blood boiled with indignation at such savage brutality on a helpless, inoffensive dog! But I was unable to give utterance or action to my feelings.

Seeing that the crew had been every one dispatched, I began

to think more of myself. My old enemy, who seemed to forget me, once more approached me, but shockingly besmeared with blood and brains. He had stood by the side of the unfortunate sailor who suffered before the swivel, and supported him with the point of his bayonet. He drew a stiletto from his side, placed its point upon my heart, and gave it a heavy thrust. I felt its point touch my skin; but the quilting of my bank bills prevented its further entrance. This savage monster then ran it up my breast, as if intending to divide my lungs, and in doing so the bank notes fell upon the deck. He snatched them up greedily and exclaimed, "Ah! laissez mois voir ce qui reste!"[5] My clothes in a few moments were ripped to pieces, at the peril of my life. He frequently came so near as to tear my skin and deluge me with blood; but by the mercy of Providence, I escaped from every danger. At this moment a heavy flaw struck the schooner, and I heard one of the pirates say, "Voila un vaisseau!"[6] They all retreated precipitately, and gaining their own vessel, were soon out of sight.

Helpless as I now was, I had the satisfaction of knowing that the pirates had been frightened by the appearance of a strange sail, but it was impossible for me to see it. Still tied to the foremast, I knew not what was my prospect of release. An hour or two had elapsed after they left me, and it was now noon. The sun played violently upon my head, and I felt a languor and debility that indicated approaching fever. My head gradually sank upon my breast, when I was shocked by hearing the water pouring into the cabin windows. The wretches had scuttled the schooner, and left me pinioned to go down with her. I commended my spirit to my Maker, and gave myself up for lost. I felt myself gradually dying away, and the last thing I remembered was the foaming noise of the waves. This was occasioned by a ship passing by me. I was taken in, restored to health, and am now a poor, ruined, helpless man.

THE *NEW PRISCILLA*

Salem, Massachusetts, and Havana

1829

It was common in the nineteenth century for newspapers, specifically newspapers in port communities like Salem, to have detailed lists of ships' comings and goings, including word passed from vessels that had hailed each other at sea, or correspondence giving accounts of ships of whom news had not arrived. The New Priscilla *is an example of the maritime networks of information transmission in an age much slower than our own. It also has some ghostly elements, including an abandoned ship and sailors' superstitions about ill fortune on voyages to come.*

Probably one of the worst cases of piracy against an American vessel was in February, 1829, when the brig *New Priscilla*, Captain Hart, was found apparently abandoned a few miles out from Havana.[1] The account of this tragic affair, which, as there were no survivors, is shrouded in mystery, is as follows, compiled from the newspaper files of the day.

The brig *New Priscilla*, Captain Hart, of and from Salem, sailed on a voyage, the ultimate destination of which was Sumatra and the pepper coast, but she never again saw her home port. Pepper cargoes were paid for in Spanish dollars, and the specie for this voyage was driven down from the banks in Essex Street in several four-horse stages, and delivered at the

wharf, so that it need not be on deposit overnight. Upon receiving it the brig made sail, and later was found abandoned in
the Gulf Stream, all on board murdered by pirates. And yet
there are those who pretend to think there was nothing exciting in Salem's past!

"It was no uncommon sight," said an old stage driver, "to
see several coaches coming from Boston driven down Essex
Street to the Asiatic Bank,[2] loaded with silver dollars in kegs
of $3000 each and canvas bags of $1000 each."

The Philadelphia *Gazette* contains the details of a horrible
tragedy, communicated in a private letter from Havana, and a
notarial certificate from Matanzas. The statement is made
by John Conega, master of the brig *Mary Jane* of New York.
He says:

"'On the 14th Feb. inst[ant], the wind at S. W. entered the
Keysal Bank in sight of the Dog Keys; at 2.30 P.M. saw a herm.
brig [hermaphrodite brig] and schooner in company, lying to
the wind; at 4 P.M., not wishing to leave the Bank, tacked to
the Southward, when they immediately filled away. At 4.15,
finding we were coming up with them, they both tacked for
about fifteen minutes, when the schooner again filled away and
left the brig in the situation above mentioned. At 5 P.M., being
aboard the brig the *New Priscilla* of Salem, on her stern, observed that her stern boat tackles were hanging in the water,
her boat gone, and not a soul to be seen on board; called three
or four times, but receiving no answer, stood off.'"

. . . It is worth noting, also, that there is nowhere to be
found any mention of a boy having been spiked to the deck by
the pirates. This blood-curdling yarn has generally been told
in connection with the piracy of the *New Priscilla*. Another incident in connection with this unfortunate vessel is a story told
of two sailors belonging to her. They had been allowed a day's
liberty on shore at Charleston, and, returning at night, were
about to go on board, just as a large black dog came to the ship's
side and howled. That was enough for the men. Possessing a sail-
or's superstition, they felt that something was surely going to
happen to the brig. So off they ran and secreted themselves until
the vessel had proceeded to sea, and thus their lives were spared.

THE *FRIENDSHIP*

Salem, Massachusetts, and Sumatra

1831

So far our nineteenth-century vessels have been at-
tacked in the Caribbean, in the Gulf of Mexico, and
along the Atlantic seaboard of the United States.
This account shows that American shipping con-
tinued to be beset by piracy even as far away as Su-
matra. But are these pirates, exactly? The passage
describes residents of Sumatra attacking a vessel that
is there to trade for pepper. Presumably the trade
would stand to benefit people in power on Sumatra
rather than those who elected to attack the vessel
and keep it for themselves. From a Malay perspec-
tive, the pirates described here might not be all that
different from the Bostonians of the Boston Tea
Party, or if acting at the behest of their leaders, the
supposed pirates of the South China Sea or the Bar-
bary Coast.

This Friendship *was originally built in 1797 as an*
East Indiaman. The Friendship of Salem *is a modern-*
day replica of this exact ship, run by the National
Park Service, and can be toured in Salem Harbor
today.[1]

On the 7th of February, 1831, the ship *Friendship*, Capt. Endicott, of Salem (Mass.,) was captured by the Malays while
lying at Qualla Battoo, on the coast of Sumatra.[2] In the forenoon

of the fatal day, Capt. Endicott, Mr. Barry, second mate, and four of the crew, it seems went on shore as usual, for the purpose of weighing pepper, expecting to obtain that day two boat loads, which had been promised them by the Malays. After the first boat was loaded, they observed that she delayed some time in passing down the river, and her crew being composed of Malays, was supposed by the officers to be stealing pepper from her, and secreting it in the bushes. In consequence of this conjecture, two men were sent off to watch them, who on approaching the boat, saw five or six Malays leap from the jungle, and hurry on board of her. The former, however, supposed them to be the boat's crew, as they had seen an equal number quit her previous to their own approach. In this they were mistaken, as will subsequently appear. At this time a brig hove in sight, and was seen standing towards Soo Soo, another pepper port, distant about five miles. Capt. Endicott, on going to the beach to ascertain whether the brig had hoisted any colors, discovered that the boat with pepper had approached within a few yards of the *Friendship*, manned with an unusual number of natives.

It appears that when the pepper boats came alongside of the *Friendship*, as but few of the hands could work at a time, numbers of the Malays came on board, and on being questioned by Mr. Knight, the first officer, who was in the gangway, taking an account of the pepper, as to their business, their reply was, that they had come to see the vessel. Mr. Knight ordered them into their boat again, and some of them obeyed, but only to return immediately to assist in the work of death, which was now commenced by attacking Mr. Knight and the rest of the crew on board. The crew of the vessel being so scattered, it was impossible to concentrate their force so as to make a successful resistance. Some fell on the forecastle,[3] one in the gangway, and Mr. Knight fell upon the quarter deck, severely wounded by a stab in the back while in the act of snatching from the bulwarks a boarding pike with which to defend himself.

The two men who were taking the pepper on a stage, having vainly attempted to get on board to the assistance of their comrades, were compelled to leap into the sea. One of them,

Charles Converse, of Salem, being severely wounded, succeeded in swimming to the bobstays,[4] to which he clung until taken on board by the natives, and from some cause he was not afterwards molested. His companion, John Davis, being unable to swim, drifted with the tide near the boat tackle, or davit falls, the blocks being overhauled down near the water; one of these he laid hold of, which the Malays perceiving, dropped their boat astern and dispatched him! The cook sprang into a canoe alongside, and in attempting to push off she was capsized; and being unable to swim, he got on the bottom, and paddled ashore with his hands, where he was made prisoner. Gregory, an Italian, sought shelter in the foretopgallant cross-trees, where he was fired at several times by the Malays with the muskets of the *Friendship*, which were always kept loaded and ready for use while on the coast.

Three of the crew leaped into the sea, and swam to a point of land near a mile distant, to the northward of the town; and, unperceived by the Malays on shore, pursued their course to the northward towards Cape Felix, intending to go to the port of Annalaboo, about forty-five miles distant. Having walked all night, they found themselves, on the following morning, near the promontory, and still twenty-five miles distant from Annalaboo.

When Mr. Endicott, Mr. Barry, and the four seamen arrived at the beach, they saw the crew jumping into the sea; the truth now, with all its horrors, flashed upon his mind, that the vessel was attacked, and in an instant they jumped on board the boat and pushed off; at the same time a friendly rajah named Po Adam, sprang into the boat; he was the proprietor of a port and considerable property at a place called Pulo Kio, but three miles distant from the mouth of the river Quallah Battoo. More business had been done by the rajah during the eight years past than by any other on the pepper coast; he had uniformly professed himself friendly to the Americans, and he has generally received the character of their being honest. Speaking a little English as he sprang into the boat, he exclaimed, "Captain, you got trouble; Malay kill you, he kill Po Adam too!" Crowds of Malays assembled on both sides of the river, brandishing their weapons in a menacing manner, while a ferry boat, manned with eight or ten of the natives, armed with spears and krisses,[5] pushed off to prevent the officers' regaining their ship. The latter exhibited no fear, and flourished the cutlass of Po Adam in a menacing manner from the bows of the boat; it so intimidated the Malays that they fled to the shore, leaving a free passage to the ship; but as they got near her they found that the Malays had got entire possession of her; some of them were promenading the deck, others were making signals of success to the people on shore, while, with the exception of one man aloft, not an individual of the crew could be seen. Three Malay boats, with about fifty men, now issued from the river in the direction of the ship, while the captain and his men, concluding that their only hope of recovering their vessel was to obtain assistance from some other ships, directed their course towards Muchie, where they knew that several American vessels were lying at anchor. Three American captains, upon hearing the misfortunes of their countrymen, weighed anchor immediately for Quallah Battoo, determined, if possible, to recover the ship. By four o'clock on the same day they gained an anchorage off that place; the Malays, in the meantime, had removed on shore every moveable article belonging to the ship, including specie, besides several cases of opium, amounting in all to upwards of thirty thousand dollars. This was done on the night of the 9th, and on the morning of the 10th, they contrived to heave in the chain cable, and get the anchor up to the bows; and the ship was drifting finely towards the beach, when the cable, not being stopped abaft[6] the bitts,[7] began suddenly to run out with great velocity; but a bight[8] having by accident been thrown forward of the windlass,[9] a riding turn[10] was the consequence, and the anchor, in its descent, was suddenly checked about fifteen fathoms from the hawse.[11] A squall soon after coming on, the vessel drifted obliquely towards the shore, and grounded upon a coral reef near half a mile to the southward of the town. The next day, having obtained a convenient anchorage, a message was sent by a friendly Malay who came on board at Soo Soo, demanding the restoration of the ship. The rajah[12] replied that he would not give her up, but that they were welcome to take her if they could; a fire was now opened upon the Friendship by the vessels, her decks were crowded with Malays, who promptly returned the fire, as did also the forts on shore. This mode of warfare appeared undecisive, and it was determined to decide the contest by a close action. A number of boats being manned and armed with about thirty officers and men, a movement was made to carry the ship by boarding. The Malays did not wait the approach of this determined attack, but all deserted the vessel to her lawful owners, when she was taken possession of and warped out into deep water. The appearance of the ship, at the time she was boarded, beggars all description; every part of her bore ample testimony of the scene of violence and destruction with which she had been visited. The objects of the voyage were abandoned, and the *Friendship* returned to the United States.

THE *MEXICAN*

Salem, Massachusetts, and Rio de Janeiro

1832

Slavers and pirates were often interchangeable at this point, during the period of time when slavery was legal in the United States but importation of slaves was not. The crew of the Panda *who attacked the* Mexican *were later captured off the west coast of Africa and brought to trial in Boston, where half of them were put to death by hanging.*

The *Mexican*, a craft of 227 tons register, owned by Joseph Peabody of Salem, and commanded by Captain John G. Butman of the same place, sailed from Salem for Rio Janeiro and a market[1] on August 29, 1832.[2] In view of subsequent purchases, she sailed from this port in ballast, with the exception of about one hundred bags of salt peter and one hundred chests of tea, also having concealed in the run some twenty thousand dollars in specie.

Exclusive of the captain, the crew of the *Mexican* consisted of two mates, eight hands before the mast, colored cook and steward; thirteen men all told.

On September 20, 1832, when in latitude 33 north and longitude 34 1-2 west, the *Mexican* fell in with and was captured by the piratical schooner *Panda*, by whom she was robbed of her specie, the crew maltreated and robbed of their own belongings. The pirates also nearly stripped the brig of provisions, sails, and ship's furniture of all kinds.

They then drove the officers and crew of the *Mexican* below, all means of egress securely fastened, the running rigging and sails of the brig cut and mutilated, her galley filled with combustibles and set on fire, and then both the crew and the brig were abandoned to the flames. Luckily, however, before the fire had gained much headway, the crew were able to break out and slowly extinguish it. They were afraid to do this too quickly, for as long as the pirates were in sight any sudden checking of the flames would be sure to draw their attention and return, which latter fact would assuredly have settled the fate of everyone on board the *Mexican*. The pirates had left the unfortunate brig in a bad plight, but Captain Butman and his crew, esteeming themselves fortunate to escape with their lives, at once set to work repairing damages as speedily as possible, and before dark had bent new sails, repaired the running gear, etc.

Thanks, also, to the foresight of Captain Butman, who, when he discovered the true character of the strange vessel, had managed to hide some of the most necessary navigating appliances, such as a compass, quadrant and chart, the *Mexican* was eventually able to reach Salem, on Oct. 12, 1832.

LA AMISTAD

Havana and Montauk

1839

Our final example is an intriguing one, particularly given that the concept of piracy vacillates so wildly between conditions of extreme freedom and extreme unfreedom. In July 1839, Spanish schooner La Amistad *was moving a group of fifty-three Mende captives who had been illegally sold and transported to Cuba, in violation of international treaties outlawing the importation of enslaved people across the Atlantic. Four of the group were children. Supposedly the tenor of the trip took an even darker turn when the ship's cook joked to the captives that they were going to be murdered and eaten. A couple of days later a Mende man named Sengbe Pieh, commonly Anglicized to Joseph Cinque, led the captives in a bloody and violent revolt. They seized the ship, killed the captain and the cook with the sense of humor, and demanded of their former captors to be sailed back to Africa.*

The two Spaniards who had imprisoned them, Don Jose Ruiz and Don Pedro Montes, deceived the Mende, instead sailing for the East Coast of the United States with the knowledge that the US Navy would certainly intercept them if they thought the schooner had fallen into the hands of pirates. Ruiz and Montes assumed that the mutineers would then be forced to return to Cuba as their property. Off Long Island, the Amistad *was waylaid by the US revenue cutter* Washington. *Pieh and some of his confederates escaped the* Washington *but were eventually caught and imprisoned with the other rebels. The* Amistad *was towed into New Haven, Connecticut, and the mutineers were charged with murder and piracy—rather surreally, the property they were accused of having seized as pirates was not only the vessel itself, but also their own bodies. Two notable court cases emerged from this incident: the* Washington *officers claiming salvage rights to the ship and the value of the human cargo and the Spanish captors being charged with enslaving the Mende. Spain demanded of the US president that the* Amistad *mutineers be returned to Cuba as slaves. Eventually the case,* United States v. The Amistad *(1841) was tried before the Supreme Court and decided in favor of the Mende, serving as a landmark moment in the abolitionist movement. The* Amistad *pirates (who were not, in the end, pirates at all) were defended by John Quincy Adams, an excerpt of whose argument appears below.*

During the night of the 30th of said month, or about daybreak on the following day, the slaves rose upon the crew, and killed the captain, a slave of his, and two sailors—sparing only two persons, after ill treating and wounding them, namely, Don Jose Ruiz and Don Pedro Montes: of whom the former was owner of forty-nine of the slaves, and the latter of the other four.[1] These they retained, that they might navigate the vessel and take her to the coast of Africa. Montes, availing himself of his knowledge of nautical affairs, and under favor of Divine Providence—"the favor of Divine Providence!"—succeeded in directing the vessel to these shores. He was spoken by various vessels, from the captains of which the negroes bought provisions, but to whom, it seems, he was unable to make known his distress, being closely watched. At length, by good fortune, he reached Long Island, where the *Amistad* was detained by the American brig-of-war *Washington*, Captain Gedney, who, on learning the circumstances of the case, secured the negroes, and took them with the vessel to New London, in the state of Connecticut.

MAY IT PLEASE YOUR HONORS—

In rising to address this Court as one of its attorneys and counsellors, regularly admitted at a great distance of time, I feel that an apology might well be expected where I shall perhaps be more likely to exhibit at once the infirmities of age and the inexperience of youth, than to render those services to the individuals whose lives and liberties are at the disposal of this Court which I would most earnestly desire to render.[2] But as I am unwilling to employ one moment of the time of the Court in anything that regards my own personal situation, I shall reserve what few observations I may think necessary to offer as an apology till the close of my argument on the merits of the question.

I therefore proceed immediately to say that, in a consideration of this case, I derive, in the distress I feel both for myself and my clients, consolation from two sources—first, that the rights of my clients to their lives and liberties have already been defended by my learned friend and colleague in so able and complete a manner as leaves me scarcely anything to say, and I feel that such full justice has been done to their interests, that any fault or imperfection of mine will merely be attributed to its true cause; and secondly, I derive consolation from the thought that this Court is a Court of JUSTICE. And in saying so very trivial a thing, I should not on any other occasion, perhaps, be warranted in asking the Court to consider what justice is. Justice, as defined in the Institutes of Justinian, nearly 2000 years ago, and as it is felt and understood by all who understand human relations and human rights, is—

"Constans et perpetua voluntas, jus suum cuique tribuendi."
"The constant and perpetual will to secure to everyone HIS OWN right."

And in a Court of Justice, where there are two parties present, justice demands that the rights of each party should be allowed to himself, as well as that each party has a right, to be secured and protected by the Court. This observation is important, because I appear here on the behalf of thirty-six individuals, the life and liberty of every one of whom depend on the decision of this Court. The Court, therefore, I trust, in deciding this case, will form no lumping judgment on these thirty-six individuals, but will act on the consideration that the life and the liberty of every one of them must be determined by its decision for himself alone.

They are here, individually, under very different circumstances, and in very different characters. Some are in one predicament, some in another. In some of the proceedings by which they have been brought into the custody and under the protection of this Court, thirty-two or three of them have been charged with the crime of murder. Three or four of them are female children, incapable, in the judgment of our laws, of the crime of murder or piracy, or, perhaps, of any other crime. Yet, from the day when the vessel was taken possession of by one of our naval officers, they have all been held as close prisoners, now for the period of eighteen long months, under custody and by authority of the Courts of the United States. I trust, therefore, that before the ultimate decision of this Court is established, its honorable members will pay due attention to the circumstances and condition of every individual concerned.

When I say I derive consolation from the consideration that I stand before a Court of Justice, I am obliged to take this ground, because, as I shall show, another Department of the Government of the United States has taken, with reference to this case, the ground of utter injustice, and these individuals for whom I appear, stand before this Court, awaiting their fate from its decision, under the array of the whole Executive power of this nation against them, in addition to that of a foreign nation. And here arises a consideration, the most painful of all others, in considering the duty I have to discharge, in which, in supporting the motion to dismiss the appeal, I shall be obliged not only to investigate and submit to the censure of this Court, the form and manner of the proceedings of the Executive in this case, but the validity, and the motive of the reasons assigned for its interference in this unusual manner in a suit between parties for their individual rights.

[. . .]

The charge I make against the present Executive administration is that in all their proceedings relating to those unfortunate men, instead of that Justice, which they were bound not less than this honorable Court itself to observe, they have substituted Sympathy. Sympathy with one of the parties in this conflict of justice, and antipathy to the other. Sympathy with the white, antipathy to the black—and in proof of this charge I adduce the admission and avowal of the Secretary of State himself. In the letter of Mr. Forsyth to the Spanish Minister d'Argaiz, of 13th of December, 1839, defending the course of the administration against the reproaches utterly groundless, but not the less bitter of the Spanish Envoy, he says:

"The undersigned cannot conclude this communication without calling the attention of the Chevalier d'Argaiz to the fact, that with the single exception of the vexatious detention to which Messrs. Montes and Ruiz have been subjected in consequence of the civil suit instituted against them, all the proceedings in the matter, on the part both the Executive and Judicial branches of the government have had their foundation in the ASSUMPTION that these persons ALONE were the parties aggrieved; and that their claims to the surrender of the property was founded in fact and in justice."

At the date of this letter, this statement of Mr. Forsyth was strictly true. All the proceedings of the government, Executive and Judicial, in this case had been founded on the assumption that the two Spanish slave-dealers were the only parties aggrieved—that all the right was on their side, and all the wrong on the side of their surviving self-emancipated victims. I ask your honors, was this JUSTICE. No. It was not so considered by Mr. Forsyth himself. It was sympathy, and he so calls it, for in the preceding page of the same letter referring to the proceedings of this Government from the very first intervention of Lieut. Gedney, he says:

"Messrs. Ruiz and Montes were first found near the coast of the United States, deprived of their property and of their freedom, suffering from lawless violence in their persons, and in imminent and constant danger of being deprived of their lives also.

They were found in this distressing and perilous situation by officers of the United States, who, moved towards them *by sympathetic feeling which subsequently became as it were national*, immediately rescued them from personal danger, restored them to freedom, secured their oppressors that they might abide the consequences of the acts of violence perpetrated upon them, and placed under the safeguard of the laws all the property which they claimed as their own, to remain in safety until the competent authority could examine their title to it, and pronounce upon the question of ownership agreeably to the provisions of the 9th article of the treaty of 1795."

This sympathy with Spanish slave-traders is declared by the Secretary to have been first felt by Lieutenant Gedney. I hope this is not correctly represented. It is imputed to him and declared to have become in a manner national. The national sympathy with the slave-traders of the barracoons[3] is officially declared to have been the prime motive of action of the government: And this fact is given as an answer to all the claims, demands and reproaches of the Spanish minister! I cannot urge the same objection to this that was brought against the assertion in the libel—that it said the thing which is not—too unfortunately it was so, as he said. The sympathy of the Executive government, and as it were of the nation, in favor of the slave-traders, and against these poor, unfortunate, helpless, tongueless, defenseless Africans, was the cause and foundation and motive of all these proceedings, and has brought this case up for trial before your honors.

[. . .]

For I inquire by what *right*, all this sympathy, from Lieut. Gedney to the Secretary of State, and from the Secretary of State, *as it were*, to the nation, was extended to the two Spaniards from Cuba exclusively, and utterly denied to the fifty-two victims of *their* lawless violence? By what *right* was it denied to the men who had restored themselves to freedom, and secured their oppressors to abide the consequences of the acts of violence perpetrated by them, and why was it extended to the perpetrators of those acts of violence themselves? When the *Amistad* first came within the territorial jurisdiction of the United States, acts of violence had passed between the two parties, the Spaniards and Africans on board of her, but on which side these acts were *lawless*, on which side were the *oppressors*, was a question of right and wrong, for the settlement of which, if the government and people of the United States interfered at all, they were bound in duty to extend their sympathy to them all; and if they intervened at all *between* them, the duty incumbent upon this intervention was not of favor, but of impartiality—not of sympathy, but of JUSTICE dispensing to every individual *his own right*.

[. . .]

The Africans were in possession, and had the presumptive right of ownership; they were in peace with the United States; the Courts have decided, and truly, that they were not pirates; they were on a voyage to their native homes—their *dulces Argos*; they had acquired the right and so far as their knowledge extended they had the power of prosecuting the voyage; the ship was theirs, and being in immediate communication with the shore, was in the territory of the State of New York; or, if not, at least half the number were actually on the soil of Now York, and entitled to all the provisions of the law of nations, and the protection and comfort which the laws of that State secure to every human being within its limits.

In this situation Lieut. Gedney, without any charge or authority from his government, without warrant of law, by force of fire arms, seizes and disarms them, then being in the peace of that Commonwealth and of the United States, drives them on board the vessel, seizes the vessel and transfers it against the will of its possessors to another State. I ask in the name of justice, by what law was this done? Even admitting that it had been a case of actual piracy, which your courts have properly found it was not, there are questions arising here of the deepest interest to the liberties of the people of this Union, and especially of the State of New York. Have the officers of the U.S. Navy a right to seize men by force, on the territory of New York, to fire at them, to overpower them, to disarm them, to put them on board of a vessel and carry them by force and against their will to another State, without warrant or form of law? I am not arraigning Lieut. Gedney, but I ask this Court, in the name of justice, to settle it in their minds, by what law it was done, and how far the principle it embraces is to be carried.

The whole of my argument to show that the appeal should be dismissed, is founded on an averment that the proceedings on the part of the United States are all wrongful from the beginning. The first act, of seizing the vessel, and these men, by an officer of the navy, was a wrong. The forcible arrest of these men, or a part of them, on the soil of New York, was a wrong. After the vessel was brought into the jurisdiction of the District Court of Connecticut, the men were first seized and imprisoned under a criminal process for murder and piracy on the high seas. Then they were libeled by Lieut. Gedney, as property, and salvage claimed on them, and under that process were taken into the custody of the marshal as property. Then they were claimed by Ruiz and Montes and again taken into custody by the court. The District Attorney of Connecticut wrote to the Secretary of State, September 5th, giving him an account of the matter, stating that "the blacks are indicted for the murder of the captain and mate," and "are now in jail at New Haven;" that "the next term of our Circuit Court sits on the 17th instant, at which time I suppose,"—that is in italics in the printed document—"I *suppose* it will be my duty to bring them to trial, unless they are in some other way disposed of." This is the first intimation of the District Attorney; it is easy to understand in what "other way" he wished them disposed of. And he closes by saying—"should you have any instructions to give on the subject, I should like to receive them as soon as may be."

Appendix

The purpose of this volume is to provide informative and entertaining primary sources about the real history of piracy during the Golden Age. But as we have seen, even in the primary sources, pirate lore is rife with exaggeration, rumor, and myth. As such, it's worthwhile to take a brief look at the two main fictional sources of pirate lore in popular culture, both of whom we know without necessarily having read them.

Long John Silver, whose name persists in a chain of seafood restaurants and whose missing leg informs every children's storybook picture of a pirate, was the villain of Robert Louis Stevenson's adventure novel *Treasure Island*, which was first published as *The Sea Cook: A Story for Boys* in 1883. The novel is a widely adapted[1] and dramatized coming-of-age story, in which a young boy named Jim Hawkins goes on a voyage hunting for pirate treasure but discovers that the cook on the voyage is not to be trusted. Though published in the nineteenth century, the action takes place in the eighteenth, at the height of the Golden Age of piracy. The chapter "What I Heard in the Apple Barrel," excerpted below, gives us Jim's view of Long John Silver first confessing that he is a pirate while Jim is concealed nearby.

Similarly, the pirate Captain James Hook first appears in a J. M. Barrie play from 1904, called *Peter Pan; or, The Boy Who Wouldn't Grow Up*, and then in the novel version *Peter and Wendy*, published in 1911. Hook is so named for the hook he wears in place of a hand that was cut off and fed to a crocodile, who continues to stalk him with a ticking clock in his belly. Hook's ship is called the *Jolly Roger*, named of course for the skull-and-crossbones colors flown by pirates 150 years earlier. In his many cartoon and toy iterations, Hook looks like a Restoration courtier in a long flowing wig, his evil designs on Peter and the Lost Boys being rendered comical, even unmanly, by Hook's ineptitude, vanity, and cowardice.

Both these notorious villains reinforce ableist stereotypes, in which the mutilation of their bodies are meant to stand in, narratively, for the corruption of their souls. Though they also speak to the hard facts of life at sea, as evidenced by the provision made for mutilation in the actual pirate articles referenced above. Both of them are represented as pitiless men made all the more evil by the threats they pose to children. Jim emerges triumphant, in contrast to Henry Avery, say, who was raped as a boy and turned pirate himself, or the children in Jamaica locked up and starved by Henry Morgan. Peter makes Hook ridiculous, in contrast to the boy whose fibula was excavated in the twenty-first century from the shattered wreckage of the *Whydah*, who winds up as dead as Black Sam Bellamy. In each case, the pirates are effectively brought under the domination and control of children. The fictionalization of pirates finally accomplishes what all the Puritan ministers, privateers, navies, carronades, international agreements, public hangings, and royal pardons could never do: it renders pirates harmless.

Only in fiction are the high seas made safe.

From
Treasure Island
by Robert Louis Stevenson

"WHAT I HEARD IN THE APPLE BARREL"

"NO, not I," said Silver. "Flint was cap'n; I was quartermaster, along of my timber leg. The same broadside I lost my leg, old Pew lost his deadlights. It was a master surgeon, him that ampytated me—out of college and all—Latin by the bucket, and what not; but he was hanged like a dog, and sun-dried like the rest, at Corso Castle. That was Roberts'[2] men, that was, and comed of changing names to their ships—*Royal Fortune* and so on. Now, what a ship was christened, so let her stay, I says. So it was with the *Cassandra*, as brought us all safe home from Malabar, after England[3] took the viceroy of the Indies; so it was with the old *Walrus*, Flint's old ship, as I've seen amuck with the red blood and fit to sink with gold."

"Ah!" cried another voice, that of the youngest hand on board, and evidently full of admiration. "He was the flower of the flock, was Flint!"

"Davis[4] was a man too, by all accounts," said Silver. "I never sailed along of him; first with England, then with Flint, that's my story; and now here on my own account,[5] in a manner of speaking. I laid by nine hundred safe, from England, and two thousand after Flint. That ain't bad for a man before the mast—all safe in bank. 'Tain't earning now, it's saving does it, you may lay to that. Where's all England's men now? I dunno. Where's Flint's? Why, most on 'em aboard here, and glad to get the duff[6]—been begging before that, some on 'em. Old Pew, as had lost his sight, and might have thought shame, spends twelve hundred pound in a year, like a lord in Parliament. Where is he now? Well, he's dead now and under hatches; but for two year before that, shiver my timbers, the man was starving! He begged, and he stole, and he cut throats, and starved at that, by the powers!"

"Well, it ain't much use, after all," said the young seaman.

"'Tain't much use for fools, you may lay to it—that, nor nothing," cried Silver. "But now, you look here: you're young, you are, but you're as smart as paint. I see that when I set my eyes on you, and I'll talk to you like a man."

You may imagine how I felt when I heard this abominable old rogue addressing another in the very same words of flattery as he had used to myself. I think, if I had been able, that I would have killed him through the barrel. Meantime, he ran on, little supposing he was overheard.

"Here it is about gentlemen of fortune. They lives rough, and they risk swinging, but they eat and drink like fighting-cocks, and when a cruise is done, why, it's hundreds of pounds instead of hundreds of farthings in their pockets. Now, the most goes for rum and a good fling, and to sea again in their shirts. But that's not the course I lay. I puts it all away, some here, some there, and none too much anywheres, by reason of suspicion. I'm fifty, mark you; once back from this cruise, I set up gentleman in earnest. Time enough too, says you. Ah, but I've lived easy in the meantime, never denied myself o' nothing heart desires, and slep' soft and ate dainty all my days but when at sea. And how did I begin? Before the mast, like you!"

"Well," said the other, "but all the other money's gone now, ain't it? You daren't show face in Bristol after this."

"Why, where might you suppose it was?" asked Silver derisively.

"At Bristol, in banks and places," answered his companion.

"It were," said the cook; "it were when we weighed anchor. But my old missis has it all by now. And the Spy-glass is sold, lease and goodwill and rigging; and the old girl's off to meet me. I would tell you where, for I trust you, but it'd make jealousy among the mates."

"And can you trust your missis?" asked the other.

"Gentlemen of fortune," returned the cook, "usually trusts little among themselves, and right they are, you may lay to it. But I have a way with me, I have. When a mate brings a slip on his cable—one as knows me, I mean—it won't be in the same world with old John. There was some that was feared of Pew, and some that was feared of Flint; but Flint his own self was feared of me. Feared he was, and proud. They was the roughest crew afloat, was Flint's; the devil himself would have been feared to go to sea with them. Well now, I tell you, I'm not a boasting man, and you seen yourself how easy I keep company, but when I was quartermaster, *lambs* wasn't the word for Flint's old buccaneers. Ah, you may be sure of yourself in old John's ship."

"Well, I tell you now," replied the lad, "I didn't half a quarter like the job till I had this talk with you, John; but there's my hand on it now."

"And a brave lad you were, and smart too," answered Silver, shaking hands so heartily that all the barrel shook, "and a finer figurehead for a gentleman of fortune I never clapped my eyes on."

By this time I had begun to understand the meaning of their terms. By a "gentleman of fortune" they plainly meant neither more nor less than a common pirate, and the little scene that I had overheard was the last act in the corruption of one of the honest hands—perhaps of the last one left aboard. But on this point I was soon to be relieved, for Silver giving a little whistle, a third man strolled up and sat down by the party.

"Dick's square," said Silver.

"Oh, I know'd Dick was square," returned the voice of the coxswain, Israel Hands. "He's no fool, is Dick." And he turned his quid and spat. "But look here," he went on, "here's what I want to know, Barbecue: how long are we a-going to stand off and on like a blessed bumboat?[7] I've had a'most enough o' Cap'n Smollett; he's hazed me long enough, by thunder! I want to go into that cabin, I do. I want their pickles and wines, and that."

"Israel," said Silver, "your head ain't much account, nor ever was. But you're able to hear, I reckon; leastways, your ears is big enough. Now, here's what I say: you'll berth forward, and you'll live hard, and you'll speak soft, and you'll keep sober till I give the word; and you may lay to that, my son."

"Well, I don't say no, do I?" growled the coxswain. "What I say is, when? That's what I say."

"When! By the powers!" cried Silver. "Well now, if you want to know, I'll tell you when. The last moment I can manage, and that's when. Here's a first-rate seaman, Cap'n Smollett, sails the blessed ship for us. Here's this squire and doctor with a map and such—I don't know where it is, do I? No more do you, says you. Well then, I mean this squire and doctor shall find the stuff, and help us to get it aboard, by the powers. Then we'll see. If I was sure of you all, sons of double Dutchmen, I'd have Cap'n Smollett navigate us half-way back again before I struck."

"Why, we're all seamen aboard here, I should think," said the lad Dick.

"We're all forecastle hands, you mean," snapped Silver. "We can steer a course, but who's to set one?[8] That's what all you gentlemen split on, first and last. If I had my way, I'd have Cap'n Smollett work us back into the trades at least; then we'd have no blessed miscalculations and a spoonful of water a day. But I know the sort you are. I'll finish with 'em at the island, as soon's the blunt's on board, and a pity it is. But you're never happy till you're drunk. Split my sides, I've a sick heart to sail with the likes of you!"

"Easy all, Long John," cried Israel. "Who's a-crossin' of you?"

"Why, how many tall ships, think ye, now, have I seen laid aboard? And how many brisk lads drying in the sun at Execution Dock?" cried Silver. "And all for this same hurry and hurry and hurry. You hear me? I seen a thing or two at sea, I have. If you would on'y lay your course, and a p'int to windward, you would ride in carriages, you would. But not you! I know you. You'll have your mouthful of rum tomorrow, and go hang."

From
J. M. Barrie,
Peter and Wendy

CHAPTER XIV

THE PIRATE SHIP

One green light squinting over Kidd's Creek,[9] which is near the mouth of the pirate river, marked where the brig, the *Jolly Roger*, lay, low in the water; a rakish-looking craft foul to the hull, every beam in her detestable like ground strewn with mangled feathers. She was the cannibal of the seas, and scarce needed that watchful eye, for she floated immune in the horror of her name.

She was wrapped in the blanket of night, through which no sound from her could have reached the shore. There was little sound, and none agreeable save the whir of the ship's sewing machine at which Smee sat, ever industrious and obliging, the essence of the commonplace, pathetic Smee. I know not why he was so infinitely pathetic, unless it were because he was so pathetically unaware of it; but even strong men had to turn hastily from looking at him, and more than once on summer evenings he had touched the fount of Hook's tears and made it flow. Of this, as of almost everything else, Smee was quite unconscious.

A few of the pirates leant over the bulwarks drinking in the miasma of the night; others sprawled by barrels over games of

dice and cards; and the exhausted four who had carried the little house lay prone on the deck, where even in their sleep they
rolled skillfully to this side or that out of Hook's reach, lest he
should claw them mechanically in passing.

Hook trod the deck in thought. O man unfathomable. It
was his hour of triumph. Peter had been removed for ever from
his path, and all the other boys were on the brig, about to
walk the plank. It was his grimmest deed since the days when
he had brought Barbecue[10] to heel; and knowing as we do how
vain a tabernacle is man, could we be surprised had he now
paced the deck unsteadily, bellied out by the winds of his success?

But there was no elation in his gait, which kept pace with
the action of his somber mind. Hook was profoundly dejected.

He was often thus when communing with himself on board
ship in the quietude of the night. It was because he was so ter-
ribly alone. This inscrutable man never felt more alone than
when surrounded by his dogs. They were socially so inferior
to him.

Hook was not his true name. To reveal who he really was
would even at this date set the country in a blaze; but as those
who read between the lines must already have guessed, he had
been at a famous public school;[11] and its traditions still clung
to him like garments, with which indeed they are largely concerned. Thus it was offensive to him even now to board a ship
in the same dress in which he grappled her; and he still ad-
hered in his walk to the school's distinguished slouch. But
above all he retained the passion for good form.

Good form! However much he may have degenerated, he
still knew that this is all that really matters.

From far within him he heard a creaking as of rusty portals,
and through them came a stern tap-tap-tap, like hammering in
the night when one cannot sleep. "Have you been good form
today?" was their eternal question.

"Fame, fame, that glittering bauble, it is mine," he cried.

"Is it quite good form to be distinguished at anything?" the
tap-tap from his school replied.

"I am the only man whom Barbecue feared," he urged; "and Flint himself feared Barbecue."

"Barbecue, Flint—what house?"[12] came the cutting retort.

Most disquieting reflection of all, was it not bad form to think about good form?

His vitals were tortured by this problem. It was a claw within him sharper than the iron one; and as it tore him, the perspiration dripped down his tallow countenance and streaked his doublet.[13] Ofttimes he drew his sleeve across his face, but there was no damming that trickle.

Ah, envy not Hook.

There came to him a presentiment of his early dissolution. It was as if Peter's terrible oath had boarded the ship. Hook felt a gloomy desire to make his dying speech, lest presently there should be no time for it.

"Better for Hook," he cried, "if he had had less ambition." It was in his darkest hours only that he referred to himself in the third person.

"No little children love me."

Strange that he should think of this, which had never troubled him before; perhaps the sewing machine brought it to his mind. For long he muttered to himself, staring at Smee, who was hemming placidly, under the conviction that all children feared him.

Feared him! Feared Smee! There was not a child on board the brig that night who did not already love him. He had said horrid things to them and hit them with the palm of his hand, because he could not hit with his fist; but they had only clung to him the more. Michael had tried on his spectacles.

To tell poor Smee that they thought him lovable! Hook itched to do it, but it seemed too brutal. Instead, he revolved this mystery in his mind: why do they find Smee lovable? He pursued the problem like the sleuth-hound that he was. If Smee was lovable, what was it that made him so? A terrible answer suddenly presented itself: "Good form?"

Had the bo'sun good form without knowing it, which is the best form of all?

He remembered that you have to prove you don't know you have it before you are eligible for Pop.[14]

With a cry of rage he raised his iron hand over Smee's head; but he did not tear. What arrested him was this reflection:

"To claw a man because he is good form, what would that be?"

"Bad form!"

The unhappy Hook was as impotent as he was damp, and he fell forward like a cut flower.

His dogs thinking him out of the way for a time, discipline instantly relaxed; and they broke into a bacchanalian dance, which brought him to his feet at once; all traces of human weakness gone, as if a bucket of water had passed over him.

"Quiet, you scugs," he cried, "or I'll cast anchor in you"; and at once the din was hushed. "Are all the children chained, so that they cannot fly away?"

"Ay, ay."

"Then hoist them up."

The wretched prisoners were dragged from the hold, all except Wendy, and ranged in line in front of him. For a time he seemed unconscious of their presence. He lolled at his ease, humming, not unmelodiously, snatches of a rude song, and fingering a pack of cards. Ever and anon the light from his cigar gave a touch of color to his face.

"Now then, bullies," he said briskly, "six of you walk the plank tonight, but I have room for two cabin boys. Which of you is it to be?"

"Don't irritate him unnecessarily," had been Wendy's instructions in the hold; so Tootles stepped forward politely. Tootles hated the idea of signing under such a man, but an instinct told him that it would be prudent to lay the responsibility on an absent person; and though a somewhat silly boy, he knew that mothers alone are always willing to be the buffer. All children know this about mothers,[15] and despise them for it, but make constant use of it.

So Tootles explained prudently, "You see, sir, I don't think my mother would like me to be a pirate. Would your mother like you to be a pirate, Slightly?"

He winked at Slightly, who said mournfully, "I don't think so," as if he wished things had been otherwise. "Would your mother like you to be a pirate, Twin?"

"I don't think so," said the first twin, as clever as the others. "Nibs, would——"

"Stow this gab," roared Hook, and the spokesmen were dragged back. "You, boy," he said, addressing John, "you look as if you had a little pluck in you. Didst never want to be a pirate, my hearty?"

Now John had sometimes experienced this hankering at maths prep.;[16] and he was struck by Hook's picking him out.

"I once thought of calling myself Red-handed Jack," he said diffidently.

"And a good name too. We'll call you that here, bully, if you join."

"What do you think, Michael?" asked John.

"What would you call me if I join?" Michael demanded.

"Blackbeard Joe."

Michael was naturally impressed. "What do you think, John?" He wanted John to decide, and John wanted him to decide.

"Shall we still be respectful subjects of the King?" John inquired.

Through Hook's teeth came the answer: "You would have to swear, 'Down with the King.'"

Perhaps John had not behaved very well so far, but he shone out now.

"Then I refuse," he cried, banging the barrel in front of Hook.

"And I refuse," cried Michael.

"Rule Britannia!" squeaked Curly.

The infuriated pirates buffeted them in the mouth; and Hook roared out, "That seals your doom. Bring up their mother. Get the plank ready."

They were only boys, and they went white as they saw Jukes and Cecco preparing the fatal plank. But they tried to look brave when Wendy[17] was brought up.

No words of mine can tell you how Wendy despised those pirates. To the boys there was at least some glamour in the pirate calling; but all that she saw was that the ship had not been scrubbed for years. There was not a porthole, on the grimy glass of which you might not have written with your finger "Dirty pig"; and she had already written it on several. But as the boys gathered round her she had no thought, of course, save for them.

"So, my beauty," said Hook, as if he spoke in syrup, "you are to see your children walk the plank."

Fine gentleman though he was, the intensity of his communings had soiled his ruff,[18] and suddenly he knew that she was gazing at it. With a hasty gesture he tried to hide it, but he was too late.

"Are they to die?" asked Wendy, with a look of such frightful contempt that he nearly fainted.

"They are," he snarled. "Silence all," he called gloatingly, "for a mother's last words to her children."

At this moment Wendy was grand. "These are my last words, dear boys," she said firmly. "I feel that I have a message to you from your real mothers, and it is this: 'We hope our sons will die like English gentlemen.'"

Even the pirates were awed; and Tootles cried out hysterically, "I am going to do what my mother hopes. What are you to do, Nibs?"

"What my mother hopes. What are you to do, Twin?"

"What my mother hopes. John, what are——"

But Hook had found his voice again.

"Tie her up," he shouted.

It was Smee who tied her to the mast. "See here, honey," he whispered, "I'll save you if you promise to be my mother."

But not even for Smee would she make such a promise. "I would almost rather have no children at all," she said disdainfully.

It is sad to know that not a boy was looking at her as Smee tied her to the mast; the eyes of all were on the plank: that last little walk they were about to take. They were no longer able to hope that they would walk it manfully, for the capacity to think had gone from them; they could stare and shiver only.

Hook smiled on them with his teeth closed, and took a step toward Wendy. His intention was to turn her face so that she should see the boys walking the plank one by one. But he never reached her, he never heard the cry of anguish he hoped to wring from her. He heard something else instead.

It was the terrible tick-tick of the crocodile.

They all heard it—pirates, boys, Wendy; and immediately every head was blown in one direction; not to the water whence the sound proceeded, but toward Hook. All knew that what was about to happen concerned him alone, and that from being actors they were suddenly become spectators.

Very frightful was it to see the change that came over him. It was as if he had been clipped at every joint. He fell in a little heap.

The sound came steadily nearer; and in advance of it came this ghastly thought, "The crocodile is about to board the ship."

Even the iron claw hung inactive; as if knowing that it was no intrinsic part of what the attacking force wanted. Left so fearfully alone, any other man would have lain with his eyes shut where he fell: but the gigantic brain of Hook was still working, and under its guidance he crawled on his knees along the deck as far from the sound as he could go. The pirates respectfully cleared a passage for him, and it was only when he brought up against the bulwarks that he spoke.

"Hide me!" he cried hoarsely.

They gathered round him; all eyes averted from the thing that was coming aboard. They had no thought of fighting it. It was Fate.

Only when Hook was hidden from them did curiosity loosen the limbs of the boys so that they could rush to the ship's side to see the crocodile climbing it. Then they got the strangest surprise of this Night of Nights; for it was no crocodile that was coming to their aid. It was Peter.

He signed to them not to give vent to any cry of admiration that might rouse suspicion. Then he went on ticking.

Notes

THE SEVENTEENTH CENTURY
AND BEFORE

FRANCIS DRAKE

1. It's hard to overstate how challenging a circumnavigation is. Rich Wilson, an American sailor who has competed in the Vendée Globe twice, writes in his book *Race France to France: Leave Antarctica to Starboard* that the number of people who have completed a solo circumnavigation in a sailboat without stopping is smaller than the number of people who have been to space. Drake wasn't alone, of course, and he stopped at several ports, but he also didn't have GPS, and nobody told him about the Roaring Forties. See Wilson, Rich, *Race France to France: Leave Antarctica to Starboard: An American in the Vendée Globe, Racing Solo, Non-Stop, Around the World* (SitesALIVE, independently published, 2012).

2. From Nuttall, Zelia, ed. and trans., *New Light on Drake: A Collection of Documents Relating to His Voyage of Circumnavigation, 1577–1580* (London: Hakluyt Society, 1914), 201–8.

3. We don't typically think of "ship" as having a technical definition today, but in the age of sail it was used primarily as an indicator of size. A ship is large while a boat is small. In the modern era, a "ship" was, per the OED, "a vessel having a bowsprit and three masts, each of which consists of a lower, top, and topgallant mast."

4. A "bark" is usually meant as a general term for a small sailing vessel. Here they are probably suggesting that the bark was used as a tender, or a smaller vessel meant to ferry crew back and forth to shore from a larger vessel lying at anchor. The bark was the water taxi of the age of sail.

5. The "prow" is the pointed front section of a boat or ship, now more commonly called the bow.

6. The OED defines "poop" in this context as "the aftermost part of a ship; the stern; the aftermost and highest deck often forming (esp. in a wooden ship) the roof of a cabin in the stern."

7. The OED defines "arquebus" as "a portable firearm of varying size and weight, esp. one supported when in use on a tripod, forked rest, etc. Now historical."

8. The OED defines "galleon" as follows: "a kind of vessel, shorter but higher than the galley; a ship of war, esp. Spanish; also, the large vessels used by the Spanish in carrying on trade with their American possessions (in modern usage chiefly in this connection)."

9. A note in the 1914 text inserted here remarks that the expression "on the ballast" was sometimes used to mean "in the hold."

10. On the Pacific Coast of what is now Mexico, the Gulf of Tehuantepec is a common site for the formation of Pacific hurricanes, and often features a steady gale-force wind called the Tehuano.

11. A seaport city on the Pacific coast of modern day Peru, one of the most important ports during the Spanish colonial period.

12. A note in the 1914 translation inserted here says, "The owner of this ship having very costly apparel, earnestly entreated Drake and besought him not to take away from him his apparel, which he promised not to doo, and the gentleman gave him a falcon of gold . . . for his favourable dealing with him." *The World Encompassed By Sir Francis Drake. Being His next Voyage to that to Nombre de Dios, formerly imprinted; Carefully collected out of the Notes of Master Francis Fletcher, Preacher in this imployment, and divers others his followers in the same. Offered now at last to publike view, both for the honour of the Actor, but especially for the stirring up of Heroick spirits, to benefit their Country, and eternize their names by like noble attempts.* London, Printed by E[lizabeth] P[urslow] for Nicholas Bourne, 1635.

13. A note in the 1914 translation here reads, "Zarate's 'ship was laden with lynen cloth and fine China silks and there were also in her divers chests full of fine earthen dishes, very finely wrought, of fine white erth, brought by the Spanyards from the country of Chyna which dishes the Spanyards greatly esteem. Of these dishes Drake tooke four chests full from them also about [?] packs of fine lynen cloth and good store of taffeta and other fine silks.'" *World Encompassed*, 182.

14. A note in the 1914 translation here reads "'diome por ellos un

alfanje y un braserillo de plata y yo prometon a V. E que no per-
dio nada en las ferias.' In Spanish dictionaries 'alfanje' is given
as the Catalan name, derived from the Arabic, for a kind of
short, broad and recurved sword, which answers to the description of the English falchion or hanger. A 'braserillo' signifies a
small brazier and was probably, in this case, a perfume-burner."
The 2022 OED defines a falchion as a "broad sword more or
less curved with the edge on the convex side."

15. A settlement of about 1,000 people in modern-day Panama,
Nombre de Dios was founded as a Spanish settlement in 1510,
making it one of the longest continuous sites of European settlement in the Americas. When Drake sacked it, it was the major
port of embarkation for Spanish treasure fleets.

16. A note in the 1914 translation remarks, "The idiom 'de altura'
particularly refers to Drake's skill in the highest branch of the
art of navigation, namely the determination of a latitude ('altura') from the measurement of the altitude ('alturna') of a heav-
enly body by means of the astrolabe, now superseded by
Hadley's quadrant and sextant."

17. Careening a ship means to tip it over on one side to make repairs
on the hull while the ship is still in the water, rather than taking
it to a shipyard or dry dock for repairs. Careening can be done
in shallow waters and shoals, but requires skilled carpenters
and shipwrights to be on board in the crew.

18. A note in the translation at this point states "So far as it is
known, the only members of Drake's company who drew maps
and painted were Francis Drake himself, his cousin John Drake,
and Francis Fletcher, of whose notes with several drawings and
maps the Sloane MS No. 61 may be a copy."

19. Sloop can have a few different meanings here. Usually it refers to
a smallish boat with a single mast and fore-and-aft rigging
(what you see on a modern sailboat, rather than square rigging).
It can also denote a smaller armed vessel, or in some cases a
large open boat.

GRACE O'MALLEY

1. I don't often trust Wikipedia, but more information can be
found here: https://en.wikipedia.org/wiki/Grace_O'Malley, retrieved December 6, 2022. See also, and foremost, Chambers,
Anne, *Grace O'Malley: The Biography of Ireland's Pirate Queen
1530–1603* (London: Gill Books, 2018), 51 [Kindle edition].

2. Chambers, *Grace O'Malley*, 11 [Kindle Edition].
3. SPI 63/170/63 (Public Record Office, National Archives, London, originally transcribed by Anne Chambers and published in an appendix in Chambers, *Grace O'Malley*).
4. Eoghan Dubhdara Ó Máille.
5. Me Ní Mháille.
6. Dónal an Chogaidh Ó Flaithbheartaigh.
7. Eóghain Ó Flaithbertaigh.
8. Murchad Ó Flaithbertaigh.
9. Richard "the Iron" Bourke.
10. Tibbott Bourke.
11. The OED defintes "cess" as "a rate levied by local authority and for local purposes. Now superseded in general English use by rate, but frequent dialect; in Ireland it is still the official term."

JACK "CHAKOUR" WARD

1. Milton, Giles, "Pirate John Ward: The Real Captain Jack Sparrow," History Extra, accessed December 6, 2022, https://www.historyextra.com/period/elizabethan/pirate-john-ward-the-real-captain-jack-sparrow/.
2. Simpson, George, "Pirates of the Caribbean: Johnny Depp based Jack Sparrow on Keith Richards and Pepé Le Pew," *Express*, accessed December 6, 2022, https://www.express.co.uk/entertainment/films/1360221/Pirates-of-the-Caribbean-Johnny-Depp-Jack-Sparrow-Keith-Richards-Pepe-Le-Pew.
3. From Barker, Andrew, *A TRVE AND CERTAINE Report of the Beginning, Proceedings, Ouerthrowes, and now present Estate of Captaine WARD and DANSEKER, the two late famous Pirates: from their first setting foorth to this present time* (London: Printed by William Hall, and are to be sold by Iohn Helme at his shop in S. Dunstans Church-yard), 1609, unpaginated.
4. Queen Elizabeth I's reign ended with her death on March 24, 1603.
5. Probably Faversham, a small village not far from Canterbury, in a marshy region abutting the Swale where it empties into the sea.
6. Not totally sure about this one. One OED definition of "toot" suggests it can refer to a drunken fit or spree, but it can also refer to a spying point or spyhole. In other contexts sources have remarked on Jack Ward's sexuality, suggesting that he especially enjoyed buggery. Your editor wonders if this is a crude reference to Ward's sexual proclivities, particularly juxtaposed with the phrase "like a good cock" immediately following.

7. Another puzzle. "Chink" in the seventeenth century meant what it does today, namely, a small fissure or opening. Your editor wonders if this might be another somewhat opaque sexual reference, given its juxtaposition to "lewdness to consume his time withal."

8. James I and VI assumed the throne of England and Ireland upon Elizabeth I's death in March 1603.

9. Sorry, worthless, or contemptible.

10. Cured salt beef, or corned beef (for the large salt grains or "corns"), was a common ration in the British Navy beginning in the seventeenth century.

11. Another tricky one. Could be "biscuit," or could be "birsle." The OED has "birsle" as a Scottish term for a toasting, or something scorched with radiant heat from this period, so perhaps a reference to warm freshly roasted meat instead of salted beef.

12. Outside the walls.

13. An archaic form of "take," as in oaths not refused, oaths willingly accepted.

14. A bark is a small sailboat used as a tender to return to the ship.

15. The OED defines "scattergood" as "one who dissipates or squanders goods or possessions; a spendthrift."

16. An archaic word meaning to disembark or off-load.

17. The OED has "sneke" as an obsolete and rare term for a cold in the head, dating from the 1500s. The word is hard to transcribe, but if it is indeed "sneke" maybe Danseker is saying the two men of the bark were sniveling.

18. The OED defines "potgun" as "a cannon with a separate chamber; (also) a short gun with a large bore, a mortar."

19. The OED defines "hostler" as "a man who attends to horses at an inn; a stableman, a groom."

SAMUEL PALACHE

1. Kritzler, Edward, *Jewish Pirates of the Caribbean* (New York: Doubleday, 2008), 87.

2. Kritzler, *Jewish Pirates*, 91.

3. *Jewish Quarterly Review* 14 (1902), 358, reprints, quoted in Kritzler, chapter 8, note 31, 285.

4. Holland, where Palache was working as an agent of Prince Maurice, son of William of Orange.

WILLIAM JACKSON

1. From Leslie, Charles, *A new history of Jamaica, from the earliest accounts, to the taking of Porto Bello by Vice-Admiral Vernon. In thirteen letters from a gentleman to his friend. . . .* (London: Printed for J. Hodges, at the Looking-Glass on London-Bridge, 1740, second edition), 58–59.

THOMAS VEAL

1. From Ellms, Charles, *The Pirates Own Book, or Authentic Narratives of the Lives, Exploits, and Executions of the Most Celebrated Sea Robbers* (Salem: Marine Research Society, 1924), 272–74.
2. Massachusetts, US, Wills and Probate Records, 1635–1991, via Ancestry.com, retrieved December 6, 2022.
3. More on Dungeon Rock here: Brooks, Rebecca, "Dungeon Rock in Lynn, Massachusetts," History of Massachusetts Blog, updated June 7, 2021, https://historyofmassachusetts.org/dungeon -rock-lynn-ma/.
4. There almost certainly was not a great earthquake in New England in 1658. With thanks to Alex More for the reference, see Ebel, John E., *New England Earthquakes: The Surprising History of Seismic Activity in the Northeast* (Lanham, MD: Globe Pequot, 2019), chapter 3, "1658: The Earthquake that May Have Never Happened."
5. It is, unsurprisingly, no longer a lonely and desolate place, but a relatively recent housing development, with the name "Pirates Glen" given to a cul-de-sac.
6. Cordwaining was a major industry in North Shore communities when this account first began to circulate, in the 1820s, though not, perhaps, in the 1650s.
7. This book was originally published in the 1820s.

HENRY MORGAN

1. See Cundall, Frank, *The Governors of Jamaica in the Seventeenth Century* (London: The West India Committee, 1936), OCLC 3262925.
2. "Sir Henry Morgan," Centre for the Study of the Legacies of British Slavery, accessed December 6, 2022, https://www.ucl.ac .uk/lbs/person/view/2146662323.
3. From Leslie, *A new history*, 107–120.

4. Henry Morgan's term of indenture is another example of the slippery state of freedom versus unfreedom for many of the people who wound up turning to piracy.

5. Edward Mansvelt, or Mansfield, a corsair of either Dutch or English antecedent, probably born in Curacao, who operated out of Port Royal, Jamaica. He raided Spanish settlements and shipping under a privateering commission.

6. The modern-day Archipelago of San Andrés, Providencia, and Santa Catalina, a department of Colombia.

7. Havana, Cuba.

8. Roughly synonymous with "ambush." The OED defines "ambuscade" as "Chiefly Military. The condition or position of lying in wait in a concealed place in order to surprise and attack an enemy, victim, etc.; a positioning of soldiers, etc., in a concealed place for this purpose. Also: the surprise attack itself."

9. Santiago, Cuba.

10. Beef carcasses.

11. Any pirate enthusiast knows the phrase "pieces of eight," but just in case, here is what Wikipedia has to say about the common currency of the Age of Sail: "The Spanish dollar, also known as the piece of eight (Spanish: *real de a ocho, dólar, peso duro, peso fuerte* or *peso*), is a silver coin of approximately 38 mm (1.5 in) diameter worth eight Spanish reales. It was minted in the Spanish Empire following a monetary reform in 1497 with content 25.563 g = (0.822 ozt) fine silver. It was widely used as the first international currency because of its uniformity in standard and milling characteristics. Some countries countermarked the Spanish dollar so it could be used as their local currency. Because the Spanish dollar was widely used in Europe, the Americas, and the Far East, it became the first world currency by the 16th century." See "Spanish dollar," Wikipedia, accessed November 30, 2022, https://en.wikipedia.org/wiki/Spanish_dollar.

12. A league at this time was equivalent to about three nautical miles.

13. The body of water between modern day Panama and Colombia.

14. From Exquemelin, A. O. (Alexandre Olivier), *The Buccaneers and Marooners of America, Being an Account of the Famous Adventures and Daring Deeds of Certain Notorious Freebooters of the Spanish Main,* ed. Howard Pyle (London: T. Fisher Unwin, 1897), 131–40.

15. Campeche, on the Yucatan peninsula.

16. The OED defines "Walloon," a variation of Vallon, as "a man or woman of the race, of Gaulish origin and speaking a French

dialect, which forms the chief portion of the population of the south-eastern provinces of Belgium."

17. The Chagres River, modern-day Panama.

18. "Sieur" in this case is an honorific, akin to "sir," rather than a proper name.

19. Charles II of Spain, the last Hapsburg king, who at the time would have been about seven years old.

20. Another term for the Isthmus of Panama, or the Spanish Main.

21. Present-day Cartagena, Colombia.

22. The meaning of "frigate" evolves over time, as by the nineteenth century the Royal Navy would class a frigate as the next smaller ship after a ship of the line. However, in Morgan's period, the OED suggests that the most common use for "frigate" was "a light and swift vessel, originally built for rowing, afterwards for sailing."

23. The OED suggests the following definition for "galleon": "a kind of vessel, shorter but higher than the galley; a ship of war, esp. Spanish; also, the large vessels used by the Spanish in carrying on trade with their American possessions (in modern usage chiefly in this connection)."

24. Perhaps it's not necessary to annotate "boat," but given the gradations of size, it seems worthwhile to note that boat in this instance is defined in the OED as follows: "A small, typically open vessel for travelling over water, propelled by oars, sail, an engine, etc. Usually contrasted with ship."

25. Organ pipes for shrapnel!

HENRY "THE DREAD PIRATE" MAINWARING

1. Knights Bachelors, accessed December 6, 2022, https://archive .org/details/knightsofenglando2shawuoft/page/n175/mode /2up?view=theater.

2. From Manwaring, G. E., *The Life and Works of Sir Henry Mainwaring, Volume 2 (London:* Navy Records Society, 1920–22).

3. A beautiful crime

4. Mamora was a fort on the Moroccan side of the Strait of Gibraltar, conquered by Spain in 1614. See here: https://www.rct.uk /group/482/content/miscellaneous/mamora-1614-forte-di -mamora-presa-da-cattolici-1614, retrieved December 5, 2022.

5. "Dey" was an honorific title in the Ottoman Empire, roughly translating to "uncle," a position held for life and with a degree of autonomy under the Sultan.

6. "Turn Turk" was a common term at this time to mean convert to Islam, like Jack Ward did.

7. Possibly Juan de Silva, IV Count of Portalegre.

8. A note in the original manuscript says "M. de Manti was a native of Marseilles, and is described as a servant of the Duke of Guise, and a man of note in navigation and similar matters."

9. Possibly Sir Arthur Mainwaring

10. "Perforstmen" does not appear in the OED, but is used here to denote men who have been impressed or otherwise forced into maritime service.

11. A note in the original text clarifies: "i.e. are not dominated by any fort or other military establishment."

12. A note in the original defines the Trade of Brittany as "the name given to that part of the sea between Ushant and Brest which is now known as the Passage de l'Iroise."

13. The OED defines a "pink" as "a small sailing vessel, usually having a narrow stern; spec. (a) a flat-bottomed boat with bulging sides, used for coasting and fishing."

14. A variant spelling of "pram," defined by the OED for this period as "an open, flat-bottomed boat or lighter, used esp. in the Baltic and the Netherlands for shipping cargo."

15. A note in the original clarifies: "Horne. Twenty miles N.N.E. of Amsterdam."

16. The OED defines "wherry" as "a light rowing-boat used chiefly on rivers to carry passengers and goods."

17. A note in the original suggests "The great recourse of pirates to the coasts of Ireland was believed to be due to the want of a statute such as that of 28 Hen. VIII in England" (Cap. XV. For the punishment of pirates and robbers of the sea), which allowed their trial by commission. From time to time all pirates in Ireland whose conduct deserved death had to be sent over to Barnstaple, Bristol, or West Cheshire.

18. A note in the original text here remarks "On August 22, 1609, Sir Richard Moryson wrote from Youghal that the continued repair of pirates to the west coast of that province was in consequence of the remoteness of the place, the wildness of the people, and their own strength and wealth both to command and entice relief. There were, he reported, 11 pirate ships with 1,000 men there then, and that he was forced to forbear any prosecution of them" (*S.P. Ireland*, 1608–10, pp. 277–78. This calendar is teeming with accounts of piracy).

19. Sides of beef or oxen.

20. A note in the original states "Mr. Oppenheim points out, that of the many pirate captains whose names continually recur in the State Papers of the reign of Elizabeth, not one is known to have been executed" (Adm. Of R.N., p. 179). I couldn't tell you who Mr. Oppenheim is, or what gives him special authority in this case, but it's true that being a pirate during the reigns of Elizabeth and James was on the whole less fatal than being a pirate one hundred years later.

21. A note in the original remarks "Paul Hentzner, who travelled in England towards the end of Elizabeth's reign, wrote that the English were 'good sailors and better pirates'" (*Travels*, 1797 ed., p. 63). Two famous pirates, Sir John Ferne and Walsingham, were employed under Mansell in the Algiers Expedition of 1620.

22. A note in the original says "By an Act of 1597–8" (39 Eliz., cap. 4), for punishing "rogues, vagabonds and sturdy beggars," among which category were included "all seafaring men pretending losses of their shippes or goods on the sea going about the Country begging," it was enacted that all who would not reform, would be banished out of the Realm, or "otherwise be judged perpetually to the Galleys of this Realm." Sir William Monson was of the opinion that the minimum period of detention in the galleys should be for seven years (N.R.S., xlv. z07). A cultural memory of this practice lingers in the lyrics to "Rule, Britannia": "Rule, Britannia! rule the waves: Britons never will be slaves."

23. A note in the original here states "Cosimo of Tuscany had a short way with proved pirates. In November 1614 two English ships laden with spoil arrived in Leghorn. Suspecting that the plunder came from Christians and not from Turks, he had the crews arrested. On enquiry, his suspicions were found to be well grounded, and he had two of the ringleaders 'hanged, quartered and gibbeted as an example,' and sent the rest to the galleys for life" (S.P. Venice, 1613–15, xliv).

24. To "lie ahull" means to drift, per the OED: "Of a ship: so as to float or drift solely with the force of the wind or current on the hull, i.e. with the sails furled or the engines turned off. Chiefly with lie."

25. A "plyer" in this instance means a ship sailing to windward.

26. Sea anchors.

27. The original has this note, clarifying the pirate strategy in play here: "This appears to have been a favorite stratagem, which was adopted also by the King's ships." Sir William Monson states that "a ship that is chased and desires to show fear, think-

ing to draw her that chases into her clutches, must counterfeit and work as though she were distressed, or lie like a wreck into the sea; she must cast drags, hogsheads, and other things overboard, to hinder her way" (*Naval Tracts*, N.R.S. xlvii, p. 142). On March 1, 1579, Drake, in the *Golden Hind*, while off Cape Francisco, fell in with the Spanish ship *Cacafuego*. "To take in sail would be to arouse the suspicions of the chase." Drake therefore hit on the ingenious idea "of trailing at his stern empty wine jars, whereby his speed was reduced, and the chase deceived as to his power of sailing" (Corbett, *Drake*, i. 274). See also *Sir Kenelm Digby's Voyage to the Mediterranean* (Camden Society, 96, p. 82).

28. "Tops" means "topgallants," or "topgallant sails," defined by the OED as "a sail set on the section of a sailing ship's mast immediately above the topmast; short for topgallant sail."

29. This is a slightly confusing turn of phrase. When I read it, it suggests to me that pirates preferred to come close and physically board the ship that they have lured into chasing them, but a note in the original suggests that the term "aboard and board" might be "on board and board," or as the notes puts it, "When two ships touch."

30. Flags.

31. A note in the original defines "floaty" as "a floaty ship is a ship which draws but little water" (vide p. 149), or rather, one that has a shallow draft.

32. A note in the original elaborates: "Lord Carew writing in 1616 records that, 'in the towne of Angire the Englishe are well enoughe intreated, but yf they be taken at sea, ether outward or homeward bound, they are esteemed good price without redemption. . . . To assure themselves of renegados, the Turkes are so carefull as in every shippe there is three Turkes for one renegado" (Carew, *Letters to Sir T. Roe*, p. 61).

33. A note in the original says "Faulcon. N.W. Coast of Algeria."

34. "Tres Forkes. On the N.E. point of Ras ed Deir, N. coast of Morocco" Manwaring, G. E., *The life and works of Sir Henry Mainwaring, Volume 2* (London: Navy Records Society, 1920–22) 9–43.

35. "Formetero. One of the Balearic Islands." Mainwaring, *The life and works*, 9–43.

36. "Euersay": Sir W. Penn spelled it Ivessy (*Memorials*, i. 332); Admiral Badiley in 1652 wrote Iversey (Spalding, *Life of Badiley*, p. 71).

37. A fathom is equivalent to two yards, so the deepest part of the channel is only about eighteen feet deep on average, and at flood tide only thirty feet, which for the drafts of ships at this period, is next to nothing.

38. Cabo de Gata, Spain.

39. "Bone is a fortified seaport town whose harbour is considered the safest on the Algerian coast" Mainwaring, *The life and works*, 9–43. Possibly modern-day Annaba, Algeria.

40. A note in the original reads "Bogee. One hundred and twelve miles E. of Algiers. The roadstead is deep and sheltered." Possibly modern-day Bejaia.

41. A note in the original reads "San Pietro, island off the S.W. point of Sardinia."

42. The original note suggests that this refers to "Cape Passer in Sicillia. Extreme S.E. of Sicily."

43. "Galee Grosse," or large galley, worked with four sails and sometimes as many as one hundred oars. These galleys could be over one hundred feet long.

44. A note in the original suggests this locale is "Apparently Susa, on the Gulf of Hammamet; 'command' being here used in the sense of 'dominion.'"

45. A note in the original suggests this site is "Porto Feryn. In the Gulf of Tunis. At one time famous for its arsenal. It was the winter port of the Tunisian fleet. Blake gained one of his celebrated victories here on 4th April, 1655."

46. A note in the original offers the following definition: "Perry, a squall or contrary wind" (*Halliwell's Dictionary*).

47. A note in the original elaborates: "The inner harbour of Algiers, originally built in 1518, consisted of a mole connecting the town with the rocks on which the lighthouse, built 1544, now stands. The citadel situated on the highest point of the city was defended by 200 guns." A mole here is defined by the OED as "a massive structure, esp. of stone, serving as a pier, breakwater, or causeway. Also: the area of water bounded by or contained within such a structure, esp. forming a harbour or port."

48. A note in the original reads "Vealls Mallego. Fourteen miles E.N.E. of Malaga."

49. A note in the original reads "Shavia. Formerly Xavea, forty-five miles N.E. of Alicante."

50. A note in the original clarifies "Allicant."

51. A note in the original identifies this locale as "Callery. Twenty-one miles S. of Valencia."

52. A note in the original offers the following definition: "I.e. Ligier; resident agent or consul."

53. Rock of Lisbon.

54. Early navigation occasionally used height or altitude in place of latitude.

55. A note in the original guesses "Lobos Island?"

56. The Azores.

57. A note in the original suggests "San Jorge."

58. A note in the original clarifies "Pico Island: has a volcanic peak."

59. A note in the original translates this as "Flowers."

60. A note in the original clarifies "Tarceres; i.e. the Azores."

61. A note in the original says "Corves. Smallest of the Azores."

62. A note in the original reads "i.e. the great fishing Banks." In Marblehead, Massachusetts, a bank still exists named National Grand Bank, for the Grand Banks where the fishing fleet used to go to make money.

63. A note in the original provides the following reference: "Travas. 'A Travers is the varietie or alteration of the Shippes motion upon the shift of windes, within any Horizontall plaine superficies, by the good collection of which Traverses the ship's uniform motion or Corse is given'" (Davis, *The Seaman's Secrets*, 1607; Hakhluyt Soc. Reprint, p. 240).

64. A note in the original offers the following discussion of convoys. "Requests to send men-of-war to guard the fishermen and convoy them home are frequently met with in the State Papers. In May 1620 John Mason, governor of Newfoundland, was granted a commission in the ship *Peter and Andrew*, of London, 320 tons burthen, to press such ships as were necessary for suppressing the pirates. Three years later two men-of-war were sent out to convoy the fishing fleet home. Lord Baltimore petitioned the King in 1628 that two of the Royal fleet at least might be appointed to guard the coast for the safety of thousands of British subjects. These appeals generally met with little response, and in 1636 the merchants of the western ports of England were petitioning Charles for protection for the 300 vessels that were then on their way home from Newfoundland" (Prowse, 108, 112; *S.P. Colonial*, vol. i. p. 93; *Weymouth Charters*, 1883, p. 178).

65. A note in the original has this to add: "On account of the alarm occasioned by the presence of pirates on the coast of Scotland, two ships under the command of Sir William Monson were dis-

patched there in 1614. 'When Sir William arrived at Caithness, he found that their number had dwindled from twenty to two. One, when admonished on the wickedness of his course, surrendered, and the other, Monson recorded, had been "not long before my boatswain's mate in the Narrow Seas." Piracy was more remunerative than service in the King's ships, and Clarke, for such was the pirate's name, had the day previous to Monson's arrival been "friendly entertained" by the Earl of Caithness, as that nobleman's "house and tenants lay open to his spoil"'" (*Naval Tracts*, N.R.S., xliii. 57).

66. A note in the original clarifies "Island."

67. A note in the original describes the following legal shifts: "In 1612 an Act was passed for punishing pirates and robbers of the sea; and in October 1614 a further Act was passed for the suppression of pirates on the Irish coasts" (*Statutes Ireland*, i. pp. 435–36; *S.P. Irdand*, 1611–14, pref. lxxi).

68. A note in the original remarks that "Piracy was almost a recognized profession in the reign of Elizabeth. In 1563 there were 400 known pirates in the four seas" (*Admin. of R.N.*, Oppenheim, p. 177).

69. A note in the original describes the enthusiasm one was likely to find among common sailors: "Sir Walter Raleigh wrote that men 'went with as great a grudging to serve in his Majesty's ships as if it were to be slaves in the galleys'" (Oppenheim, p. 187).

70. A note in the original translates this to be "Let not the cobbler judge beyond his last."

71. A note in the original remarks "Obviously in reference to Raleigh. The story as told by Oldys is to the effect that Raleigh one day approached the Queen, telling her that he had a favour to beg. 'When, Sir Walter,' said she, 'will you cease to be a beggar?' To which he replied, 'When your gracious Majesty ceases to be a benefactor'" (*Raleigh Wks.*, 1829, i. 142).

72. From Manwaring, *The life and works*, 9–43.

ALEXANDER O. EXQUEMELIN

1. From Exquemelin, A. O., *Bucaniers of America, or, A true Account of the Most Remarkable Assaults Committed of Late Years upon the Coasts of the West-Indies by the Bucaniers of Jamaica and Tortuga, Both English and French Wherein Are Contained More Especially the Unparallel'd Exploits of Sir Henry Morgan, our English Jamaican Hero Who Sack'd Puerto*

Velo, Burnt Panama, &c. / written originally in Dutch by John Esquemeling . . . ; and thence translated into Spanish by Alonso de Bonne-Maison . . . ; now faithfully rendred into English (1684).

2. Maiming and dismemberment was not uncommon in the maritime trades, which is one reason both the preeminent fictional pirates who appear in our appendix are missing limbs, with a hook for a hand or a peg for a leg. See also "Shipping Up to Boston," the song by the Dropkick Murphys, or even Rupert Murdoch, who had a finger sliced off by rigging while sailing on Larry Ellison's yacht in the 1990s, which was saved by the quick thinking of an America's Cup sailor who was along for the ride. See Soper, Taylor, "How to Save Rupert Murdoch's Finger, and Other Startup Lessons from Entrepreneur T.A. McCann," Geek-Wire, accessed December 6, 2022, https://www.geekwire.com /2019/save-rupert-murdochs-finger-startup-lessons-entrepreneur -t-mccann/.

HENRY "LONG BEN" AVERY/EVERY

1. The National Archives, SP 63/358, fols. 127–32, via "Henry Every," Wikipedia, accessed December 6, 2022, https://en.wikipe dia.org/wiki/Henry_Every.

2. Burgess, Douglas R., *The Pirates' Pact: The Secret Alliances Between History's Most Notorious Buccaneers and Colonial America* (New York: McGraw Hill, 2009), 138.

3. Kole, William, "Ancient Coins May Solve Mystery of Murderous 1600s Pirate," Associated Press, accessed December 6, 2022, https://apnews.com/article/ancient-coins-may-solve-mystery -1600s-pirate-f5a6151b74e0dcf96de585eab451f90c.

4. Anonymous (Captain Charles Johnson), *The History and Lives of All the Most Notorious Pirates, and the Crews . . . And in This Edition Continued Down to the Year 1735.* (The Eighth Edition. London: Printed for C. Hitch, in Pater-noster Row . . . MDCCLXV), 9–27.

5. The boatswain, sometimes "bosun," is the officer on a ship in charge of equipment, especially rigging, lines, cables, sails, and so forth. It's a high-ranking job.

6. An archaic and obsolete interjection now, "zounds" is short for "God's wounds."

7. Did this anecdote actually happen? It's hard to say. But certainly the suggestion of this account of Avery's life is that he was,

around the age of six, kidnapped and used as a sexual plaything by the ship captain, and tried to free himself by blowing up the ship. And if it did happen, such abuse might inform the abuse Avery meted out later in life.

8. A "groyne" is a hydraulic structure on a shore or riverbank, to interrupt water flow and sedimentation. Like a jetty.

9. I've spent some time staring at maps, and I haven't been able to decipher what the modern name of this island might be. There is a Desroches Island in the Seychelles, off Madagascar, and a number of smaller islands between them. Do you know what island this is? Share your thoughts at katherinehowe.com/contact.

10. Clothes. At this period of history, clothing and linens were the average person's most valuable possessions.

11. Martinique.

12. Trepassey Harbour in Newfoundland, Canada.

13. Another spelling of the island I am, so far, unable to identify.

14. Muhi al-Din Muhammad, c. 1618–March 3, 1707, commonly known as Aurangzeb. Though Avery's exploits seizing the dhow definitely heightened tensions between England, the East India Company, and the Mughal Empire, no mention is made here of a daughter, ravished or not. More on the Anglo-Mughal War and Avery's part in stoking the hostilities here: "Aurangzeb," Wikipedia, accessed December 7, 2022, https://en.wikipedia.org /wiki/Aurangzeb#Relations_with_the_English_and_the _Anglo-Mughal_War.

15. This part, at least, is true: the Mughal barricaded the English-controlled colony of Bombay, and the East India Company finally had to buy him off with a tribute of what one historian has estimated at 600,000 pounds. See Burgess, Douglas R., "Piracy in the Public Sphere: The Henry Every Trials and the Battle for Meaning in Seventeenth-Century Print Culture," *Journal of British Studies* 48, no. 4 (Oct 2009): 887–913.

16. The OED has "tarpaulin" as a now archaic slang for common sailor, viz. "a nickname for a mariner or sailor, esp. a common sailor." Often abbreviated to "tar," like Jack Tar.

17. Flip was a mixture of beer and spirits sweetened with sugar and heated with a hot iron.

18. A small seal used to ensure the authenticity of documents sealed with wax, used as a stamp, like a signet ring.

19. At various points the English crown offered pardons to pirates, in an attempt to bring them back under official control, and smooth trading relationships. One of these pardons will open

part II, as it in some respects kicked off the last stage of the Golden Age of piracy.

20. Bideford, in Devon, England.

WILLIAM KIDD

1. Skowronek, Russell K., and Charles R. Ewen, eds., *X Marks the Spot: The Archaeology of Piracy* (Gainesville: University Press of Florida, 2006), 102.

2. Skowronek and Ewen, *X Marks the Spot*, 103.

3. From *A Full Account of the Proceedings in Relation to Capt. Kidd. In Two Letters*. Written by "a person of Quality to a Kinsman of the Earl of Bellomont in Ireland" (London: Booksellers of London and Westminster, 1701).

4. Presumably the Nine Years' War, of which the Glorious Revolution in England and the Indian Wars in colonial North America were a part. See "Nine Years' War," Wikipedia, accessed December 7, 2022, https://en.wikipedia.org/wiki/Nine_Years%27_War.

5. Sarah Bradley Cox Oort. They were married in 1691.

6. Henry Avery, sometimes spelled Every, discussed earlier.

7. Genoese.

8. Pennsylvania.

9. Plymouth, England.

10. Probably Madeira, Portugal.

11. Could be lots of places, including present-day Colombia or Costa Rica. A Caribbean location seems likely, given his next stop, and because of the prevailing trade winds across the Atlantic.

12. Probably St. Jago, or Santiago, present-day Spanish Town in Jamaica, which at the time was a haven for pirates.

13. Calcutta, present-day Kolkata, India.

14. Isla de Mona, at present an uninhabited nature reserve between Puerto Rico and the Dominican Republic.

15. From Head, Franklin H., *Studies in Early American History: A Notable Lawsuit* (Chicago: Privately printed, 1895), collection of Columbia University libraries.

16. Supposedly Frederick Law Olmsted, landscape designer of Central Park in New York, among many other places.

17. Deer Island, Maine.

18. This name is utterly preposterous.

19. Founder, of course, of one of the great robber baron fortunes of Gilded Age New York.

THOMAS TEW

1. "Amity, as you know, means friendship," beams the mayor of Amity Island in *Jaws* (1975).
2. Skowronek and Ewen, *X Marks the Spot*, 105.
3. McDonald, Kevin P., *Pirates, Merchants, Settlers, and Slaves: Colonial America and the Indo-Atlantic World* (Oakland, CA: University of California Press, 2015), 99.
4. From Anonymous (Captain Charles Johnson), *A General History of the Pyrates . . .* (London: T. Warner, 1724), 57–58.
5. Gorée, an island off the coast of Dakar in modern-day Senegal, maintained as a UNESCO World Heritage Site because of its role in the slave trade. From the fifteenth to the nineteenth centuries, Gorée served as the largest slave-trading center on the African coast, controlled by successions of European powers including the Portuguese, Dutch, English, and French. See "Island of Gorée," UNESCO, accessed December 7, 2022, https://whc .unesco.org/en/list/26/.

THE GOLDEN AGE

THE PROCLAMATION PARDONING PIRATES

1. From Brigham, Clarence S., *British Royal Proclamations Relating to America, 1603–1783* (New York: B. Franklin, 1911), 176–77.
2. Later the deadline was extended to July 1, 1719.

HOWELL DAVIS

1. From Ellms, *Pirates Own Book*, 201–14
2. The western coast of Africa, center of the slave trade.
3. Edward England the pirate, not the country.
4. New Providence Island, Bahamas.
5. The sailing master was the officer in charge of navigation on a naval or merchant vessel.
6. I'm not confident of the contemporary name of this careening spot, as several small bays on the eastern end of Cuba could seem to fit the bill, including Taco Bay and, of course, Guantanamo. There is a "Coxen Hole" in the Bay Islands of Honduras, but that's pretty far away.
7. Sao Nicolau in the Cape Verde Islands, a Portuguese island chain off the coast of Senegal.

8. Probably not the Isle of May outside Edinburgh, but I'm not sure which Caribbean island might have once had this name.

9. Or "granado," an early form of grenade.

10. The slave trade.

11. Common sailors, sailors "before the mast."

12. Soldiers armed with muskets.

13. Per the OED, "leeward" means "situated on the side turned away from the wind; having a direction away from the wind." Also, in orientation on board a vessel, to the left side of the vessel when standing in the stern and facing toward the bow.

14. Accra, modern-day Ghana, on the Gulf of Guinea.

15. Principe.

16. For those readers finding Davis and his ilk morally repugnant, take heart in the fact that a gut shot is, by all accounts, a desperately slow and painful way to die.

CHRISTOPHER "BILLY ONE-HAND" CONDENT/CONDON

1. From Ellms, *Pirates Own Book,* 235–41

2. Per the OED, a "boom" is "a long spar run out from different places in the ship, to extend or boom out the foot of a particular sail; as jib-boom, flying jib-boom, studding-sail booms." On a basic modern sailboat, if the mast and boom form a capital L shape, the boom is the foot of the L.

3. "Rubbed salt in the wounds," per the OED: "Originally Nautical. To rub salt, brine, vinegar, or the like into (a person's back) in order to render a whipping or flogging more painful; to punish (a person) in this way. Now rare."

4. Shrouds are standing rigging used to support masts and other structures on a vessel.

5. Guessing this refers to turns of the hourglass, which were usually made in four-hour and half-hour sizes. This probably means a four-hour size, as most ship watches were organized in four-hour blocks. So the battle lasted twelve hours. More here: Isil, Olivia, "Navigation and Related Instruments in 16th-Century England," National Park Service, accessed December 7, 2022, https://www.nps.gov/fora/learn/education/navigation-and-related-instruments-in-16th-century-england.htm.

6. Rio de la Plata, Argentina, passing between Buenos Aires and Montevideo.

7. Zanzibar.

8. Per the OED, a "snow" is "a small sailing-vessel resembling a brig, carrying a main and fore mast and a supplementary trysail mast close behind the mainmast; formerly employed as a warship."

EDWARD "NED" LOW

1. From Ellms, *Pirates Own Book,* 242–51
2. George Lowther, a pirate active in the Caribbean at this time with a vessel named *Happy Delivery.*
3. "Brigantine" can have a few different definitions, but the most likely one for our purposes is this one from the OED: "A two-masted vessel, carrying square sails on her foremast, which is rigged like a ship's foremast; her main or after-mast is the mainmast of a schooner, and in Falconer's time, like that mast, carried a square topsail: but is now entirely fore-and-aft-rigged."
4. Block Island? An island in Long Island Sound, part of Rhode Island, not far from Martha's Vineyard. If so, the ship out of Amboy was probably out of New Jersey.
5. One source suggests this is a port in Rhode Island, but I haven't been able to identify what its modern name might be.
6. From the OED: "A small seagoing fore-and-aft rigged vessel, originally with only two masts, but now often with three or four masts and carrying one or more topsails. The rig characteristic of a schooner has been defined as consisting essentially of two gaff sails, the after sail not being smaller than the fore, and a head sail set on a bowsprit."
7. That is, they repeatedly hoisted the friars up from the yardarms, letting them down again before they could choke to death, only to hoist them up again.
8. In the Bay of Honduras, Low was careening the ship *Rose Pink* but accidentally ordered too many men to one side while the gunports were open, causing the ship to swamp with water and be scuttled. Oops.
9. Per the OED: "A Portuguese gold coin current in England and its colonies in the first half of the 18th cent., then worth about 27 shillings (now historical). Hence colloquial: †the sum of 27 shillings (obsolete). Also more generally (usually in plural): any gold coin. Cf. doubloon n."
10. Charles Harris, an English pirate closely associated with Ned Low.
11. It remains true that high-speed, high-octane chases in a sailboat can actually be colossally slow if the wind doesn't cooperate.
12. The mainyard is the crossbeam that supports the top of the

mainsail (the boom is at the bottom of sail). Without the yard, there's nothing for a square sail to hang off, so the vessel can't carry its largest, most powerful sail.

13. This could mean a number of different things, either beatings or sexual violence.

STEDE "GENTLEMAN PIRATE" BONNET

1. "The sailor, seen as young and manly, unattached, and unconstrained by conventional morality, epitomized the bachelor subculture in the gay cultural imagination. He served for generations as the central masculine icon in gay pornography, as the paintings of Charles Demuth and Paul Cadmus from the early decades of the [twentieth] century and the photographs produced by gay pornographers in the middle decades attest." Chauncey, George, *Gay New York: Gender, Urban Culture, and the Making of the Gay Male World, 1890–1940* (New York: Basic Books, 1994), 78.

2. Anonymous (Captain Charles Johnson), *A General History of the Pyrates* 3rd ed., 91–112.

3. North Carolina, just north of Wilmington.

4. The Triple Alliance of 1717, see "Triple Alliance (1717)," Wikipedia, accessed December 8, 2022, https://en.wikipedia.org/wiki/Triple_Alliance_(1717).

5. Boom-boat, or a little tender to a larger vessel.

6. Ocracoke Inlet, at the southernmost tip of Cape Hatteras, North Carolina.

7. A hogshead was a large cask, usually used for storing liquids like rum or molasses.

8. Since he had accepted the King's Pardon that opens this section, Stede Bonnet resumed pirating under a pseudonym, Captain Thomas.

9. Molasses.

10. Per OED, "A large, heavy boat, fitted with one or more masts and carrying fore-and-aft or lug sails and sometimes furnished with guns; a sloop."

11. Sullivan's Island, outside of Charleston, South Carolina.

12. This is one of the few instances where we can see with certainty what happened to enslaved people who were seized by pirates. In this case, they were bartered back to the syndicate who owned the seized ship in exchange for the king's pardon. Nice for Yeats; not so nice for the people he used to barter with.

13. The Cape Fear River.

14. Tricky harbors and river mouths typically had pilots, people who were familiar with the currents and navigational challenges of the area, who would come aboard solely for the purpose of navigating vessels to safety. In this case, the pilot ran them aground.

15. When a vessel runs aground at low tide, especially in a sandy bottom that doesn't do immediate damage, the vessel will generally refloat at high tide, which comes six hours later.

16. Not sure about this Bible quote, but Malachi 2:7 reads, "Then went out to him Jerusalem, and all Judaea, and all the region round about Jordan, And were baptized of him in Jordan, confessing their sins. But when he saw many of the Pharisees and Sadducees come to his baptism, he said unto them, O generation of vipers, who hath warned you to flee from the wrath to come?"

17. 2 Corinthians 5:19–20: "[19]To wit, that God was in Christ, reconciling the world unto himself, not imputing their trespasses unto them; and hath committed unto us the word of reconciliation. [20]Now then we are ambassadors for Christ, as though God did beseech you by us: we pray you in Christ's stead, be ye reconciled to God."

EDWARD "BLACKBEARD" TEACH

1. Bolster, W. Jeffrey, *Black Jacks: African American Seamen in the Age of Sail* (Cambridge: Harvard University Press, 1997), 14.

2. Per the OED, a "Ramillies wig" was "a wig with a long plait behind tied with a bow at the top and bottom."

3. Anonymous (Captain Charles Johnson), *A General History of the Pyrates*, 70–85.

4. Benjamin Hornigold was an English pirate in the Caribbean and Bahamas who eventually accepted the King's Pardon and became a pirate hunter.

5. The island in the Bahamas, not the city in Rhode Island.

6. Flour.

7. Turneffe Atoll, present-day Belize.

8. I don't see a likely waypoint between Turneffe Atoll and Grand Cayman that matches this name, as the Turks and Caicos are on the other side of Jamaica. A puzzle.

9. Charleston.

10. Charles Vane, an English pirate based out of Port Royal, Jamaica.

11. In value.

12. I'm not sure what this denotes. The James River extends past

present-day Newport News, to Jamestown outside Williamsburg, at the time the seat of colonial Virginia government.

13. This means that his draft was deeper, or rather, that the keel of his ship extended deeper into the water than the keel of Blackbeard's vessel. A ship with a deeper draft will run aground before a ship with a shallower draft, and in shoals the water can shallow up very quickly.

14. Making the vessel lighter will lessen the draft, which will allow the vessel to get closer to Blackbeard's ship aground.

15. Maynard is so focused on making his ship lighter that he orders the crew to "stave," or cave in, the barrels holding their drinking water, to reduce the weight on board.

16. Per OED, "to change the position of, shift (a block, rope, etc.)."

17. Waist, which is to say, the gunwales were pretty low, and there was nothing for Blackbeard's men to shelter behind if they were standing on deck.

18. Grape shot rather than cannonballs, good for killing large numbers of people rather than punching holes in hulls.

19. A member of Blackbeard's crew, a black pirate, ready to blow up the powder magazine in a last-ditch effort to destroy their attackers.

BARTHOLOMEW "BLACK BART" ROBERTS

1. Rediker, Marcus. *Villains of All Nations: Atlantic Pirates in the Golden Age* (Boston: Beacon Press, 2004), 33.

2. Anonymous (Captain Charles Johnson), *The History and Lives of All the Most Notorious Pirates*, 83–90.

3. Another rare example of a historical argument for a unique Jolly Roger flag for a particular pirate.

4. A name that truly beggars the imagination, even by eighteenth-century standards.

5. Calabar, originally Akwa Akpa, present-day Nigeria, at the time a Portuguese center of the slave trade.

6. Cape Lopez, present-day Gabon.

7. Anomabu, present-day Ghana.

8. Sailboats, be they big square riggers or tiny dinghies, cannot sail directly into the wind. Modern-day boats can "point" pretty close to it, but most vessels in this period were square-rigged, which means that they can pretty much only run before the wind. So what's happening here is, they are right outside the

harbor, they can see the pirates inside the harbor, but they are physically unable to sail into the harbor to meet them, due to the direction of the wind. They must "sheer off," or change direction, and try to reach them from a different angle.

9. Principe.

10. To "slip the cable" means to undo the line holding the anchor to a vessel and let it run overboard in order to make sail as quickly as possible. Weighing anchor, in contrast, was difficult, time-consuming, and required lots of crew working a windlass to bring it up. After a time, "to slip the cable" became nautical slang for dying.

11. Casnewydd Bach in Pembrokeshire, present-day Wales.

SAMUEL "BLACK SAM" BELLAMY

1. Skowronek and Ewen, *X Marks the Spot*, 131.

2. See the deposition transcribed here: Brooks, Baylus C., "Deposition of Abijah Savage at Antigua—30 Nov 1716," Baylus C. Brooks, accessed December 9, 2022, http://baylusbrooks.com /index_files/Page46036.htm.

3. Levenson, Michale, "Remains Are Identified as a Boy Pirate," Boston.com, accessed December 9, 2022, http://archive.boston .com/news/local/articles/2006/06/02/remains_are_identified _as_a_boy_pirate/.

4. *From Instructions to the Living, from the Condition of the DEAD. A Brief Relation of REMARKABLES in the Shipwreck of above One Hundred Pirates, Who Were Cast Away in the Ship Whido, on the Coast of New-England, April 26, 1717* . . . . (Boston: Printed by John Allen, for Nicholas Boone, at the Sign of the Bible in Cornhill, 1717), unpaginated.

5. As the *Whydah* was a slave ship, we can assume that the "prisoners" murdered by Bellamy and his crew were enslaved people.

6. Control of the mind.

7. The first time I read this I took it to mean that he swore, as pirates are of course known to do. But upon reflection, I wonder if "John Brown" born in Jamaica was a formerly enslaved person who reverted to his native tongue, whatever it might have been, when on the scaffold. Hard to say, but possible.

WILLIAM SNELGRAVE

1. From Snelgrave, Captain William, *A New Account of Some Parts of Guinea and the Slave-Trade* (London, 1734), 196–211.
2. "Sallec" doesn't appear in the OED, but a review of the word's use in other eighteenth- and early nineteenth-century sources suggests it refers to a slave ship seeking captives for sale in Morocco.
3. The OED defines a "pinnace" as borrowed from the French, "pinasse," or "a small light vessel, usually having two schooner-rigged (originally square-rigged) masts, often in attendance on a larger vessel and used as a tender or scout, to carry messages, etc." The term fell out of use after the eighteenth century.
4. Flood tide is high tide.

JOHN UPTON

1. From Hayward, Arthur L., ed., *Lives of the Most Remarkable Criminals Who Have Been Condemned and Executed for Murder, Highway Robberies, Housebreaking, Street Robberies, Coining or Other Offences: From the Year 1720 to the Year 1735. Collected from Original Papers and Authentic Memoir* (London, 1735; reprint New York: Dodd, Mead, 1927), volume 3.
2. Enemies of the human race.
3. An outdated term likely meaning "provisioned," i.e., readied to sail again.
4. Joseph Cooper. In 1725, Cooper would set fire to the gunpowder magazine of his own vessel, blowing it and himself up to evade capture and trial.

RICHARD LUNTLY

1. From "The Last speech and dying words, of Richard Luntly, carpenter aboard the Eagle Snow, who was executed within the flood mark at Leith, upon the 11th January, 1721, for the crimes of piracy and robbery," National Library of Scotland.
2. I'm not certain which Captain Davis this is. In addition to Howell there was at least one, possibly two, Edward Davises in the same theater of operations.
3. Principe.
4. São Tomé.
5. The equator.
6. In this usage, the OED defines "butt" as follows: "A large cask

used to store liquids, typically varying in capacity from 108 to 140 gallons (approx. 491 to 637 litres) though often much smaller in early use. In later use also: the contents of such a cask; a liquid measure of capacity equal to the capacity of a butt, equivalent to half a tun."

7. Not sure which Caribbean island this might be.

ANNE BONNY AND MARY READE

1. From Anonymous (Captain Charles Johnson), *A General History of the Pyrates*, 157–73.
2. Breda Castle, present-day Netherlands.
3. A pregnancy was said to "quicken" when the fetus could be felt moving, that is, about twenty weeks.
4. "Lying in" suggests that the wife became sick during the final stage of a pregnancy. Your editor wonders if she suffered pre-eclampsia.
5. A "groat" is a coin worth almost nothing. Per the OED, more specifically: "The English groat coined in 1351–2 was made equal to four pence. This ratio between the groat and the penny continued to be maintained; but owing to the progressive debasement of both coins, the 'old groats' which remained in circulation were valued at a higher rate (see quots. 1465, c1483, also 1552 in b). The groat ceased to be issued for circulation in 1662, and was not afterwards coined under that name. The 'fourpence' (popularly 'fourpenny bit,' 'fourpenny piece'), which was issued from 1836 to 1856 (and after 1888 reissued for colonial circulation) was occasionally called a 'groat,' but the name was neither officially recognized nor commonly used. The Scottish fourpenny piece, first struck in 1358, is called a 'groat' (Anglo-Norman grote) in an English Act of 1390, and this name was used in Scotland itself in the 15th cent. Its value was already only 3d. English in 1373, and 2d. in 1390; later it fell much lower. In Ireland the groat was first struck in 1460."
6. New Providence Island, Nassau, the Bahamas, a notorious pirate nest.

JOHN PHILIPS

1. From Dow, George Francis, and John Henry Edmonds, *The Pirates of the New England Coast, 1630–1730* (Salem, MA: Marine Research Society, 1923), 310–13.

2. A cape on the Massachusetts coast north of Boston, headquarters for much of the colonial fishing fleet.
3. The southernmost point of mainland Florida, in the Everglades.
4. Head into the wind brings a sail boat to a complete stop.
5. A note in the original reads "Babson, History of Gloucester, p. 287. This is very likely true, as Jeremiah Bumstead of Boston recorded in his diary on May 3, 1724, that 'Philip's and Burrill's heads were brought to Boston in pickle.'"—*New England Historic and Genealogical Register,* vol. 15, p. 201.

PHILIP ASHTON

1. From Barnard, John, *Ashton's Memorial: AN HISTORY OF THE Strange Adventures, AND Signal Deliverances, OF Mr. Philip Ashton, Who, after he had made his Escape from the PIRATES, liv'd alone on a Desolate Island for about Sixteen Months, &c* (Boston, 1725).
2. While drunk.
3. Newfoundland, Canada.
4. This would become the *Rose Pink*, the vessel accidentally scuttled when they leave the gunports open.
5. Hunting for birds.
6. A Trojan War allusion, to Hector's supposed arrogance that cost him his life in a battle with Achilles.
7. The highest sail on the tallest mast.
8. Another example of the tricky parts of sailing. They are right outside Tobago's harbor, but the wind is so light they cannot sail faster than the current is pushing them away.
9. Utila Island, present-day Honduras.
10. Ozenbrig was a rough, durable weave cotton not unlike burlap, used for clothing for workers and slaves in the eighteenth century.

WILLIAM FLY

1. From Mather, Cotton, *The Vial Poured Out Upon the Sea: A Remarkable Relation of Certain Pirates . . .* (Boston, 1726) and *The Tryals of Sixteen Persons for Piracy &c* (Boston, 1726).
2. "Sheets" are the ropes that control the shape and orientation of a sail. The main sheets controlled the main sail.
3. Presumably the windlass, the large geared mechanism at the bow of a vessel used to wind up the anchor chain.
4. To stave in a vessel's hull or cause it to spring a leak.

5. Per the OED, "A gallant, a free-and-easy fellow, a good fellow; 'fellow,' generally familiarly laudatory, sometimes good-naturedly contemptuous. (The original sense is difficult to seize: Bailey 1730 says, 'a bravo, an Hector; also a spruce fellow, a beau'; Johnson 'a brisk man, either fierce or gay, called so in contempt.') (Now colloquial or slangy: in literature, chiefly a reminiscence of the eighteenth century.)"

6. Beelzebub, or the devil.

FANNY CAMPBELL

1. From Ballou, Maturin Murray, *Fanny Campbell, the Female Pirate Captain: A Tale of the Revolution* (New York: E. D. Long and Co, 1844), https://www.gutenberg.org/cache/epub /47430/pg47430-images.html.

2. The Liberty Tree, which was actually a large elm that grew near Boston Common and served as an early meeting place and site of rebellion against the Stamp Acts, which grew into fervor for the American Revolution, was later adopted as a flag—often with the slogan "An Appeal to Heaven" for the frigates that served for George Washington. The Liberty Tree was abstracted into a pine. In effect, this flag was the first American naval ensign.

JOSE "GASPARILLA" GASPAR

1. From Bradlee, Francis B. C., *Piracy in the West Indies and Its Suppression* (Salem, MA: Essex Institute, 1923), 53–56.

2. Davis, William C., *The Pirates Laffite: The Treacherous World of the Corsairs of the Gulf* (Orlando, FL: Houghton Mifflin Harcourt, 2005), 449.

3. Turtle Bay and Port Charlotte are just northwest of modern-day Fort Meyers, Florida. This island name doesn't appear on current maps that I have seen, but Gasparilla State Park is on the southernmost tip of Boca Grande, across a small strait from Cayo Costa.

4. More on indigenous mound building cultures of Florida here: Edic, Robert F., "Aboriginal Occupation of Gasparilla Island," *Maritime Archaeology of Lemon Bay, Florida*, no. 14 (Spring 1999), https://bocagrandehistoricalsociety.com/wp-content/up loads/2017/04/2.2-Aboriginal-Occupation-of-Gasparilla -Island2.pdf.

5. Pierre was the brother of notorious Baratarian smuggler Jean Laffite (spelling tended to vary, but historians have largely set-

tled on two *F*s and one *T*), originally based in New Orleans, pardoned after their involvement on the United States side of the Battle of New Orleans, whose exploits on Galveston Island, Texas, open part III of this reader. Pierre was more the moneyman and Jean was more the captain, and at times they have been confused for one another.

6. A small island in the Ten Thousand Islands National Wildlife Refuge, due south of Fort Meyers, Florida.

7. Near Fort Meyers, in the same outer-harbor chain of keys as Boca Grande.

THE NINETEENTH CENTURY

FIRST BARBARY WAR

1. From McClure, James P., and J. Jefferson Looney, *The Papers of Thomas Jefferson Digital Edition* (Charlottesville: University of Virginia Press, Rotunda, 2008–2022), accessed December 7, 2022, https://rotunda-upress-virginia-edu.proxy.library.cornell .edu/founders/TSJN-01-08-02-0339. Original source: Main Series, Volume 8 (25 February–31 October 1785).

2. From McClure and Looney, *The Papers of Thomas Jefferson*. Original source: Main Series, Volume 18 (4 November 1790–24 January 1791).

3. Sterret, Andrew, "Sterret's Sea Fight."

ZHENG YI SAO

1. Antony, Robert J., *The Golden Age of Piracy in China, 1520–1810: A Short History with Documents* (Lanham, MD: Rowman and Littlefield, 2022), 34.

2. Per OED, an old Scottish term for "highwayman."

3. From Neumann, Charles Fried, *History of the Pirates who Infested the China Sea from 1807 to 1810* (London: Printed for the Oriental Translation Fund, 1831), 97–104.

4. Per OED, in addition to the usual usage with which we are all familiar, i.e., a small package of letters or correspondence, "packet" is also "colloquial (chiefly British). A large sum of money."

5. Per OED, "An establishment for traders carrying on business, especially in a foreign country; a merchant company's trading station; a trading post. Now historical."

6. Per OED, "comprador" is "Formerly, the name of a native servant employed by Europeans, in India and the East, to purchase necessaries and keep the household accounts: a house-steward."

7. Per OED, this was a term used in the China trade. "In India, China. A seal or the impression of a seal; an official impress or stamp."

8. This is a nautical term. The "roads" is a body of water that is sheltered from currents, big tides, or swells where ships can expect to lie at anchor without dragging.

9. Basically, their ship has left without them, and they are trying to chase it down in their smaller tender.

10. The length of a ship's cable, or about six hundred feet. One nautical mile is ten cable lengths. One knot of speed is equivalent to one nautical mile per hour. So they're pretty close to the ship, but then then ship tacks, i.e., changes direction by bringing the bow through the wind.

11. This is another nautical term, meaning that they trimmed in their sails so that they could sail closer to the wind, or upwind. A more common contemporary term for this point of sail is "close hauled."

12. They are trying to sail upwind, but the tide and the swells are pushing against them, and they are moving backward. They take down the masts and instead try to use oars to catch up to their ship, but it's no use.

13. A ship of their own country, flying the English flag, which they knew would be friendly.

14. A lee shore means a shore which lies in the direction the wind is blowing. If the wind and tide are pushing a sailboat toward the shore, and that boat doesn't have enough "leeway," or room to maneuver, the boat can be driven aground. Sailboats cannot sail directly into the wind. At best they can sail at about a forty-five-degree angle to the wind, and that's for a boat that points well. Square riggers don't point well. The author's tender was probably fore and aft rigged, meaning it had triangular sails much like a modern sailboat, and could sail closer to the wind than the ship they are trying to catch up to. But even boats that point well can be driven onto a lee shore.

15. In big wind, a boat can become overpowered, which leads to broaching at worst, and inefficient speed at best. Reefing sails means to reduce the available sail area. In a strong wind, a reefed boat will handle better and actually go faster and more safely than a boat with lots of sail area out.

16. Tacking means to bring the bow of a boat through the wind. Basically he's saying that he zigzagged back and forth all night, crossing the bow back and forth through the wind, just to keep them standing still. It would have been exhausting work.

17. The weather side is also the windward side, so he means the land in the direction from which the wind is coming. He's still trying to get away from the threat of the lee shore.

18. Steered closer to the wind.

19. It's not entirely clear where Glasspoole is, and I haven't been able to ascertain the modern names of the navigational clues he has supplied to us so far. However, it seems likely that he has been sailing just southeast of present-day Hong Kong, which is connected by many large and small islands with present-day Macao. He may have been stuck in modern-day Discovery Bay.

20. Since sailboats cannot sail directly "head to wind," or into the wind, Glasspoole is trying to escape the Red Banner pirates by rowing in a direction that the fleet cannot sail.

21. I'm guessing they've made it to the Zhujiang River Estuary, on the southeast side of present-day Hong Kong.

22. Per OED, "A sailing vessel of a kind used in East and South-East Asia, typically having fully-battened lugsails. Now chiefly applied to Chinese and Japanese vessels of this type; in early use applied more widely to include also vessels of Java, the Malay Archipelago, and South India."

JEAN LAFITTE

1. From Bradlee, *Piracy*, 17–20.

2. From Ellms, *Pirates Own Book*, 81–85.

3. The Sabine divides Texas from Louisiana.

4. Texas at this point was definitely not a republic. It was a part of Spanish Mexico, which was trying for its own independence from Spain, with mixed success. Texas would briefly become a republic in 1836.

5. Laffite's claims are spurious at best. He was sailing under forged letters of marque from the illegitimate Mexican government. It was piracy, under the absolutely thinnest sheen of legitimacy.

6. A bayou is a small waterway, like a creek, in Louisiana and East Texas. Bayou St. John flows from Lake Pontcharain into the Faubourg St. John neighborhood of New Orleans.

7. Control of the engagement. Well-defined in an amusing scene from the film *Master and Commander: The Far Side of the World* (2003).

8. A brigantine is a two masted sailing ship with a square rigged foremast and a fore and aft rigged mainmast. Sometimes called a "hermaphrodite brig." In contrast, a brig is usually square rigged on both masts.

9. No one actually knows how Jean Laffite died. But this is a pretty exciting imagination of one way it could easily have happened.

SCHOONER *JANE*

1. From Stuart, Alexander, *Report of the Trial of Peter Heaman and Francois Gautiez or Gautier, for the Crimes of Piracy and Murder: Before the High Court of Admiralty, Held at Edinburgh on the 26th and 27th of November 1821* (Edinburgh: Charles Guthrie, 1821).

2. Per OED, "A vessel with two masts square-rigged like a ship's fore- and main-masts, but carrying also on her main-mast a lower fore-and-aft sail with a gaff and boom. A brig differs from a snow in having no try-sail mast, and in lowering her gaff to furl the sail. Merchant snows are often called 'brigs.' This vessel was probably developed from the brigantine by the men-of-war brigs, so as to obtain greater sail-power."

3. Per OED, "2. spec. Scots Law. To appear in a court, as a party to a cause, either in person or by counsel."

4. This is the first instance I have found to actually mention buried treasure.

5. Another term for this sail plan is a "hermaphrodite rig."

6. Per OED, "A large container of definite capacity for storing solids or liquids, such as meat, fish, or oil. Now: spec. a large cask for storing wine or cider."

7. This is also the first mention I've found of walking the plank in an actual primary source.

8. A marlinspike is a long, pointed metal knife end, used for loosening knots. Even today marlinspikes are a standard part of a sailing knife or rigging knife.

9. Per the OED, "An 'incident' of feudal law, whereby a fief reverted to the lord when the tenant died without leaving a successor qualified to inherit under the original grant. Hence, the lapsing of land to the Crown (in U.S., to the state), or to the lord of the manor, on the death of the owner intestate without heirs.

As an attainted person, according to the doctrine of 'corruption of blood' (see attainder n.), could have no legal heir, his property suffered escheat. This 'escheat by corruption of blood,' theoretically distinct from the 'forfeiture' inflicted as a penalty for treason and felony, was abolished together with the latter by the Felony Act, 1870."

THE *DOVER*

1. Per OED, "A West Indian coasting vessel; hence transferred to other slow clumsy coasting craft."
2. From Bradlee, *Piracy in the West Indies*, 32.

THE *PORPOISE*

1. From Bradlee, *Piracy in the West Indies*, 15–17.

THE *ALLIGATOR*

1. From Bradlee, *Piracy in the West Indies*, 30–31.
2. Oars.

THE *BELVIDERE*

1. The customs entry point to Louisiana, on the Gulf Coast, leading into a networks of bayous and Mississippi tributaries to ferry goods for sale to New Orleans.
2. From Bradlee, *Piracy in the West Indies*, 2–3.
3. Hanged and then cut down.
4. Per OED, "A warship carrying 74 guns. Now historical."
5. A historical term, now this would be called the port bow, or to the left of the vessel if standing in the stern and facing the bow.
6. A schooner has two masts and usually several sails, including multiple foresails like a jib and a flying jib. To be lying under mainsail and jib means they are using very little sail power for their size, and so are going slowly on purpose.
7. Per OED, "To haul up (the sails) by means of the brails."
8. This is probably more sail trim detail than you need, but Lamson is recording these details in the ship's log, which is mainly concerned with sail trim and weather. The age of the great clipper ships crossing the Atlantic in record time—some speed records that were only recently broken—was still twenty years

away, but ship captains would have stood to benefit from making the fastest passages of which they were capable.

9. Two points off the closest he could sail to the wind—basically he has trimmed the vessel to go as fast as it is capable of going.

10. Per OED, "A short gun with a large bore, firing many balls or slugs, and capable of doing execution within a limited range without exact aim. (Now superseded by other firearms.)"

11. The support structure for the cannon.

12. Per OED, "Nautical. Chiefly plural. An opening in a ship's side on a level with the deck to allow water to run away."

13. Halyards are lines that hoist a sail up and down from the top of the mast.

THE *MARY*

1. From Bradlee, *Piracy in the West Indies*, 23–29.
2. A bit like Blackbeard, no? Already certain pirate tropes are beginning to fall into place.
3. Misfired.
4. He is too well dressed to send to the devil.
5. Let me see what's left!
6. Here is a ship!

THE *NEW PRISCILLA*

1. From Bradlee, *Piracy in the West Indies*, 6–7.
2. Today, the facade of the Peabody Essex Museum.

THE *FRIENDSHIP*

1. "Friendship of Salem," National Park Service, accessed December 11, 2022, https://www.nps.gov/places/friendship-of-salem.htm.
2. From Ellms, *Pirates Own Book*, 226–30.
3. Per OED, "Nautical. A short raised deck at the fore end of a vessel. In early use raised like a castle to command the enemy's decks. Obsolete exc. archaic or Historical."
4. Per OED, "A rope used to confine the bowsprit of a ship downward to the stem . . . [Its use] is to draw down the bowsprit and keep it steady; and to counteract the force of the stays of the fore-mast, which draw it upwards.'" *Falconer Dict. Marine* (1769).
5. Per OED, "A Malay dagger, with a blade of a wavy form."

6. Per OED, "Chiefly Nautical. To or towards the rear; backward."
7. Per OED, "One of the strong posts firmly fastened in pairs in the deck or decks of a ship, for fastening cables, belaying ropes, etc.; generally used in the plural. The chief pair, the riding bitts, are used for fastening the cable while the ship rides at anchor; others are the topsail-sheet bitts, carrick-bitts, wind-lass bitts, etc. Also attrib., as bitt-head, bitt-pin."
8. Per OED, "Nautical. A length of rope when looped or folded, esp. distinguishing the body of the rope from its ends; a loop in a length of rope."
9. Per OED, "A mechanical contrivance working on the principle of the wheel and axle, on a horizontal axis (thus distinguished from a capstan); consisting of a roller or beam, resting on supports, round which a rope or chain is wound; used for various purposes, esp. on board ship for weighing the anchor or hauling upon a purchase, at the head of a mine-shaft for hoisting coal or other mineral, or for raising a bucket from a well."
10. Per OED, "Originally and chiefly Nautical a section of a rope, etc., which passes over another section in the construction of a knot." Basically, they hauled up the anchor, but didn't wind the cable tightly enough or secure it well enough, so the anchors fell again at a high speed, snarling the lines holding them in a knot, and leaving the anchors dangling uselessly, and dangerously, from the bow of the vessel.
11. Per OED, "That part of the bows of a ship in which the hawse-holes are cut for the cables to pass through; hence, sometimes, in plural, the hawse-holes themselves."
12. This account suggests that the "pirates" who claimed the *Friendship* were functioning in the same way as the Barbary Coast pirates, namely, that they were acting on the command of a local leader or warlord, in order to exact tribute, rather than as renegades.

THE *MEXICAN*

1. Almost certainly a slave market.
2. From Bradlee, *Piracy in the West Indies*, 7–8.

LA AMISTAD

1. *Argument of John Quincy Adams, before the Supreme Court of the United States in the case of the United States, Appellants,*

vs. Cinqud, and others, Africans, captured in the Schooner Amistad, by Lieut. Gedney, delivered on the 24th of February and 1st of March, 1841.

2. From *Argument of John Quincy Adams.* . . . (New York: S. W. Benedict, 128 Fulton Street, 1841).

3. Per OED, "A rough barrack, set of sheds, or enclosure, in which black slaves (originally), convicts, etc., are temporarily detained. Also figurative."

APPENDIX

1. There's even a Muppet version, though unfortunately I can't quite recommend it.

2. Bartholomew Roberts.

3. Edward England.

4. Howell Davis, probably.

5. "Going out on the account" was a term of art that meant going pirating.

6. Per OED, "Originally Nautical slang. A boiled or steamed sweet pudding, usually containing fruit, and made in a bag." Stevenson has fallen into a common trap for writers of historical fiction—he used historical slang that sounded right, but wasn't. This use of "duff" dates from the early nineteenth century, not the eighteenth.

7. Per OED, "Originally: a small boat used to carry provisions to, and remove refuse from, ships lying at anchor in a harbour; (from the eighteenth century) a small trading boat carrying provisions for sale to moored or anchored ships, and (later also, esp. in Singapore) ferrying cargo between ships and the shore."

8. To be rated able, a seaman had to be able to hand, reef, and steer. But navigation was a different animal all together. Most maritime communities had navigation schools to teach the math and calculations necessary for wayfinding at sea.

9. Named, presumably, for William Kidd.

10. Quite possibly a reference to Long John Silver, whose nickname, as briefly seen in the foregoing chapter, was "Barbecue."

11. A gentleman pirate, like Stede Bonnet. "Public school" in Great Britain is equivalent to private school in the United States.

12. Probably a reference to which "house" he was in at public school, like Gryffindor at Hogwarts.

13. Per OED, "A close-fitting body-garment, with or without sleeves, worn by men from the fourteenth to the eighteenth centuries.

(Rarely applied to a similar garment worn by women.) Obsolete exc. Historical." Sort of like a vest, worn over a blouse but under a coat.

14. Per OED, "At Eton College: (originally) a social club and debating society, founded in 1811; (now) the body of prefects at the college." Eton is one of the premier public schools in the UK, a feeder school for Oxford and Cambridge. Hook presumably went to Eton.

15. Alas, so true.

16. John used to wish to be a pirate instead of doing his math homework.

17. Wendy, of course, is one of the Darling children, but at this point in the story has nominated herself mother of all the Lost Boys.

18. Per OED, "A ruffle or frill around the sleeve of a garment at the wrist."

Index

THE PENGUIN BOOK OF WITCHES

Edited by Katherine Howe

From a manual for witch hunters written by King James himself in 1597, to court documents from the Salem witch trials of 1692, *The Penguin Book of Witches* is a treasury of historical accounts of accused witches that sheds light on the reality behind the legends.

THE PENGUIN BOOK OF MERMAIDS

Edited by Cristina Bacchilega and Marie Alohalani Brown

Among the oldest and most popular mythical beings, merfolk have captured the imagination long before Ariel sold her voice to a sea witch in *The Little Mermaid*. *The Penguin Book of Mermaids* is a treasury of tales showing us how public perceptions of this popular mythical hybrid illuminate issues of spirituality, ecology, and sexuality.

THE PENGUIN BOOK OF DRAGONS

Edited by Scott G. Bruce

The most popular mythological creature in the human imagination, dragons have provoked fear and fascination for their lethal venom and crushing coils. *The Penguin Book of Dragons* features accounts spanning millennia and continents of these monsters that mark the boundary between the known and the unknown.

Ⓟ PENGUIN CLASSICS

Ready to find your next great classic? Let us help. Visit prh.com/penguinclassics

ALSO AVAILABLE

THE PENGUIN BOOK OF THE UNDEAD

Fifteen Hundred Years of Supernatural Encounters
Edited by Scott G. Bruce

Since ancient times, accounts of supernatural activity have mystified us. *The Penguin Book of the Undead* charts our relationship with spirits and apparitions over fifteen hundred years, showing the evolution in our thinking about the ability of dead souls to return to the realm of the living.

THE PENGUIN BOOK OF HELL

Edited by Scott G. Bruce

From the Hebrew Bible's shadowy realm of Sheol to twenty-first-century visions of Hell on earth, *The Penguin Book of Hell* takes us through three thousand years of eternal damnation. Drawing upon religious poetry, theological treatises, and accounts of saints' lives, this fascinating volume of hellscapes illuminates how Hell has long haunted us, in both life and death.

THE PENGUIN BOOK OF EXORCISMS

Edited by Joseph P. Laycock

Levitation. Speaking in tongues. A hateful, glowing stare. The signs of spirit possession have been documented for thousands of years and across religions and cultures. *The Penguin Book of Exorcisms* brings together the most astonishing accounts. Fifty-seven percent of Americans profess to believe in demonic possession; after reading this book, you may too.

PENGUIN CLASSICS

Ready to find your next great classic? Let us help. Visit prh.com/penguinclassics